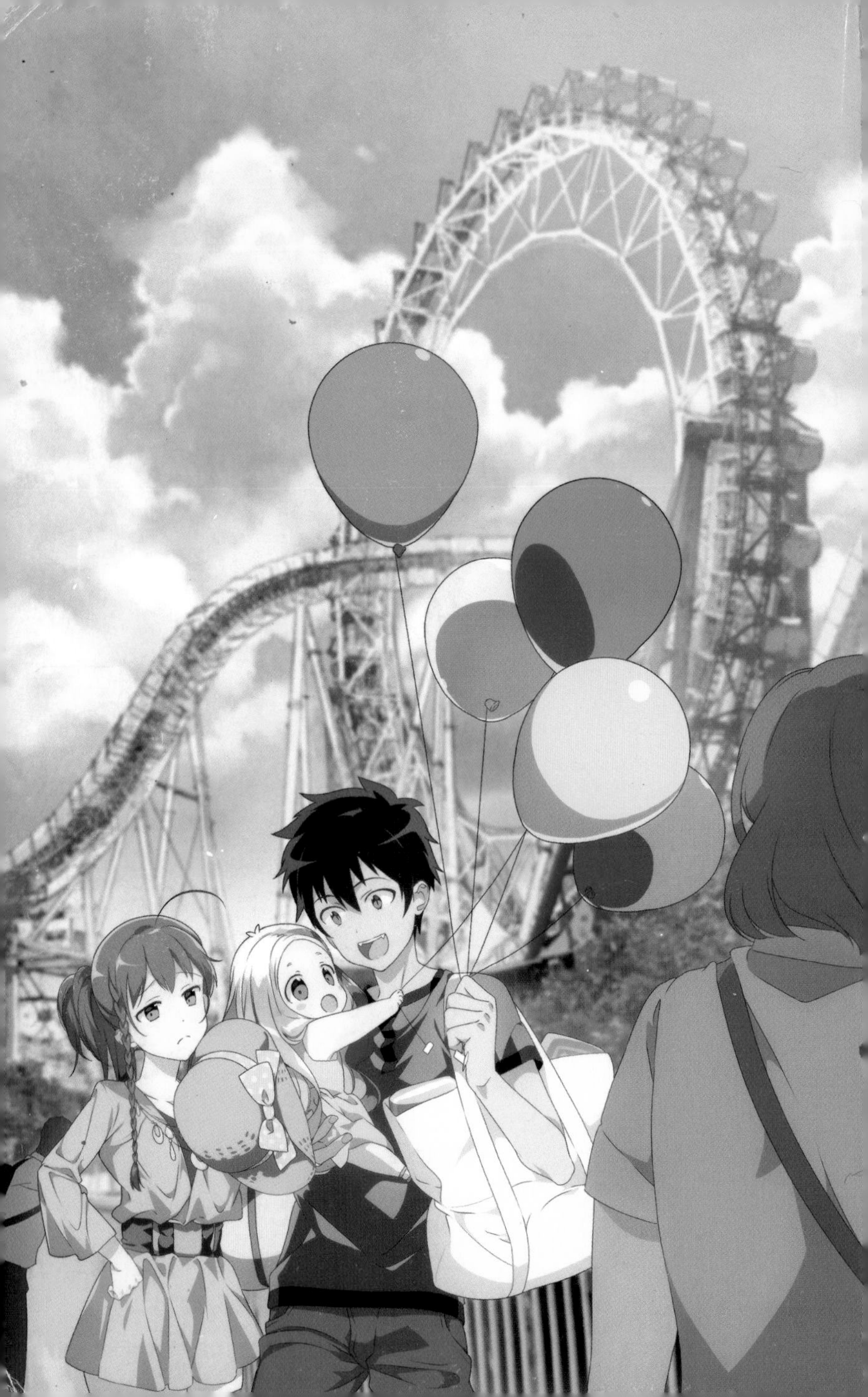

Chapter 32: The Devil and the Hero Converse on the Ferris Wheel • • • • p4

Chapter 33: The Devil Is Asked for His Child Back • • • • • • • • • • • • • p35

Chapter 34: The Devil and the Hero Share the Floor for the Night • • • • p63

Chapter 35: The Hero Declares She Will Clean Up Her Own Messes • • • p99

Chapter 36: The Hero Kicks Out an Uninvited Guest • • • • • • • • • • • p131

Chapter 37: The Devil Feels the Pain of Loss • • • • • • • • • • • • • • • p163

Afterword • p192

Emi
Yusa

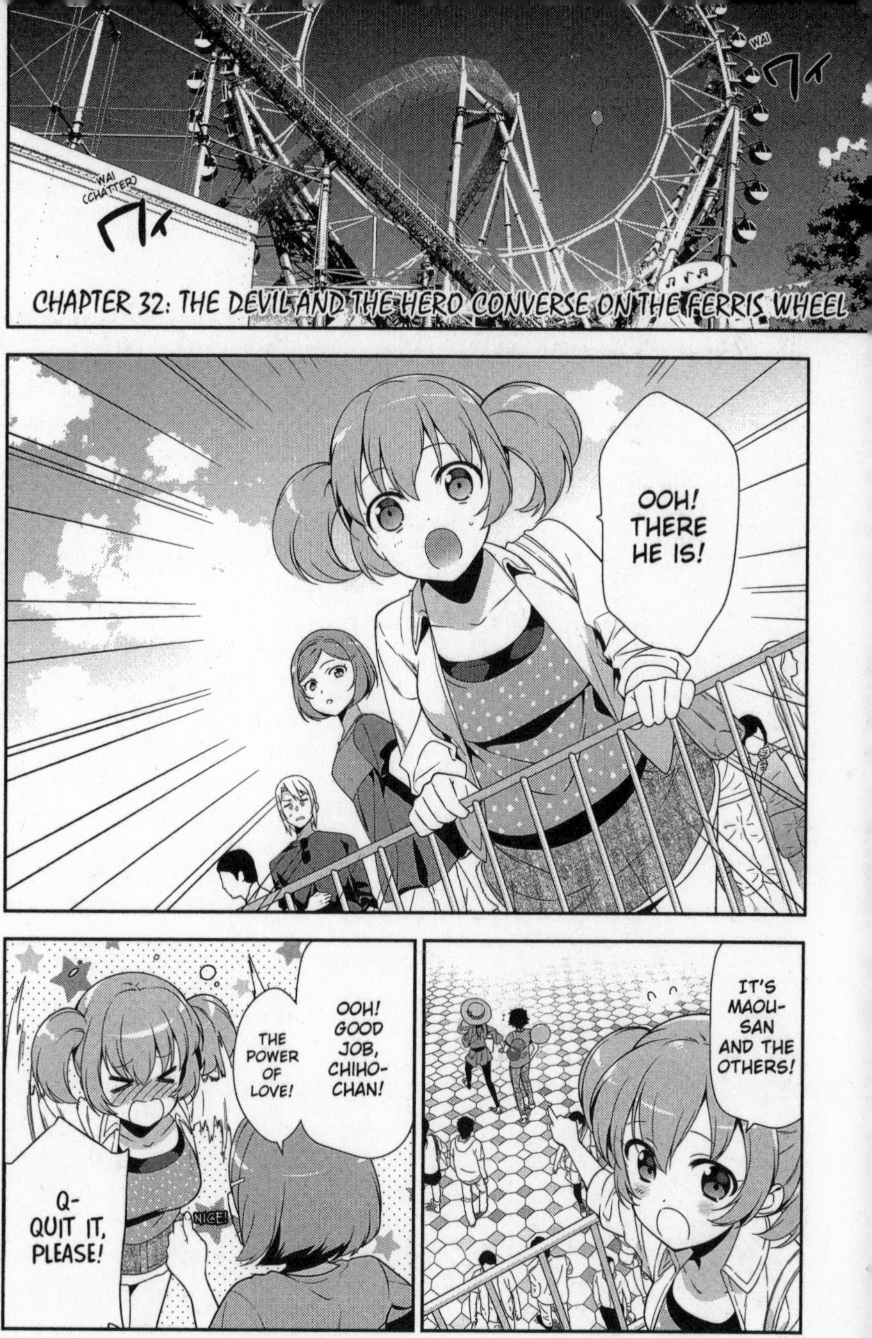
WAI
WAI (CHATTER)
CHAPTER 32: THE DEVIL AND THE HERO CONVERSE ON THE FERRIS WHEEL
OOH! THERE HE IS!
IT'S MAOU-SAN AND THE OTHERS!
OOH! GOOD JOB, CHIHO-CHAN!
THE POWER OF LOVE!
NICE!
Q-QUIT IT, PLEASE!

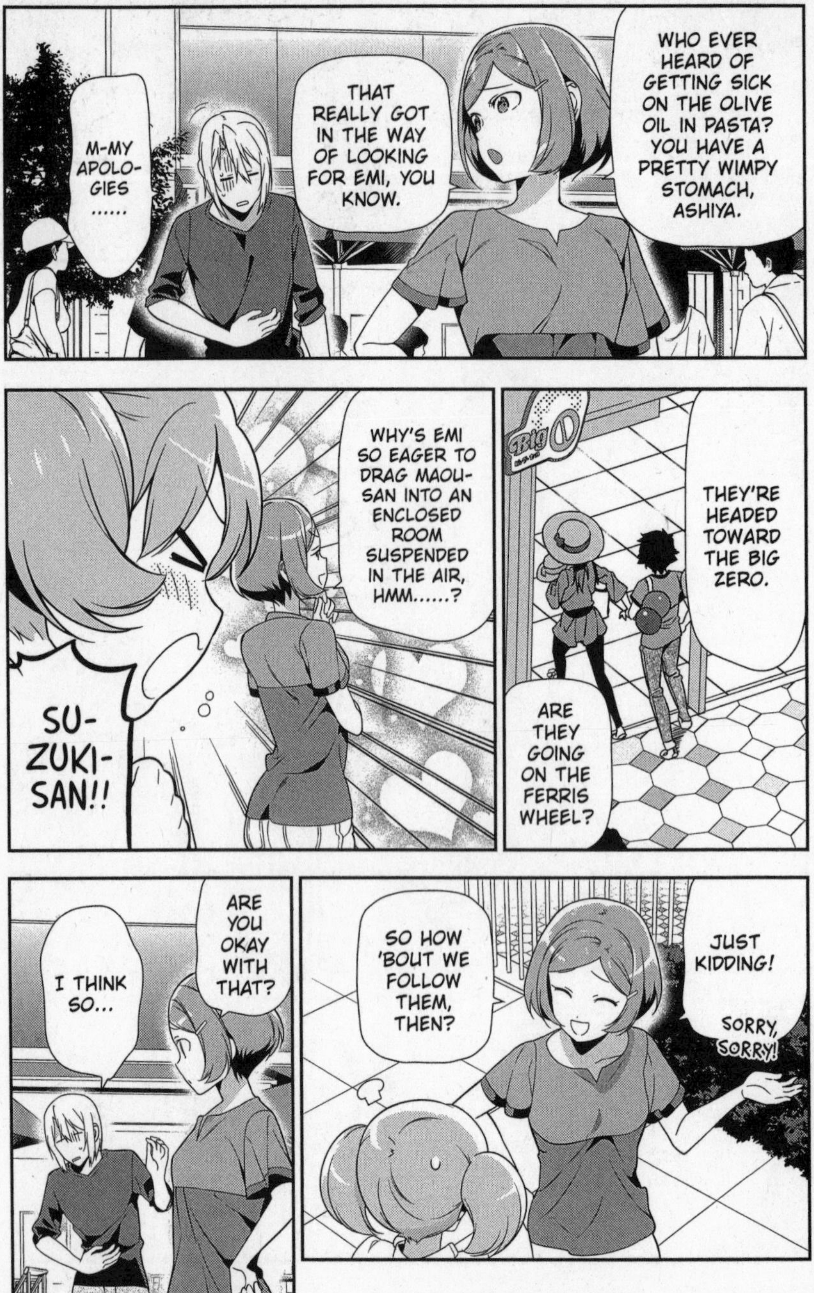
WHO EVER HEARD OF GETTING SICK ON THE OLIVE OIL IN PASTA? YOU HAVE A PRETTY WIMPY STOMACH, ASHIYA.
THAT REALLY GOT IN THE WAY OF LOOKING FOR EMI, YOU KNOW.
M-MY APOLOGIES......
THEY'RE HEADED TOWARD THE BIG ZERO.
ARE THEY GOING ON THE FERRIS WHEEL?
WHY'S EMI SO EAGER TO DRAG MAOU-SAN INTO AN ENCLOSED ROOM SUSPENDED IN THE AIR, HMM......?
SU-ZUKI-SAN!!
JUST KIDDING!
SORRY, SORRY!
SO HOW 'BOUT WE FOLLOW THEM, THEN?
ARE YOU OKAY WITH THAT?
I THINK SO...

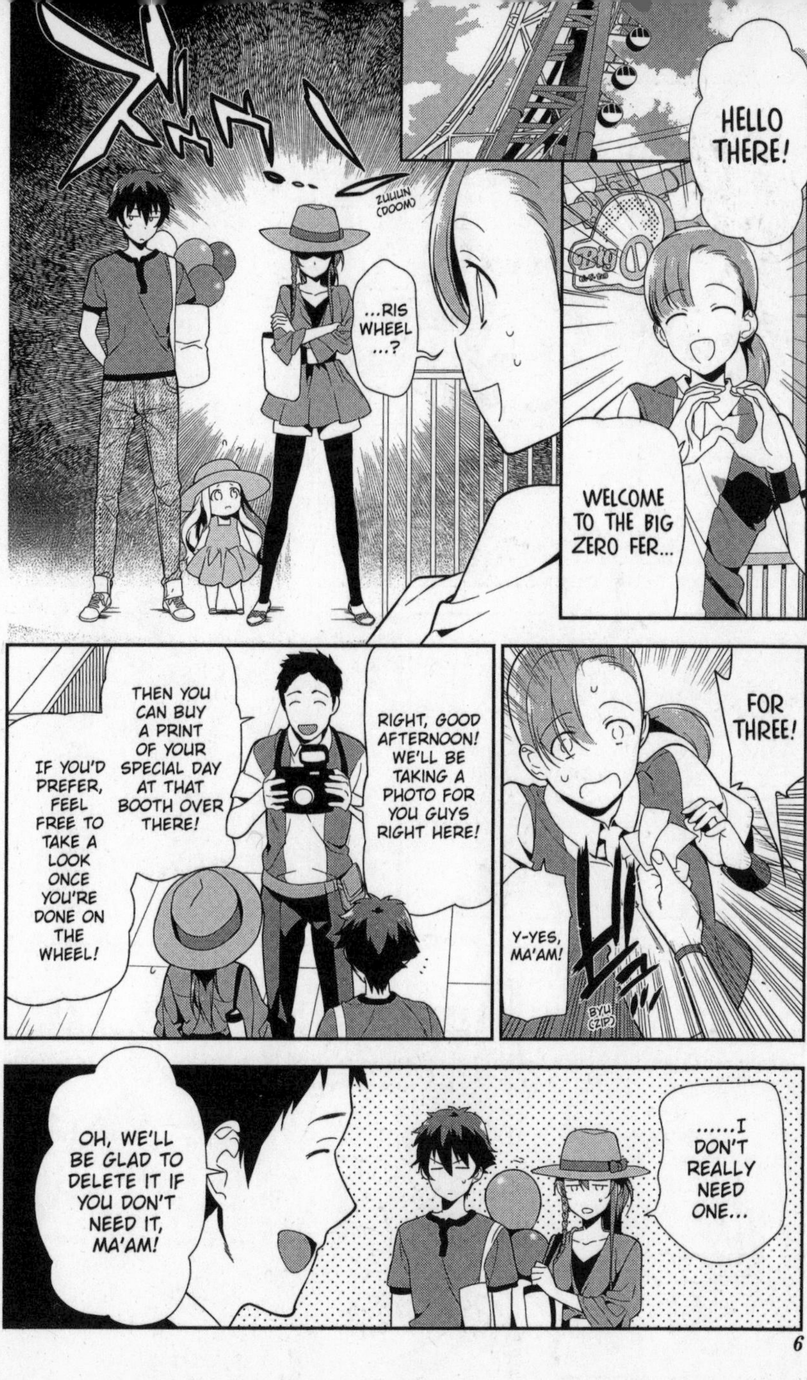
HELLO THERE!
WELCOME TO THE BIG ZERO FER...
ZUUUN (DOOM)
...RIS WHEEL ...?
FOR THREE!
Y-YES, MA'AM!
BYU (ZIP)
RIGHT, GOOD AFTERNOON! WE'LL BE TAKING A PHOTO FOR YOU GUYS RIGHT HERE!
THEN YOU CAN BUY A PRINT OF YOUR SPECIAL DAY AT THAT BOOTH OVER THERE!
IF YOU'D PREFER, FEEL FREE TO TAKE A LOOK ONCE YOU'RE DONE ON THE WHEEL!
......I DON'T REALLY NEED ONE...
OH, WE'LL BE GLAD TO DELETE IT IF YOU DON'T NEED IT, MA'AM!

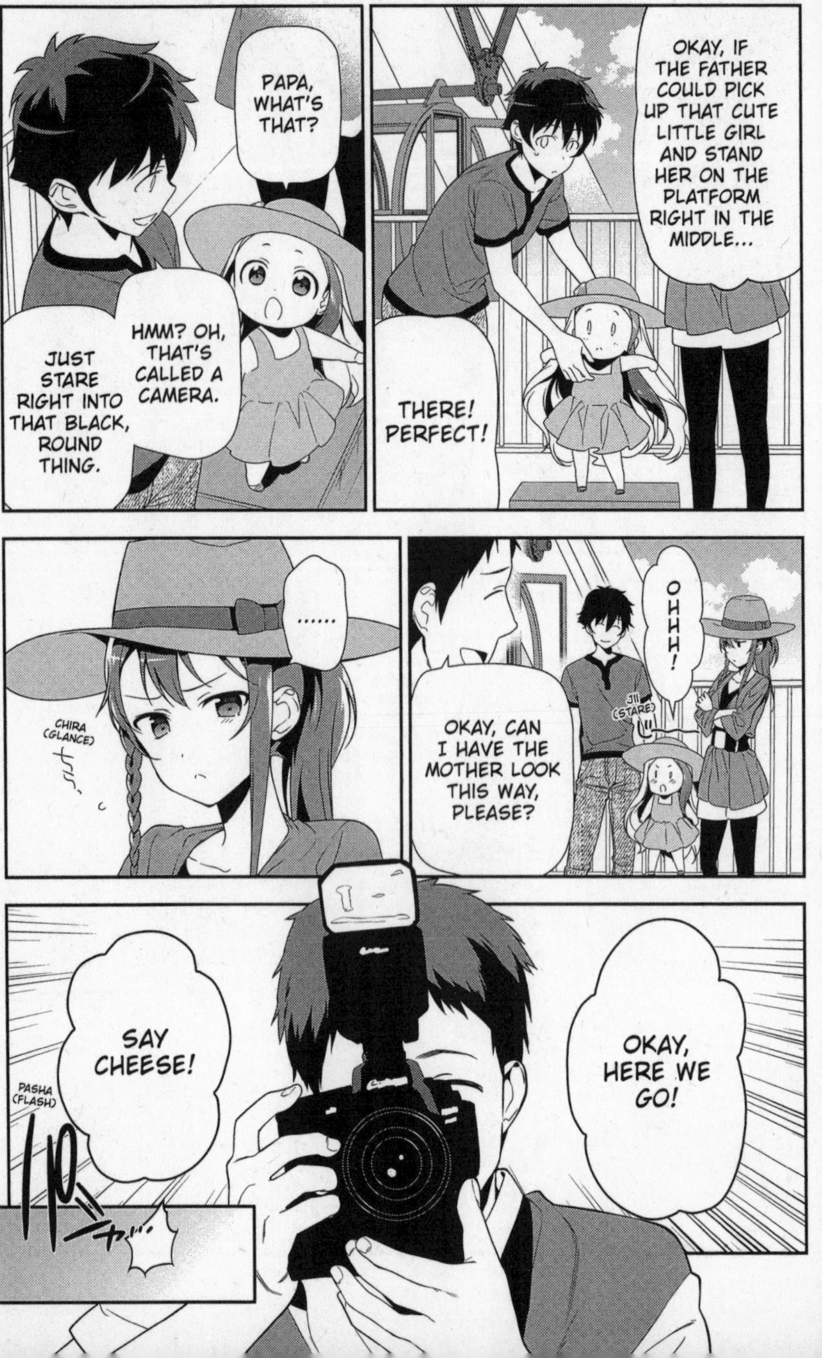
OKAY, IF THE FATHER COULD PICK UP THAT CUTE LITTLE GIRL AND STAND HER ON THE PLATFORM RIGHT IN THE MIDDLE...
THERE! PERFECT!
PAPA, WHAT'S THAT?
HMM? OH, THAT'S CALLED A CAMERA.
JUST STARE RIGHT INTO THAT BLACK, ROUND THING.
OHHH!
JII (STARE)
OKAY, CAN I HAVE THE MOTHER LOOK THIS WAY, PLEASE?
......
CHIRA (GLANCE)
OKAY, HERE WE GO!
SAY CHEESE!
PASHA (FLASH)

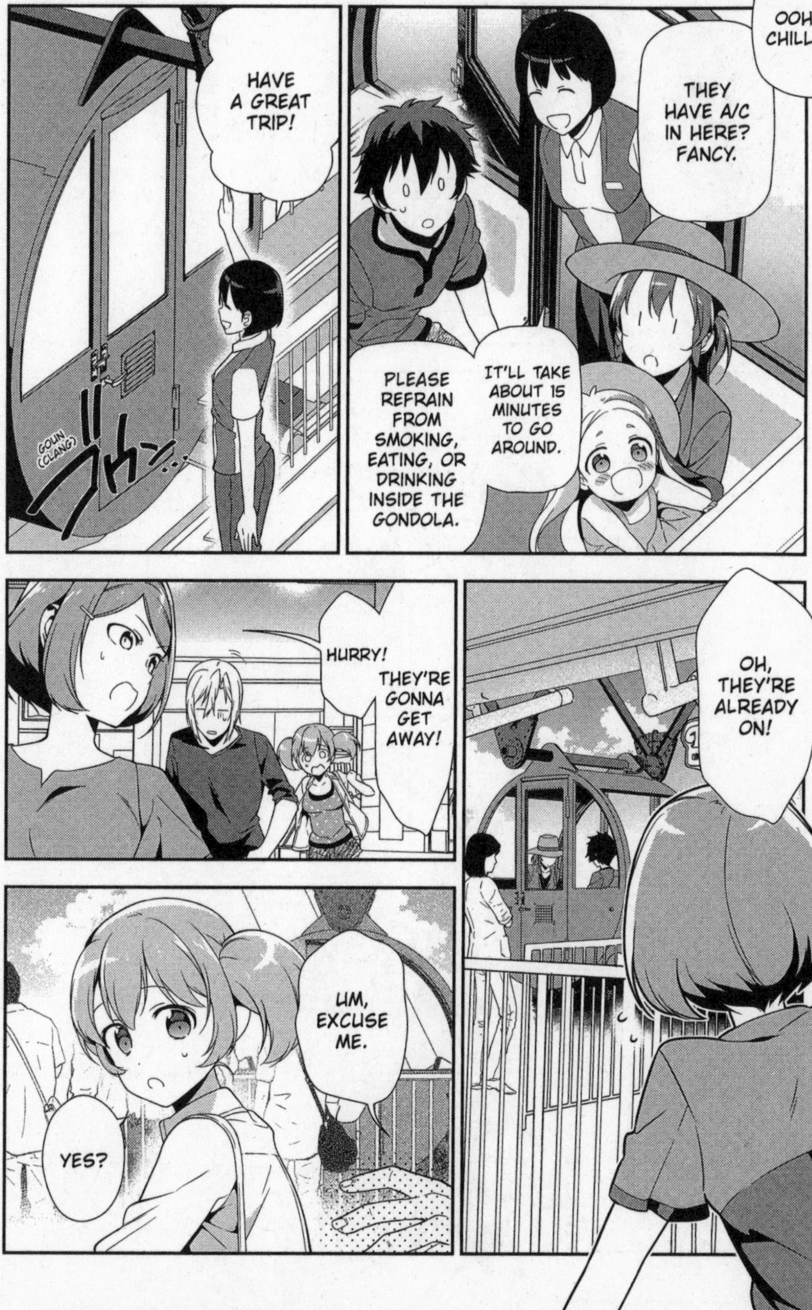
OOH, CHILLY.
THEY HAVE A/C IN HERE? FANCY.
IT'LL TAKE ABOUT 15 MINUTES TO GO AROUND.
PLEASE REFRAIN FROM SMOKING, EATING, OR DRINKING INSIDE THE GONDOLA.
HAVE A GREAT TRIP!
GOUN (CLANG)
OH, THEY'RE ALREADY ON!
HURRY!
THEY'RE GONNA GET AWAY!
UM, EXCUSE ME.
YES?

SIGN: ATTRACTIONS

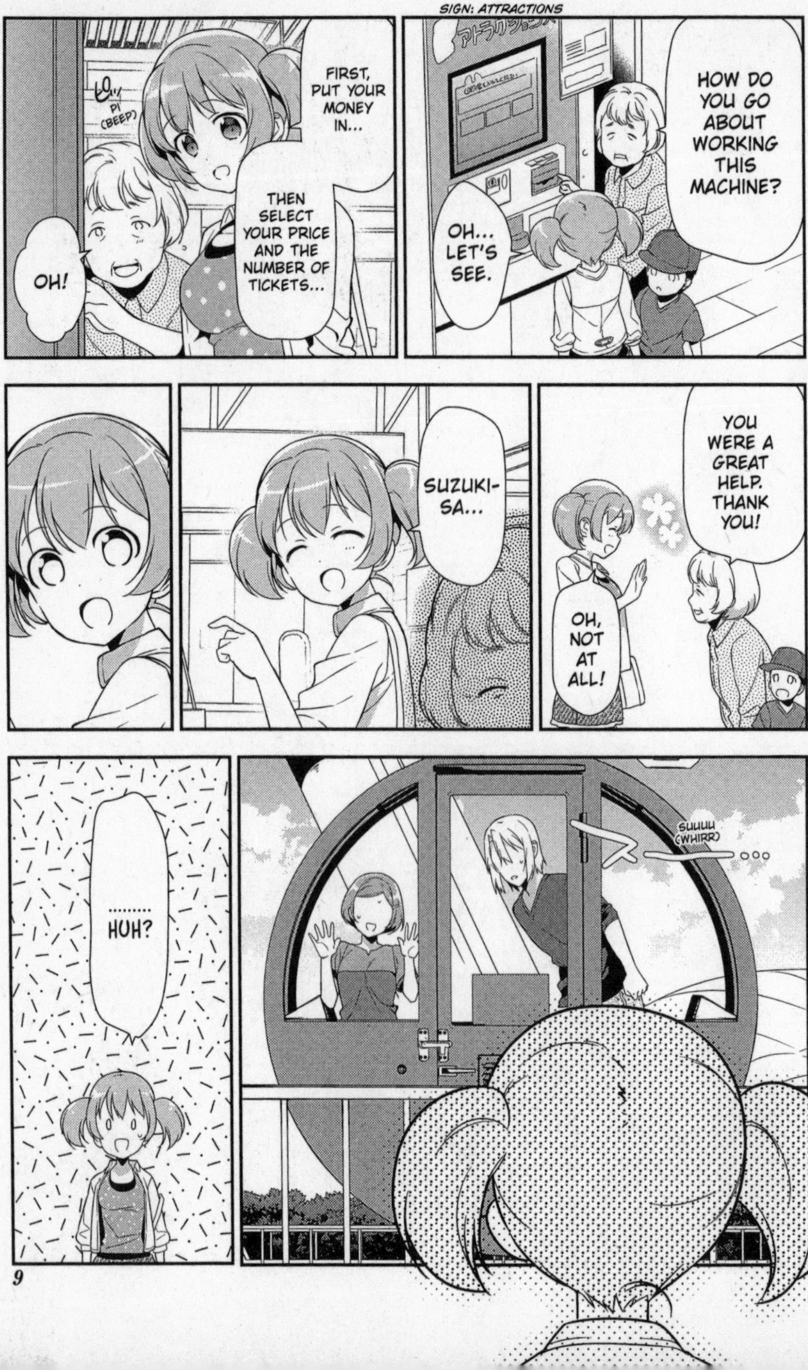

HOW DO YOU GO ABOUT WORKING THIS MACHINE?
OH... LET'S SEE.
FIRST, PUT YOUR MONEY IN...
PI (BEEP)
THEN SELECT YOUR PRICE AND THE NUMBER OF TICKETS...
OH!
YOU WERE A GREAT HELP. THANK YOU!
OH, NOT AT ALL!
SUZUKI-SA...
SUUUU (WHIRR)
.... HUH?

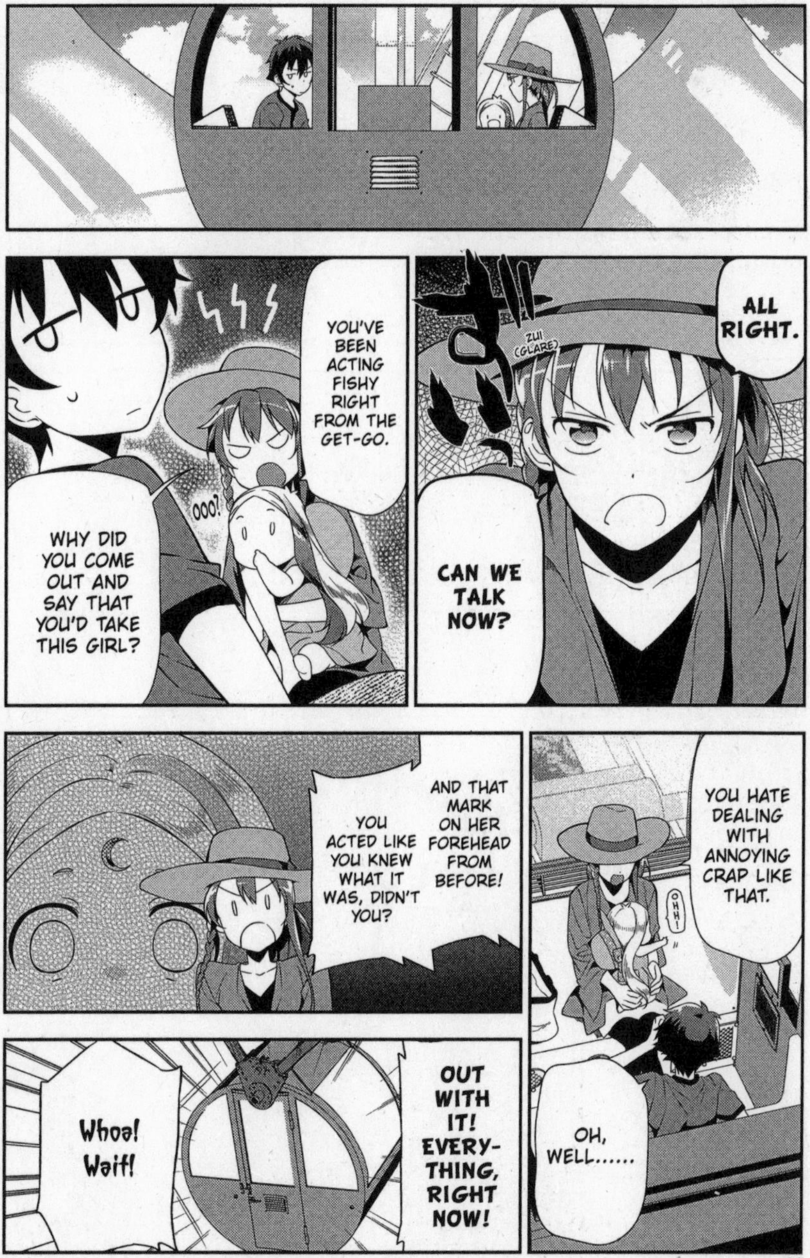
ALL RIGHT.
ZUI (GLARE)
CAN WE TALK NOW?
YOU'VE BEEN ACTING FISHY RIGHT FROM THE GET-GO.
OOO?
WHY DID YOU COME OUT AND SAY THAT YOU'D TAKE THIS GIRL?
YOU HATE DEALING WITH ANNOYING CRAP LIKE THAT.
OHH!
OH, WELL......
AND THAT MARK ON HER FOREHEAD FROM BEFORE!
YOU ACTED LIKE YOU KNEW WHAT IT WAS, DIDN'T YOU?
OUT WITH IT! EVERYTHING, RIGHT NOW!
Whoa! Wait!

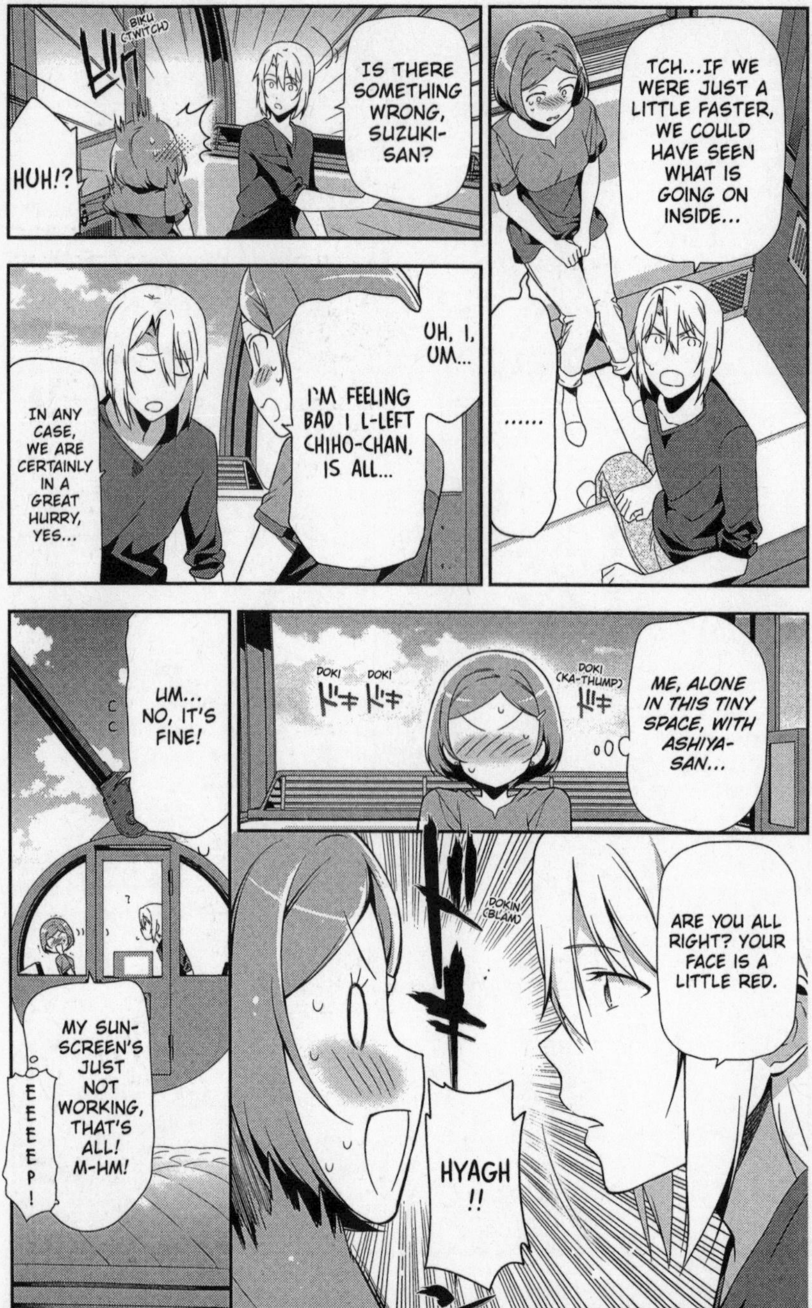
TCH...IF WE WERE JUST A LITTLE FASTER, WE COULD HAVE SEEN WHAT IS GOING ON INSIDE...
......
BIKU (TWITCH)
IS THERE SOMETHING WRONG, SUZUKI-SAN?
HUH!?
UH, I, UM...
I'M FEELING BAD I L-LEFT CHIHO-CHAN, IS ALL...
IN ANY CASE, WE ARE CERTAINLY IN A GREAT HURRY, YES...
ME, ALONE IN THIS TINY SPACE, WITH ASHIYA-SAN...
DOKI (KA-THUMP)
DOKI DOKI
ARE YOU ALL RIGHT? YOUR FACE IS A LITTLE RED.
DOKIN (BLAM)
HYAGH!!
UM... NO, IT'S FINE!
MY SUN-SCREEN'S JUST NOT WORKING, THAT'S ALL! M-HM!
EEEEEP!

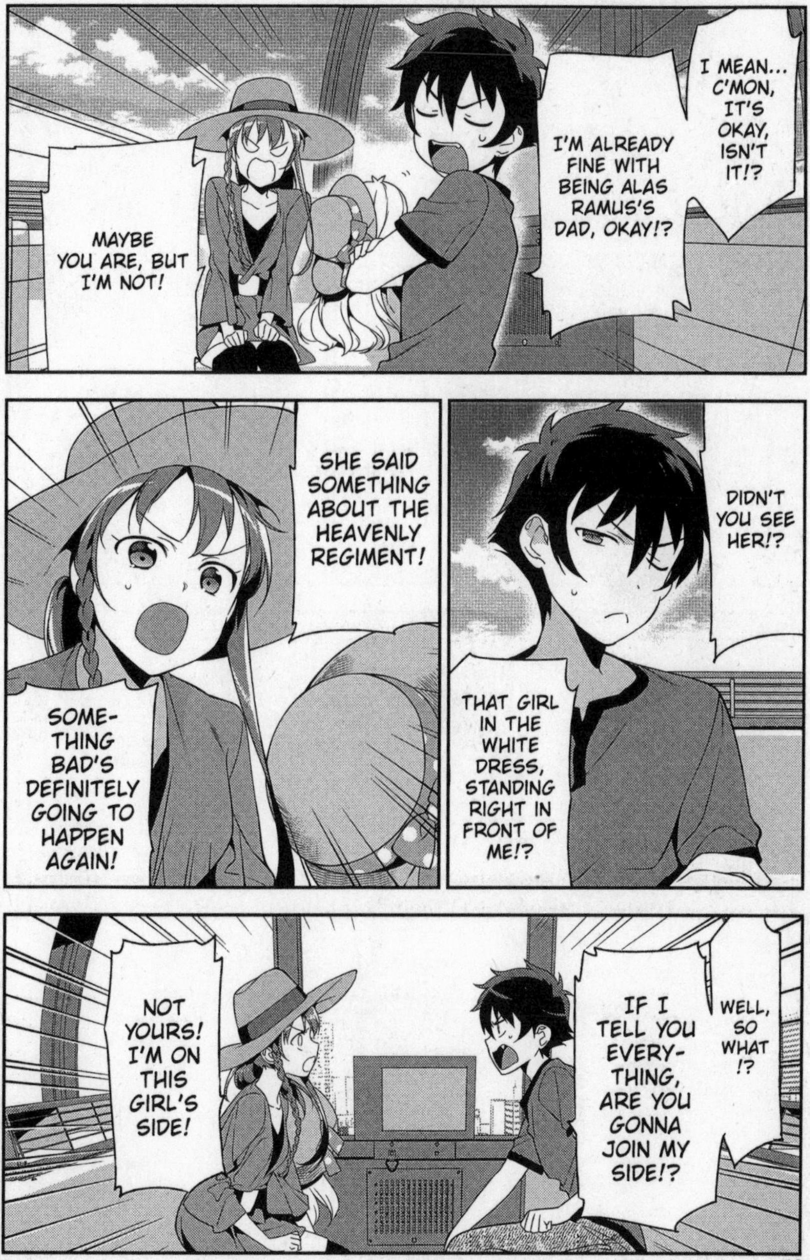
I MEAN... C'MON, IT'S OKAY, ISN'T IT!?
I'M ALREADY FINE WITH BEING ALAS RAMUS'S DAD, OKAY!?
MAYBE YOU ARE, BUT I'M NOT!
DIDN'T YOU SEE HER!?
THAT GIRL IN THE WHITE DRESS, STANDING RIGHT IN FRONT OF ME!?
SHE SAID SOMETHING ABOUT THE HEAVENLY REGIMENT!
SOME-THING BAD'S DEFINITELY GOING TO HAPPEN AGAIN!
WELL, SO WHAT!?
IF I TELL YOU EVERY-THING, ARE YOU GONNA JOIN MY SIDE!?
NOT YOURS! I'M ON THIS GIRL'S SIDE!

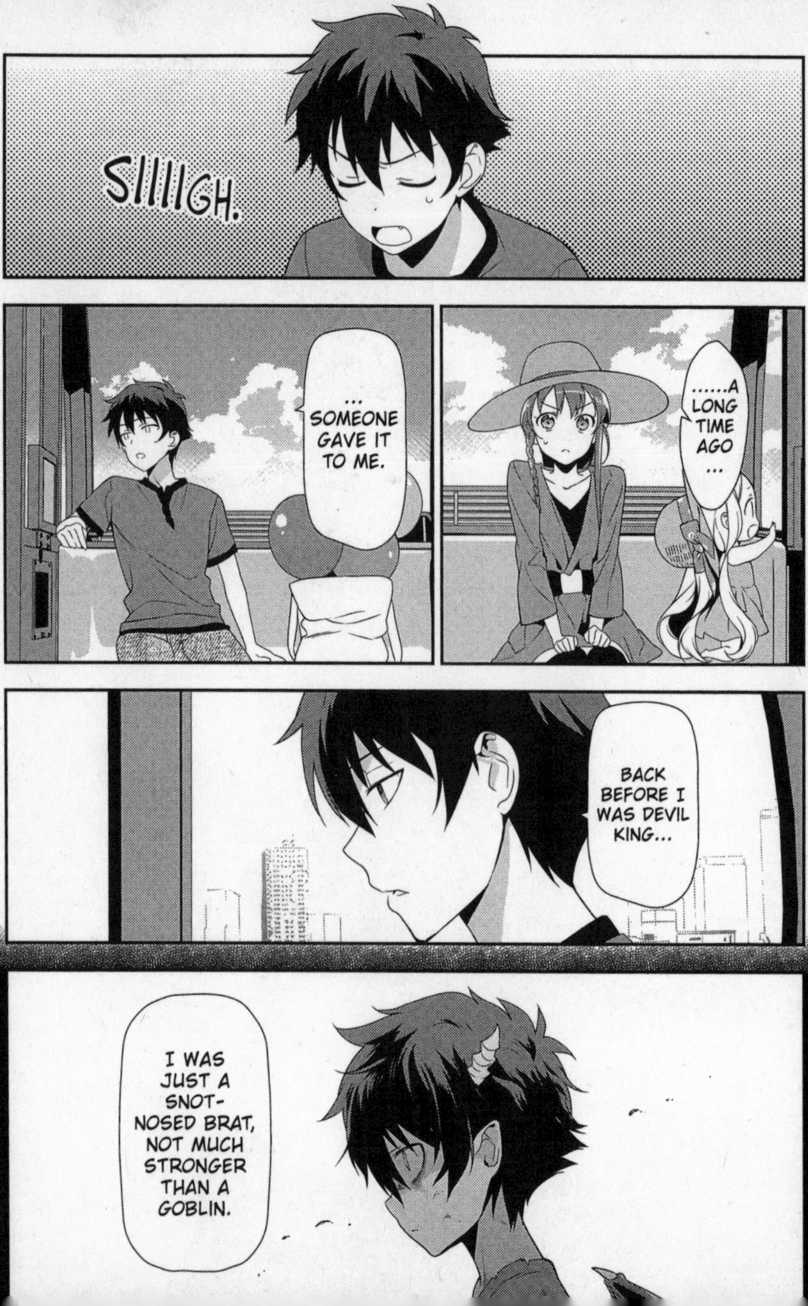
SIIIGH.
......A LONG TIME AGO ...
... SOMEONE GAVE IT TO ME.
BACK BEFORE I WAS DEVIL KING...
I WAS JUST A SNOT-NOSED BRAT, NOT MUCH STRONGER THAN A GOBLIN.

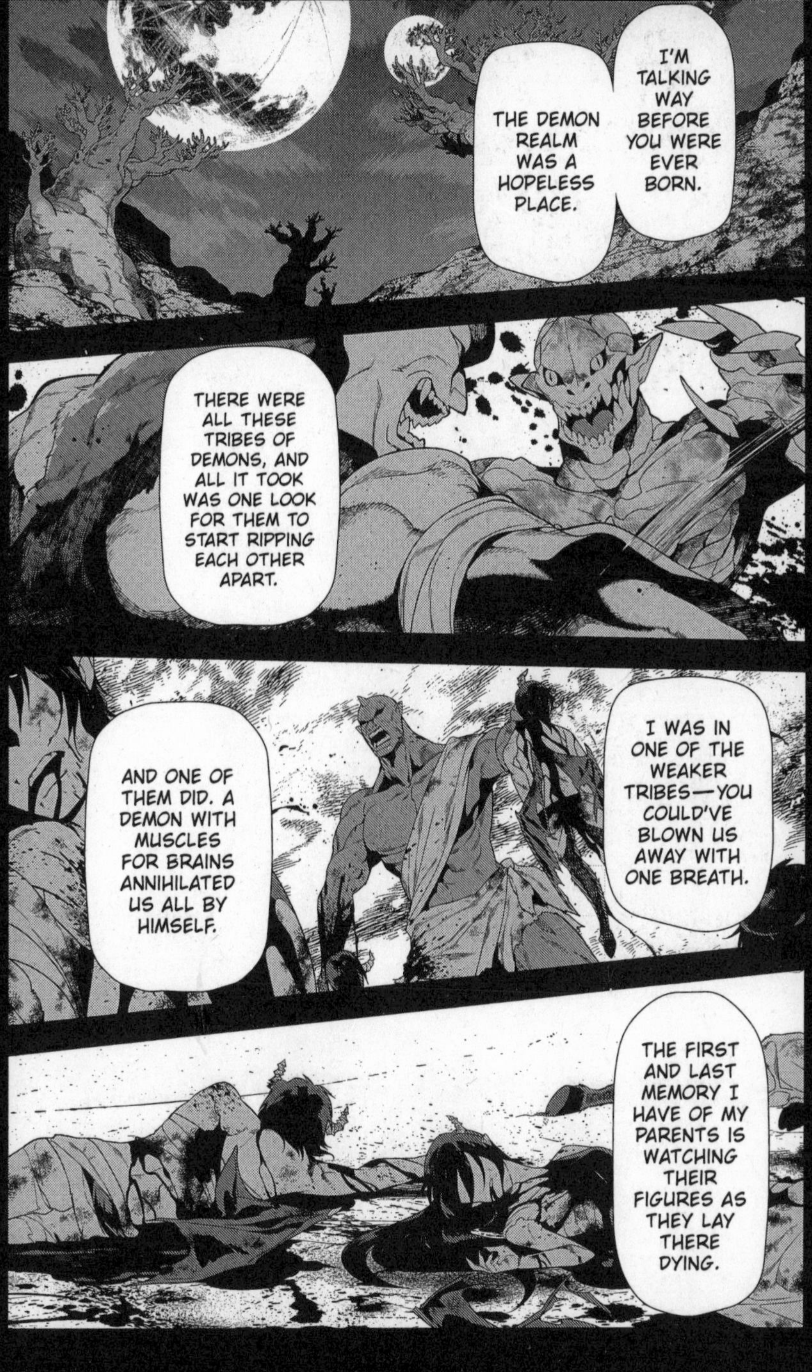
I'M TALKING WAY BEFORE YOU WERE EVER BORN.
THE DEMON REALM WAS A HOPELESS PLACE.
THERE WERE ALL THESE TRIBES OF DEMONS, AND ALL IT TOOK WAS ONE LOOK FOR THEM TO START RIPPING EACH OTHER APART.
I WAS IN ONE OF THE WEAKER TRIBES—YOU COULD'VE BLOWN US AWAY WITH ONE BREATH.
AND ONE OF THEM DID. A DEMON WITH MUSCLES FOR BRAINS ANNIHILATED US ALL BY HIMSELF.
THE FIRST AND LAST MEMORY I HAVE OF MY PARENTS IS WATCHING THEIR FIGURES AS THEY LAY THERE DYING.

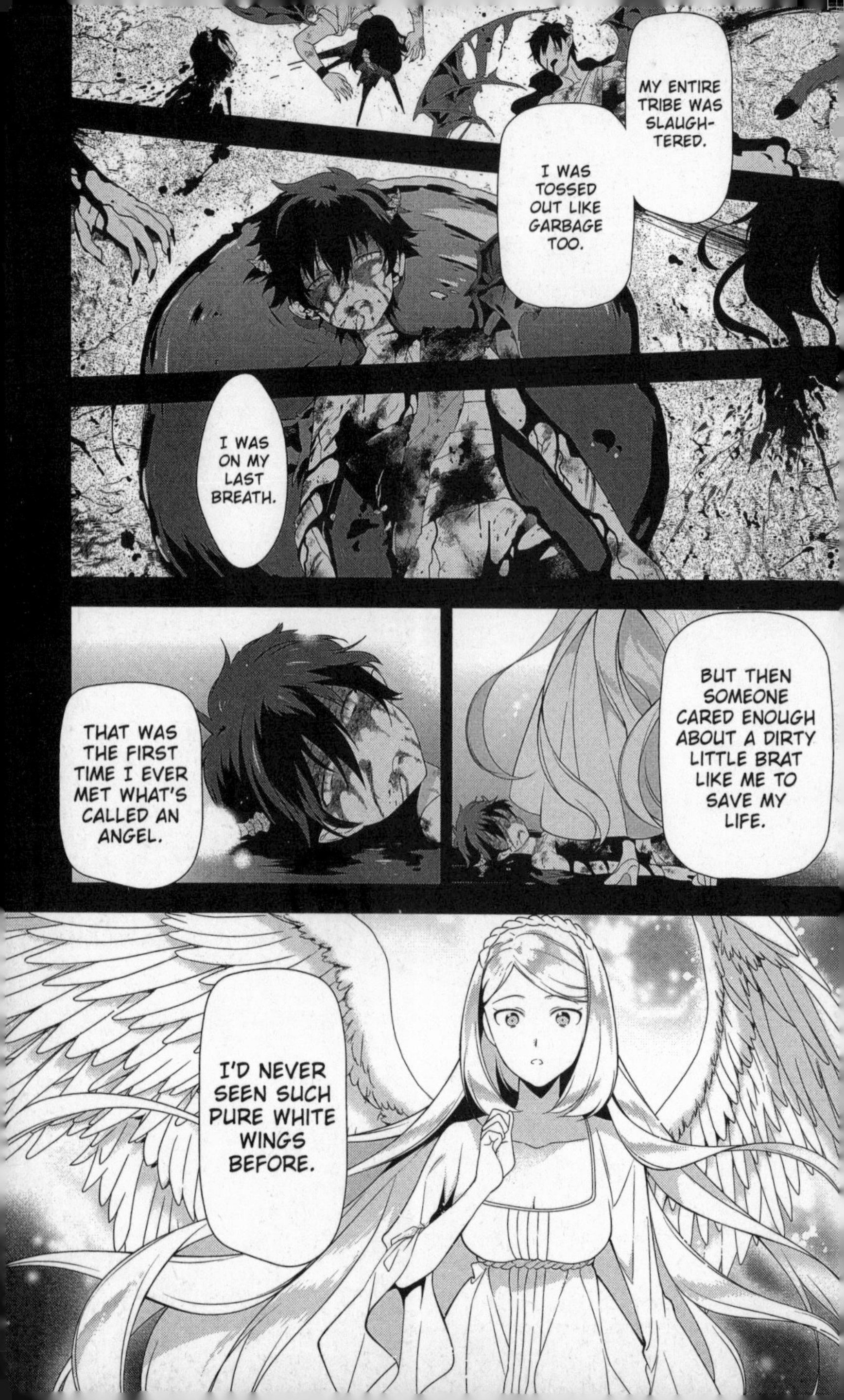
MY ENTIRE TRIBE WAS SLAUGHTERED.
I WAS TOSSED OUT LIKE GARBAGE TOO.
I WAS ON MY LAST BREATH.
BUT THEN SOMEONE CARED ENOUGH ABOUT A DIRTY LITTLE BRAT LIKE ME TO SAVE MY LIFE.
THAT WAS THE FIRST TIME I EVER MET WHAT'S CALLED AN ANGEL.
I'D NEVER SEEN SUCH PURE WHITE WINGS BEFORE.

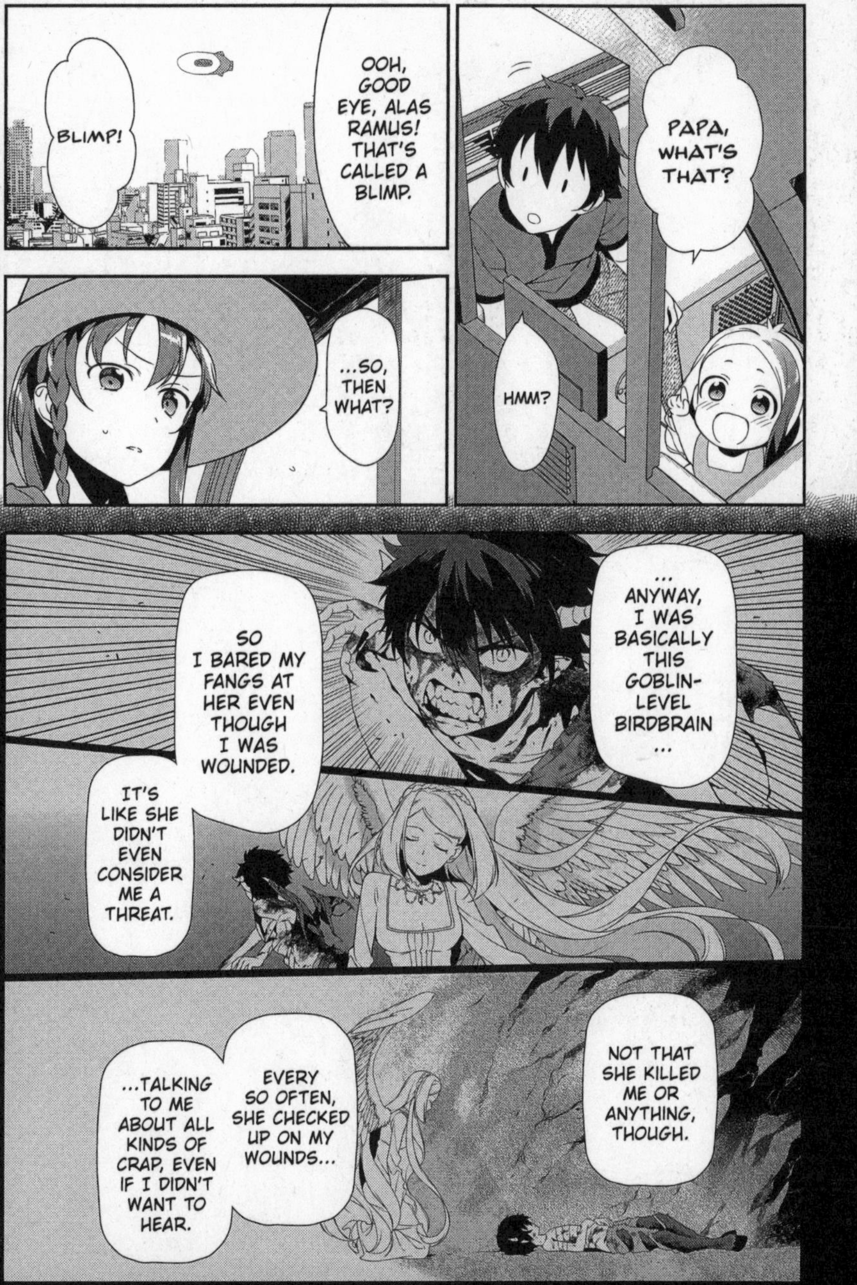
PAPA, WHAT'S THAT?
HMM?
OOH, GOOD EYE, ALAS RAMUS! THAT'S CALLED A BLIMP.
BLIMP!
...SO, THEN WHAT?
... ANYWAY, I WAS BASICALLY THIS GOBLIN-LEVEL BIRDBRAIN ...
SO I BARED MY FANGS AT HER EVEN THOUGH I WAS WOUNDED.
IT'S LIKE SHE DIDN'T EVEN CONSIDER ME A THREAT.
NOT THAT SHE KILLED ME OR ANYTHING, THOUGH.
EVERY SO OFTEN, SHE CHECKED UP ON MY WOUNDS...
...TALKING TO ME ABOUT ALL KINDS OF CRAP, EVEN IF I DIDN'T WANT TO HEAR.

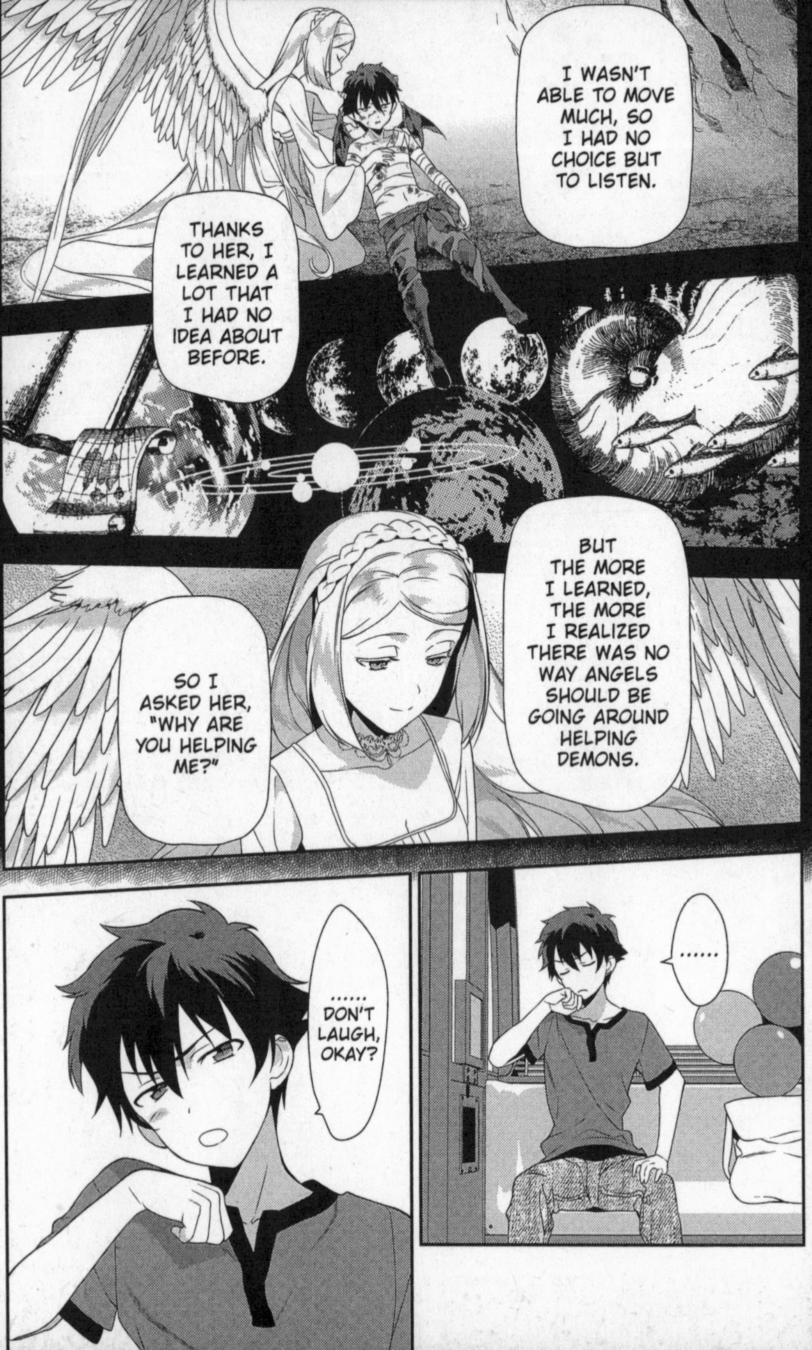
I WASN'T ABLE TO MOVE MUCH, SO I HAD NO CHOICE BUT TO LISTEN.
THANKS TO HER, I LEARNED A LOT THAT I HAD NO IDEA ABOUT BEFORE.
BUT THE MORE I LEARNED, THE MORE I REALIZED THERE WAS NO WAY ANGELS SHOULD BE GOING AROUND HELPING DEMONS.
SO I ASKED HER, "WHY ARE YOU HELPING ME?"
......
...... DON'T LAUGH, OKAY?

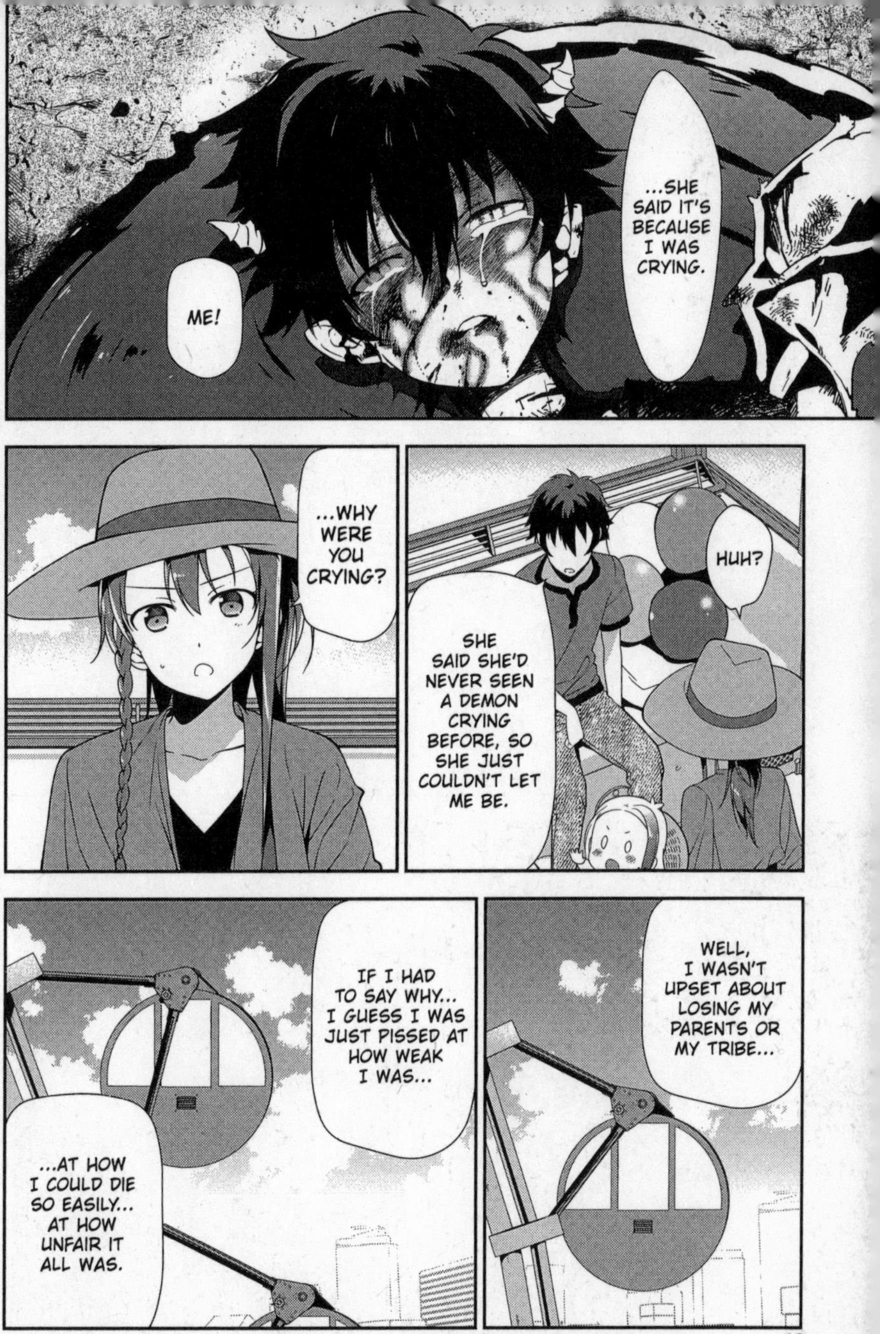
...SHE SAID IT'S BECAUSE I WAS CRYING.
ME!
HUH?
SHE SAID SHE'D NEVER SEEN A DEMON CRYING BEFORE, SO SHE JUST COULDN'T LET ME BE.
...WHY WERE YOU CRYING?
WELL, I WASN'T UPSET ABOUT LOSING MY PARENTS OR MY TRIBE...
IF I HAD TO SAY WHY... I GUESS I WAS JUST PISSED AT HOW WEAK I WAS...
...AT HOW I COULD DIE SO EASILY... AT HOW UNFAIR IT ALL WAS.

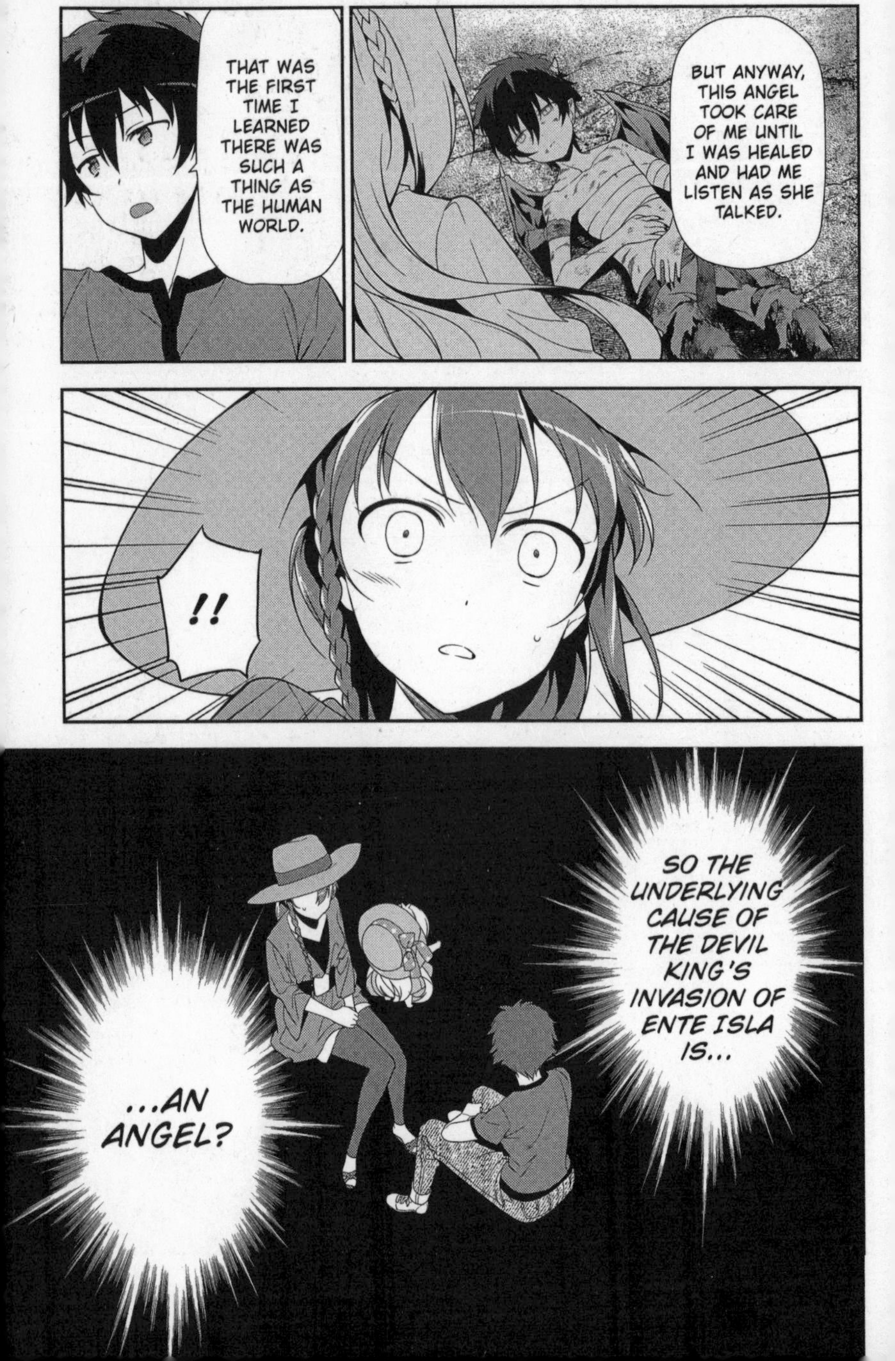
BUT ANYWAY, THIS ANGEL TOOK CARE OF ME UNTIL I WAS HEALED AND HAD ME LISTEN AS SHE TALKED.
THAT WAS THE FIRST TIME I LEARNED THERE WAS SUCH A THING AS THE HUMAN WORLD.
!!
SO THE UNDERLYING CAUSE OF THE DEVIL KING'S INVASION OF ENTE ISLA IS...
...AN ANGEL?

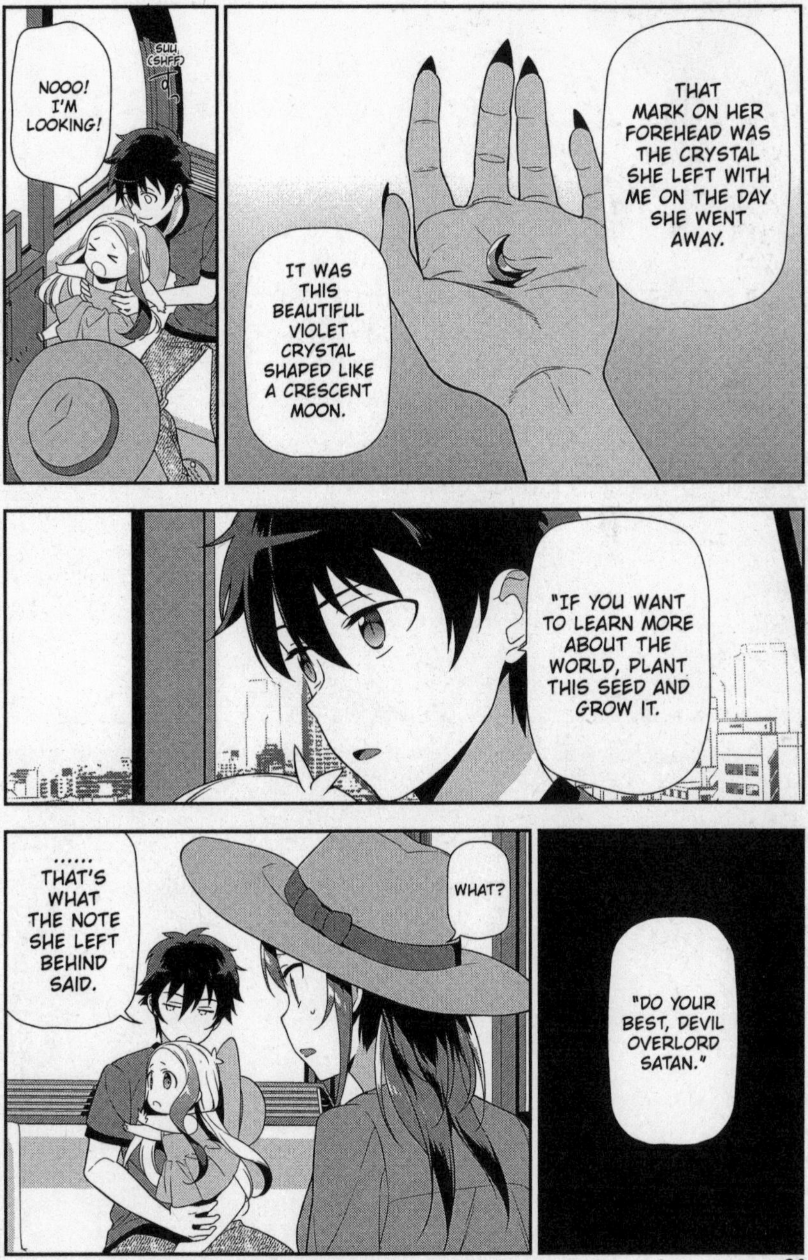
THAT MARK ON HER FOREHEAD WAS THE CRYSTAL SHE LEFT WITH ME ON THE DAY SHE WENT AWAY.
IT WAS THIS BEAUTIFUL VIOLET CRYSTAL SHAPED LIKE A CRESCENT MOON.
SUU, (SHFF)
NOOO! I'M LOOKING!
"IF YOU WANT TO LEARN MORE ABOUT THE WORLD, PLANT THIS SEED AND GROW IT.
"DO YOUR BEST, DEVIL OVERLORD SATAN."
WHAT?
...... THAT'S WHAT THE NOTE SHE LEFT BEHIND SAID.

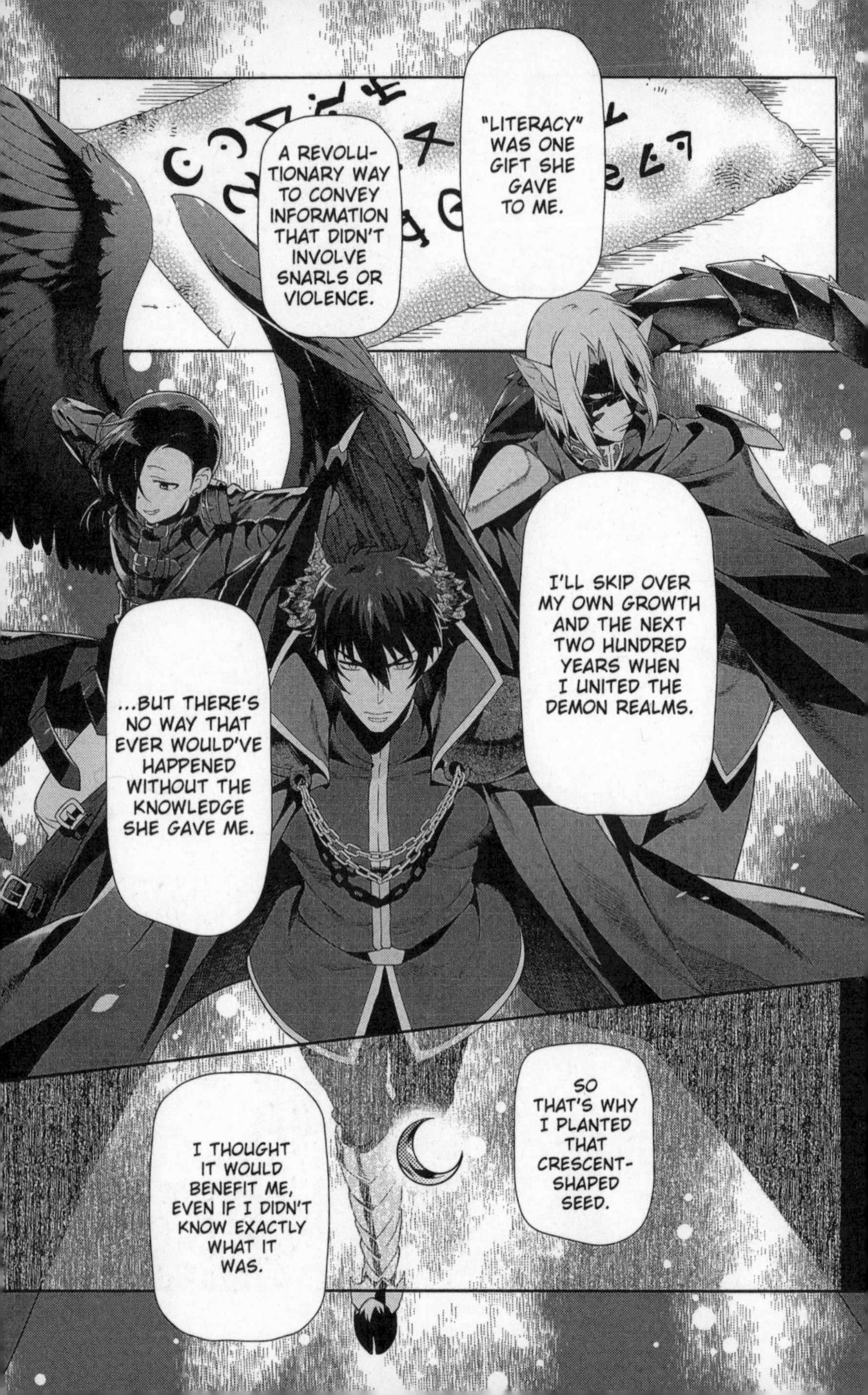
"LITERACY" WAS ONE GIFT SHE GAVE TO ME.
A REVOLUTIONARY WAY TO CONVEY INFORMATION THAT DIDN'T INVOLVE SNARLS OR VIOLENCE.
I'LL SKIP OVER MY OWN GROWTH AND THE NEXT TWO HUNDRED YEARS WHEN I UNITED THE DEMON REALMS.
...BUT THERE'S NO WAY THAT EVER WOULD'VE HAPPENED WITHOUT THE KNOWLEDGE SHE GAVE ME.
SO THAT'S WHY I PLANTED THAT CRESCENT-SHAPED SEED.
I THOUGHT IT WOULD BENEFIT ME, EVEN IF I DIDN'T KNOW EXACTLY WHAT IT WAS.

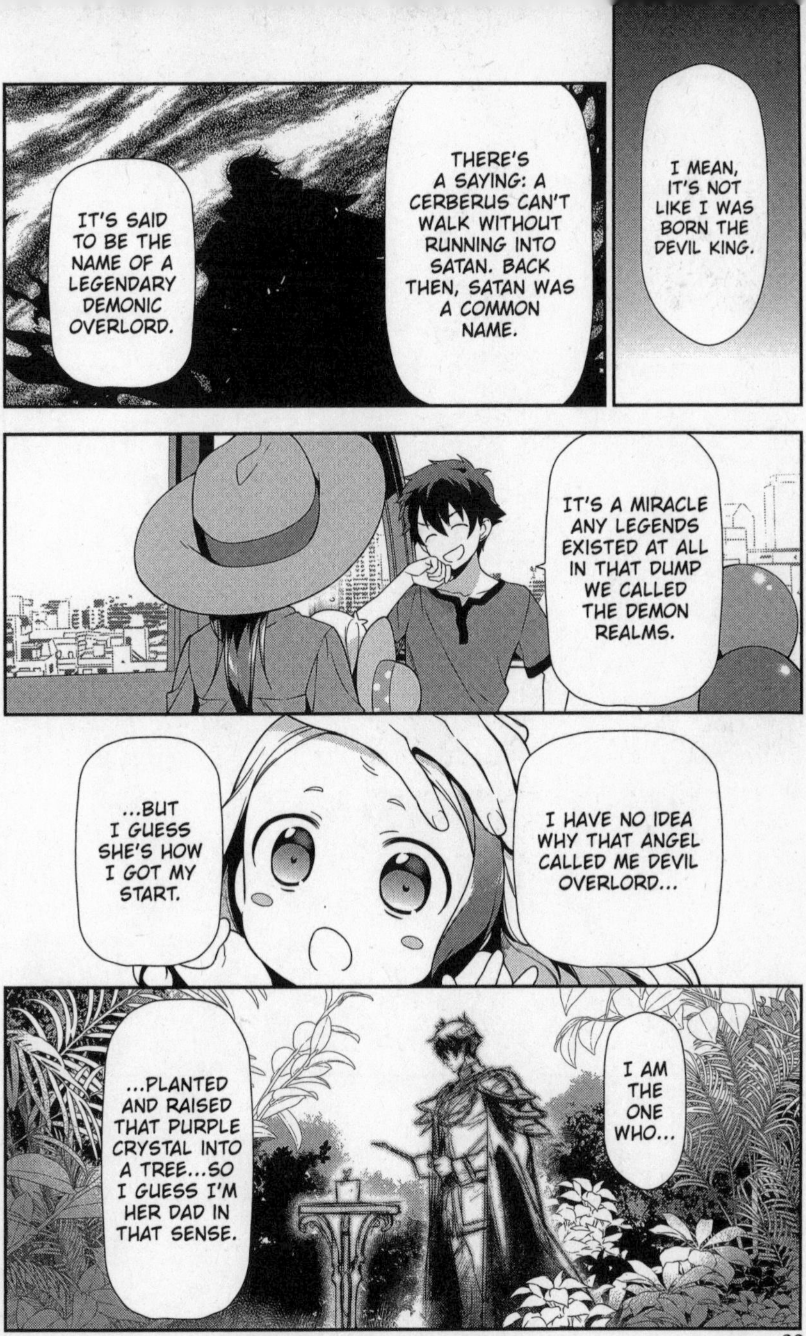
I MEAN, IT'S NOT LIKE I WAS BORN THE DEVIL KING.
THERE'S A SAYING: A CERBERUS CAN'T WALK WITHOUT RUNNING INTO SATAN. BACK THEN, SATAN WAS A COMMON NAME.
IT'S SAID TO BE THE NAME OF A LEGENDARY DEMONIC OVERLORD.
IT'S A MIRACLE ANY LEGENDS EXISTED AT ALL IN THAT DUMP WE CALLED THE DEMON REALMS.
I HAVE NO IDEA WHY THAT ANGEL CALLED ME DEVIL OVERLORD...
...BUT I GUESS SHE'S HOW I GOT MY START.
I AM THE ONE WHO...
...PLANTED AND RAISED THAT PURPLE CRYSTAL INTO A TREE...SO I GUESS I'M HER DAD IN THAT SENSE.

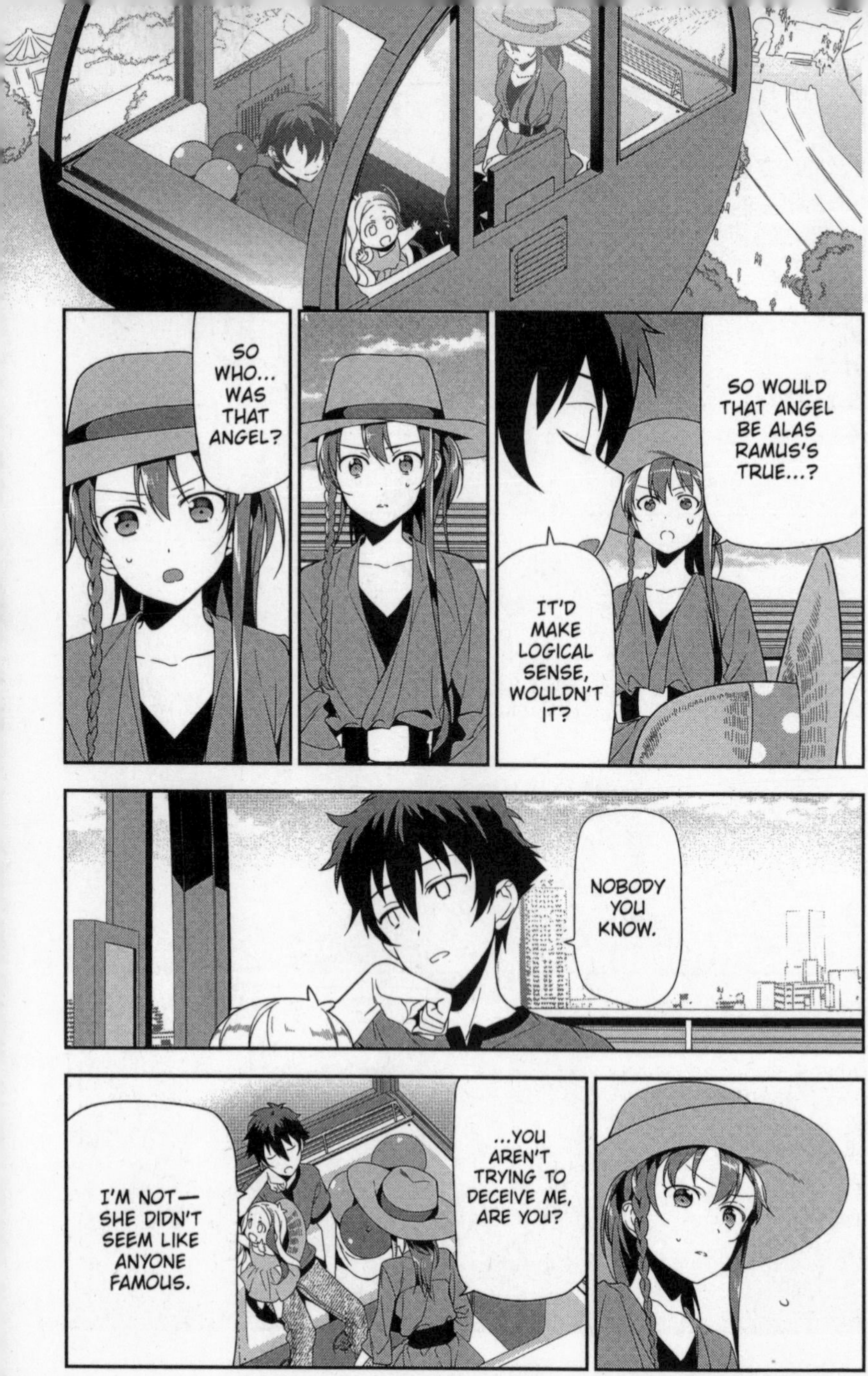
SO WOULD THAT ANGEL BE ALAS RAMUS'S TRUE...?
IT'D MAKE LOGICAL SENSE, WOULDN'T IT?
SO WHO... WAS THAT ANGEL?
NOBODY YOU KNOW.
...YOU AREN'T TRYING TO DECEIVE ME, ARE YOU?
I'M NOT— SHE DIDN'T SEEM LIKE ANYONE FAMOUS.

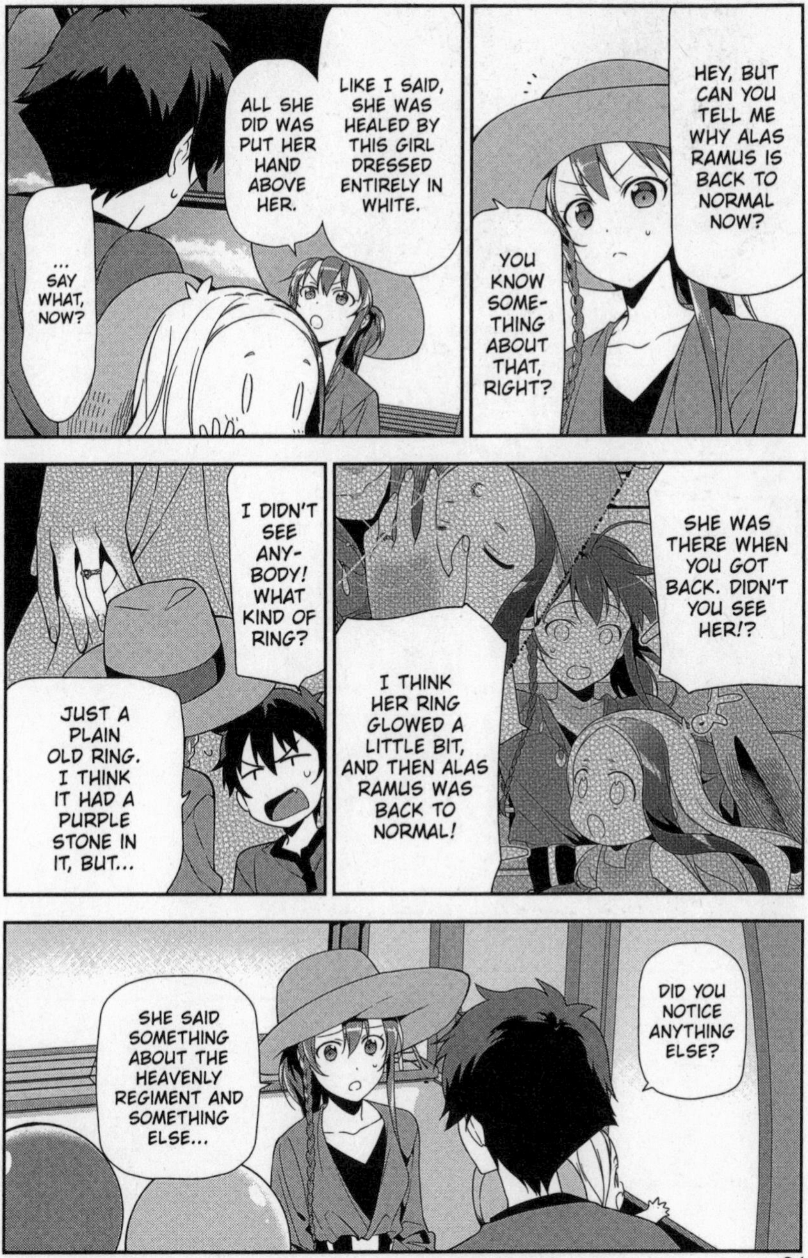
HEY, BUT CAN YOU TELL ME WHY ALAS RAMUS IS BACK TO NORMAL NOW?
YOU KNOW SOME-THING ABOUT THAT, RIGHT?
LIKE I SAID, SHE WAS HEALED BY THIS GIRL DRESSED ENTIRELY IN WHITE.
ALL SHE DID WAS PUT HER HAND ABOVE HER.
... SAY WHAT, NOW?
SHE WAS THERE WHEN YOU GOT BACK. DIDN'T YOU SEE HER!?
I THINK HER RING GLOWED A LITTLE BIT, AND THEN ALAS RAMUS WAS BACK TO NORMAL!
I DIDN'T SEE ANY-BODY! WHAT KIND OF RING?
JUST A PLAIN OLD RING. I THINK IT HAD A PURPLE STONE IN IT, BUT...
DID YOU NOTICE ANYTHING ELSE?
SHE SAID SOMETHING ABOUT THE HEAVENLY REGIMENT AND SOMETHING ELSE...

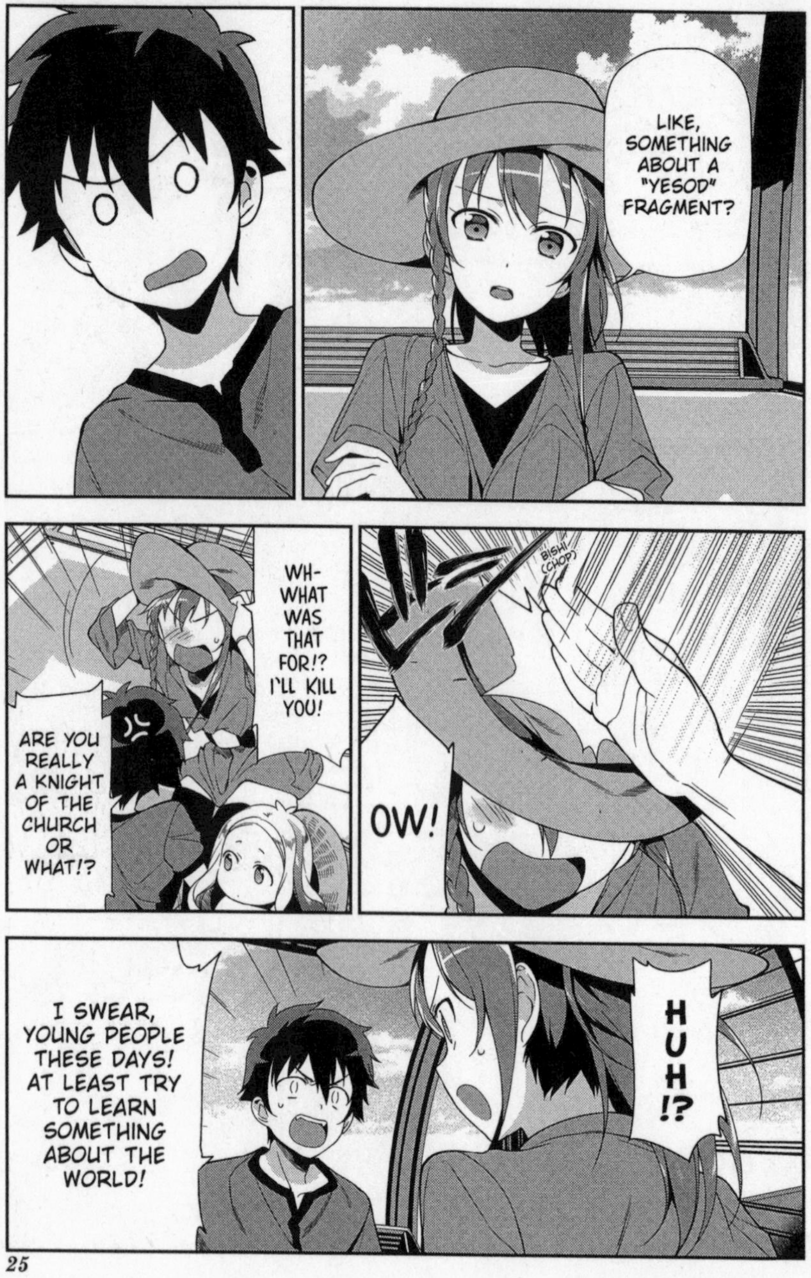
LIKE, SOMETHING ABOUT A "YESOD" FRAGMENT?
BISHI (CHOP)
OW!
WH-WHAT WAS THAT FOR!? I'LL KILL YOU!
ARE YOU REALLY A KNIGHT OF THE CHURCH OR WHAT!?
HUH!?
I SWEAR, YOUNG PEOPLE THESE DAYS! AT LEAST TRY TO LEARN SOMETHING ABOUT THE WORLD!

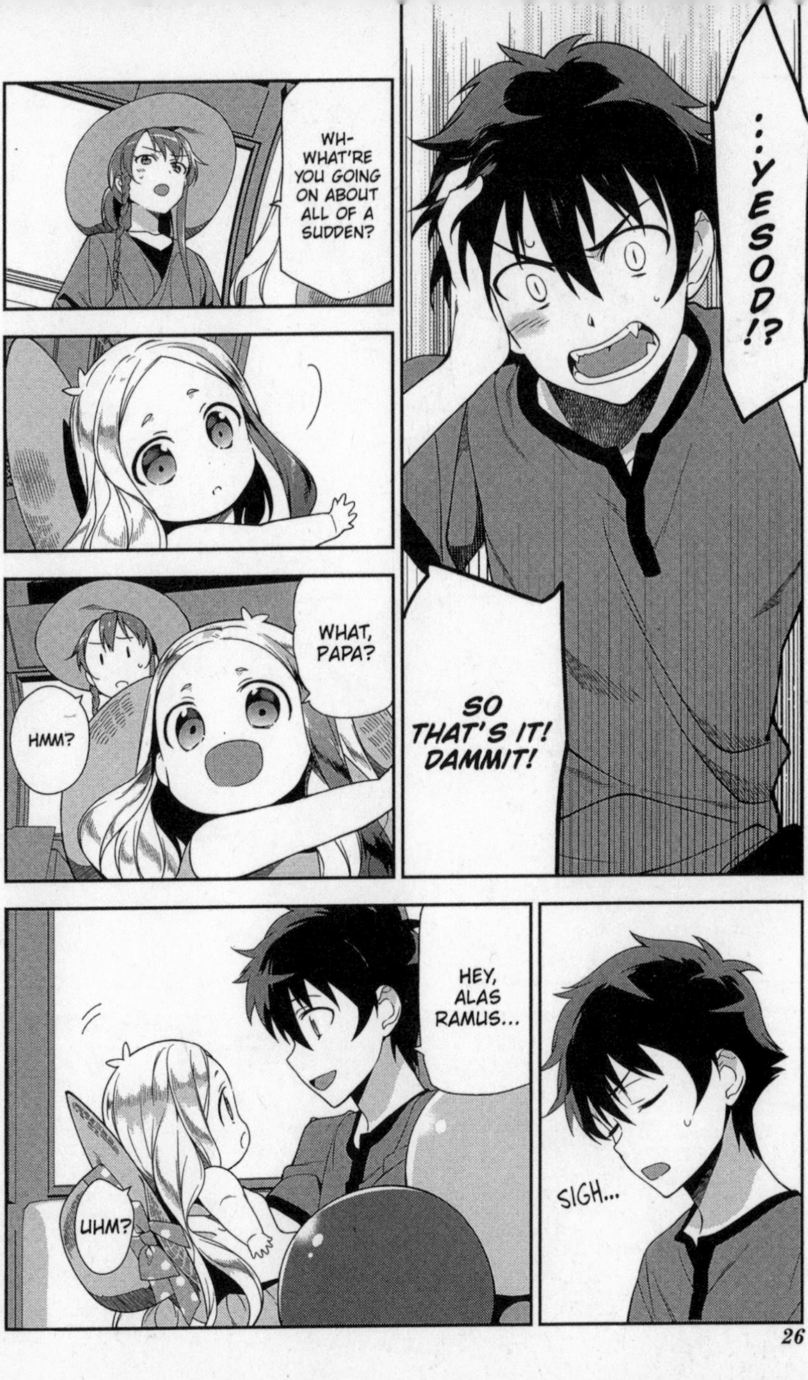
...YESOD!?
SO THAT'S IT! DAMMIT!
WH- WHAT'RE YOU GOING ON ABOUT ALL OF A SUDDEN?
WHAT, PAPA?
HMM?
SIGH...
HEY, ALAS RAMUS...
UHM?

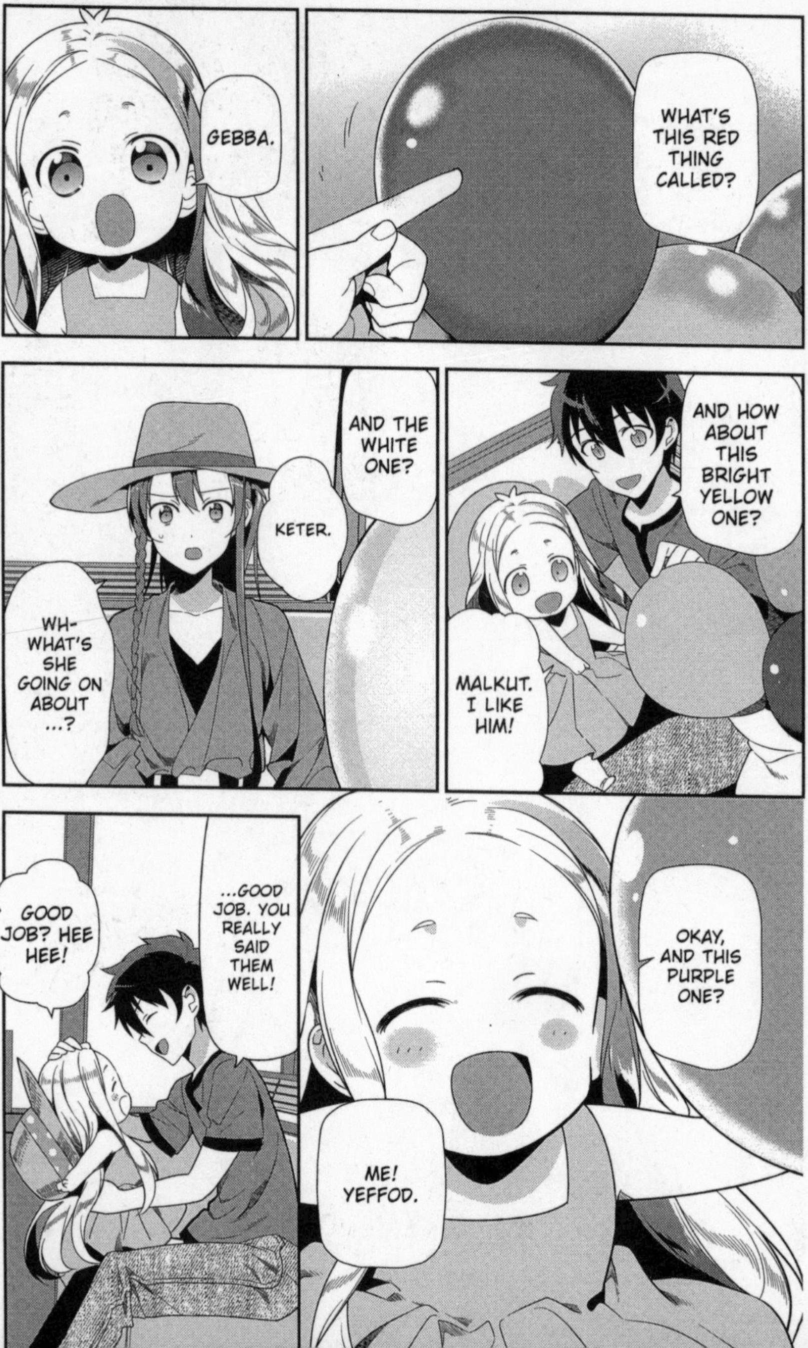
WHAT'S THIS RED THING CALLED?
GEBBA.
AND HOW ABOUT THIS BRIGHT YELLOW ONE?
MALKUT. I LIKE HIM!
AND THE WHITE ONE?
KETER.
WH-WHAT'S SHE GOING ON ABOUT ...?
OKAY, AND THIS PURPLE ONE?
ME! YEFFOD.
...GOOD JOB. YOU REALLY SAID THEM WELL!
GOOD JOB? HEE HEE!

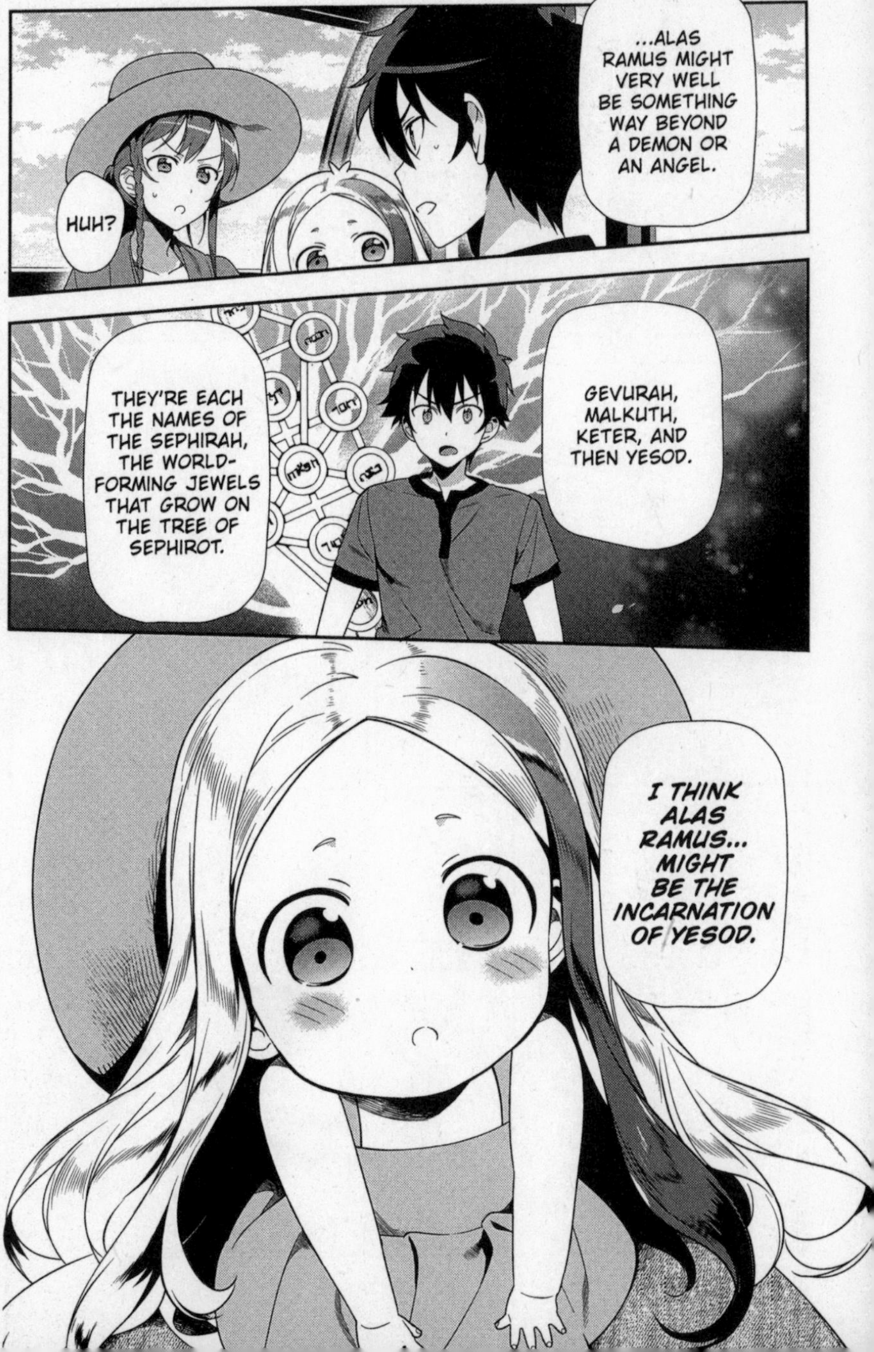
...ALAS RAMUS MIGHT VERY WELL BE SOMETHING WAY BEYOND A DEMON OR AN ANGEL.
HUH?
GEVURAH, MALKUTH, KETER, AND THEN YESOD.
THEY'RE EACH THE NAMES OF THE SEPHIRAH, THE WORLD-FORMING JEWELS THAT GROW ON THE TREE OF SEPHIROT.
I THINK ALAS RAMUS... MIGHT BE THE INCARNATION OF YESOD.

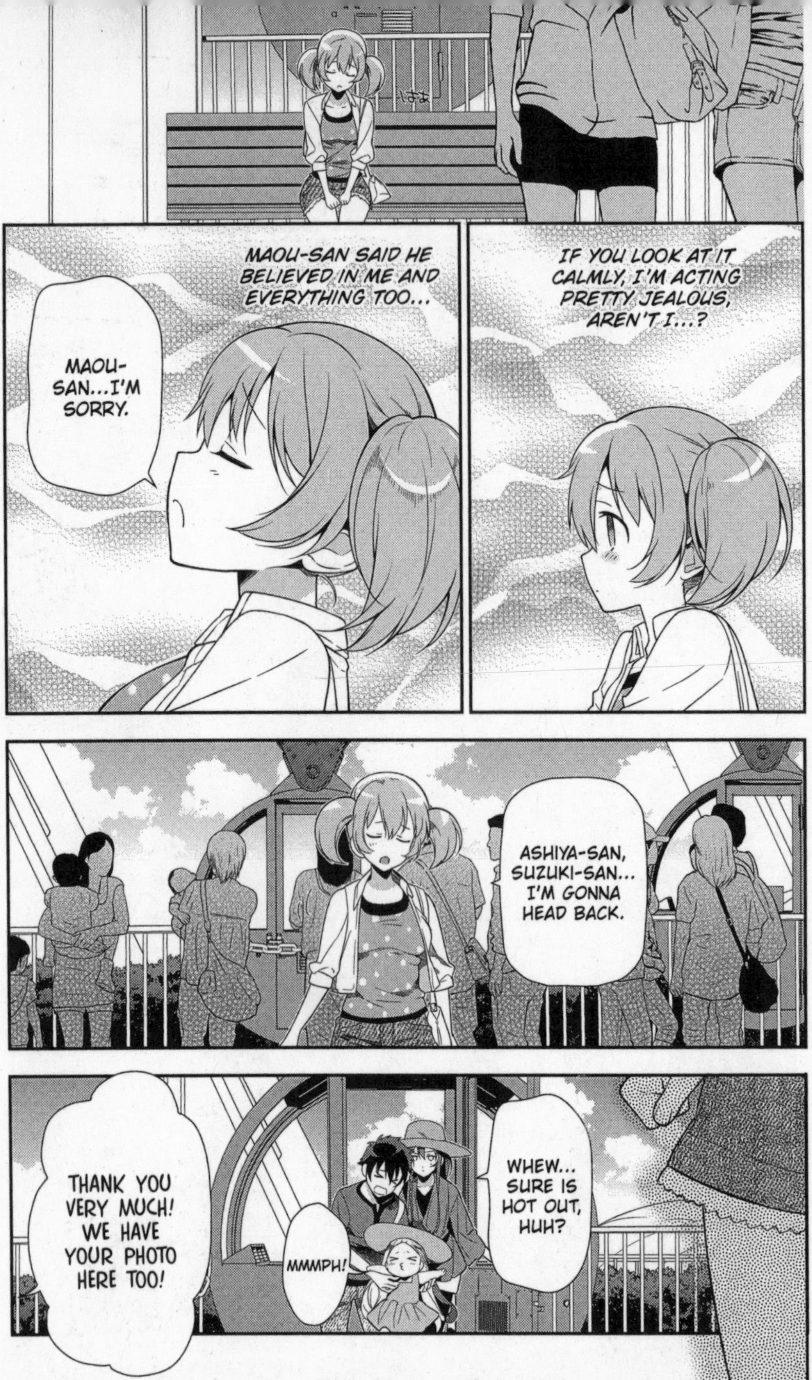
IF YOU LOOK AT IT CALMLY, I'M ACTING PRETTY JEALOUS, AREN'T I...?
MAOU-SAN SAID HE BELIEVED IN ME AND EVERYTHING TOO...
MAOU-SAN...I'M SORRY.
ASHIYA-SAN, SUZUKI-SAN... I'M GONNA HEAD BACK.
WHEW... SURE IS HOT OUT, HUH?
MMMPH!
THANK YOU VERY MUCH! WE HAVE YOUR PHOTO HERE TOO!

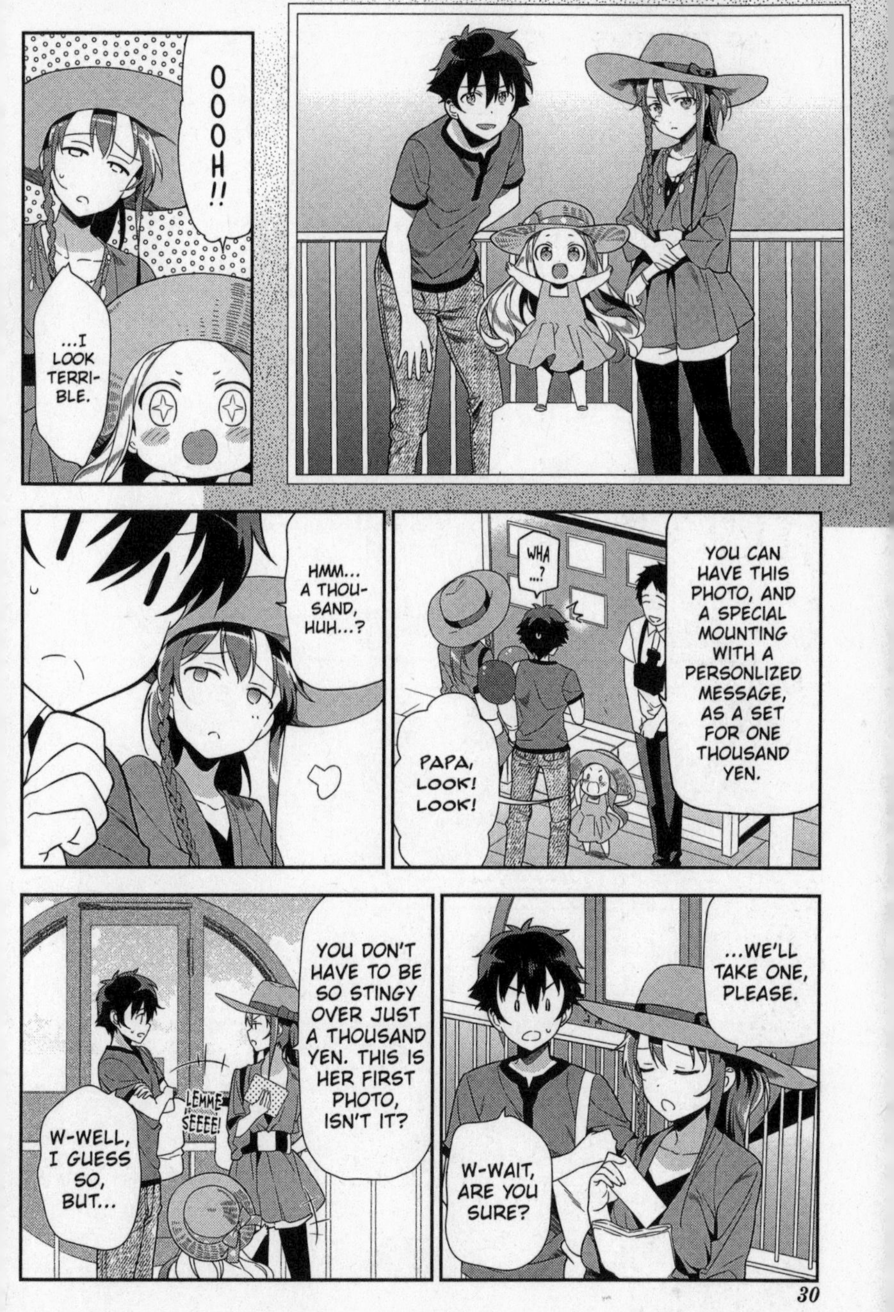
OOOH!!
...I LOOK TERRIBLE.
YOU CAN HAVE THIS PHOTO, AND A SPECIAL MOUNTING WITH A PERSONLIZED MESSAGE, AS A SET FOR ONE THOUSAND YEN.
WHA...?
PAPA, LOOK! LOOK!
HMM... A THOUSAND, HUH...?
...WE'LL TAKE ONE, PLEASE.
W-WAIT, ARE YOU SURE?
YOU DON'T HAVE TO BE SO STINGY OVER JUST A THOUSAND YEN. THIS IS HER FIRST PHOTO, ISN'T IT?
LEMME SEEEE!
W-WELL, I GUESS SO, BUT...

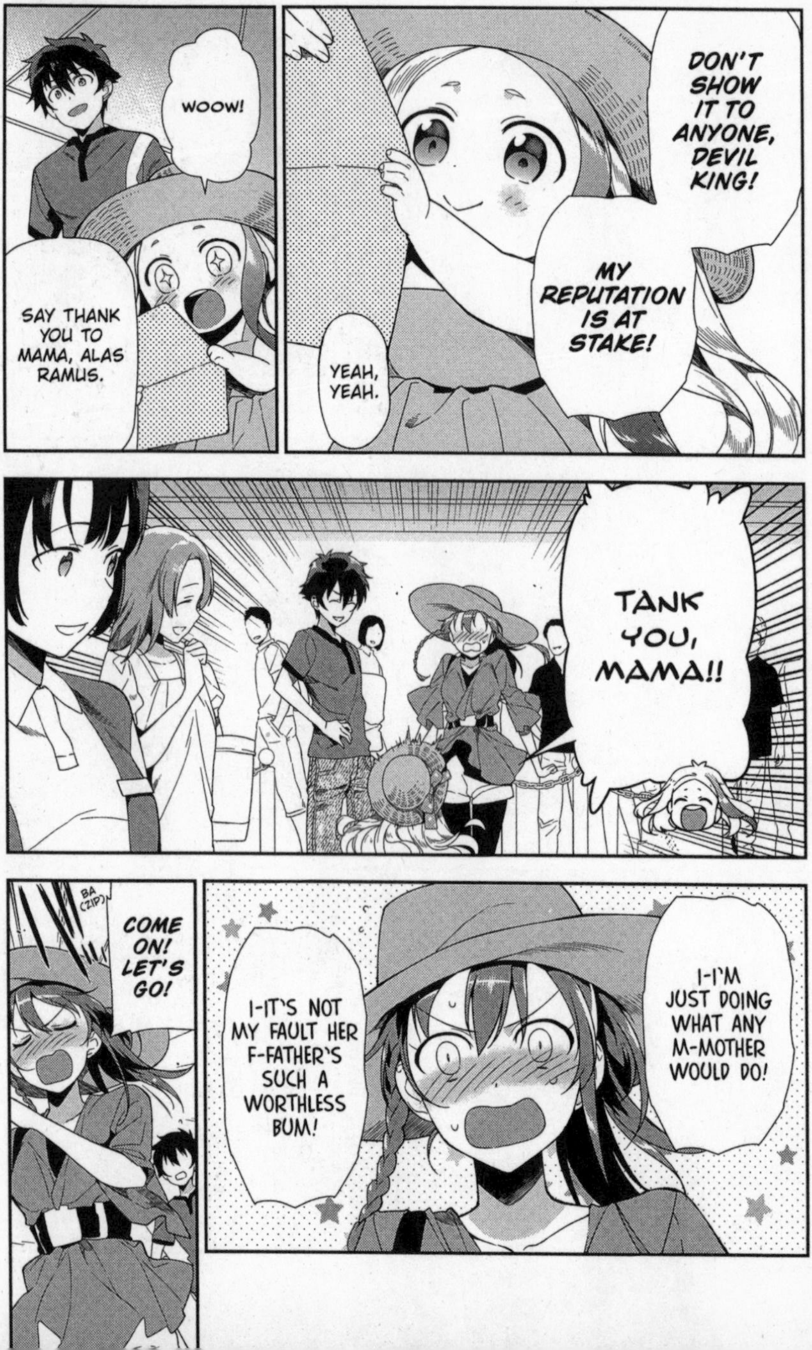
DON'T SHOW IT TO ANYONE, DEVIL KING!
MY REPUTATION IS AT STAKE!
YEAH, YEAH.
WOOW!
SAY THANK YOU TO MAMA, ALAS RAMUS.
TANK YOU, MAMA!!
I-I'M JUST DOING WHAT ANY M-MOTHER WOULD DO!
I-IT'S NOT MY FAULT HER F-FATHER'S SUCH A WORTHLESS BUM!
BA (ZIP)
COME ON! LET'S GO!

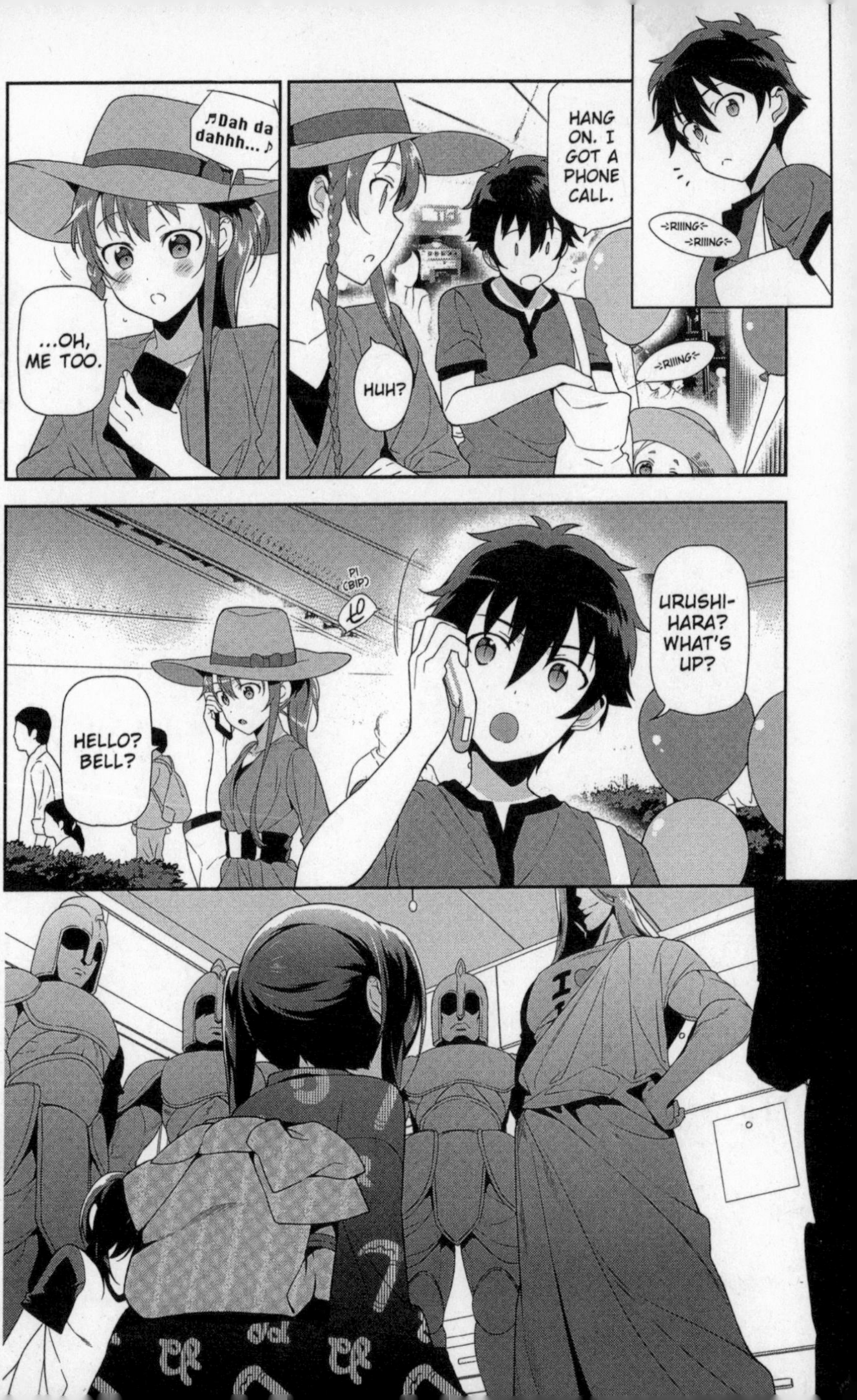
-RIIING-
-RIIING-
HANG ON. I GOT A PHONE CALL.
-RIIING-
HUH?
♪Dah da dahhh...♪
...OH, ME TOO.
URUSHI-HARA? WHAT'S UP?
PI (BIP)
HELLO? BELL?

Satan

THE DEVIL IS A PART-TIMER!

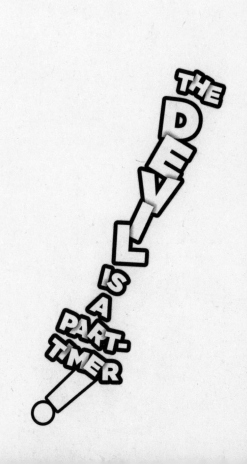

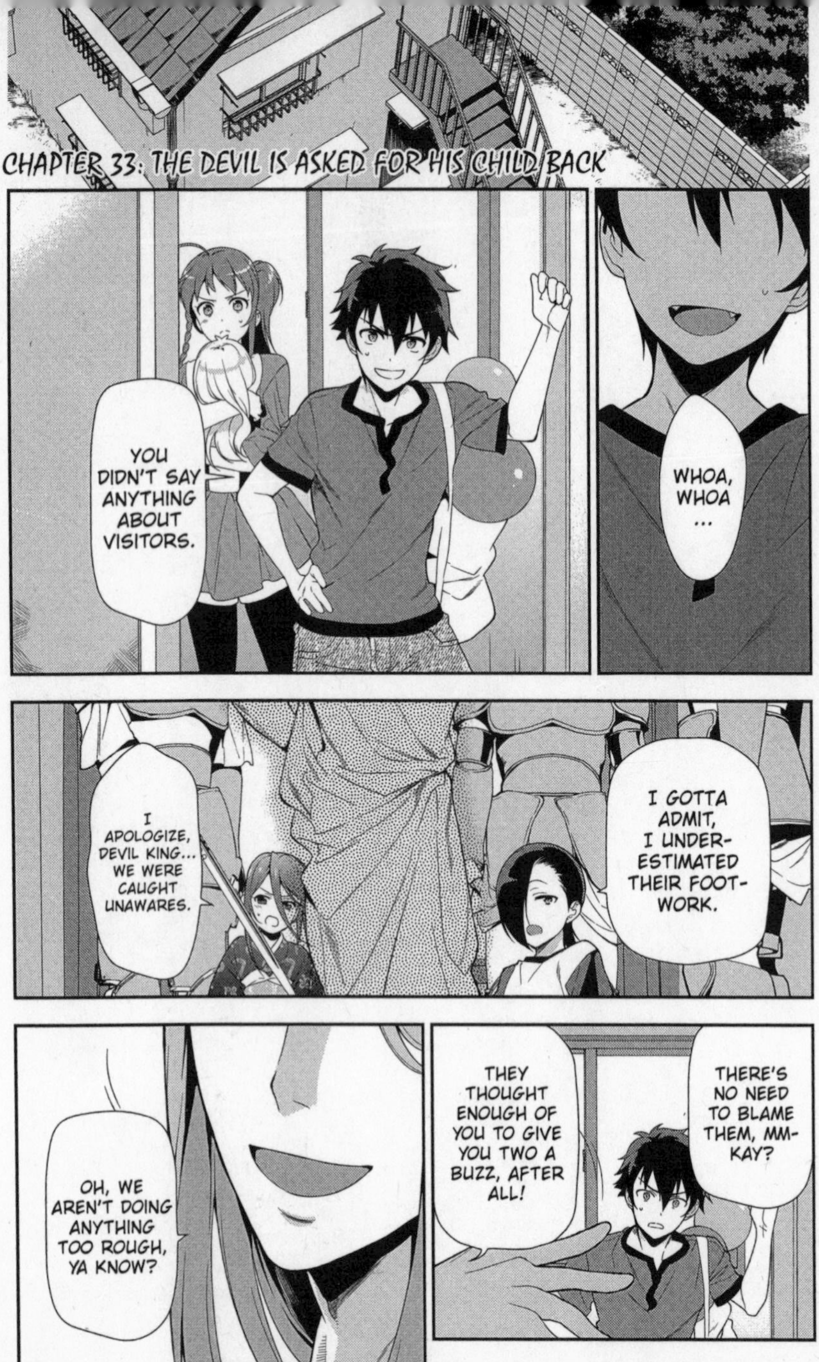
CHAPTER 33: THE DEVIL IS ASKED FOR HIS CHILD BACK
WHOA, WHOA ...
YOU DIDN'T SAY ANYTHING ABOUT VISITORS.
I GOTTA ADMIT, I UNDER-ESTIMATED THEIR FOOT-WORK.
I APOLOGIZE, DEVIL KING... WE WERE CAUGHT UNAWARES.
THERE'S NO NEED TO BLAME THEM, MM-KAY?
THEY THOUGHT ENOUGH OF YOU TO GIVE YOU TWO A BUZZ, AFTER ALL!
OH, WE AREN'T DOING ANYTHING TOO ROUGH, YA KNOW?

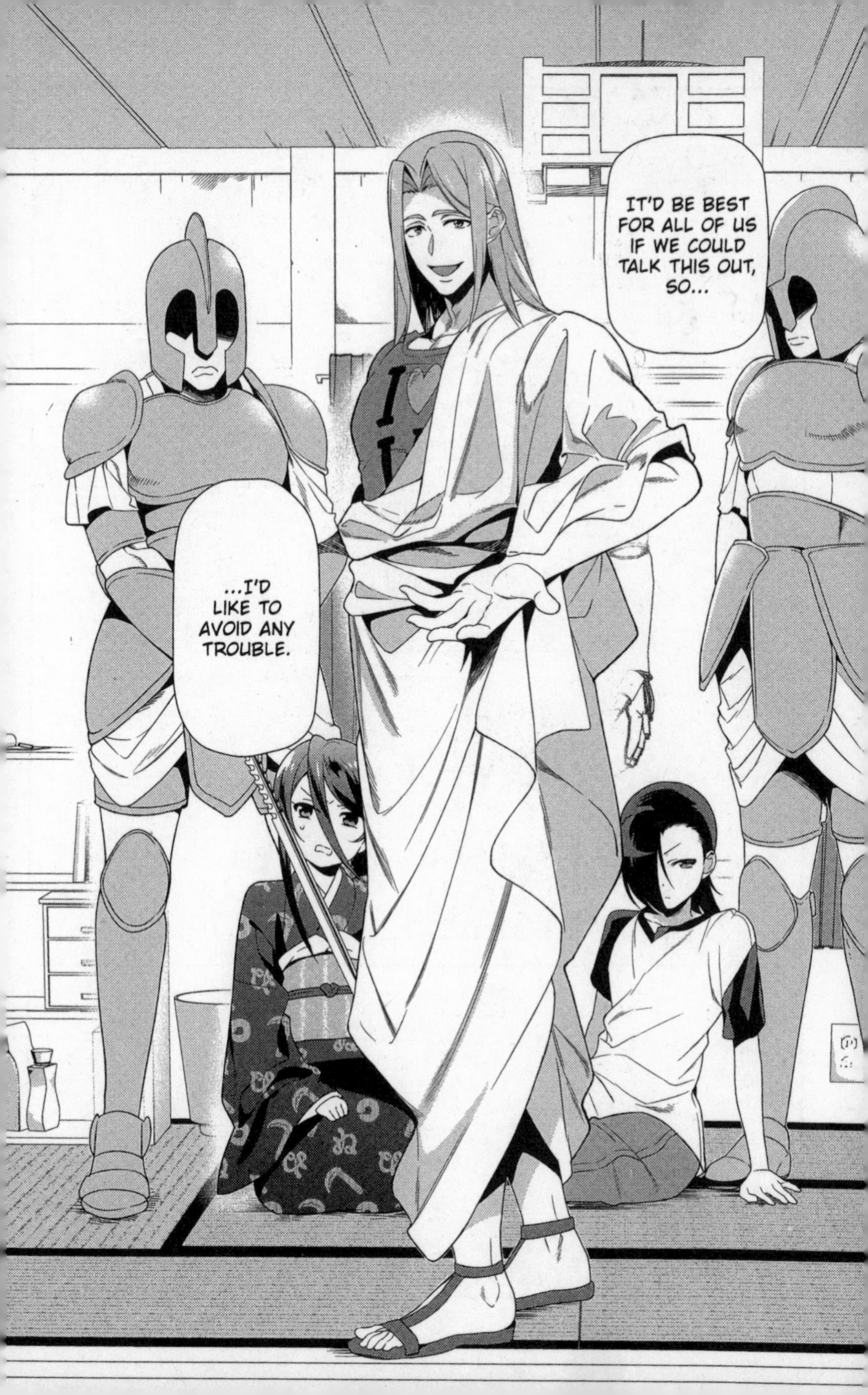
IT'D BE BEST FOR ALL OF US IF WE COULD TALK THIS OUT, SO...
...I'D LIKE TO AVOID ANY TROUBLE.

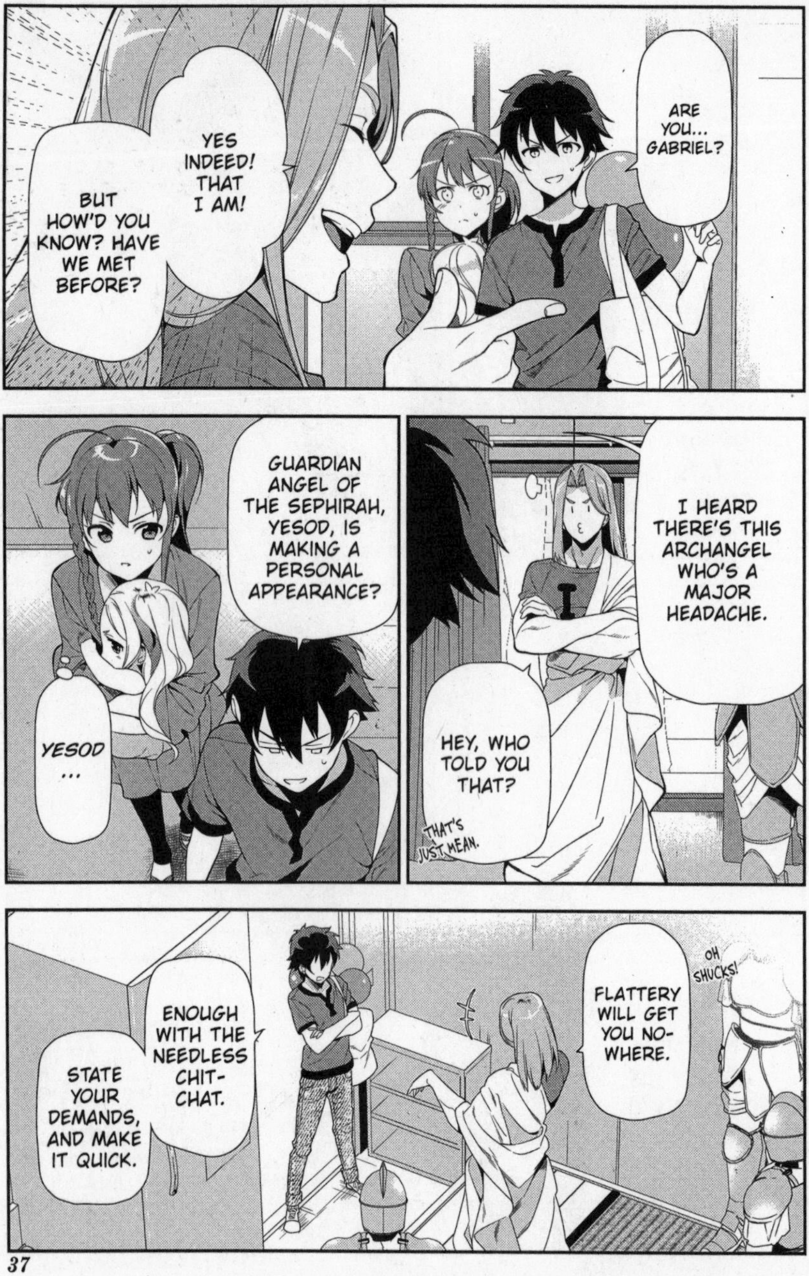
ARE YOU... GABRIEL?
YES INDEED! THAT I AM!
BUT HOW'D YOU KNOW? HAVE WE MET BEFORE?
I HEARD THERE'S THIS ARCHANGEL WHO'S A MAJOR HEADACHE.
HEY, WHO TOLD YOU THAT?
THAT'S JUST MEAN.
GUARDIAN ANGEL OF THE SEPHIRAH, YESOD, IS MAKING A PERSONAL APPEARANCE?
YESOD...
OH SHUCKS!
FLATTERY WILL GET YOU NO-WHERE.
ENOUGH WITH THE NEEDLESS CHIT-CHAT.
STATE YOUR DEMANDS, AND MAKE IT QUICK.

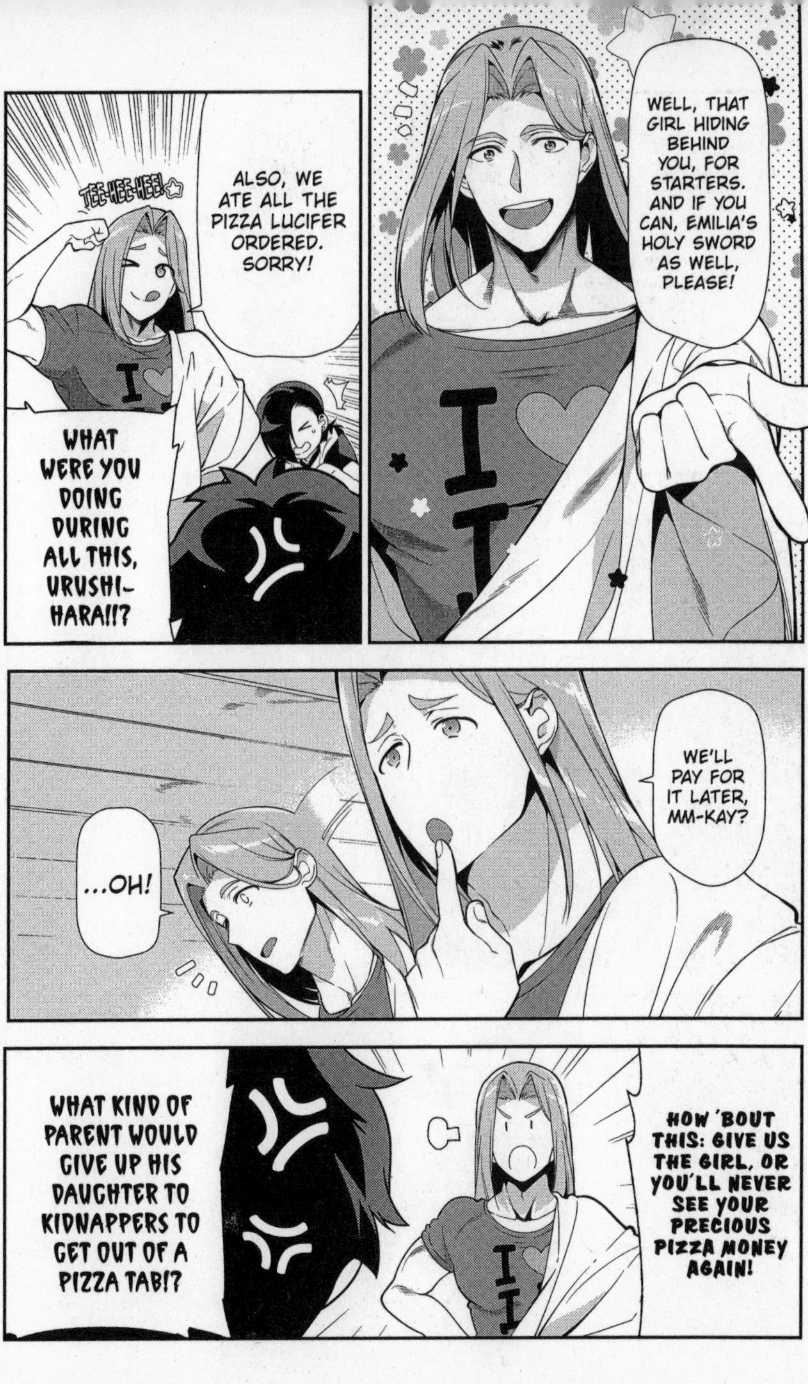
WELL, THAT GIRL HIDING BEHIND YOU, FOR STARTERS. AND IF YOU CAN, EMILIA'S HOLY SWORD AS WELL, PLEASE!
ALSO, WE ATE ALL THE PIZZA LUCIFER ORDERED. SORRY!
TEE-HEE-HEE!
WHAT WERE YOU DOING DURING ALL THIS, URUSHI-HARA!!?
WE'LL PAY FOR IT LATER, MM-KAY?
...OH!
HOW 'BOUT THIS: GIVE US THE GIRL, OR YOU'LL NEVER SEE YOUR PRECIOUS PIZZA MONEY AGAIN!
WHAT KIND OF PARENT WOULD GIVE UP HIS DAUGHTER TO KIDNAPPERS TO GET OUT OF A PIZZA TAB!?

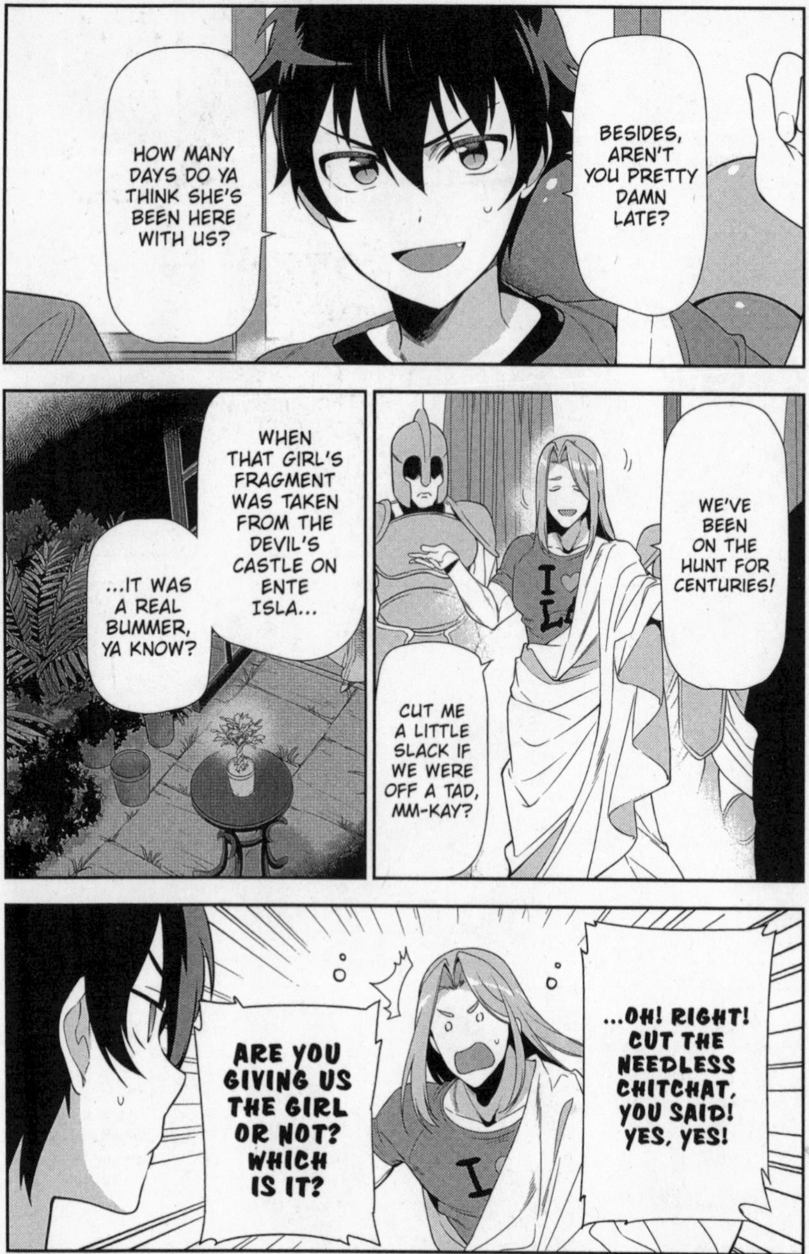
BESIDES, AREN'T YOU PRETTY DAMN LATE?
HOW MANY DAYS DO YA THINK SHE'S BEEN HERE WITH US?
WE'VE BEEN ON THE HUNT FOR CENTURIES!
CUT ME A LITTLE SLACK IF WE WERE OFF A TAD, MM-KAY?
WHEN THAT GIRL'S FRAGMENT WAS TAKEN FROM THE DEVIL'S CASTLE ON ENTE ISLA...
...IT WAS A REAL BUMMER, YA KNOW?
...OH! RIGHT! CUT THE NEEDLESS CHITCHAT, YOU SAID! YES, YES!
ARE YOU GIVING US THE GIRL OR NOT? WHICH IS IT?

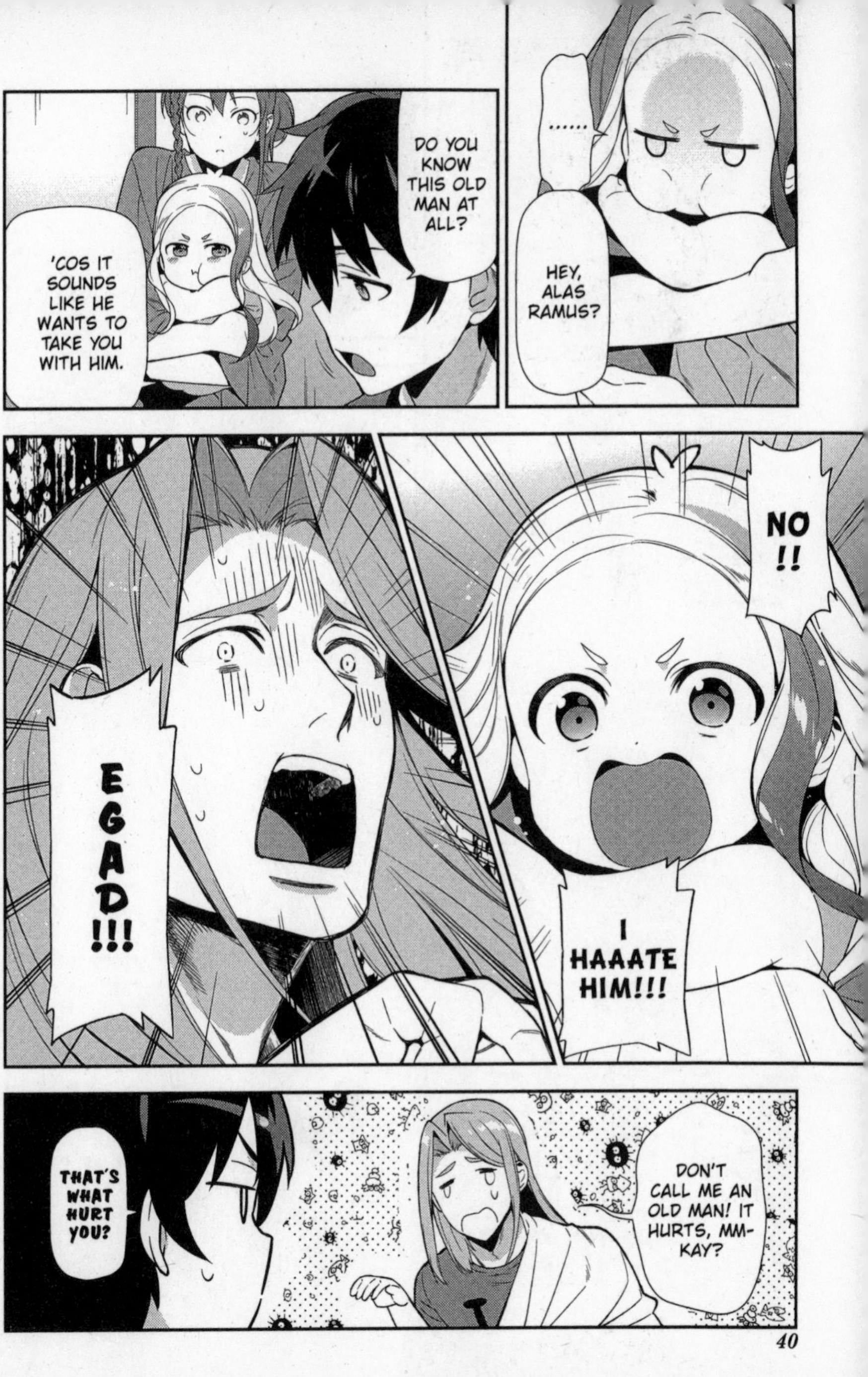

......
HEY, ALAS RAMUS?
DO YOU KNOW THIS OLD MAN AT ALL?
'COS IT SOUNDS LIKE HE WANTS TO TAKE YOU WITH HIM.
NO!!
I HAAATE HIM!!!
EGAD!!!
DON'T CALL ME AN OLD MAN! IT HURTS, MM-KAY?
THAT'S WHAT HURT YOU?

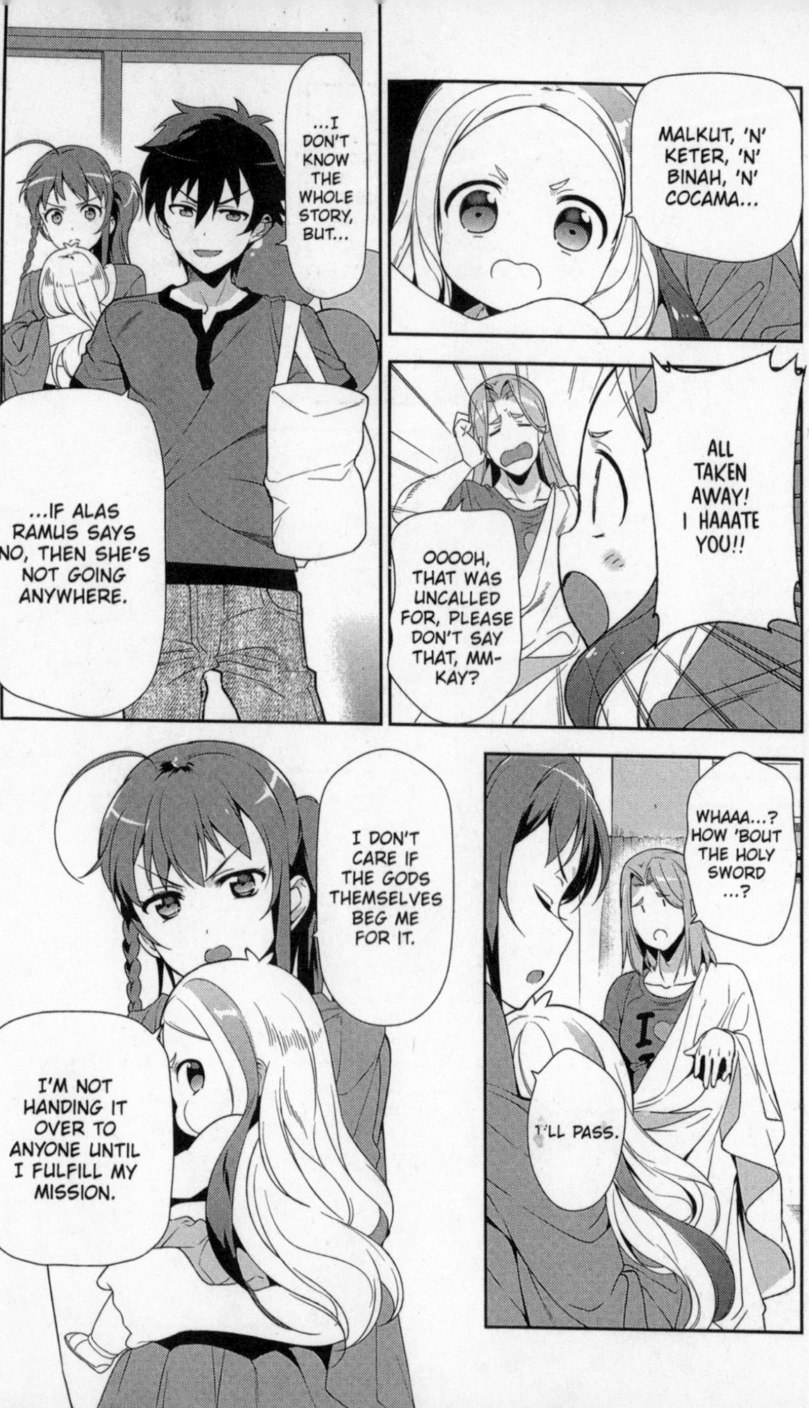
MALKUT, 'N' KETER, 'N' BINAH, 'N' COCAMA...
ALL TAKEN AWAY! I HAAATE YOU!!
OOOOH, THAT WAS UNCALLED FOR, PLEASE DON'T SAY THAT, MM-KAY?
...I DON'T KNOW THE WHOLE STORY, BUT...
...IF ALAS RAMUS SAYS NO, THEN SHE'S NOT GOING ANYWHERE.
WHAAA...? HOW 'BOUT THE HOLY SWORD ...?
I'LL PASS.
I DON'T CARE IF THE GODS THEMSELVES BEG ME FOR IT.
I'M NOT HANDING IT OVER TO ANYONE UNTIL I FULFILL MY MISSION.

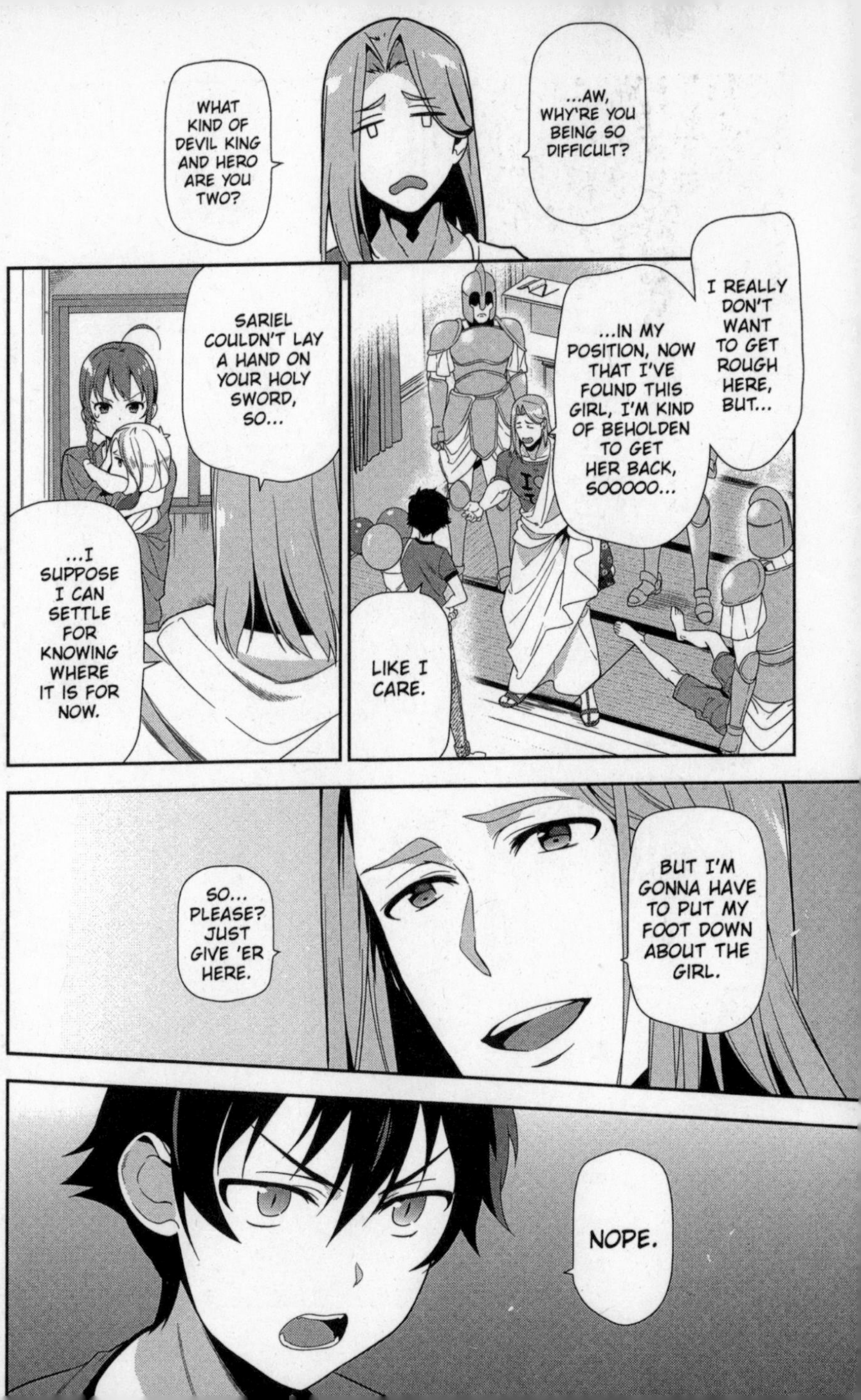
...AW, WHY'RE YOU BEING SO DIFFICULT?
WHAT KIND OF DEVIL KING AND HERO ARE YOU TWO?
I REALLY DON'T WANT TO GET ROUGH HERE, BUT...
...IN MY POSITION, NOW THAT I'VE FOUND THIS GIRL, I'M KIND OF BEHOLDEN TO GET HER BACK, SOOOOO...
LIKE I CARE.
SARIEL COULDN'T LAY A HAND ON YOUR HOLY SWORD, SO...
...I SUPPOSE I CAN SETTLE FOR KNOWING WHERE IT IS FOR NOW.
BUT I'M GONNA HAVE TO PUT MY FOOT DOWN ABOUT THE GIRL.
SO... PLEASE? JUST GIVE 'ER HERE.
NOPE.

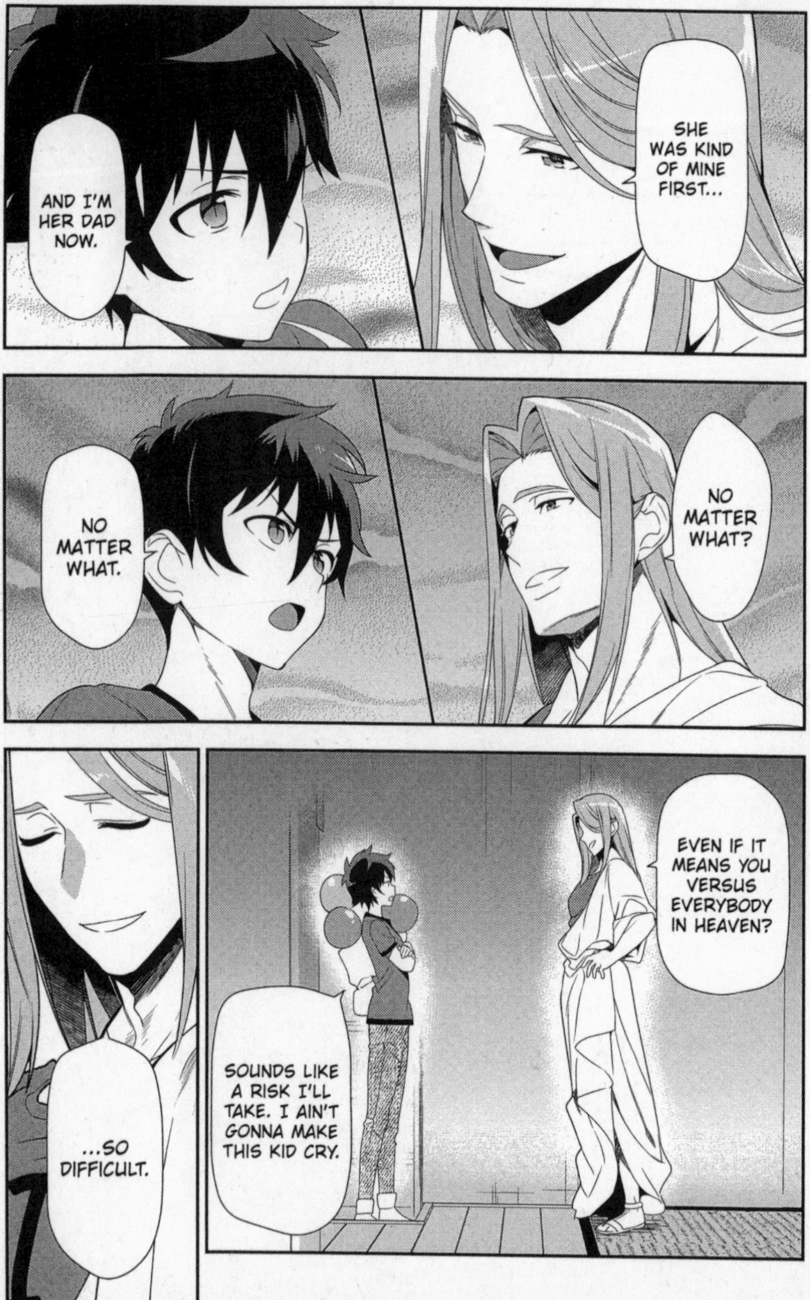
SHE WAS KIND OF MINE FIRST...
AND I'M HER DAD NOW.
NO MATTER WHAT?
NO MATTER WHAT.
EVEN IF IT MEANS YOU VERSUS EVERYBODY IN HEAVEN?
SOUNDS LIKE A RISK I'LL TAKE. I AIN'T GONNA MAKE THIS KID CRY.
...SO DIFFICULT.

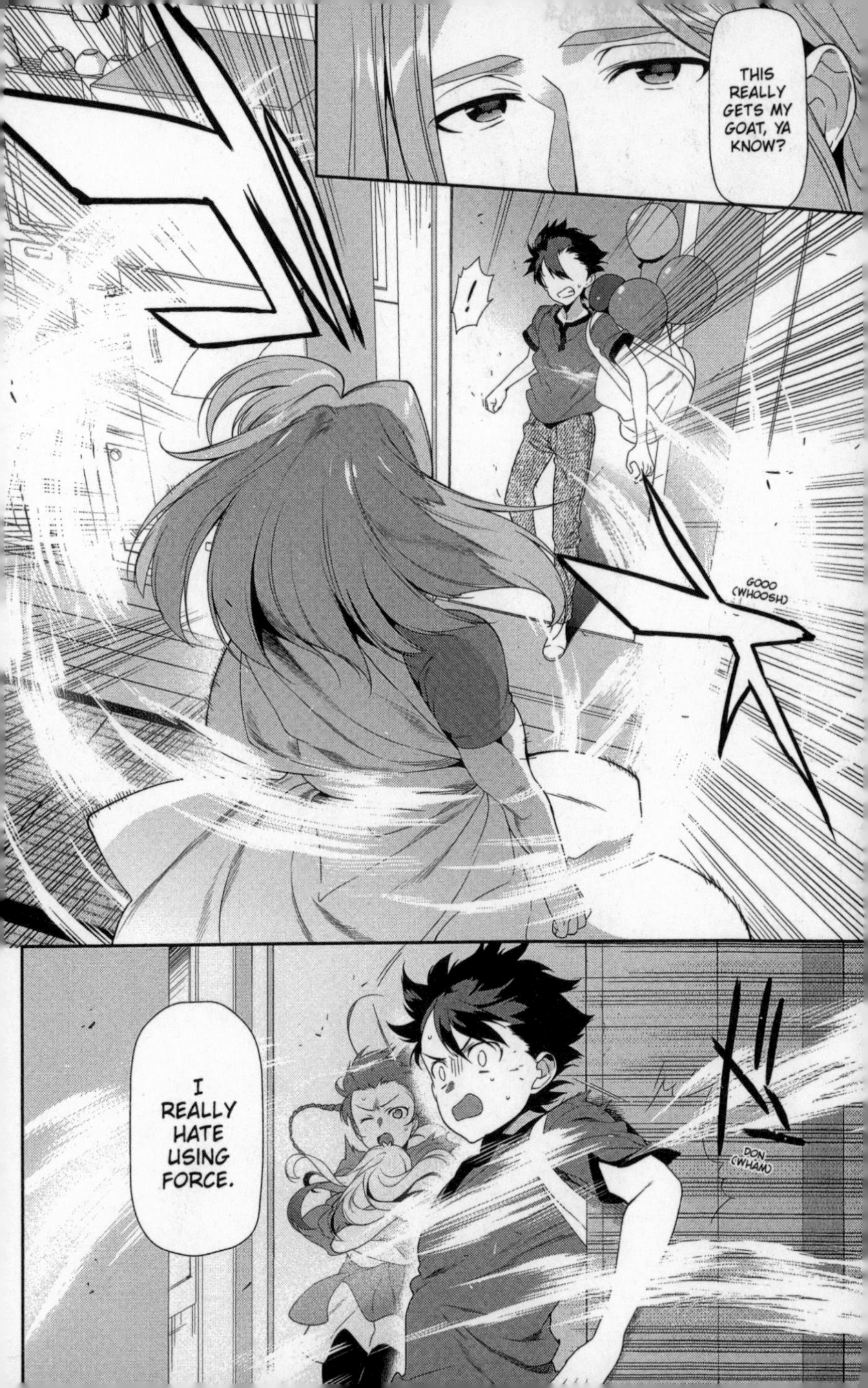
THIS REALLY GETS MY GOAT, YA KNOW?
!
GOOO (WHOOSH)
!!
DON (WHAM)
I REALLY HATE USING FORCE.

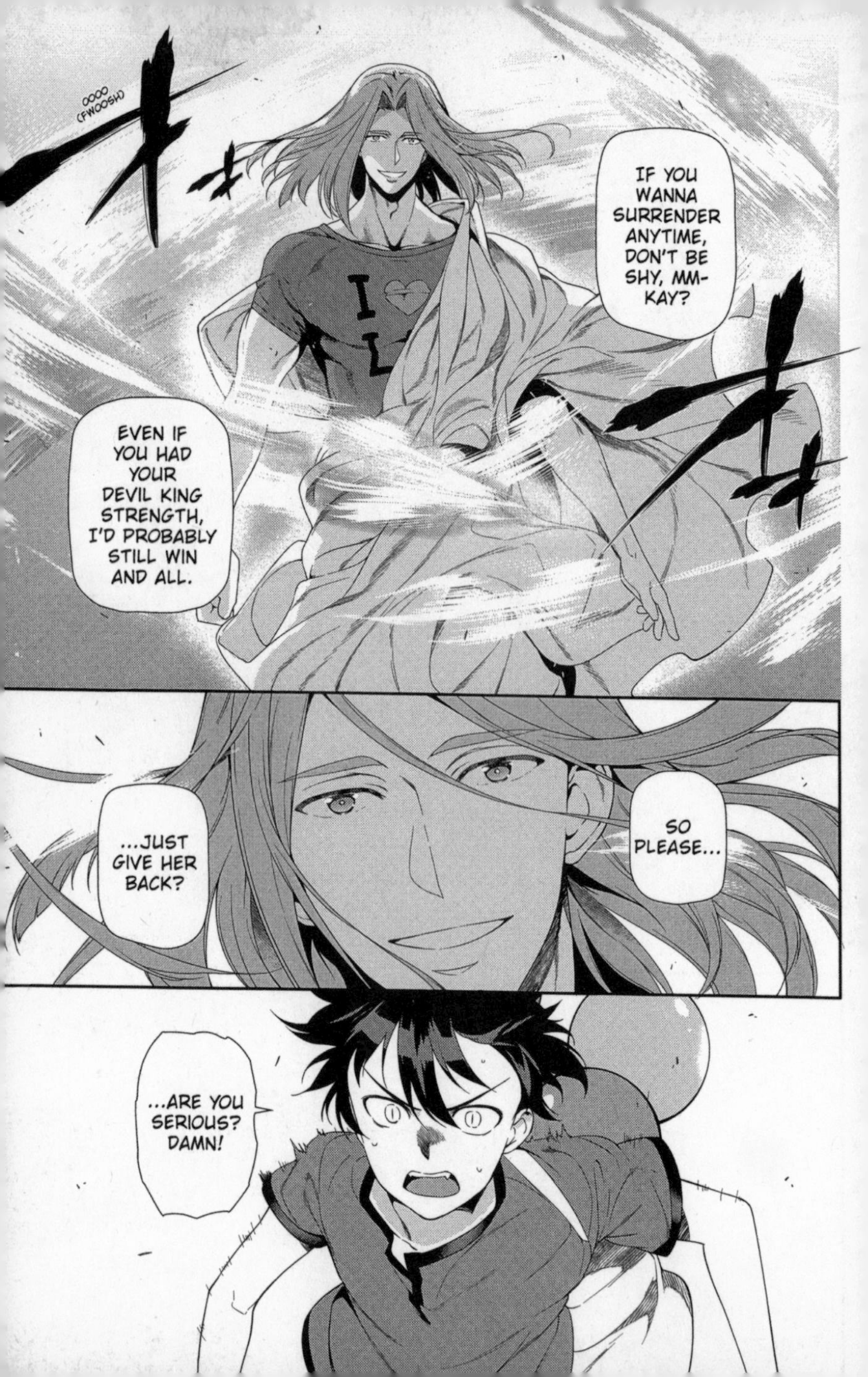
IF YOU WANNA SURRENDER ANYTIME, DON'T BE SHY, MM-KAY?
OOOO (FWOOSH)
EVEN IF YOU HAD YOUR DEVIL KING STRENGTH, I'D PROBABLY STILL WIN AND ALL.
SO PLEASE...
...JUST GIVE HER BACK?
...ARE YOU SERIOUS? DAMN!

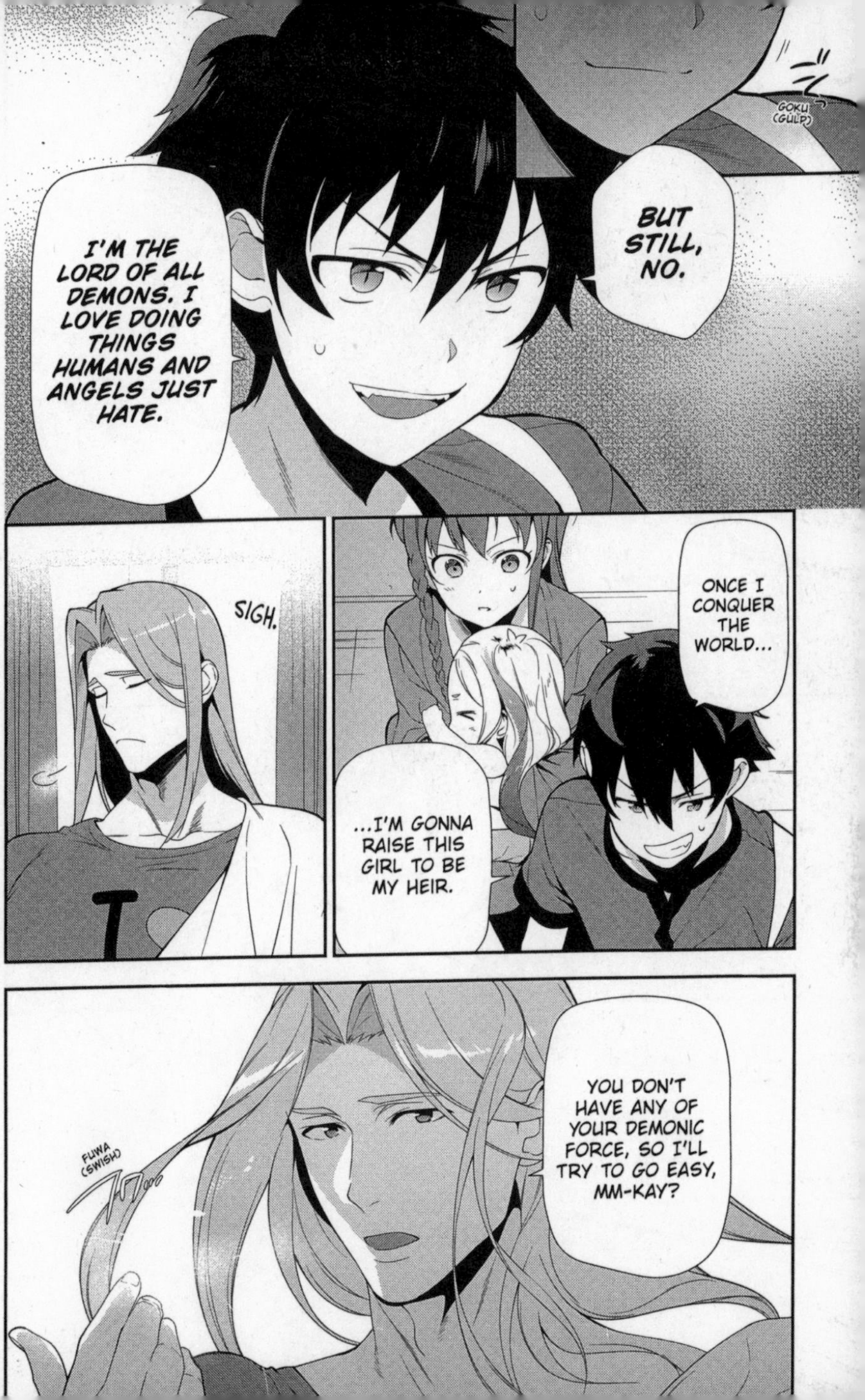
GOKU (GULP)
BUT STILL, NO.
I'M THE LORD OF ALL DEMONS. I LOVE DOING THINGS HUMANS AND ANGELS JUST HATE.
ONCE I CONQUER THE WORLD...
...I'M GONNA RAISE THIS GIRL TO BE MY HEIR.
SIGH.
YOU DON'T HAVE ANY OF YOUR DEMONIC FORCE, SO I'LL TRY TO GO EASY, MM-KAY?
FUWA (SWISH)

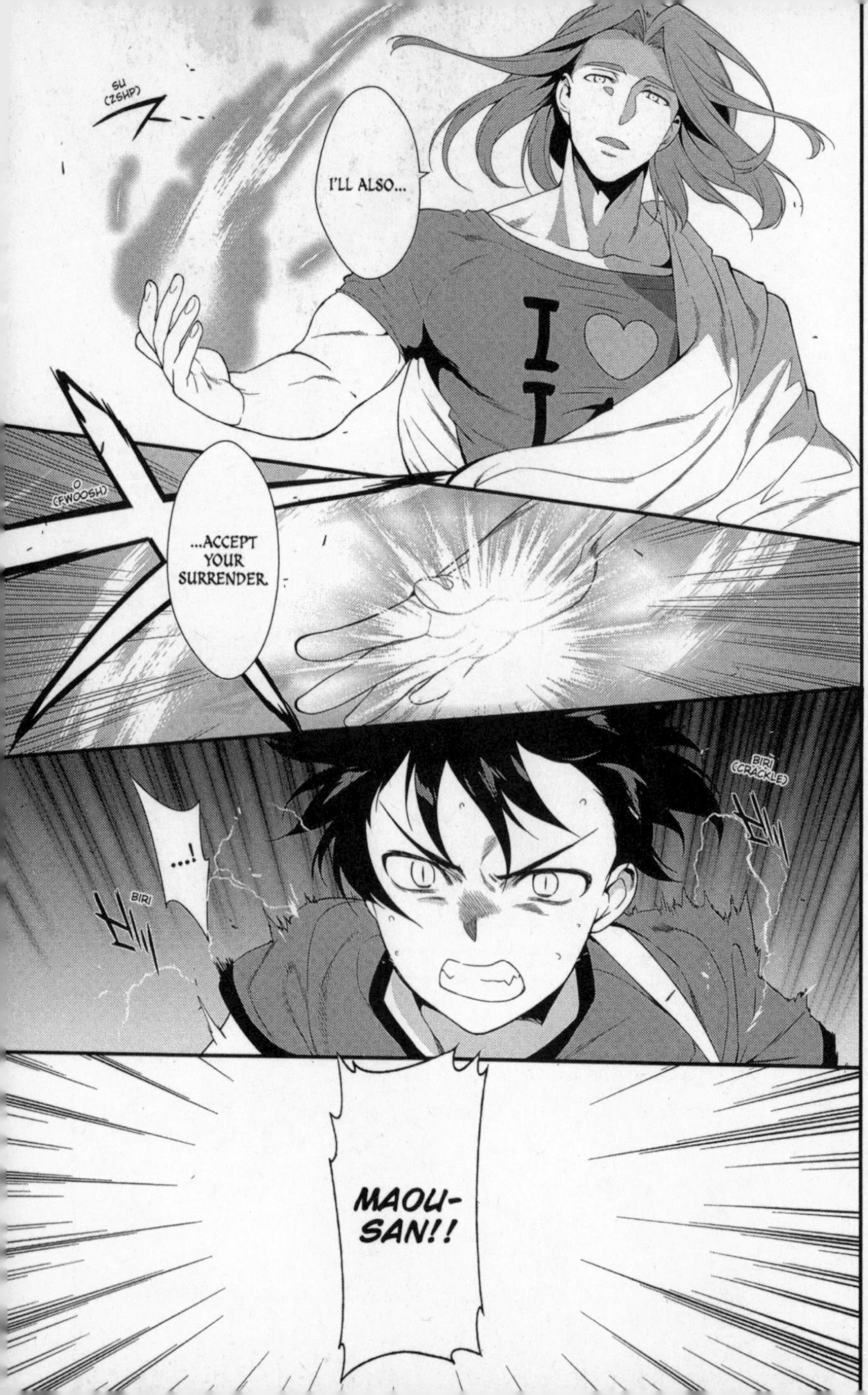
I'LL ALSO...
SU (ZSHP)
...ACCEPT YOUR SURRENDER.
O (FWOOSH)
BIRI (CRACKLE)
...!
BIRI
MAOU-SAN!!

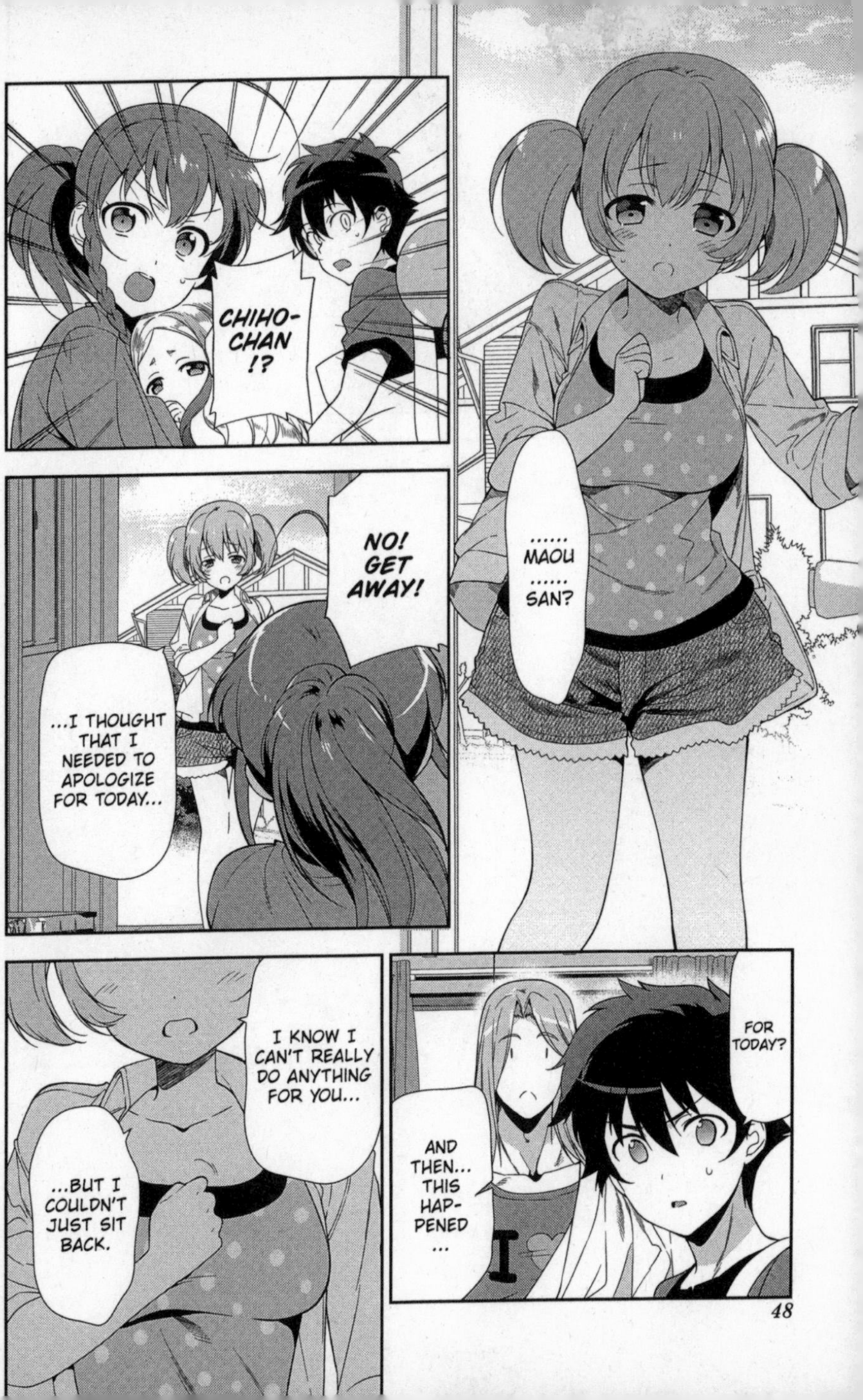
......MAOU ...... SAN?
CHIHO-CHAN !?
NO! GET AWAY!
...I THOUGHT THAT I NEEDED TO APOLOGIZE FOR TODAY...
FOR TODAY?
AND THEN... THIS HAPPENED ...
I KNOW I CAN'T REALLY DO ANYTHING FOR YOU...
...BUT I COULDN'T JUST SIT BACK.

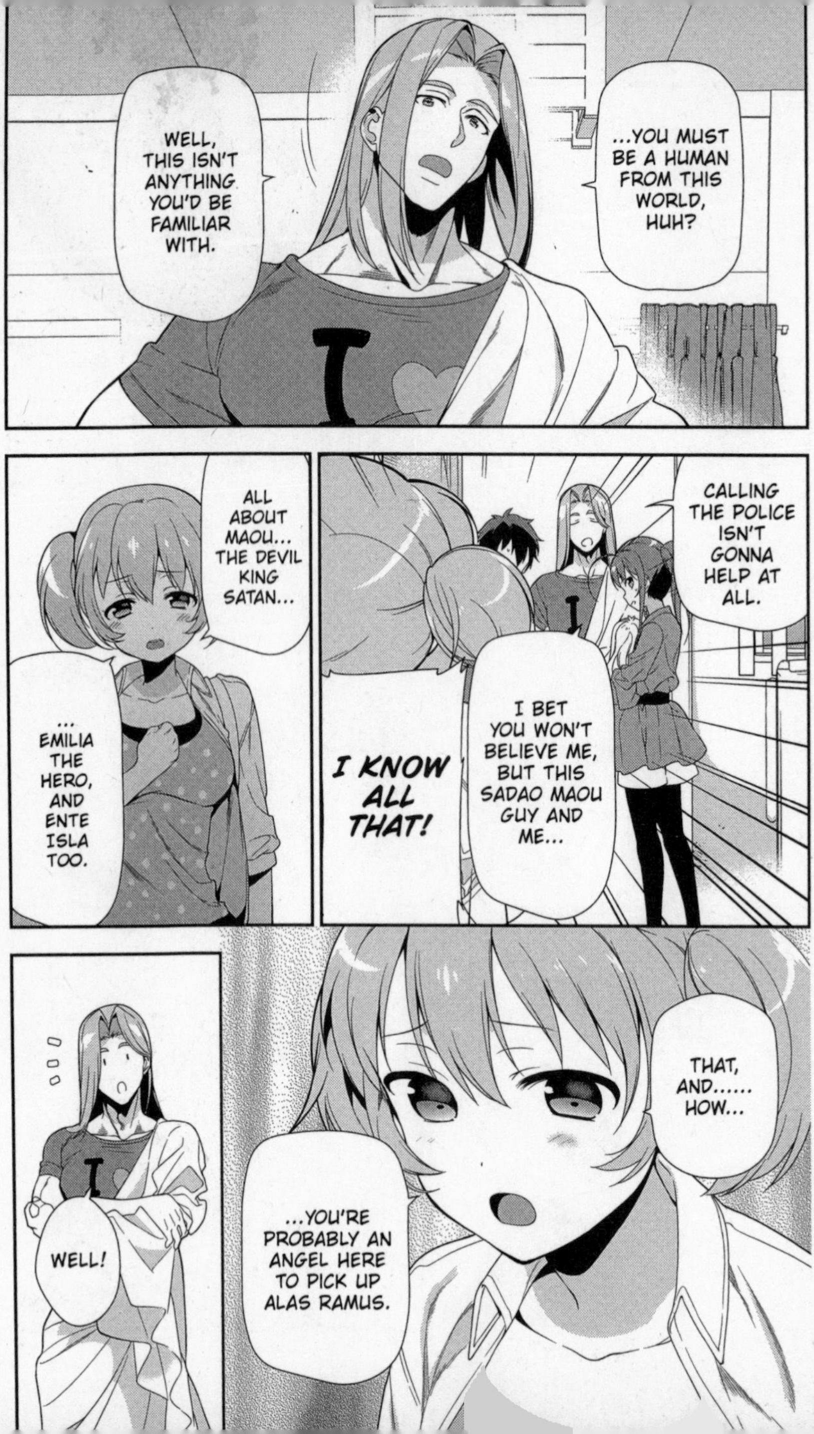
...YOU MUST BE A HUMAN FROM THIS WORLD, HUH?
WELL, THIS ISN'T ANYTHING YOU'D BE FAMILIAR WITH.
CALLING THE POLICE ISN'T GONNA HELP AT ALL.
I BET YOU WON'T BELIEVE ME, BUT THIS SADAO MAOU GUY AND ME...
I KNOW ALL THAT!
ALL ABOUT MAOU... THE DEVIL KING SATAN...
...EMILIA THE HERO, AND ENTE ISLA TOO.
THAT, AND...... HOW...
...YOU'RE PROBABLY AN ANGEL HERE TO PICK UP ALAS RAMUS.
WELL!

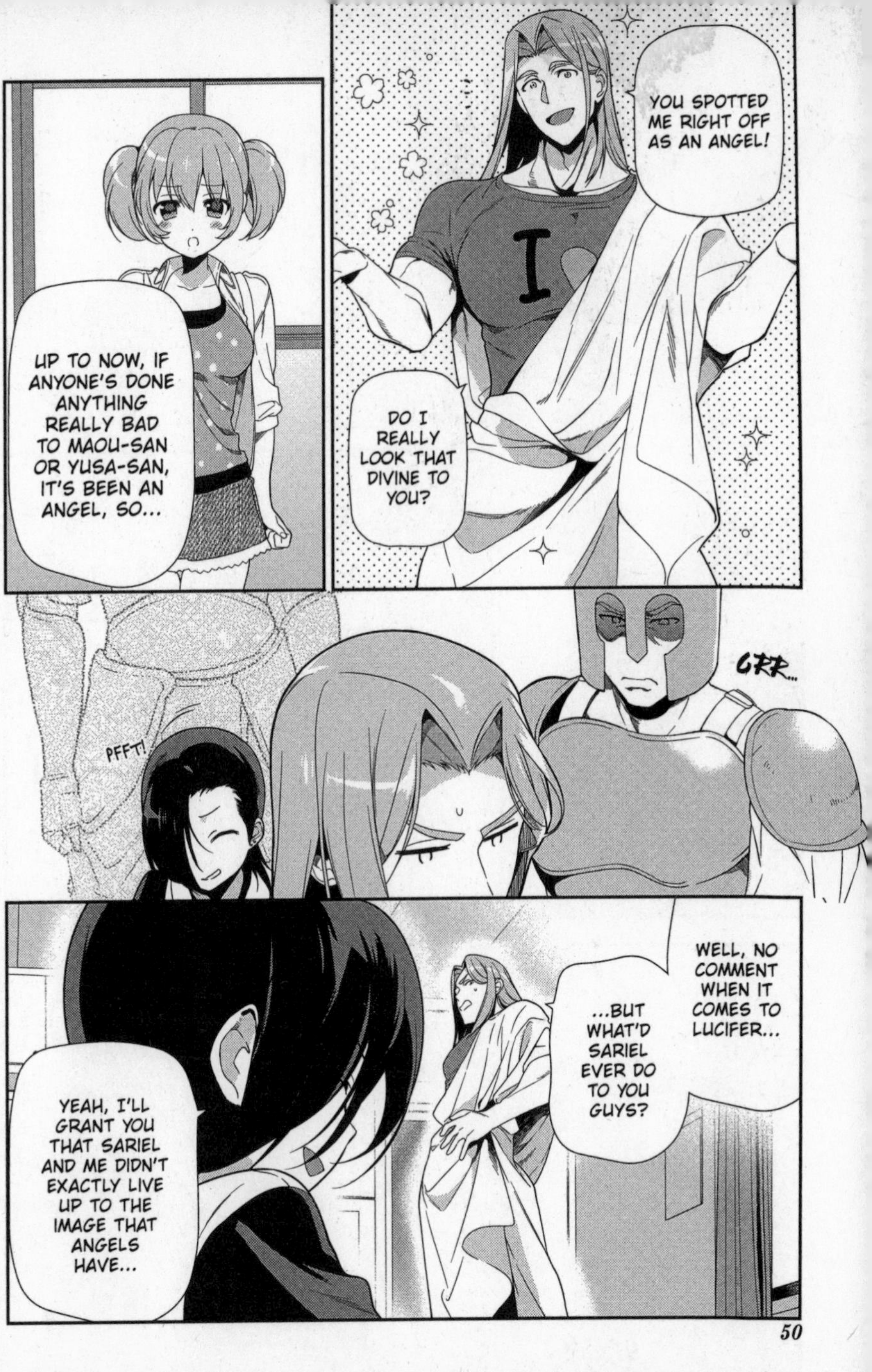
YOU SPOTTED ME RIGHT OFF AS AN ANGEL!
DO I REALLY LOOK THAT DIVINE TO YOU?
UP TO NOW, IF ANYONE'S DONE ANYTHING REALLY BAD TO MAOU-SAN OR YUSA-SAN, IT'S BEEN AN ANGEL, SO...
GRR...
PFFT!
WELL, NO COMMENT WHEN IT COMES TO LUCIFER...
...BUT WHAT'D SARIEL EVER DO TO YOU GUYS?
YEAH, I'LL GRANT YOU THAT SARIEL AND ME DIDN'T EXACTLY LIVE UP TO THE IMAGE THAT ANGELS HAVE...

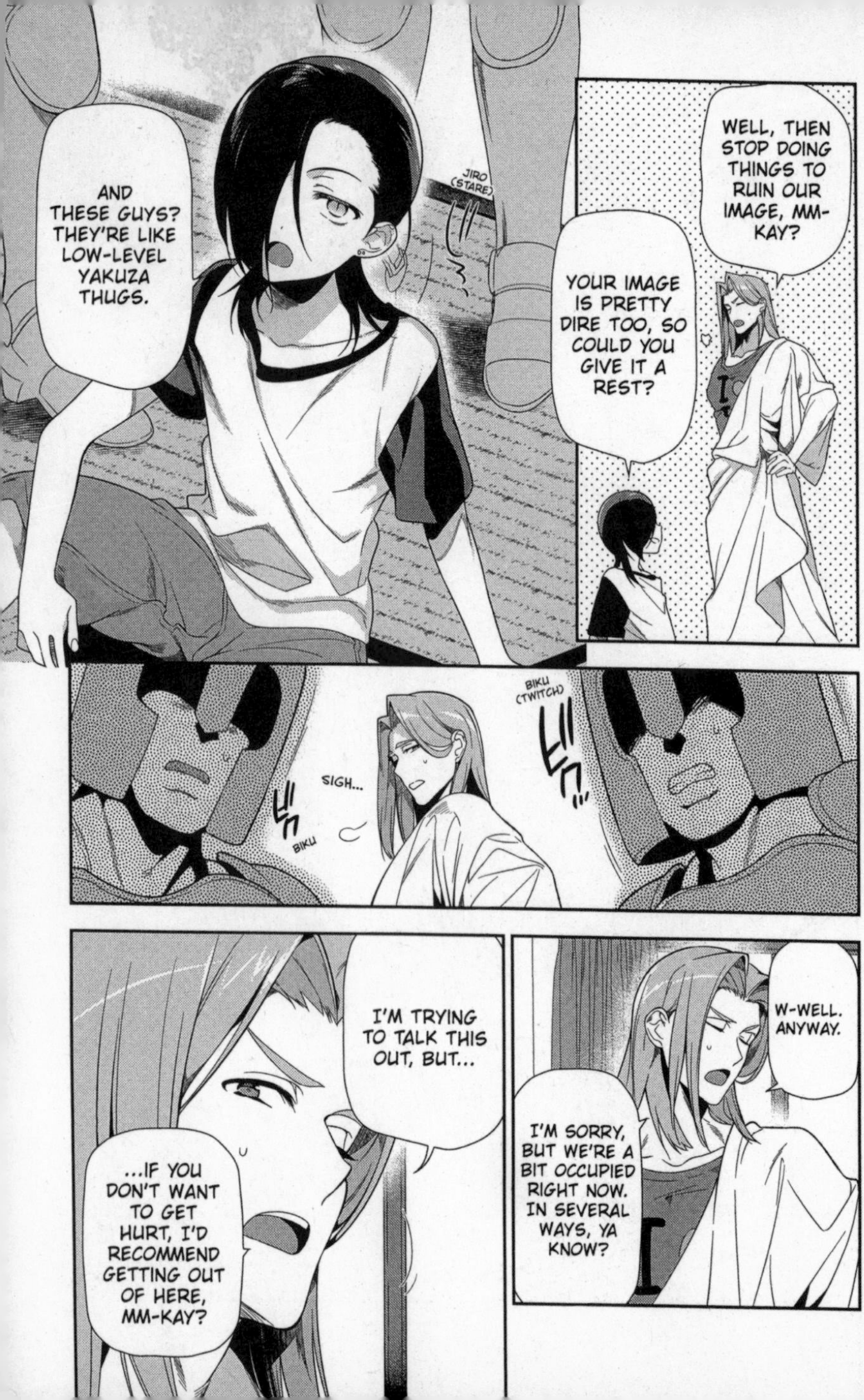
WELL, THEN STOP DOING THINGS TO RUIN OUR IMAGE, MM-KAY?
YOUR IMAGE IS PRETTY DIRE TOO, SO COULD YOU GIVE IT A REST?
JIRO (STARE)
AND THESE GUYS? THEY'RE LIKE LOW-LEVEL YAKUZA THUGS.
BIKU (TWITCH)
SIGH...
BIKU
W-WELL. ANYWAY.
I'M SORRY, BUT WE'RE A BIT OCCUPIED RIGHT NOW. IN SEVERAL WAYS, YA KNOW?
I'M TRYING TO TALK THIS OUT, BUT...
...IF YOU DON'T WANT TO GET HURT, I'D RECOMMEND GETTING OUT OF HERE, MM-KAY?

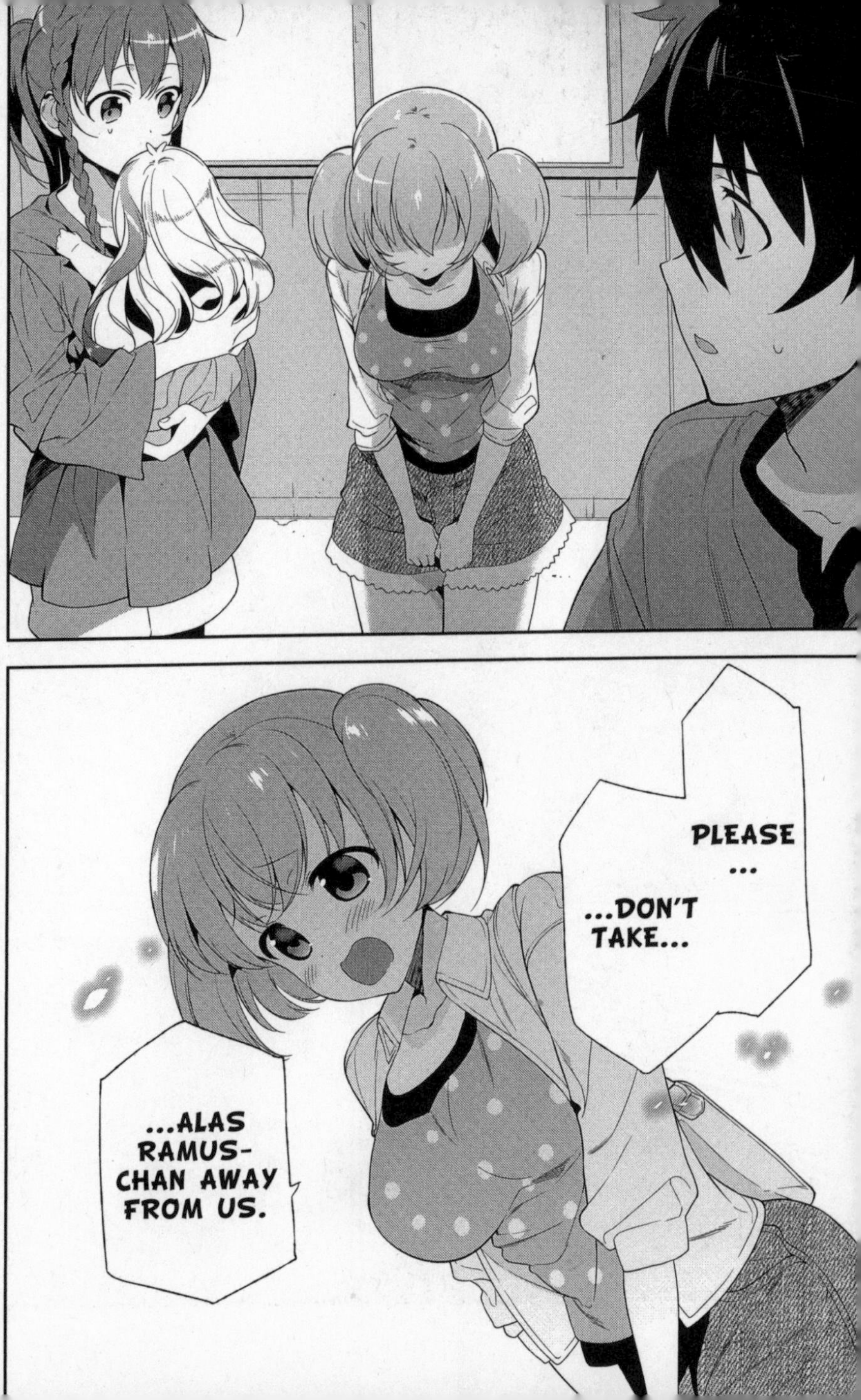
...
PLEASE ... ...DON'T TAKE...
...ALAS RAMUS-CHAN AWAY FROM US.

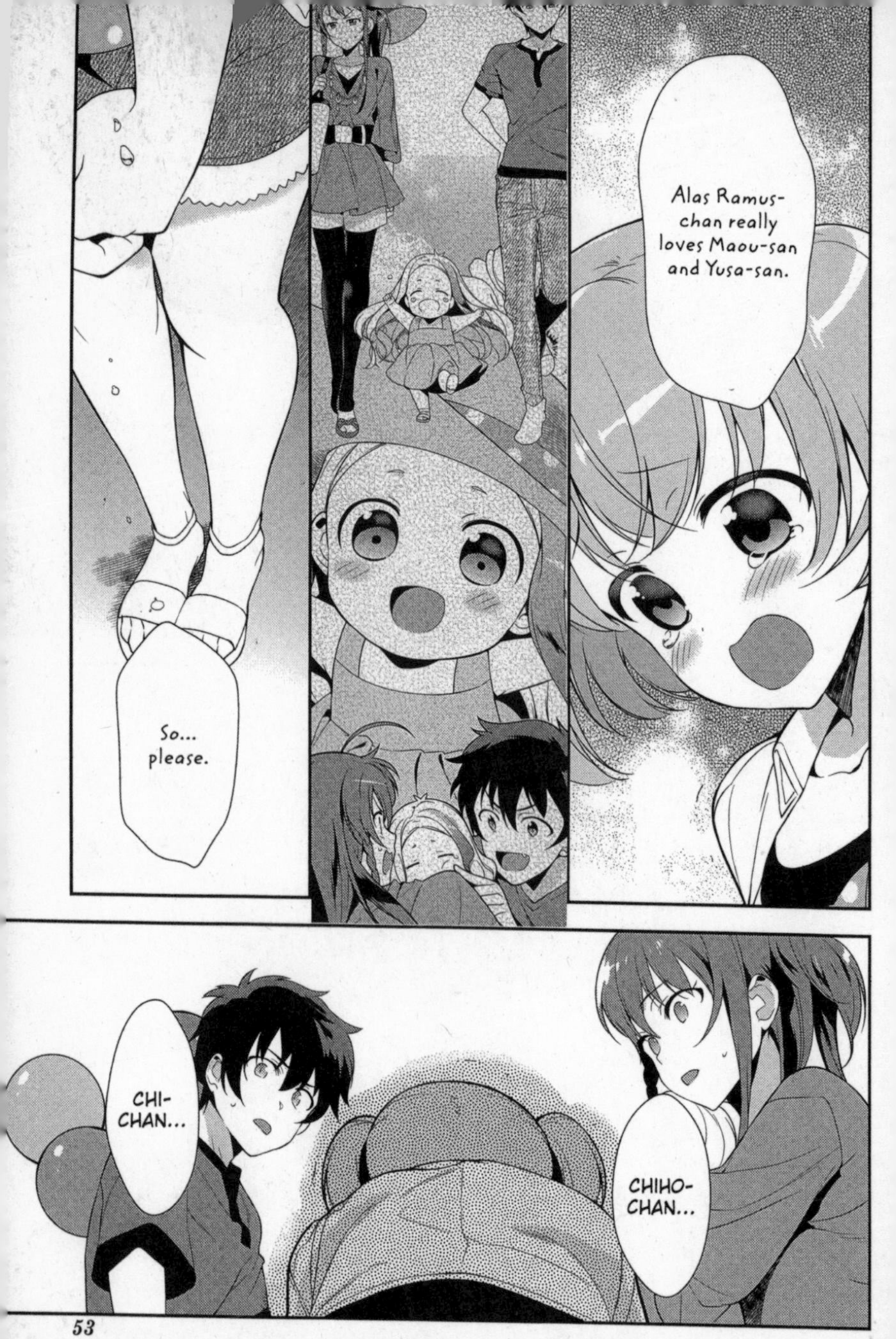
Alas Ramus-chan really loves Maou-san and Yusa-san.
So... please.
CHIHO-CHAN...
CHI-CHAN...

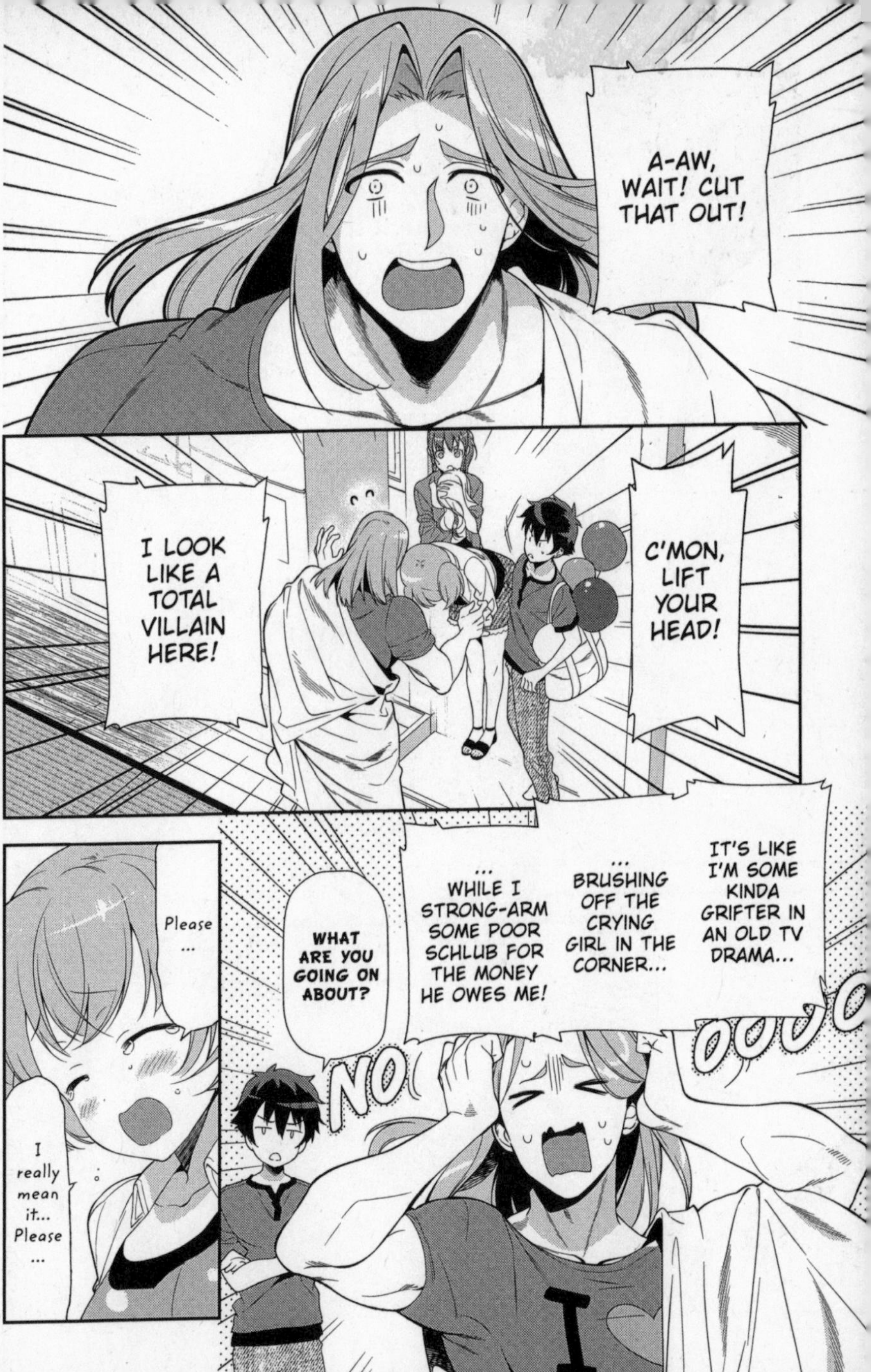
A-AW, WAIT! CUT THAT OUT!
C'MON, LIFT YOUR HEAD!
I LOOK LIKE A TOTAL VILLAIN HERE!
IT'S LIKE I'M SOME KINDA GRIFTER IN AN OLD TV DRAMA...
... BRUSHING OFF THE CRYING GIRL IN THE CORNER...
... WHILE I STRONG-ARM SOME POOR SCHLUB FOR THE MONEY HE OWES ME!
WHAT ARE YOU GOING ON ABOUT?
NO
OOOO
Please ...
I really mean it... Please ...

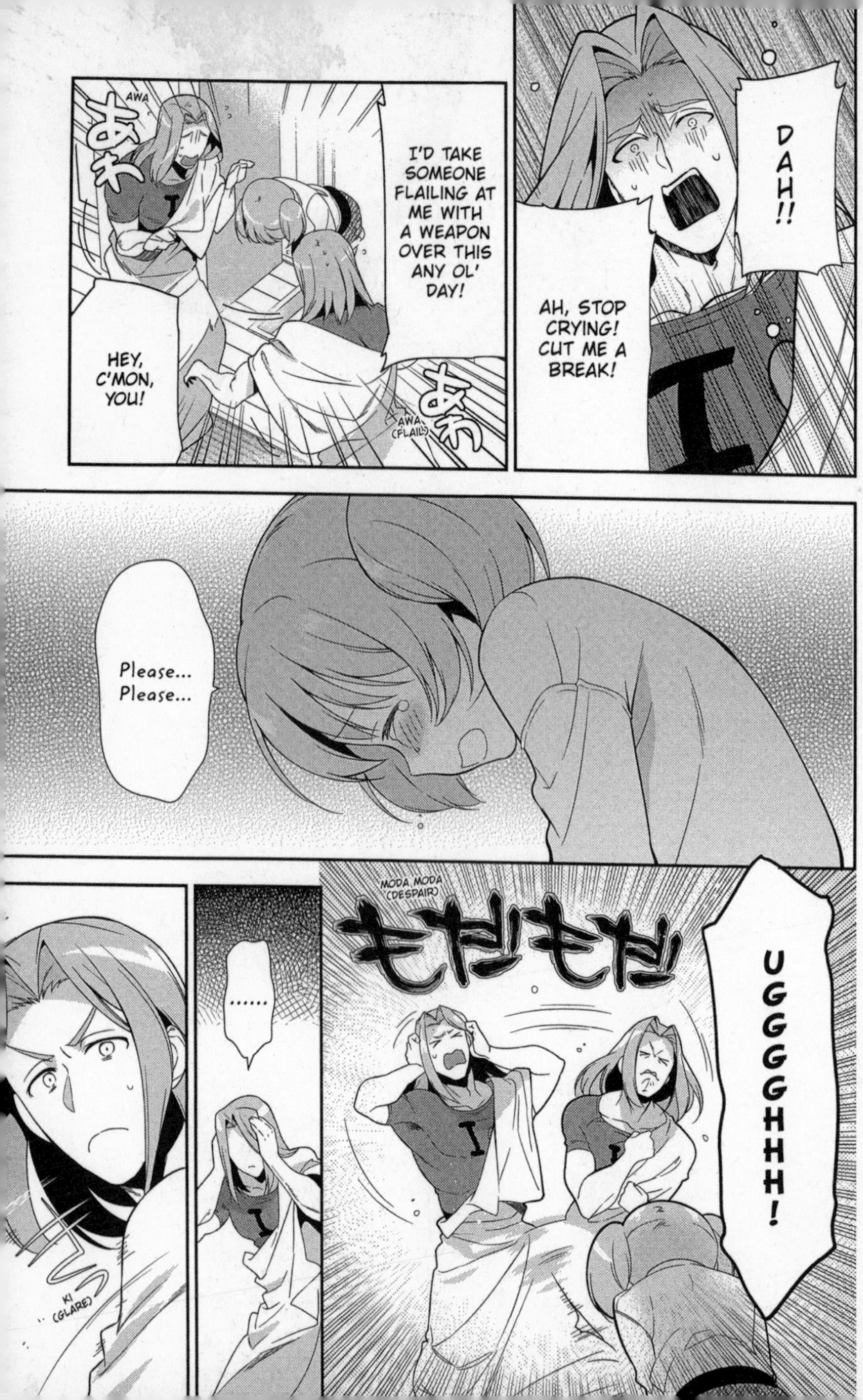
DAH!!
AH, STOP CRYING! CUT ME A BREAK!
I'D TAKE SOMEONE FLAILING AT ME WITH A WEAPON OVER THIS ANY OL' DAY!
AWA
あわ
HEY, C'MON, YOU!
AWA (FLAIL)
あわ
Please... Please...
UGGGGHHHH!
MODA MODA (DESPAIR)
もだもだ
......
KI (GLARE)

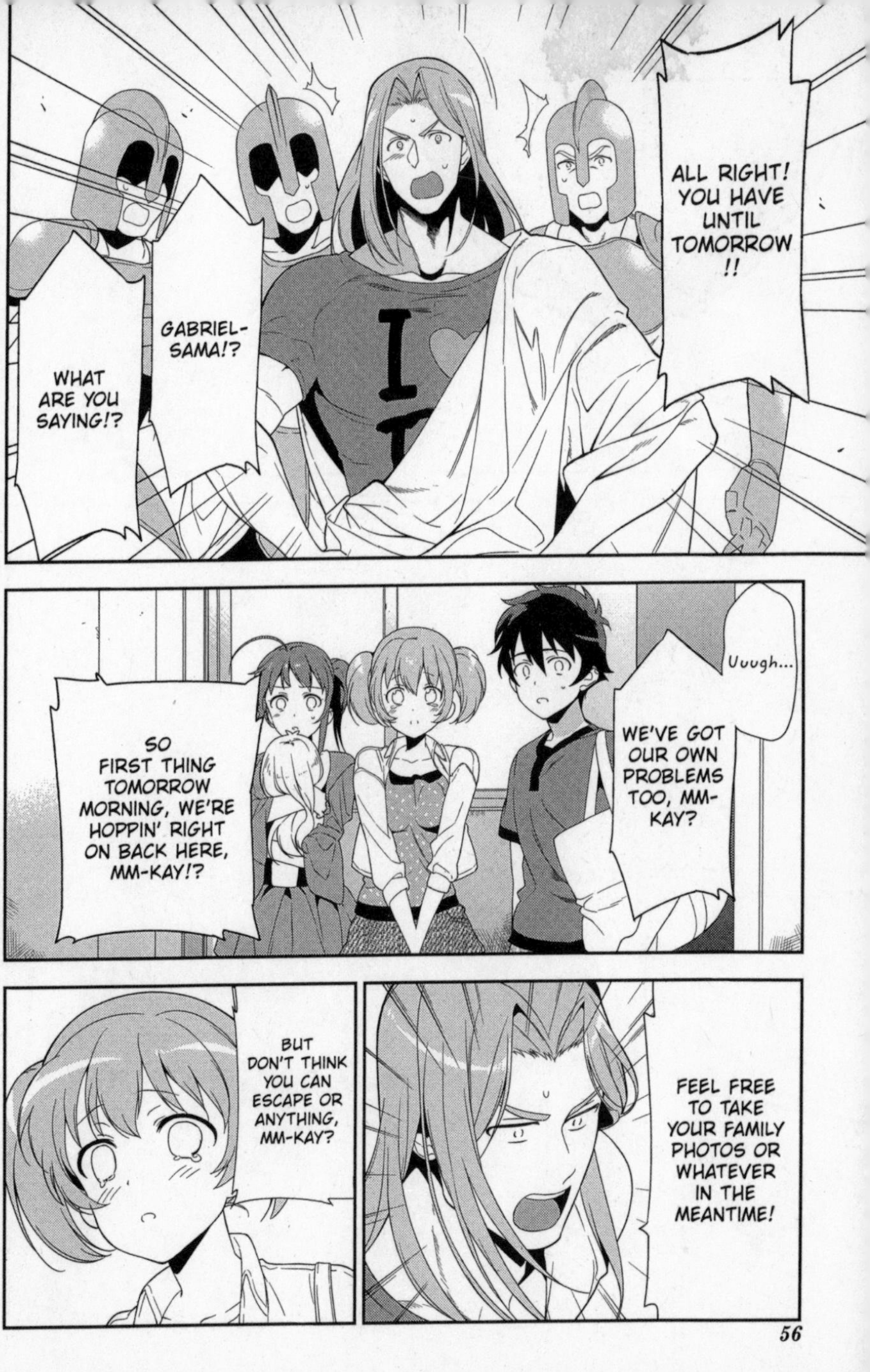
ALL RIGHT! YOU HAVE UNTIL TOMORROW!!
GABRIEL-SAMA!?
WHAT ARE YOU SAYING!?
Uuugh...
WE'VE GOT OUR OWN PROBLEMS TOO, MM-KAY?
SO FIRST THING TOMORROW MORNING, WE'RE HOPPIN' RIGHT ON BACK HERE, MM-KAY!?
FEEL FREE TO TAKE YOUR FAMILY PHOTOS OR WHATEVER IN THE MEANTIME!
BUT DON'T THINK YOU CAN ESCAPE OR ANYTHING, MM-KAY?

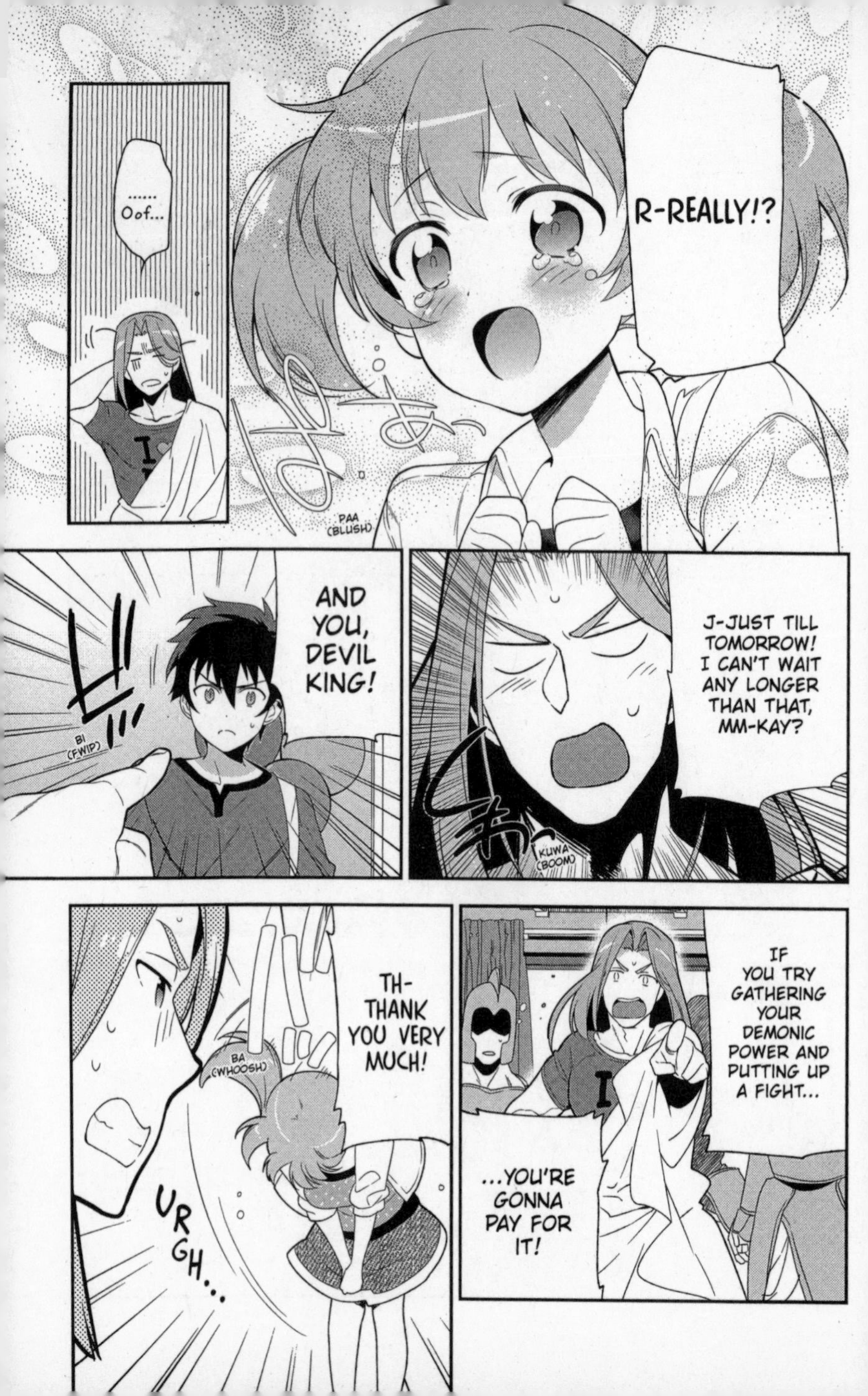
R-REALLY!?
PAA (BLUSH)
...... Oof...
J-JUST TILL TOMORROW! I CAN'T WAIT ANY LONGER THAN THAT, MM-KAY?
KUWA (BOOM)
AND YOU, DEVIL KING!
BI (FWIP)
IF YOU TRY GATHERING YOUR DEMONIC POWER AND PUTTING UP A FIGHT...
...YOU'RE GONNA PAY FOR IT!
TH-THANK YOU VERY MUCH!
BA (WHOOSH)
URGH...

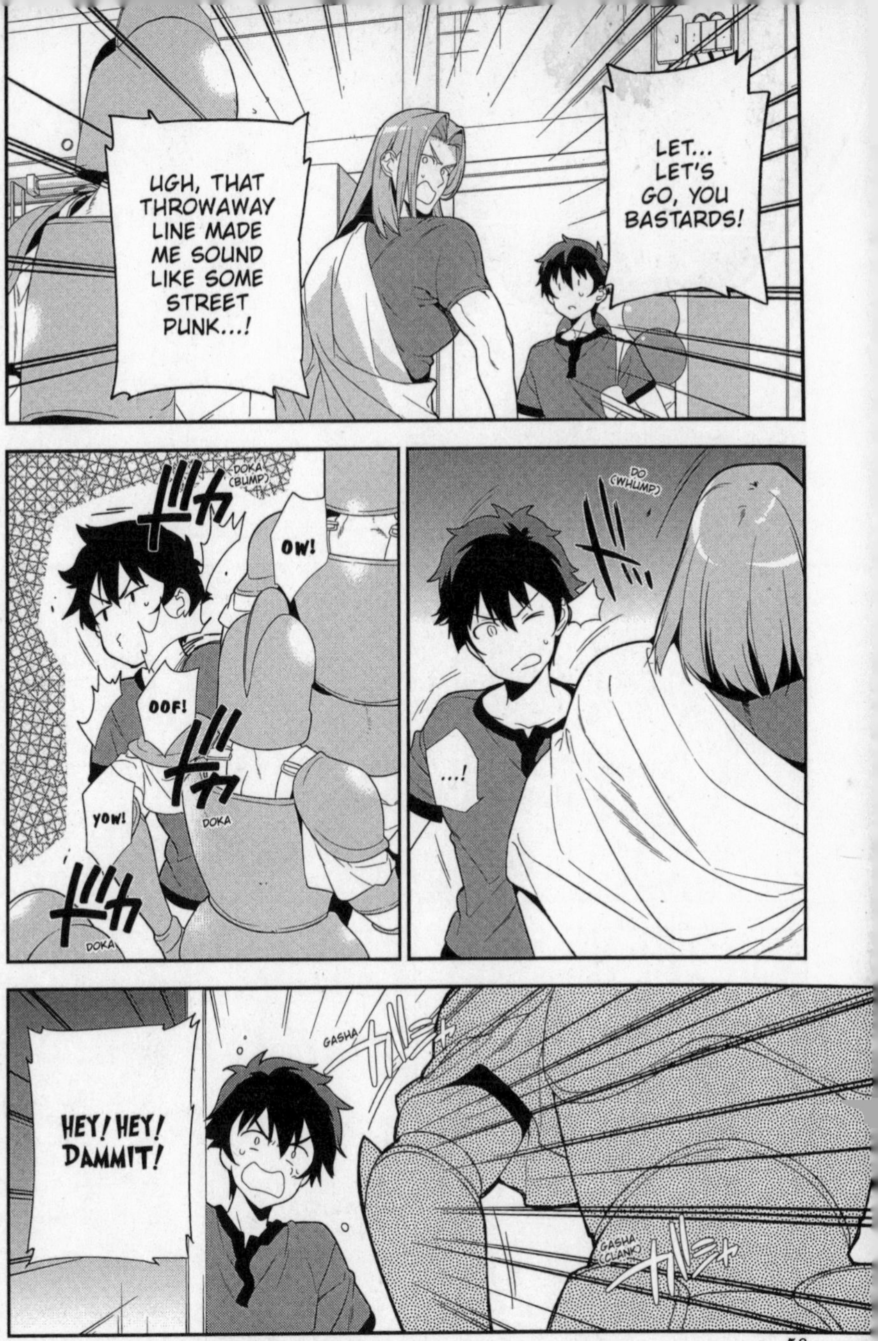
LET... LET'S GO, YOU BASTARDS!
UGH, THAT THROWAWAY LINE MADE ME SOUND LIKE SOME STREET PUNK...!
DO (WHUMP)
...!
DOKA (BUMP)
OW!
OOF!
DOKA
YOW!
DOKA
GASHA
HEY! HEY! DAMMIT!
GASHA (CLANK)

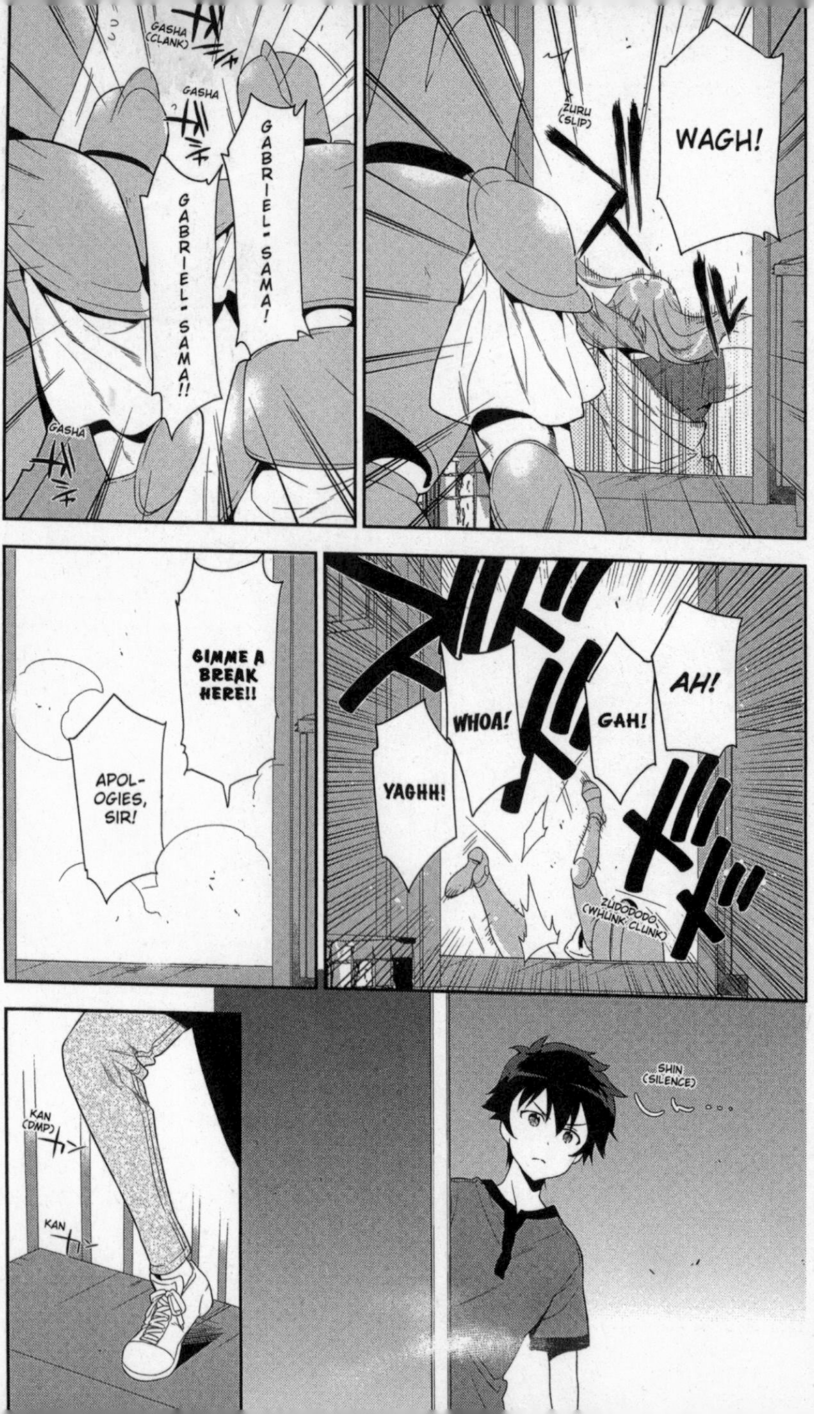
WAGH!
ZURU (SLIP)
GASHA (CLANK)
GASHA
GABRIEL-SAMA!
GABRIEL-SAMA!!
GASHA
AH!
GAH!
WHOA!
YAGHH!
ZUDODODO (WHUNK CLUNK)
GIMME A BREAK HERE!!
APOLOGIES, SIR!
SHIN (SILENCE)
KAN (DMP)
KAN

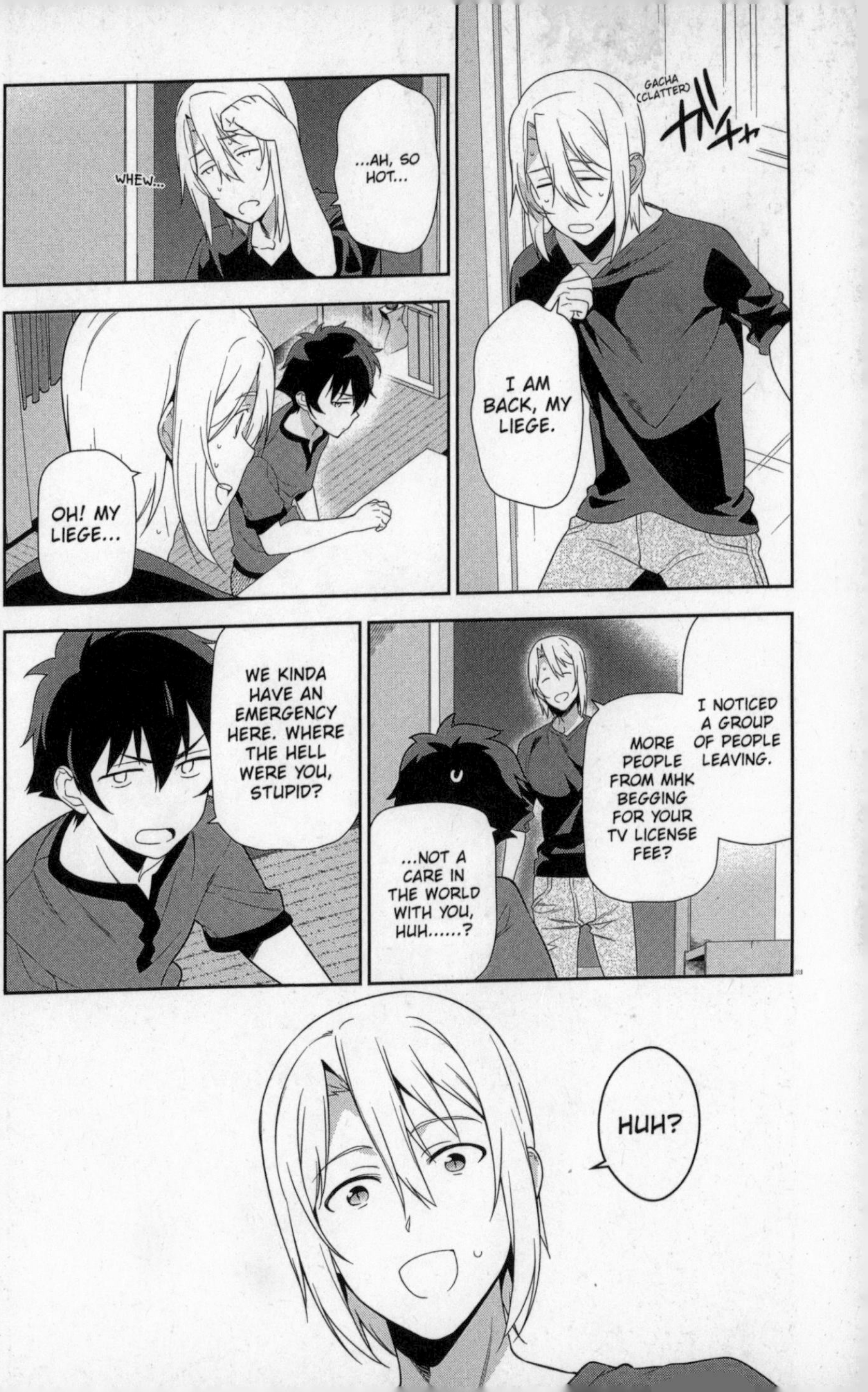
GACHA (CLATTER)
ガチャ
I AM BACK, MY LIEGE.
...AH, SO HOT...
WHEW...
OH! MY LIEGE...
I NOTICED A GROUP OF PEOPLE LEAVING.
MORE PEOPLE FROM MHK BEGGING FOR YOUR TV LICENSE FEE?
...NOT A CARE IN THE WORLD WITH YOU, HUH......?
WE KINDA HAVE AN EMERGENCY HERE. WHERE THE HELL WERE YOU, STUPID?
HUH?

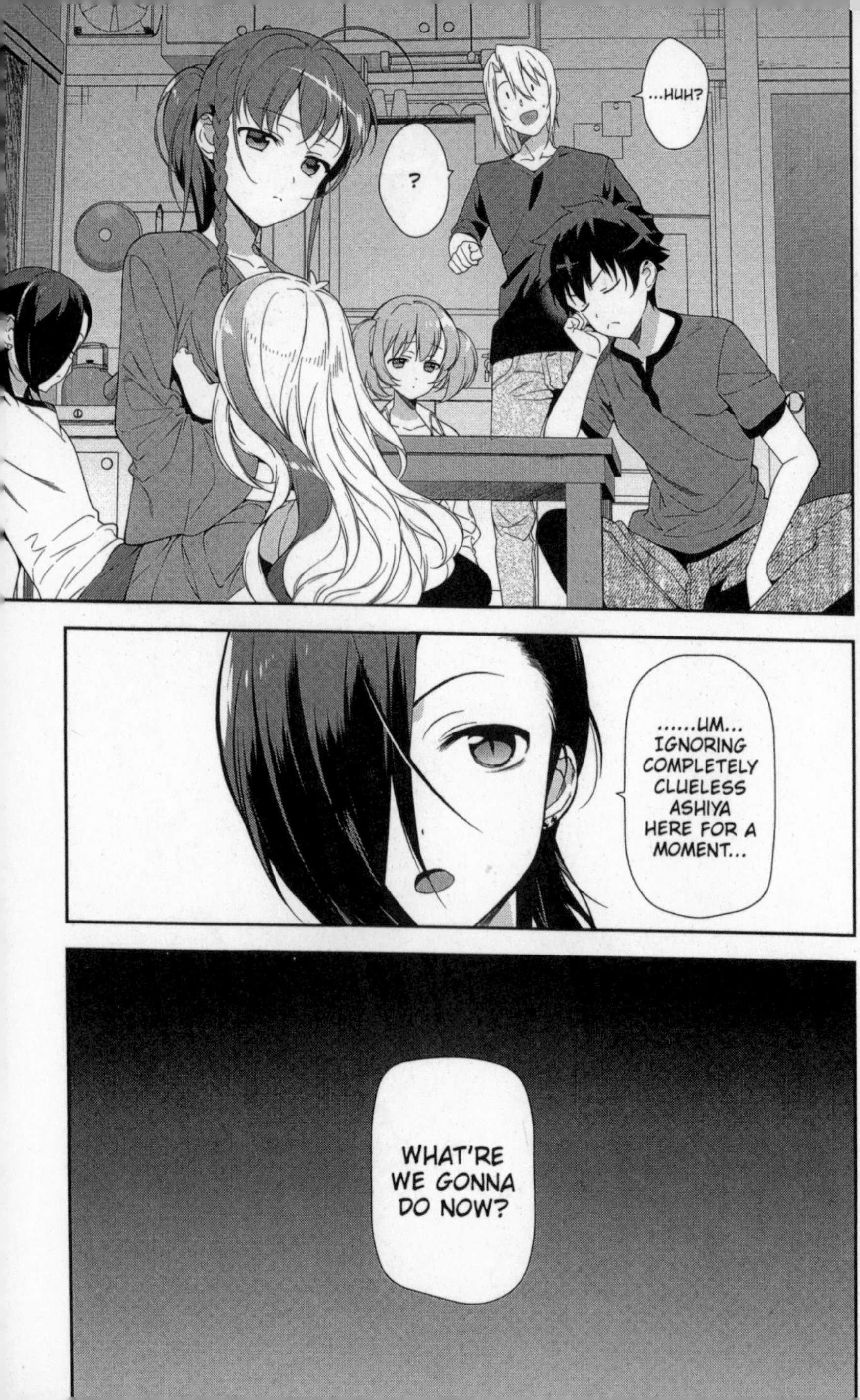
...HUH?
?
......UM... IGNORING COMPLETELY CLUELESS ASHIYA HERE FOR A MOMENT...
WHAT'RE WE GONNA DO NOW?

THE DEVIL IS A PART-TIMER!

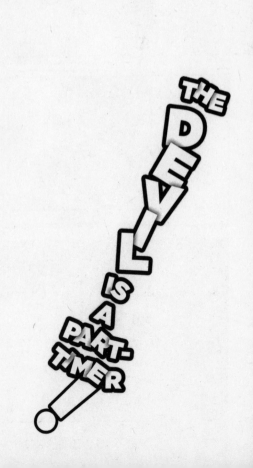

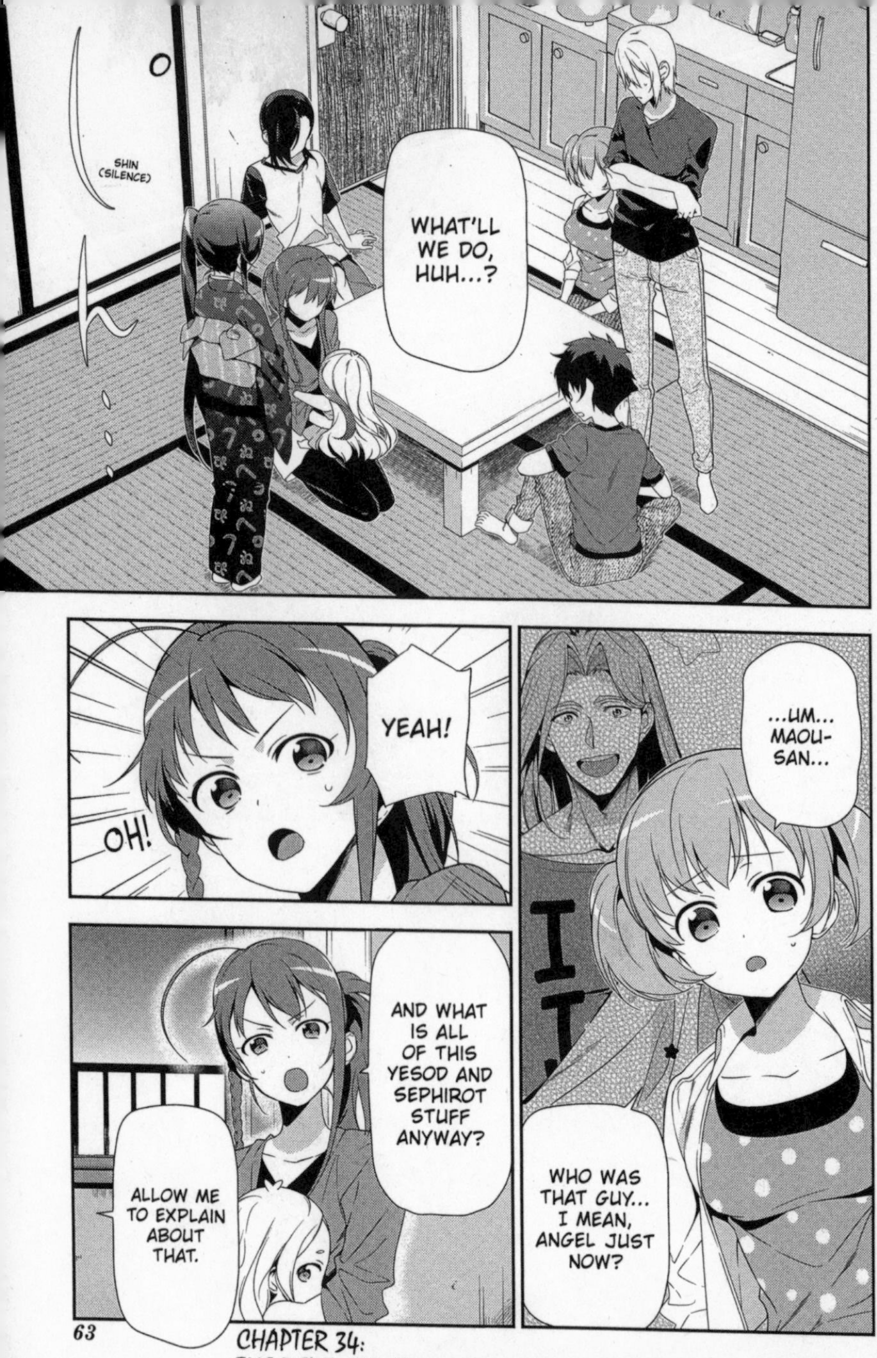
WHAT'LL WE DO, HUH...?
SHIN (SILENCE)
...UM... MAOU-SAN...
WHO WAS THAT GUY... I MEAN, ANGEL JUST NOW?
YEAH!
OH!
AND WHAT IS ALL OF THIS YESOD AND SEPHIROT STUFF ANYWAY?
ALLOW ME TO EXPLAIN ABOUT THAT.

CHAPTER 34:
THE DEVIL AND THE HERO SHARE THE FLOOR FOR THE NIGHT

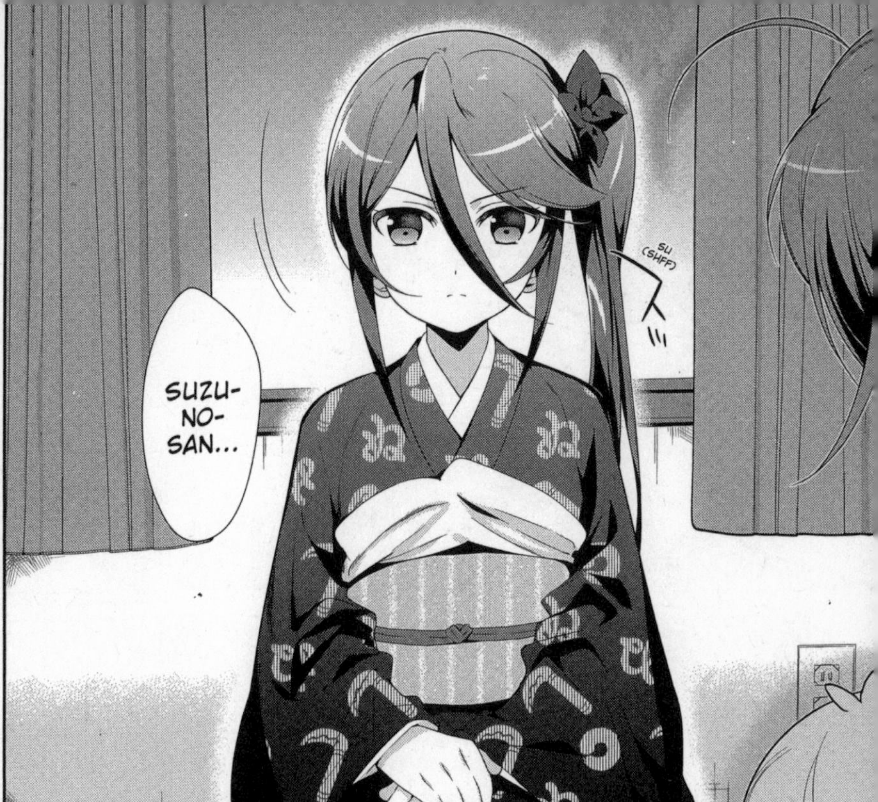
SU (SHFF)
SUZU-NO-SAN...
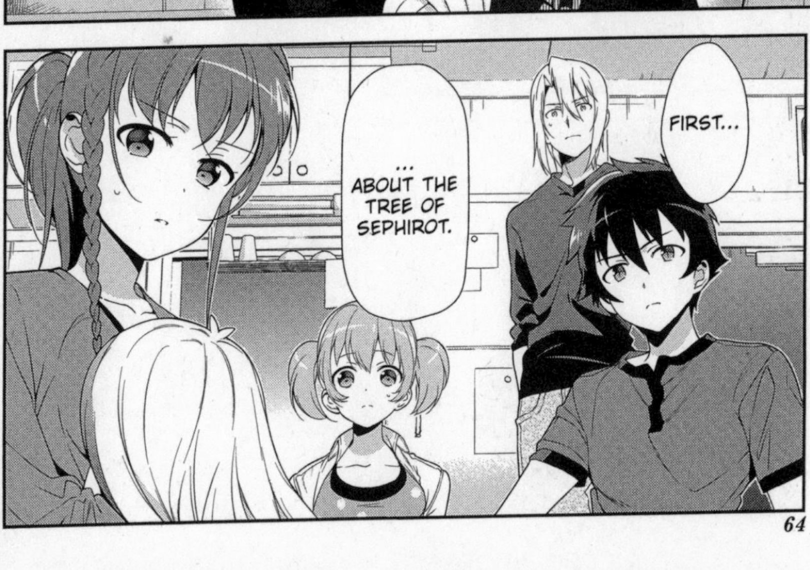
FIRST...
...ABOUT THE TREE OF SEPHIROT.

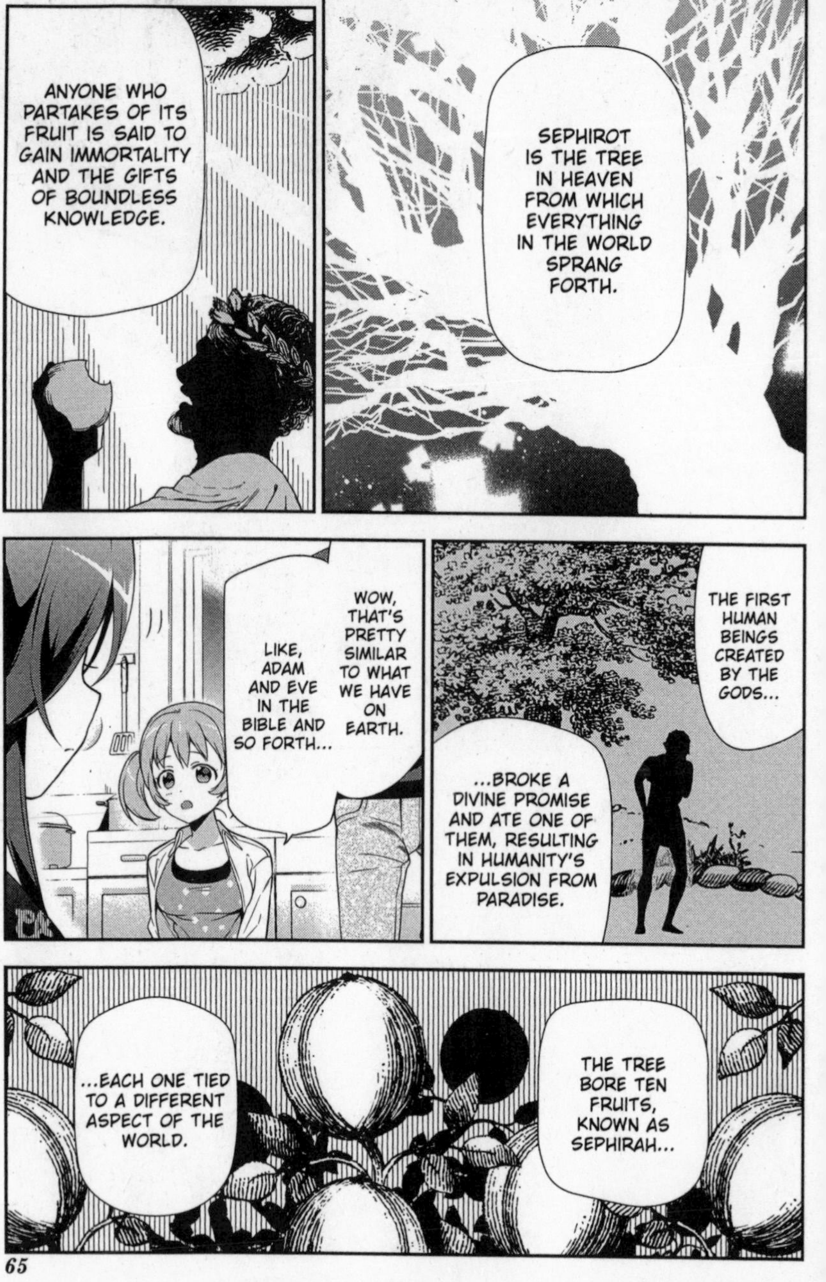
SEPHIROT IS THE TREE IN HEAVEN FROM WHICH EVERYTHING IN THE WORLD SPRANG FORTH.
ANYONE WHO PARTAKES OF ITS FRUIT IS SAID TO GAIN IMMORTALITY AND THE GIFTS OF BOUNDLESS KNOWLEDGE.
THE FIRST HUMAN BEINGS CREATED BY THE GODS...
...BROKE A DIVINE PROMISE AND ATE ONE OF THEM, RESULTING IN HUMANITY'S EXPULSION FROM PARADISE.
WOW, THAT'S PRETTY SIMILAR TO WHAT WE HAVE ON EARTH.
LIKE, ADAM AND EVE IN THE BIBLE AND SO FORTH...
THE TREE BORE TEN FRUITS, KNOWN AS SEPHIRAH...
...EACH ONE TIED TO A DIFFERENT ASPECT OF THE WORLD.

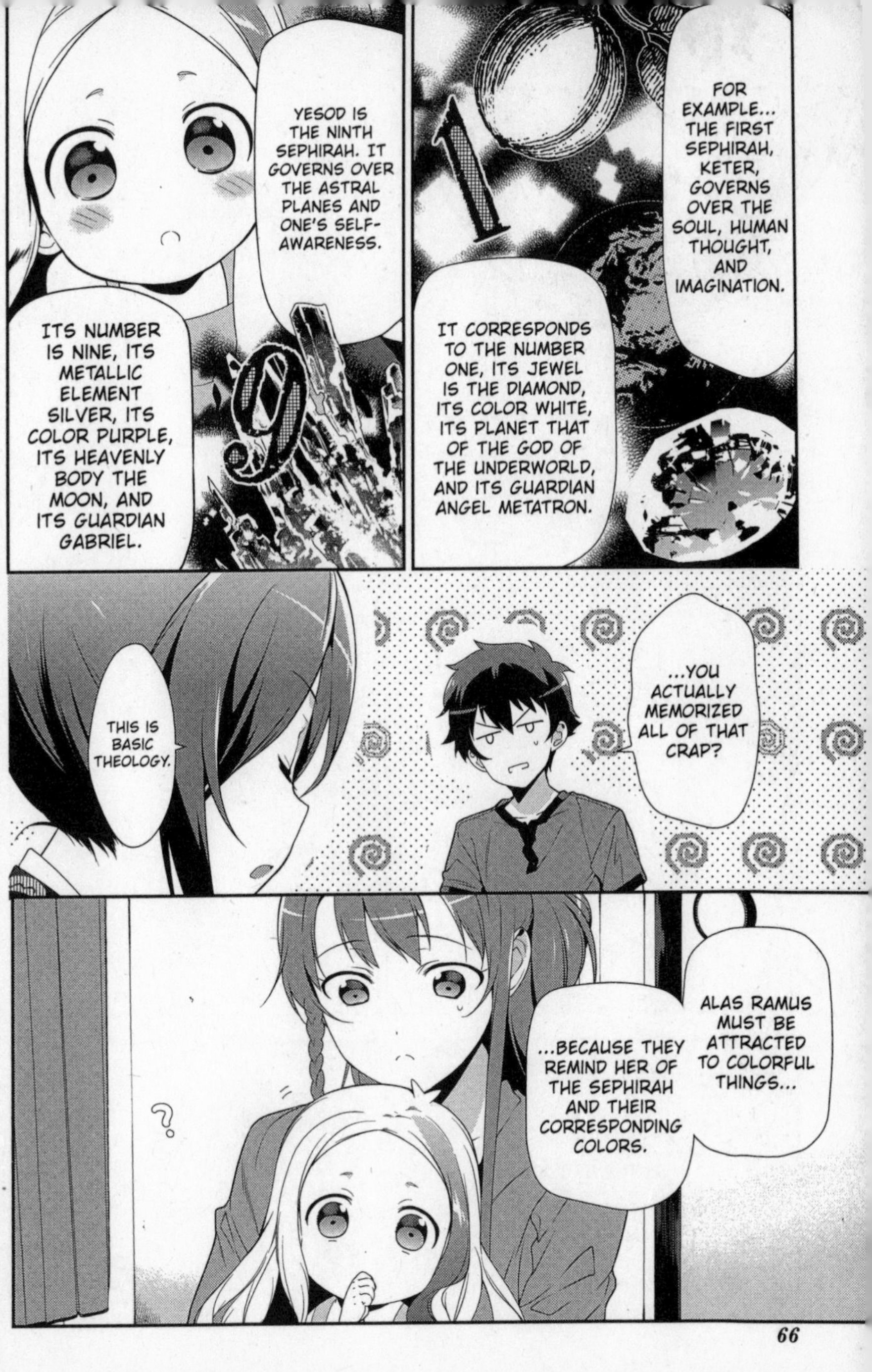
FOR EXAMPLE... THE FIRST SEPHIRAH, KETER, GOVERNS OVER THE SOUL, HUMAN THOUGHT, AND IMAGINATION.
IT CORRESPONDS TO THE NUMBER ONE, ITS JEWEL IS THE DIAMOND, ITS COLOR WHITE, ITS PLANET THAT OF THE GOD OF THE UNDERWORLD, AND ITS GUARDIAN ANGEL METATRON.
YESOD IS THE NINTH SEPHIRAH. IT GOVERNS OVER THE ASTRAL PLANES AND ONE'S SELF-AWARENESS.
ITS NUMBER IS NINE, ITS METALLIC ELEMENT SILVER, ITS COLOR PURPLE, ITS HEAVENLY BODY THE MOON, AND ITS GUARDIAN GABRIEL.
...YOU ACTUALLY MEMORIZED ALL OF THAT CRAP?
THIS IS BASIC THEOLOGY.
ALAS RAMUS MUST BE ATTRACTED TO COLORFUL THINGS...
...BECAUSE THEY REMIND HER OF THE SEPHIRAH AND THEIR CORRESPONDING COLORS.
?

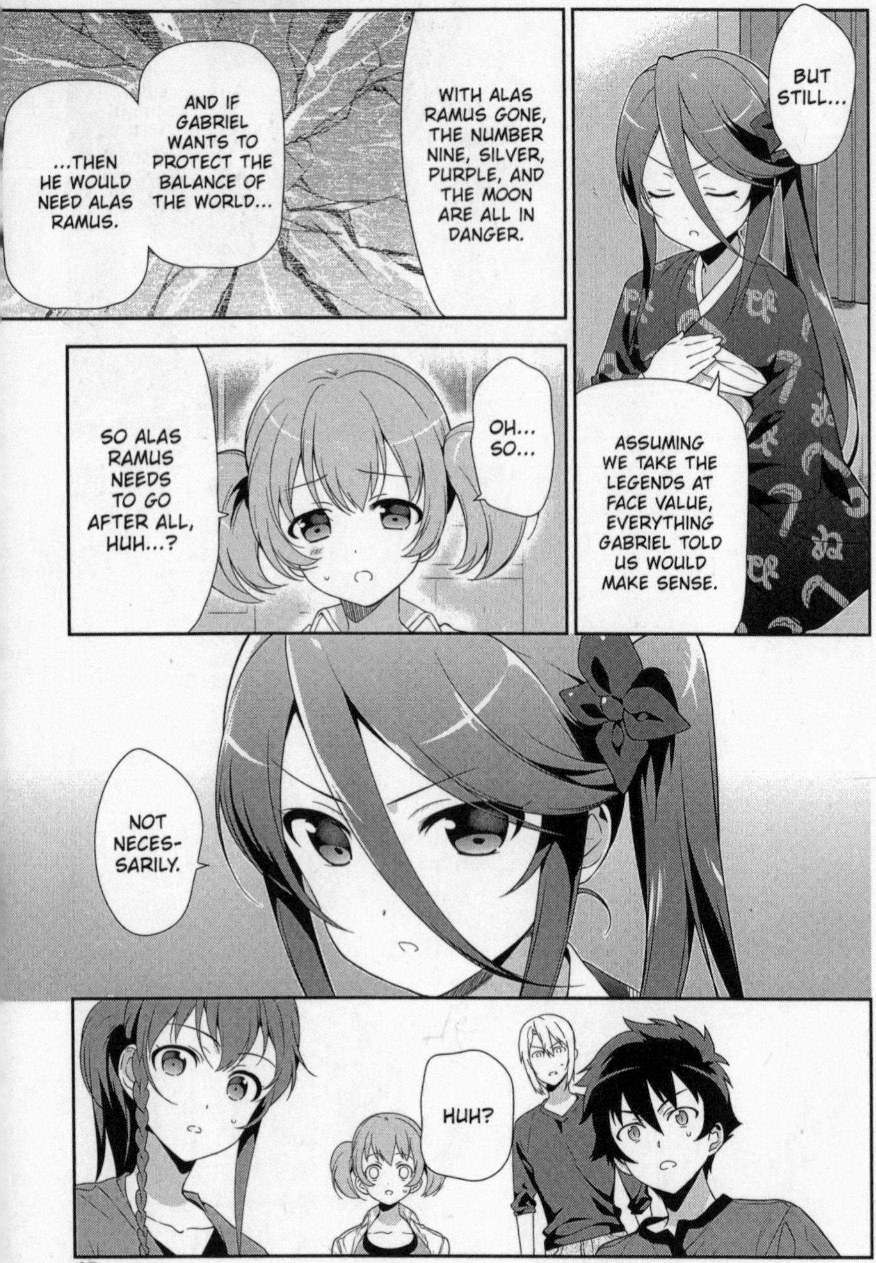

BUT STILL...
ASSUMING WE TAKE THE LEGENDS AT FACE VALUE, EVERYTHING GABRIEL TOLD US WOULD MAKE SENSE.
WITH ALAS RAMUS GONE, THE NUMBER NINE, SILVER, PURPLE, AND THE MOON ARE ALL IN DANGER.
AND IF GABRIEL WANTS TO PROTECT THE BALANCE OF THE WORLD...
...THEN HE WOULD NEED ALAS RAMUS.
OH... SO...
SO ALAS RAMUS NEEDS TO GO AFTER ALL, HUH...?
NOT NECES-SARILY.
HUH?

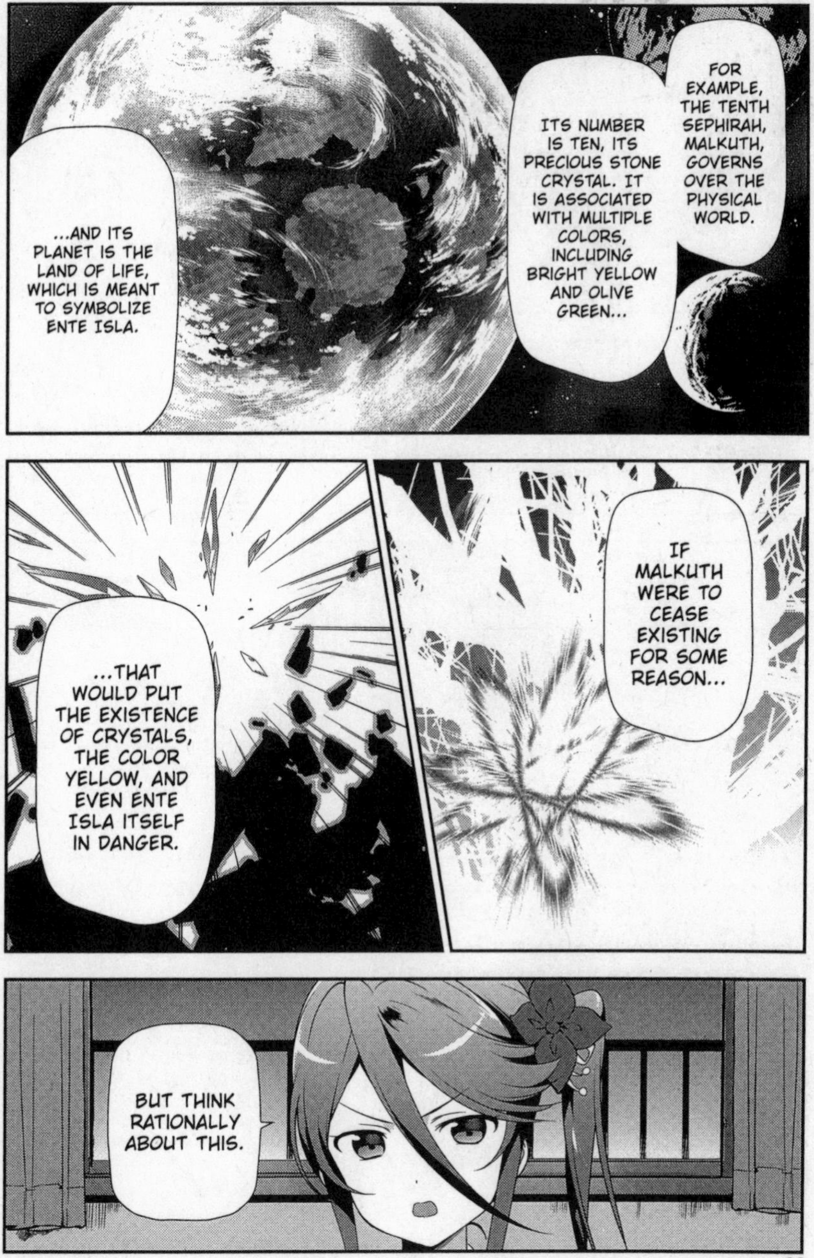
FOR EXAMPLE, THE TENTH SEPHIRAH, MALKUTH, GOVERNS OVER THE PHYSICAL WORLD.
ITS NUMBER IS TEN, ITS PRECIOUS STONE CRYSTAL. IT IS ASSOCIATED WITH MULTIPLE COLORS, INCLUDING BRIGHT YELLOW AND OLIVE GREEN...
...AND ITS PLANET IS THE LAND OF LIFE, WHICH IS MEANT TO SYMBOLIZE ENTE ISLA.
IF MALKUTH WERE TO CEASE EXISTING FOR SOME REASON...
...THAT WOULD PUT THE EXISTENCE OF CRYSTALS, THE COLOR YELLOW, AND EVEN ENTE ISLA ITSELF IN DANGER.
BUT THINK RATIONALLY ABOUT THIS.

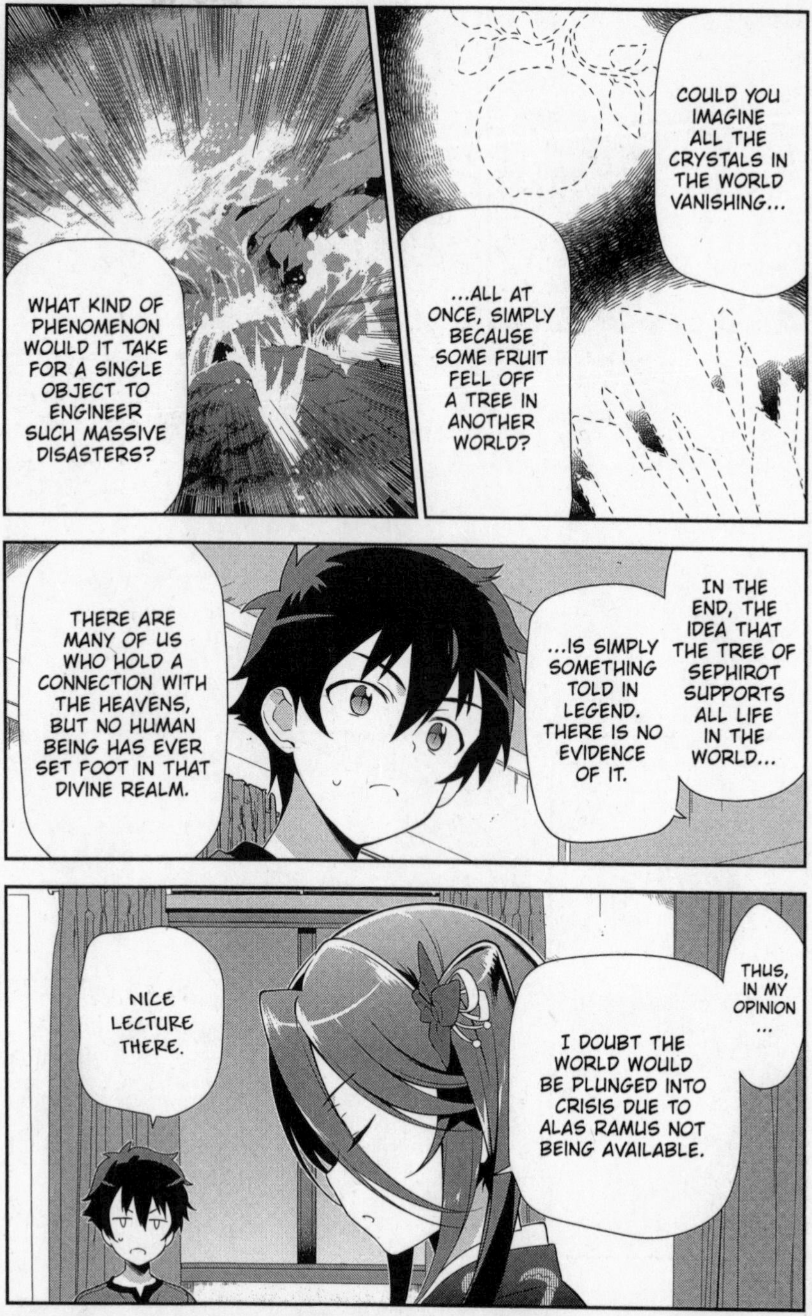
COULD YOU IMAGINE ALL THE CRYSTALS IN THE WORLD VANISHING...
...ALL AT ONCE, SIMPLY BECAUSE SOME FRUIT FELL OFF A TREE IN ANOTHER WORLD?
WHAT KIND OF PHENOMENON WOULD IT TAKE FOR A SINGLE OBJECT TO ENGINEER SUCH MASSIVE DISASTERS?
IN THE END, THE IDEA THAT THE TREE OF SEPHIROT SUPPORTS ALL LIFE IN THE WORLD...
...IS SIMPLY SOMETHING TOLD IN LEGEND. THERE IS NO EVIDENCE OF IT.
THERE ARE MANY OF US WHO HOLD A CONNECTION WITH THE HEAVENS, BUT NO HUMAN BEING HAS EVER SET FOOT IN THAT DIVINE REALM.
THUS, IN MY OPINION ...
I DOUBT THE WORLD WOULD BE PLUNGED INTO CRISIS DUE TO ALAS RAMUS NOT BEING AVAILABLE.
NICE LECTURE THERE.

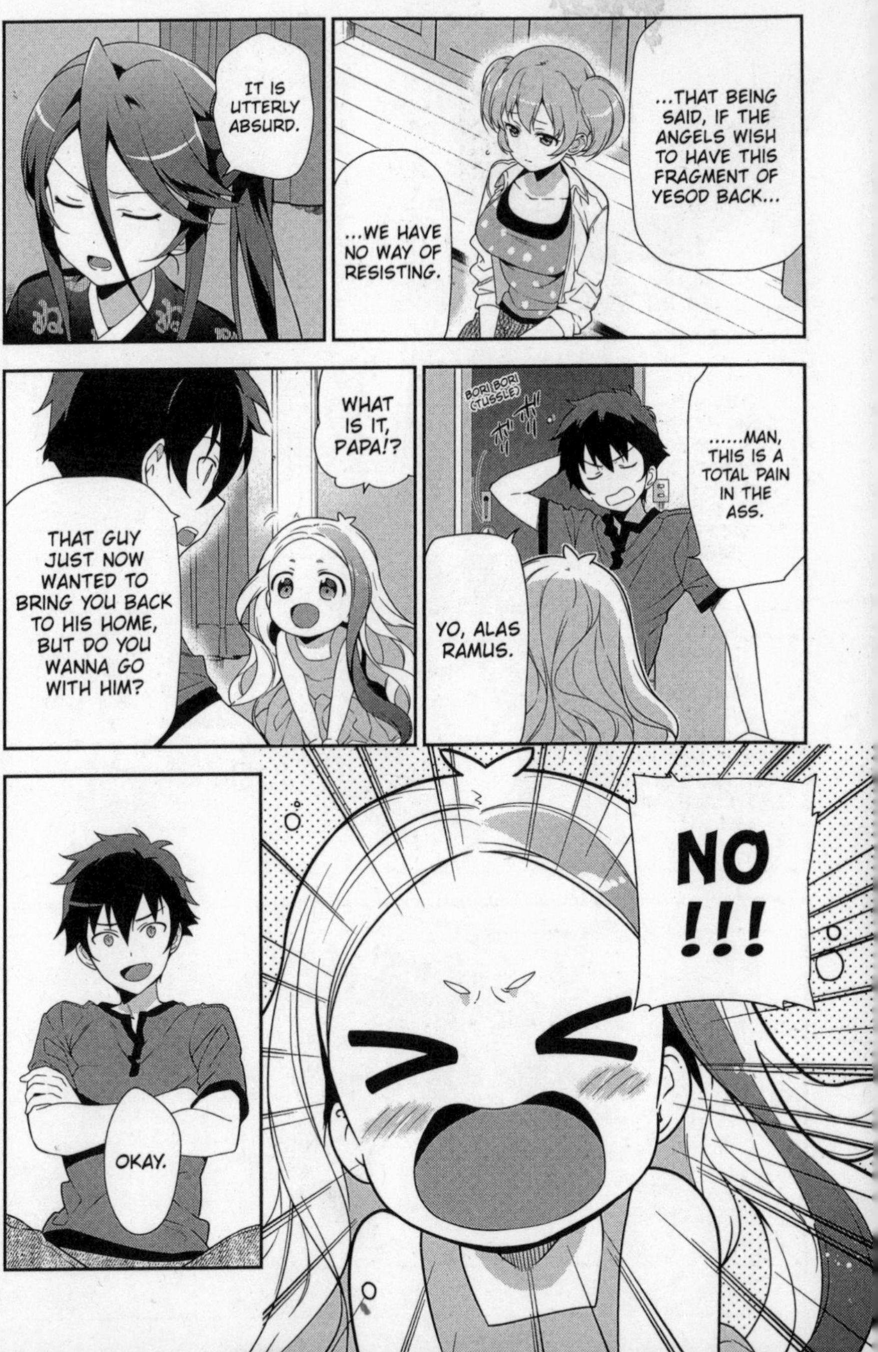
...THAT BEING SAID, IF THE ANGELS WISH TO HAVE THIS FRAGMENT OF YESOD BACK...
...WE HAVE NO WAY OF RESISTING.
IT IS UTTERLY ABSURD.
BORI BORI (TUSSLE)
......MAN, THIS IS A TOTAL PAIN IN THE ASS.
YO, ALAS RAMUS.
WHAT IS IT, PAPA!?
THAT GUY JUST NOW WANTED TO BRING YOU BACK TO HIS HOME, BUT DO YOU WANNA GO WITH HIM?
NO !!!
OKAY.

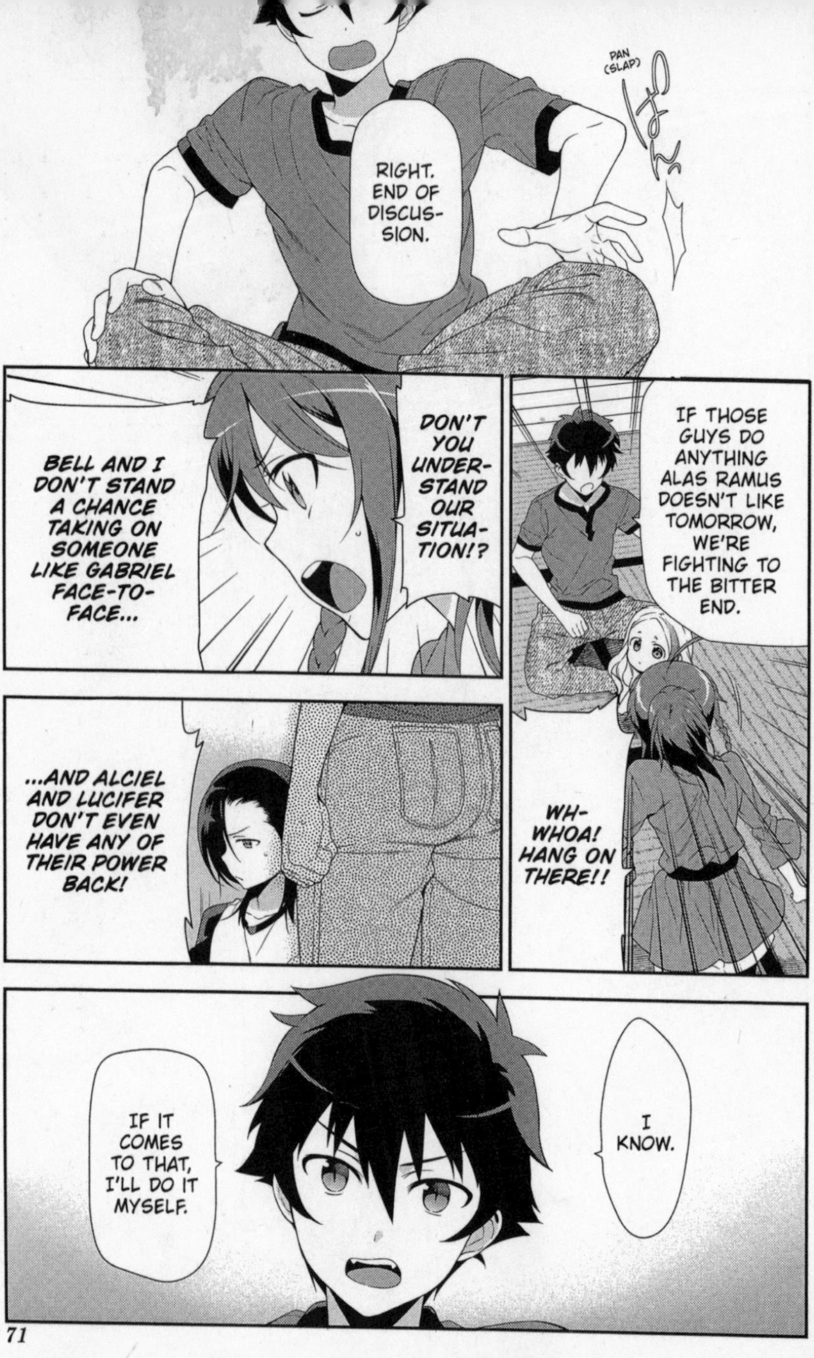
PAN (SLAP)
RIGHT. END OF DISCUS-SION.
IF THOSE GUYS DO ANYTHING ALAS RAMUS DOESN'T LIKE TOMORROW, WE'RE FIGHTING TO THE BITTER END.
WH-WHOA! HANG ON THERE!!
DON'T YOU UNDER-STAND OUR SITUA-TION!?
BELL AND I DON'T STAND A CHANCE TAKING ON SOMEONE LIKE GABRIEL FACE-TO-FACE...
...AND ALCIEL AND LUCIFER DON'T EVEN HAVE ANY OF THEIR POWER BACK!
I KNOW.
IF IT COMES TO THAT, I'LL DO IT MYSELF.

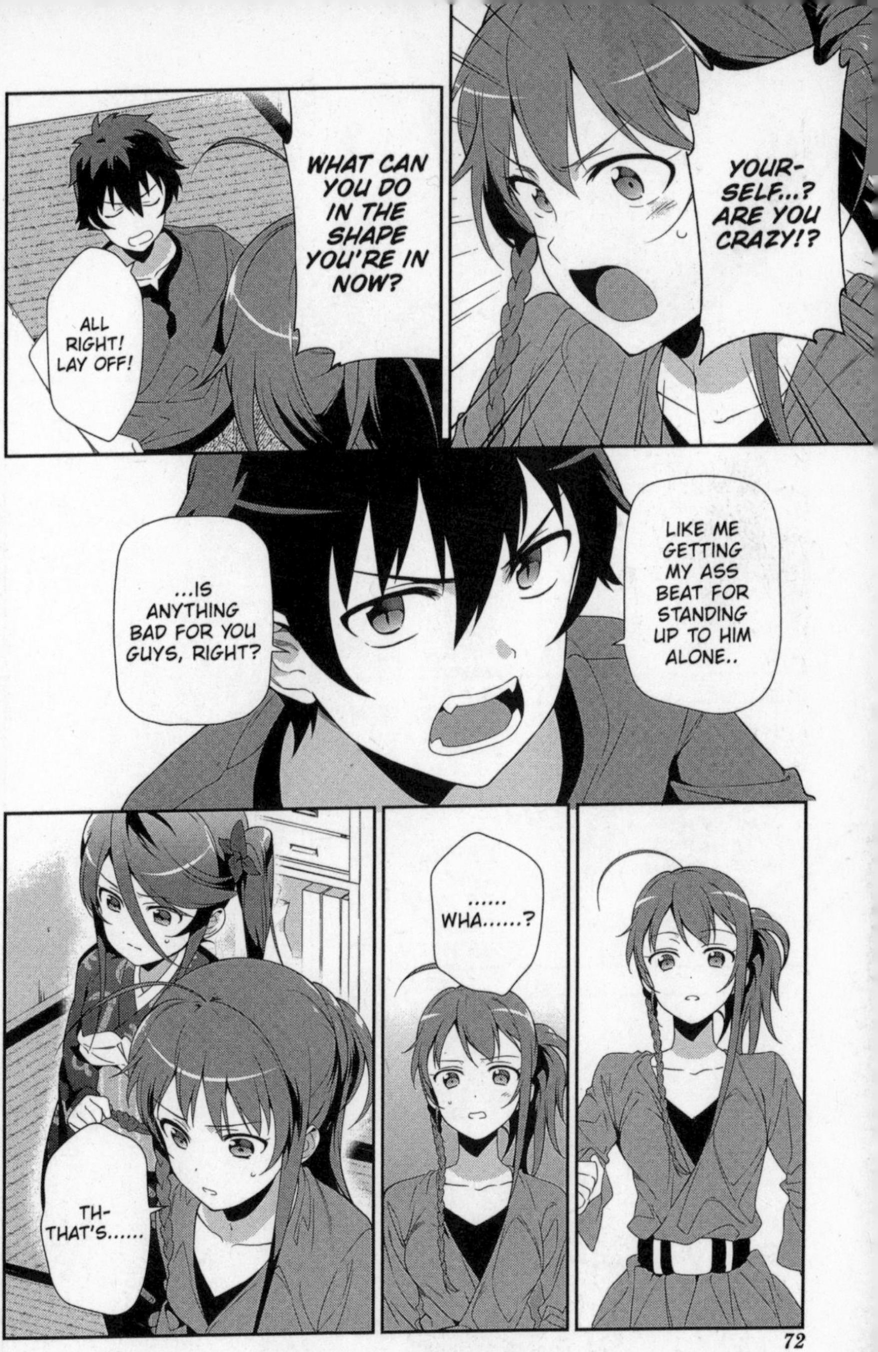
YOURSELF...? ARE YOU CRAZY!?
WHAT CAN YOU DO IN THE SHAPE YOU'RE IN NOW?
ALL RIGHT! LAY OFF!
LIKE ME GETTING MY ASS BEAT FOR STANDING UP TO HIM ALONE..
...IS ANYTHING BAD FOR YOU GUYS, RIGHT?
...... WHA......?
TH-THAT'S......

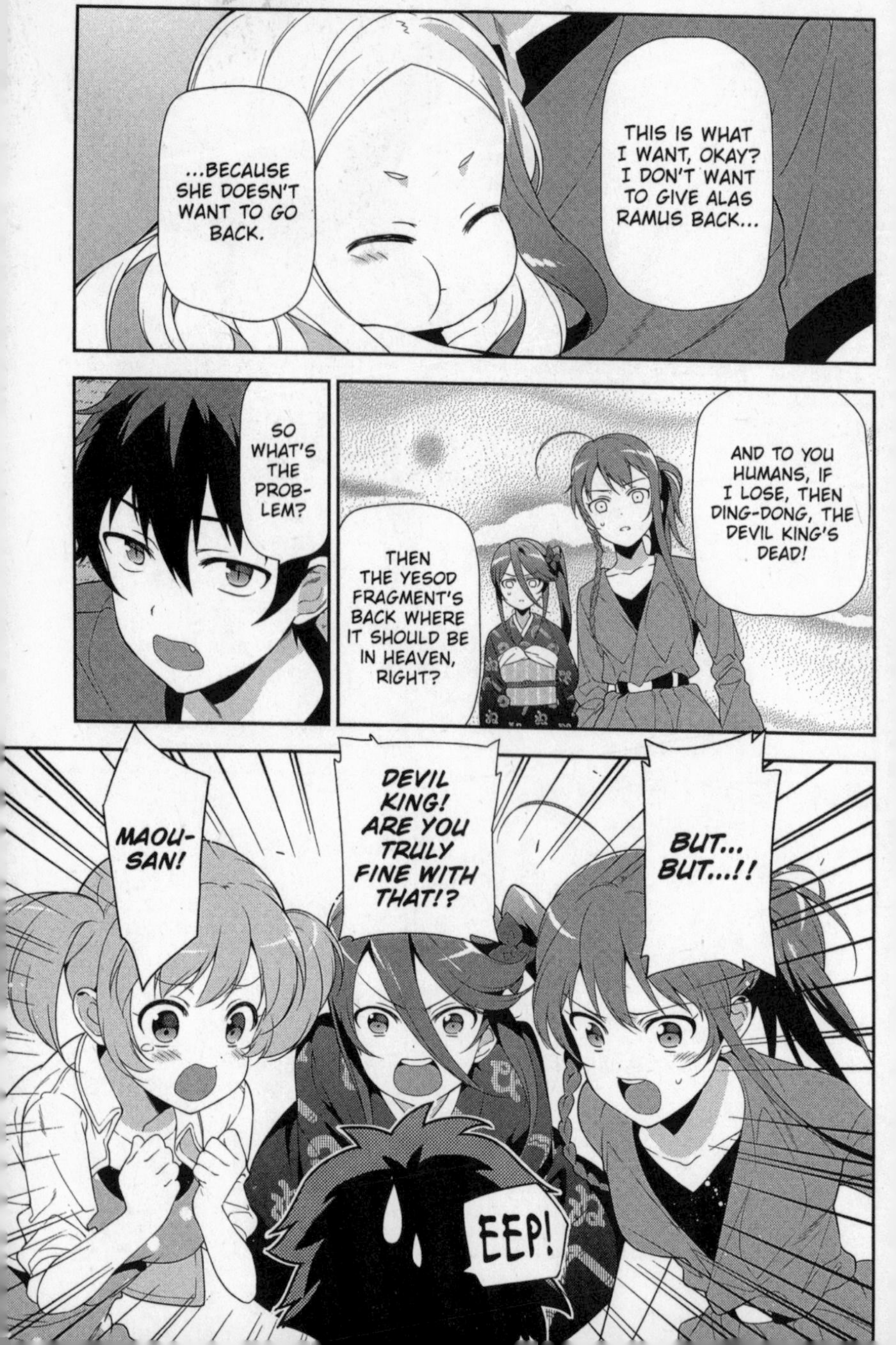
THIS IS WHAT I WANT, OKAY? I DON'T WANT TO GIVE ALAS RAMUS BACK...
...BECAUSE SHE DOESN'T WANT TO GO BACK.
AND TO YOU HUMANS, IF I LOSE, THEN DING-DONG, THE DEVIL KING'S DEAD!
THEN THE YESOD FRAGMENT'S BACK WHERE IT SHOULD BE IN HEAVEN, RIGHT?
SO WHAT'S THE PROB-LEM?
BUT... BUT...!!
DEVIL KING! ARE YOU TRULY FINE WITH THAT!?
MAOU-SAN!
EEP!

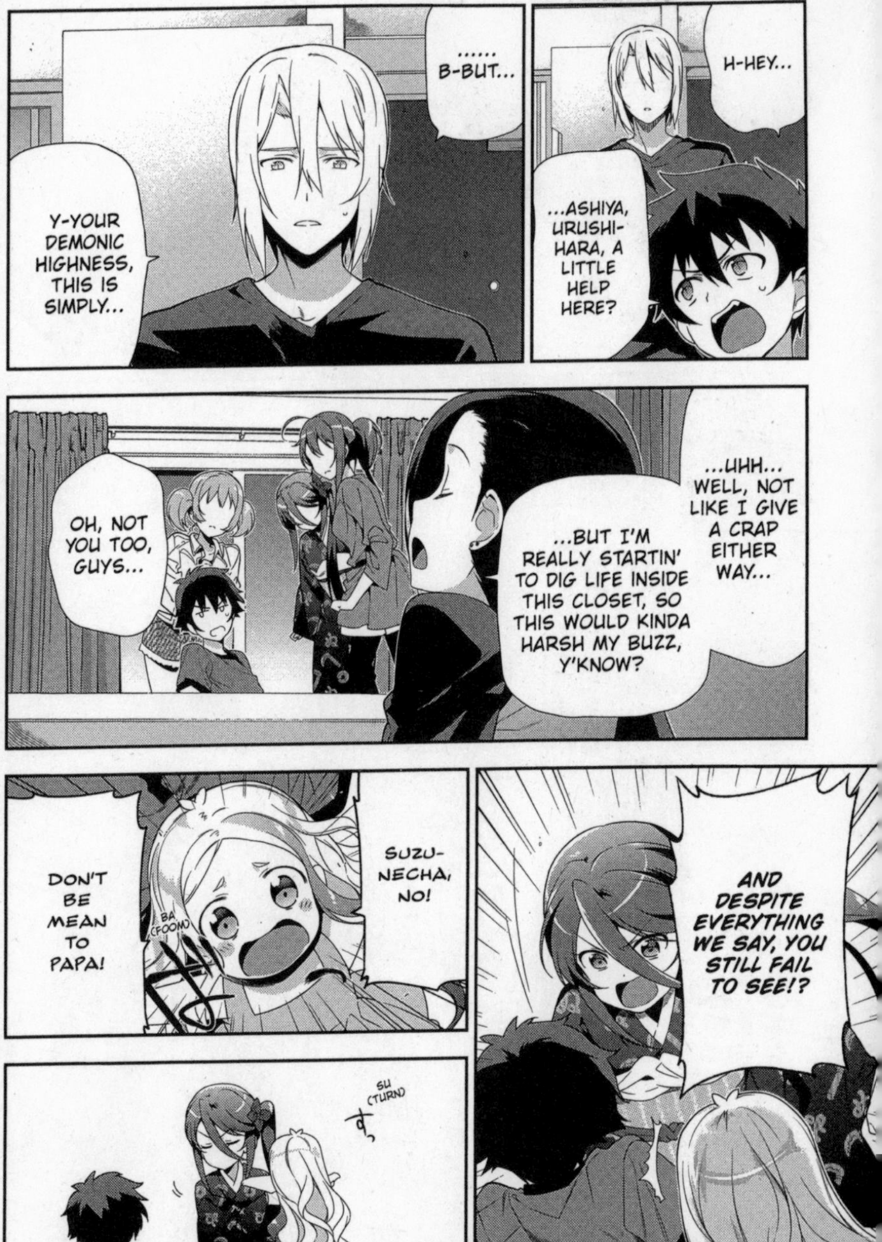
H-HEY...
...ASHIYA, URUSHI-HARA, A LITTLE HELP HERE?
......B-BUT...
Y-YOUR DEMONIC HIGHNESS, THIS IS SIMPLY...
...UHH... WELL, NOT LIKE I GIVE A CRAP EITHER WAY...
...BUT I'M REALLY STARTIN' TO DIG LIFE INSIDE THIS CLOSET, SO THIS WOULD KINDA HARSH MY BUZZ, Y'KNOW?
OH, NOT YOU TOO, GUYS...
AND DESPITE EVERYTHING WE SAY, YOU STILL FAIL TO SEE!?
SUZU-NECHA, NO!
BA (FOOM)
DON'T BE MEAN TO PAPA!
SU (TURN)

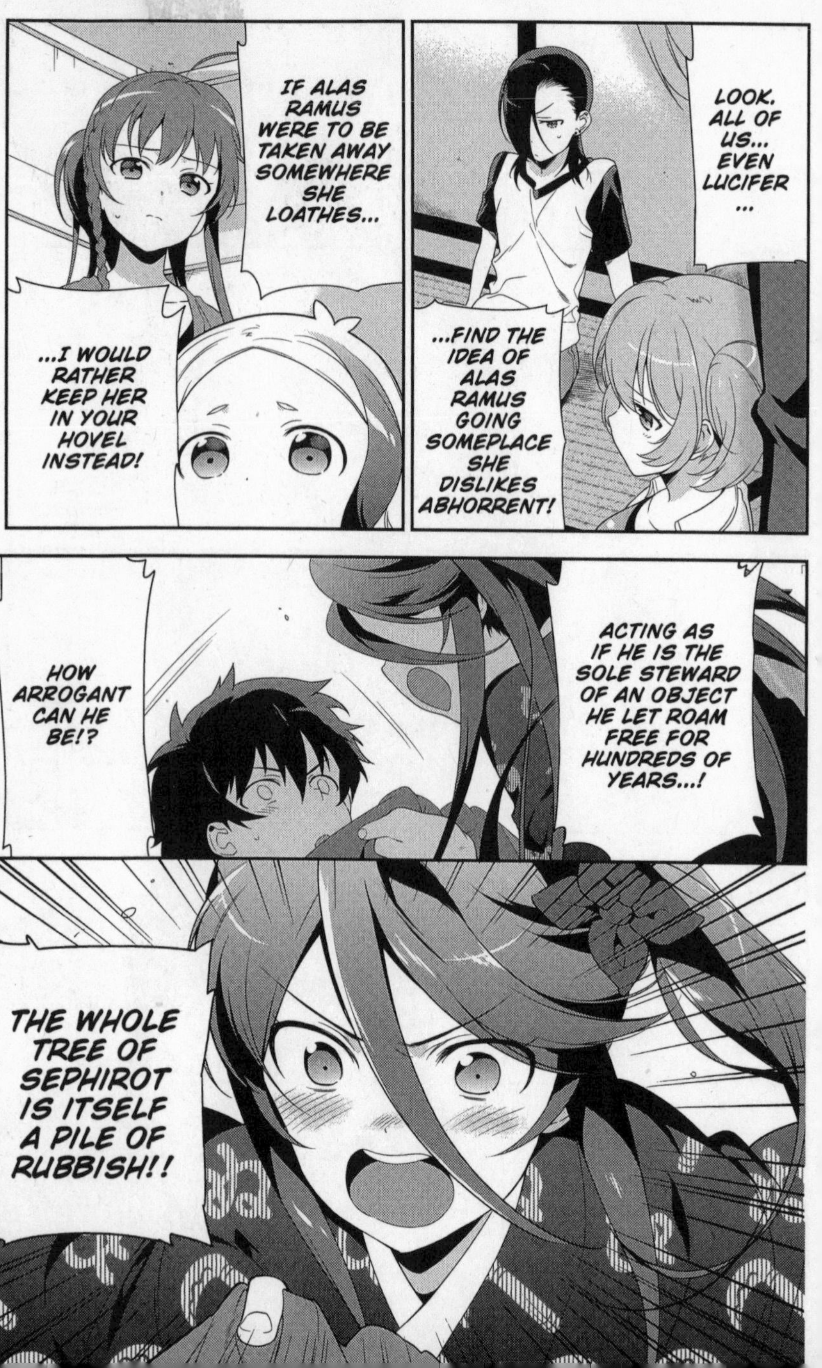
LOOK. ALL OF US... EVEN LUCIFER...
...FIND THE IDEA OF ALAS RAMUS GOING SOMEPLACE SHE DISLIKES ABHORRENT!
IF ALAS RAMUS WERE TO BE TAKEN AWAY SOMEWHERE SHE LOATHES...
...I WOULD RATHER KEEP HER IN YOUR HOVEL INSTEAD!
ACTING AS IF HE IS THE SOLE STEWARD OF AN OBJECT HE LET ROAM FREE FOR HUNDREDS OF YEARS...!
HOW ARROGANT CAN HE BE!?
THE WHOLE TREE OF SEPHIROT IS ITSELF A PILE OF RUBBISH!!

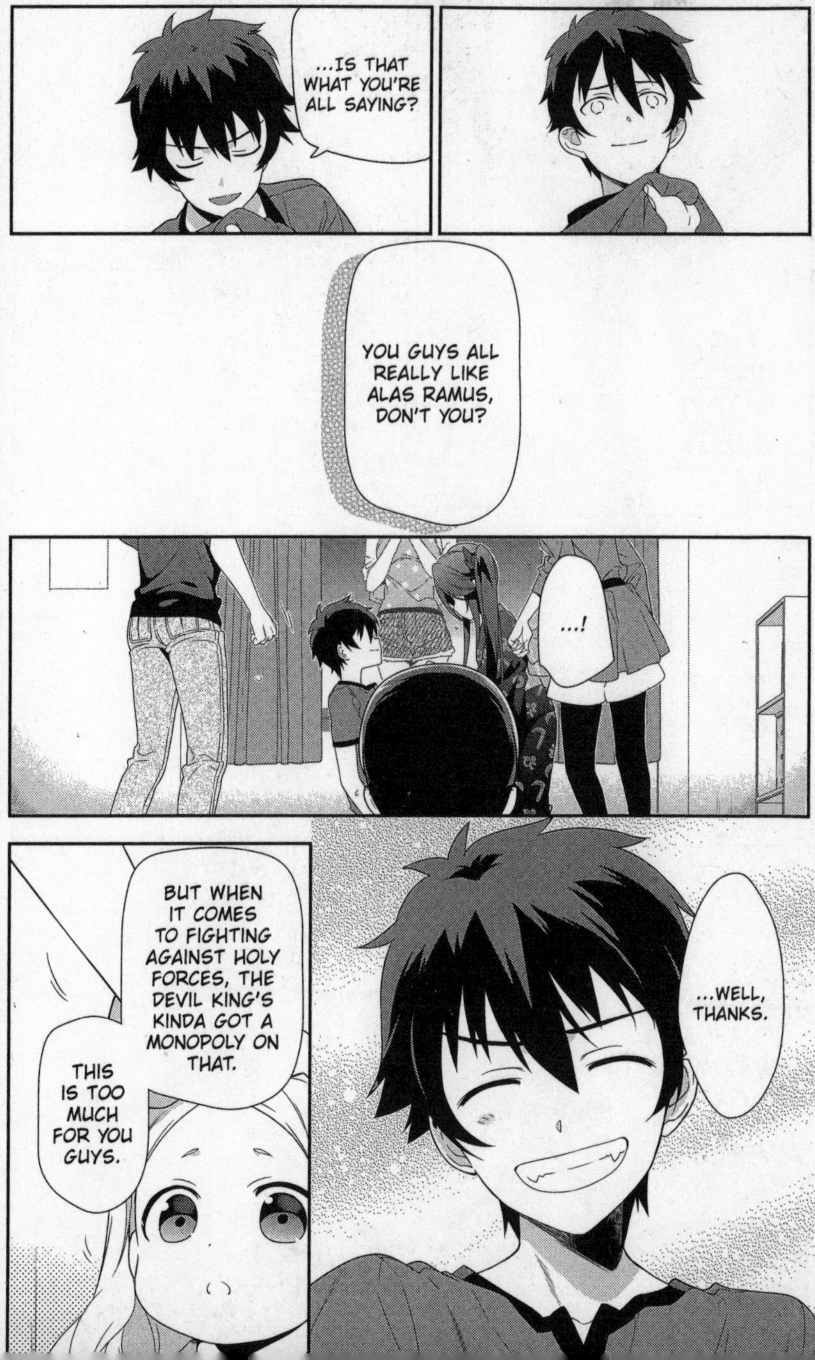
...IS THAT WHAT YOU'RE ALL SAYING?
YOU GUYS ALL REALLY LIKE ALAS RAMUS, DON'T YOU?
...!
...WELL, THANKS.
BUT WHEN IT COMES TO FIGHTING AGAINST HOLY FORCES, THE DEVIL KING'S KINDA GOT A MONOPOLY ON THAT.
THIS IS TOO MUCH FOR YOU GUYS.

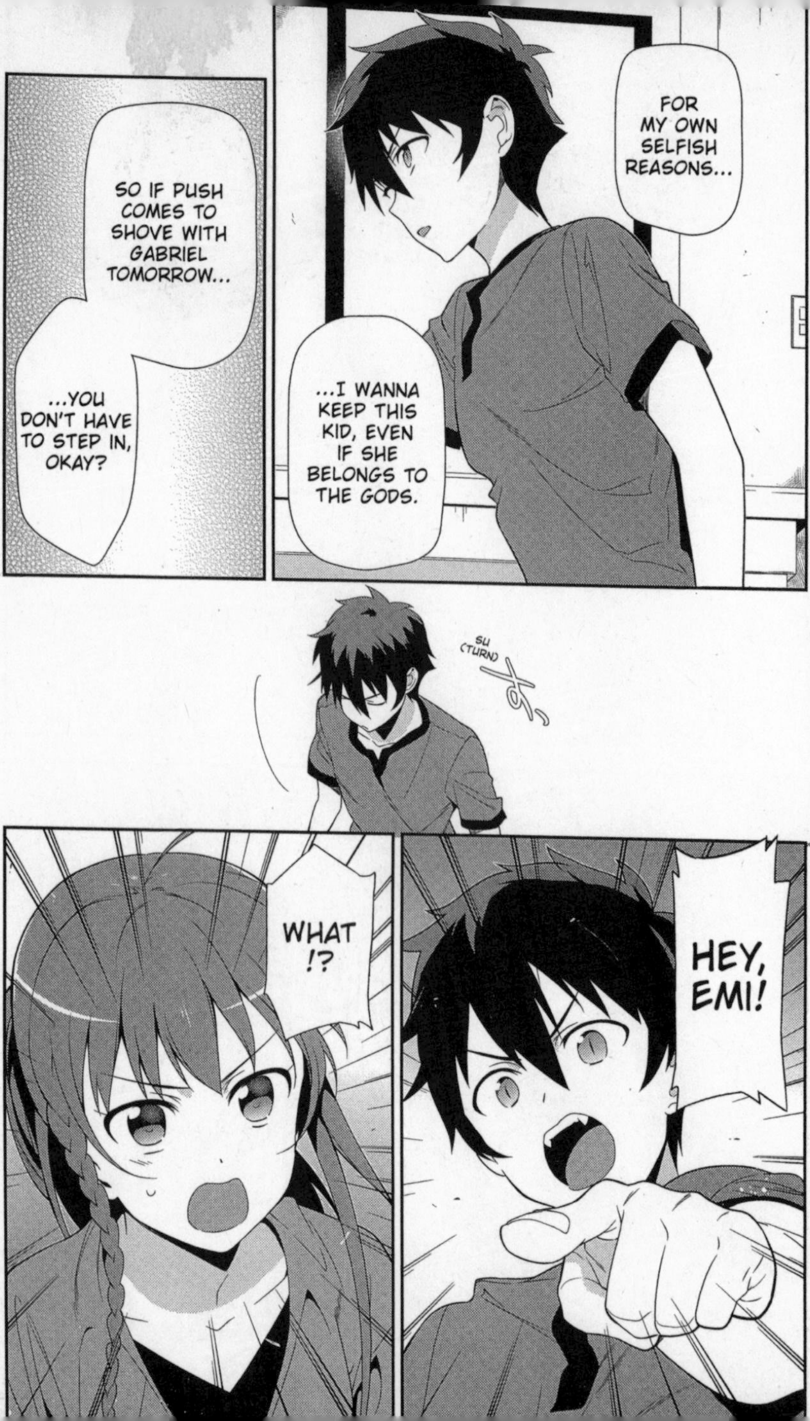
FOR MY OWN SELFISH REASONS...
...I WANNA KEEP THIS KID, EVEN IF SHE BELONGS TO THE GODS.
SO IF PUSH COMES TO SHOVE WITH GABRIEL TOMORROW...
...YOU DON'T HAVE TO STEP IN, OKAY?
SU (TURN)
すっ
HEY, EMI!
WHAT !?

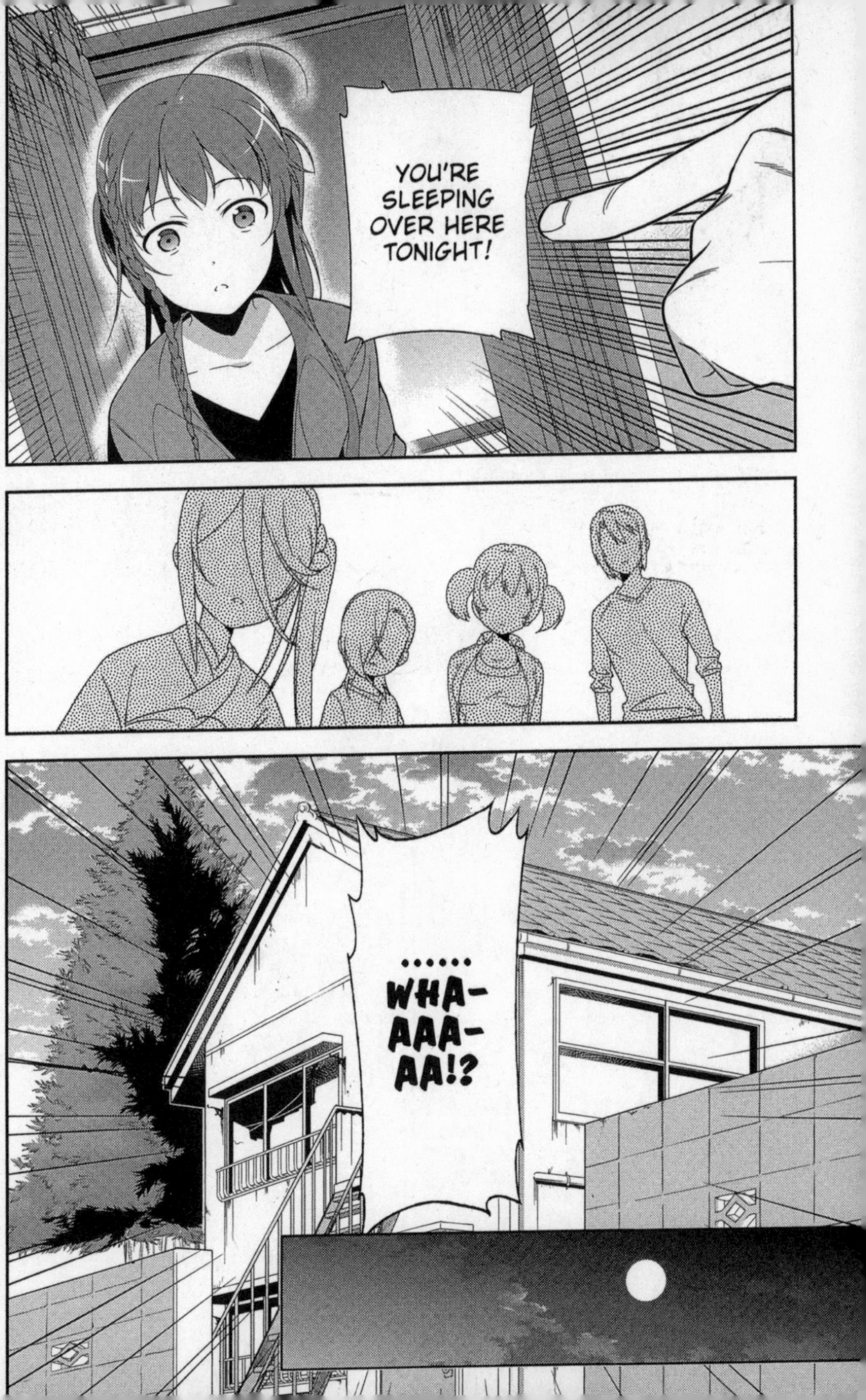
YOU'RE SLEEPING OVER HERE TONIGHT!
......
WHA-AAA-AA!?

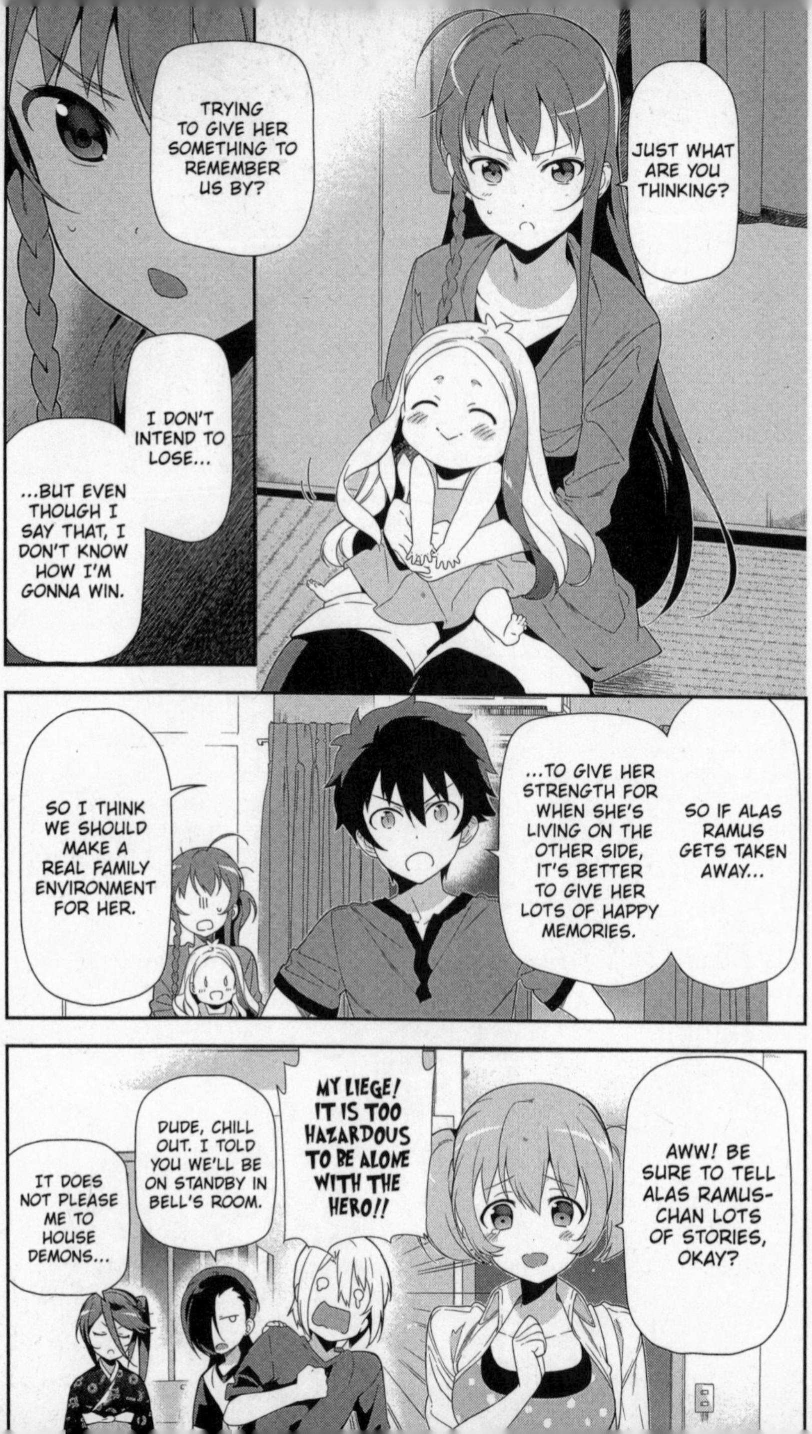
JUST WHAT ARE YOU THINKING?
TRYING TO GIVE HER SOMETHING TO REMEMBER US BY?
I DON'T INTEND TO LOSE...
...BUT EVEN THOUGH I SAY THAT, I DON'T KNOW HOW I'M GONNA WIN.
SO IF ALAS RAMUS GETS TAKEN AWAY...
...TO GIVE HER STRENGTH FOR WHEN SHE'S LIVING ON THE OTHER SIDE, IT'S BETTER TO GIVE HER LOTS OF HAPPY MEMORIES.
SO I THINK WE SHOULD MAKE A REAL FAMILY ENVIRONMENT FOR HER.
AWW! BE SURE TO TELL ALAS RAMUS-CHAN LOTS OF STORIES, OKAY?
MY LIEGE! IT IS TOO HAZARDOUS TO BE ALONE WITH THE HERO!!
DUDE, CHILL OUT. I TOLD YOU WE'LL BE ON STANDBY IN BELL'S ROOM.
IT DOES NOT PLEASE ME TO HOUSE DEMONS...

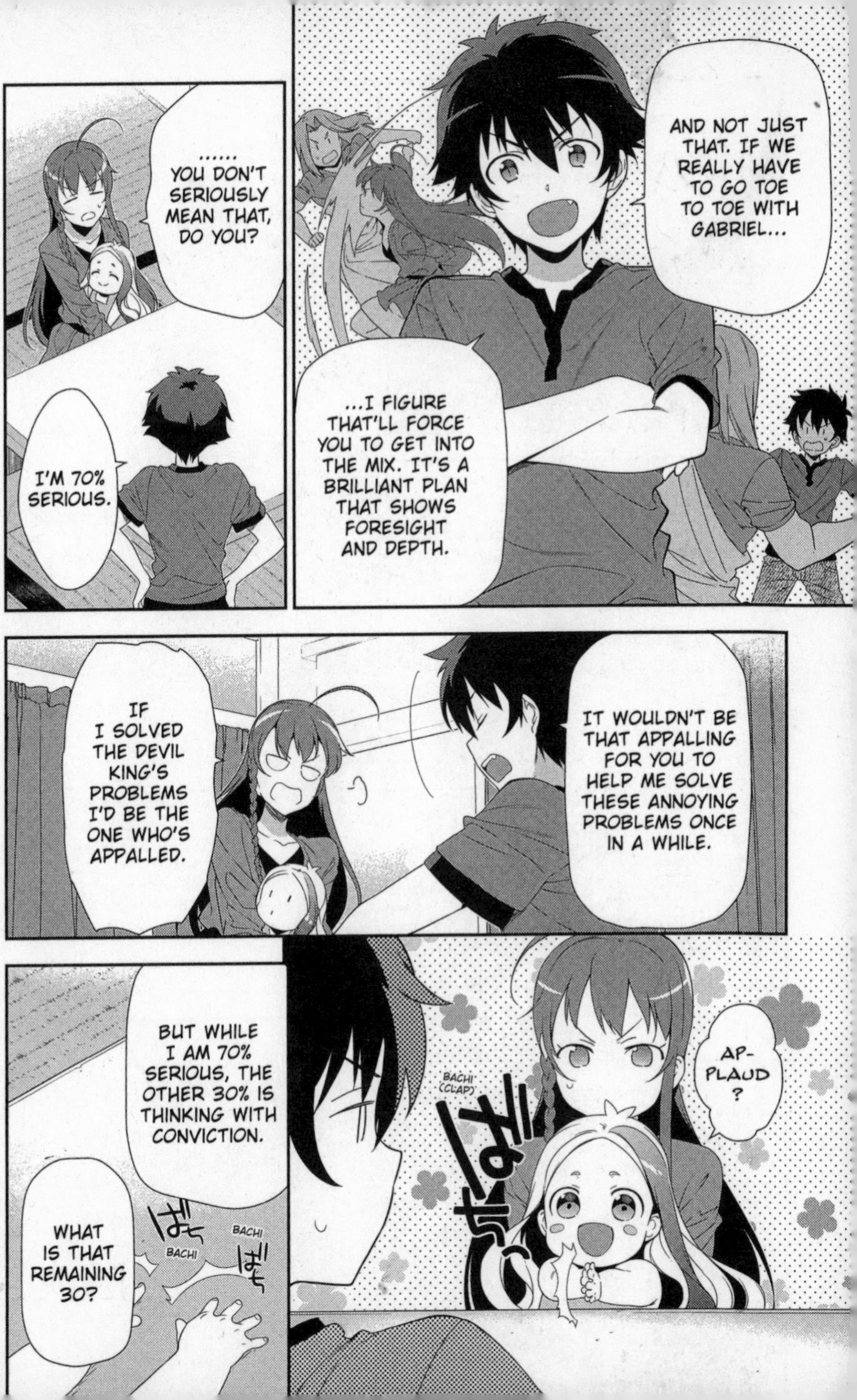
AND NOT JUST THAT. IF WE REALLY HAVE TO GO TOE TO TOE WITH GABRIEL...
...I FIGURE THAT'LL FORCE YOU TO GET INTO THE MIX. IT'S A BRILLIANT PLAN THAT SHOWS FORESIGHT AND DEPTH.
...... YOU DON'T SERIOUSLY MEAN THAT, DO YOU?
I'M 70% SERIOUS.
IT WOULDN'T BE THAT APPALLING FOR YOU TO HELP ME SOLVE THESE ANNOYING PROBLEMS ONCE IN A WHILE.
IF I SOLVED THE DEVIL KING'S PROBLEMS I'D BE THE ONE WHO'S APPALLED.
AP-PLAUD?
BACHI (CLAP)
BUT WHILE I AM 70% SERIOUS, THE OTHER 30% IS THINKING WITH CONVICTION.
WHAT IS THAT REMAINING 30?
BACHI
BACHI

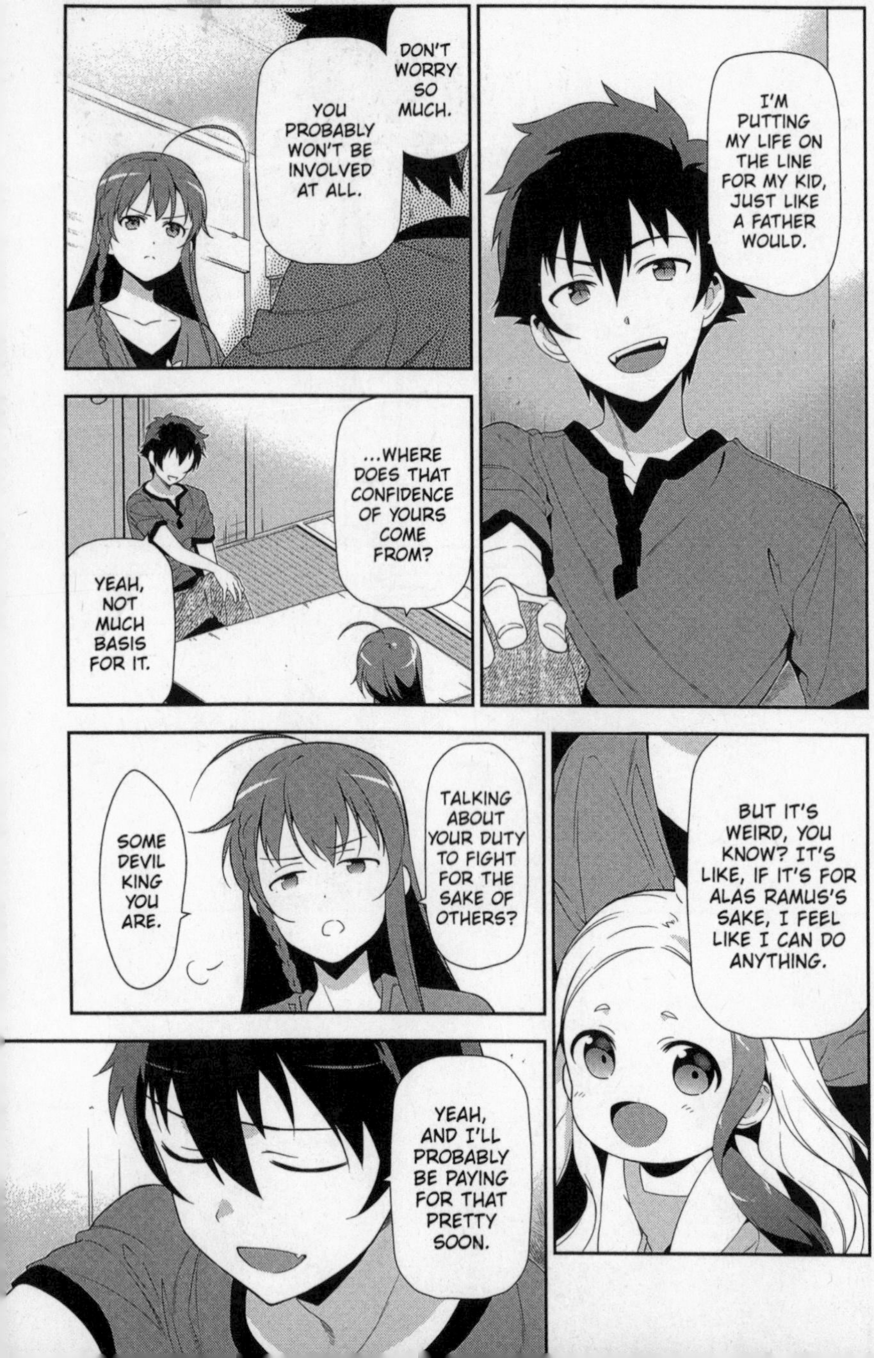
I'M PUTTING MY LIFE ON THE LINE FOR MY KID, JUST LIKE A FATHER WOULD.
DON'T WORRY SO MUCH.
YOU PROBABLY WON'T BE INVOLVED AT ALL.
...WHERE DOES THAT CONFIDENCE OF YOURS COME FROM?
YEAH, NOT MUCH BASIS FOR IT.
BUT IT'S WEIRD, YOU KNOW? IT'S LIKE, IF IT'S FOR ALAS RAMUS'S SAKE, I FEEL LIKE I CAN DO ANYTHING.
TALKING ABOUT YOUR DUTY TO FIGHT FOR THE SAKE OF OTHERS?
SOME DEVIL KING YOU ARE.
YEAH, AND I'LL PROBABLY BE PAYING FOR THAT PRETTY SOON.

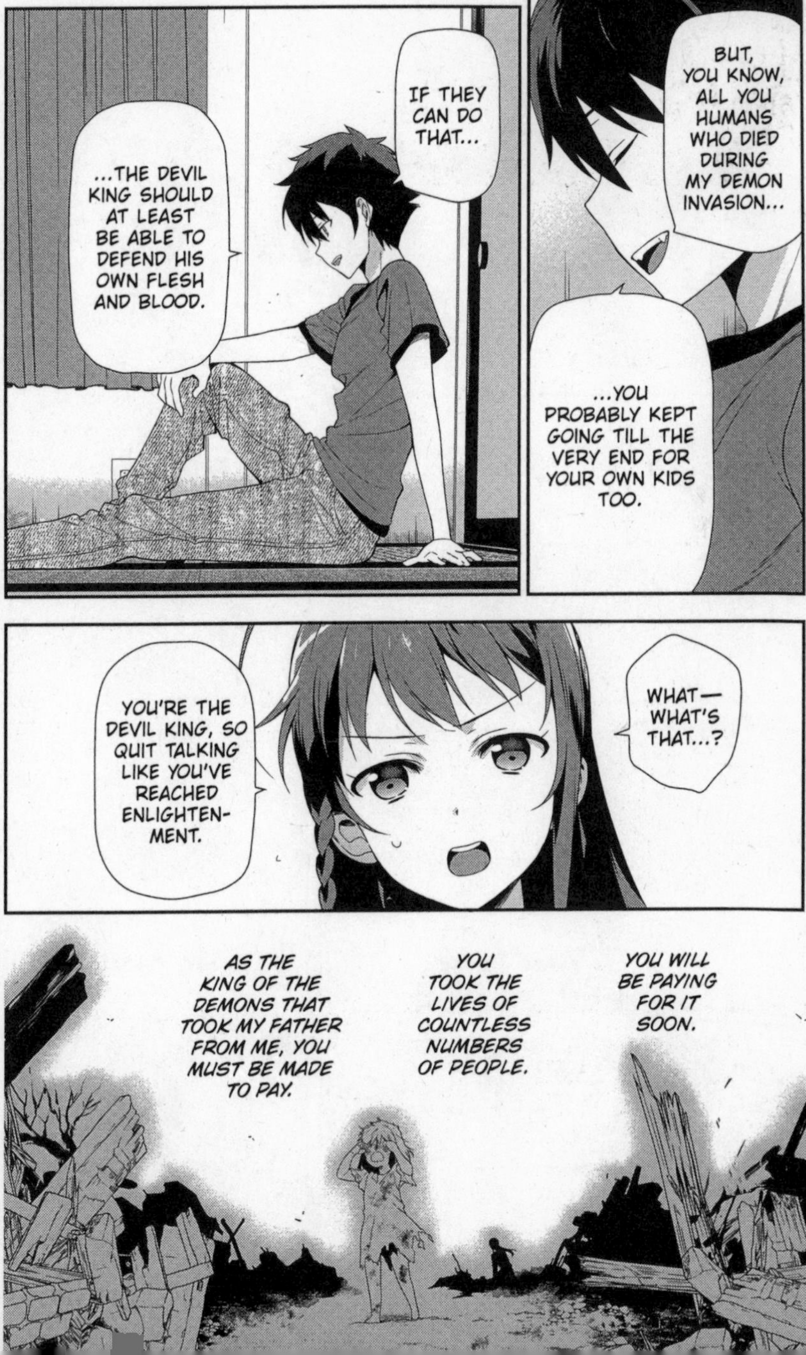
BUT, YOU KNOW, ALL YOU HUMANS WHO DIED DURING MY DEMON INVASION...
...YOU PROBABLY KEPT GOING TILL THE VERY END FOR YOUR OWN KIDS TOO.
IF THEY CAN DO THAT...
...THE DEVIL KING SHOULD AT LEAST BE ABLE TO DEFEND HIS OWN FLESH AND BLOOD.
WHAT—WHAT'S THAT...?
YOU'RE THE DEVIL KING, SO QUIT TALKING LIKE YOU'VE REACHED ENLIGHTEN-MENT.
YOU WILL BE PAYING FOR IT SOON.
YOU TOOK THE LIVES OF COUNTLESS NUMBERS OF PEOPLE.
AS THE KING OF THE DEMONS THAT TOOK MY FATHER FROM ME, YOU MUST BE MADE TO PAY.

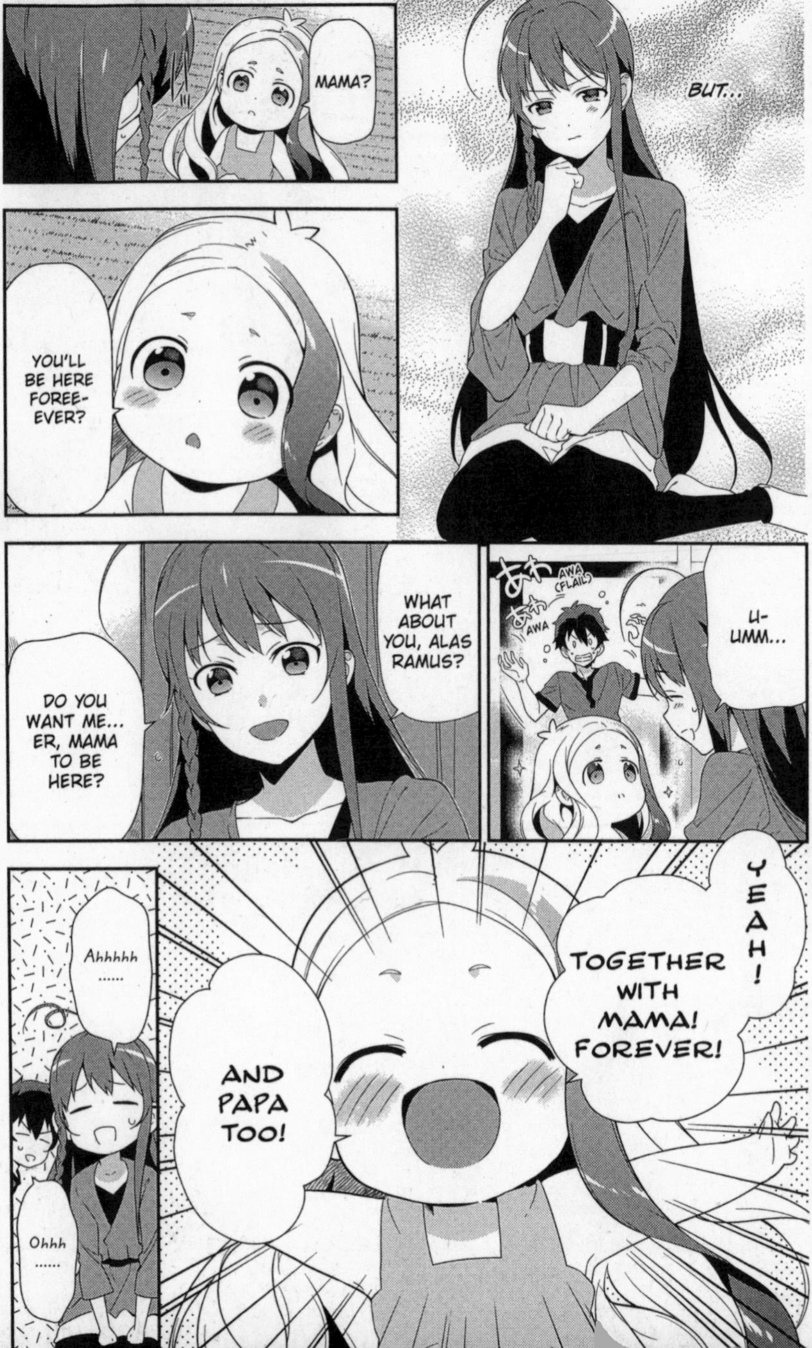
BUT...
MAMA?
YOU'LL BE HERE FOREE-EVER?
U-UMM...
あわ AWA (FLAIL)
あわ AWA
WHAT ABOUT YOU, ALAS RAMUS?
DO YOU WANT ME... ER, MAMA TO BE HERE?
YEAH!
TOGETHER WITH MAMA! FOREVER!
AND PAPA TOO!
Ahhhhh ......
Ohhh ......

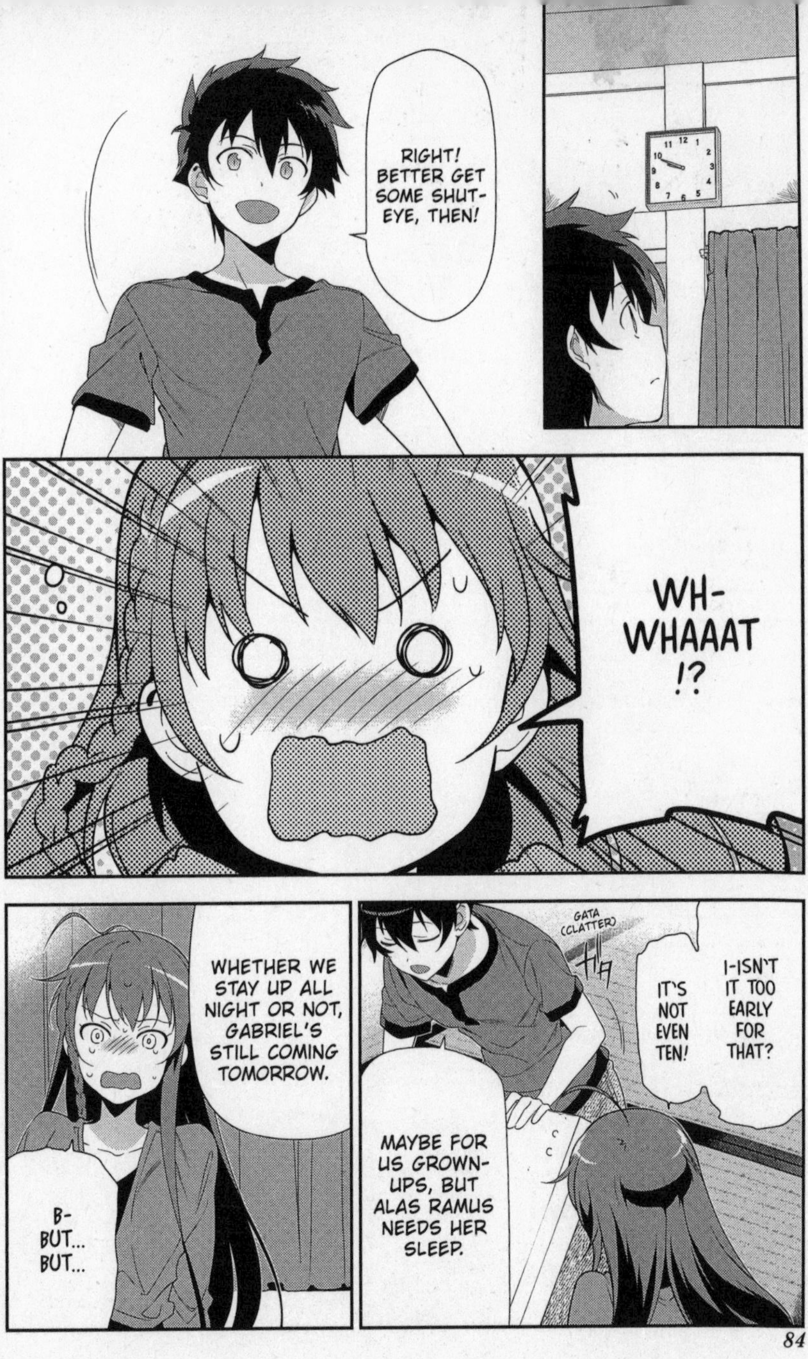
RIGHT! BETTER GET SOME SHUT-EYE, THEN!
WH-WHAAAT!?
I-ISN'T IT TOO EARLY FOR THAT?
IT'S NOT EVEN TEN!
GATA (CLATTER)
MAYBE FOR US GROWN-UPS, BUT ALAS RAMUS NEEDS HER SLEEP.
WHETHER WE STAY UP ALL NIGHT OR NOT, GABRIEL'S STILL COMING TOMORROW.
B-BUT... BUT...

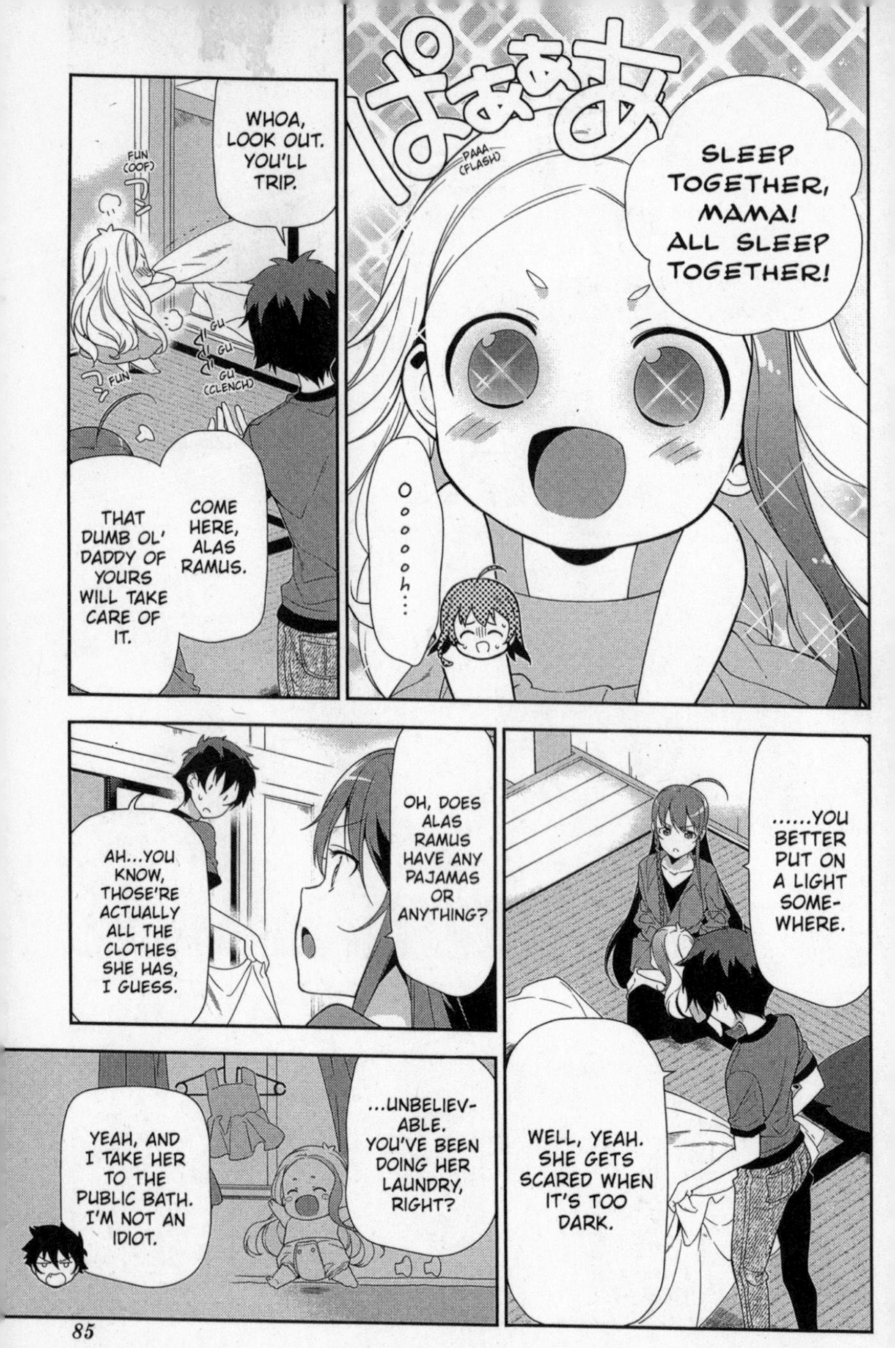

ぱぁぁぁ
PAAA (FLASH)
SLEEP TOGETHER, MAMA! ALL SLEEP TOGETHER!
Oooooh...
WHOA, LOOK OUT. YOU'LL TRIP.
FUN (OOF)
GU GU GU (CLENCH)
FUN
COME HERE, ALAS RAMUS.
THAT DUMB OL' DADDY OF YOURS WILL TAKE CARE OF IT.
......YOU BETTER PUT ON A LIGHT SOMEWHERE.
WELL, YEAH. SHE GETS SCARED WHEN IT'S TOO DARK.
OH, DOES ALAS RAMUS HAVE ANY PAJAMAS OR ANYTHING?
AH...YOU KNOW, THOSE'RE ACTUALLY ALL THE CLOTHES SHE HAS, I GUESS.
...UNBELIEVABLE. YOU'VE BEEN DOING HER LAUNDRY, RIGHT?
YEAH, AND I TAKE HER TO THE PUBLIC BATH. I'M NOT AN IDIOT.

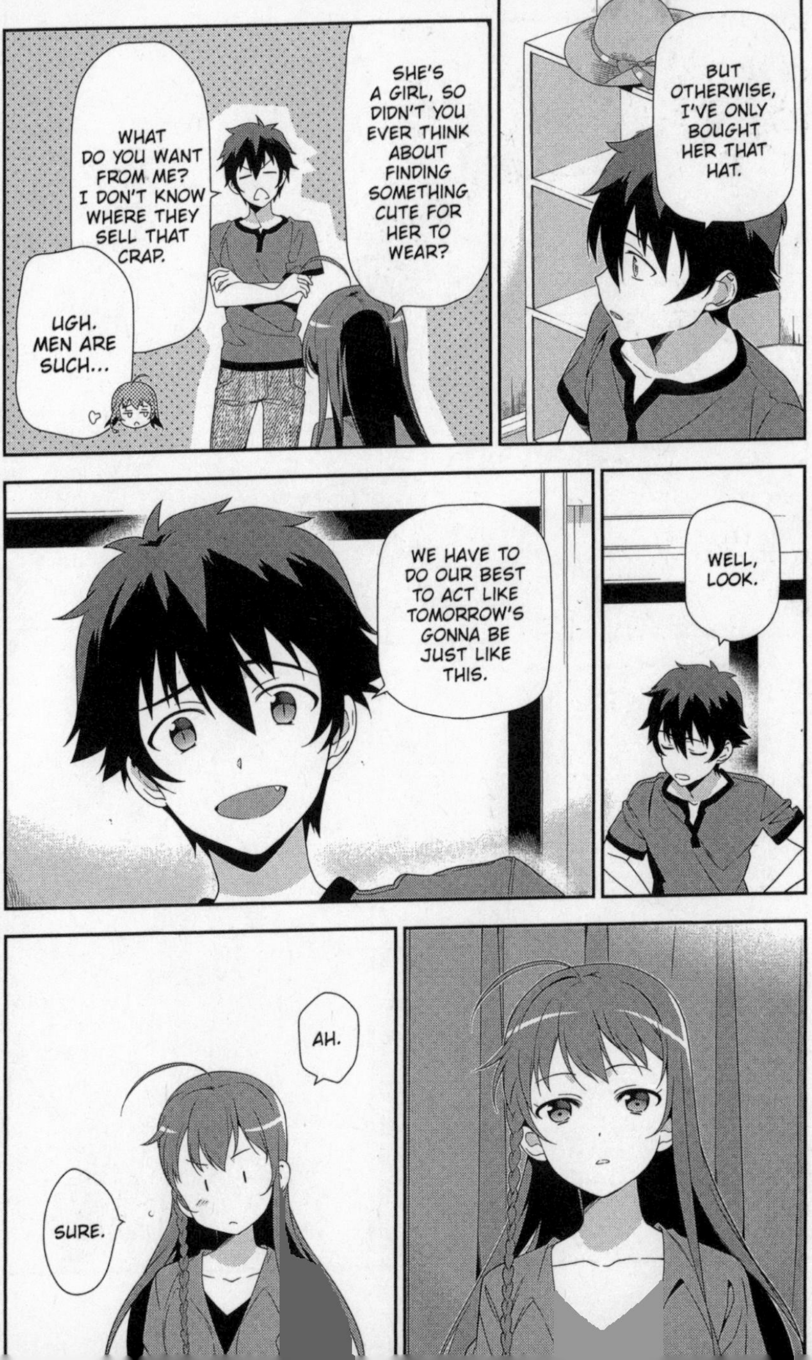
BUT OTHERWISE, I'VE ONLY BOUGHT HER THAT HAT.
SHE'S A GIRL, SO DIDN'T YOU EVER THINK ABOUT FINDING SOMETHING CUTE FOR HER TO WEAR?
WHAT DO YOU WANT FROM ME? I DON'T KNOW WHERE THEY SELL THAT CRAP.
UGH. MEN ARE SUCH...
WELL, LOOK.
WE HAVE TO DO OUR BEST TO ACT LIKE TOMORROW'S GONNA BE JUST LIKE THIS.
AH.
SURE.

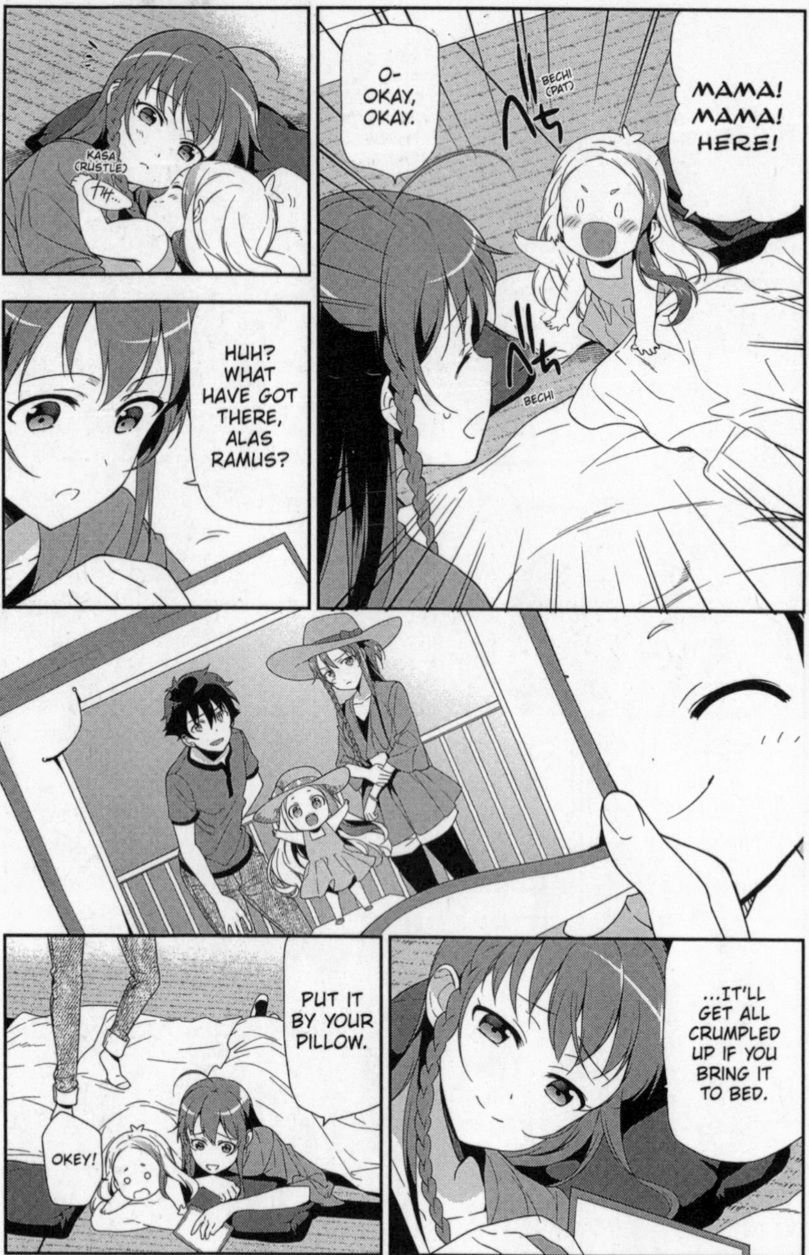
MAMA! MAMA! HERE!
BECHI (PAT)
O- OKAY, OKAY.
BECHI
KASA (RUSTLE)
カサ...
HUH? WHAT HAVE GOT THERE, ALAS RAMUS?
...IT'LL GET ALL CRUMPLED UP IF YOU BRING IT TO BED.
PUT IT BY YOUR PILLOW.
OKEY!

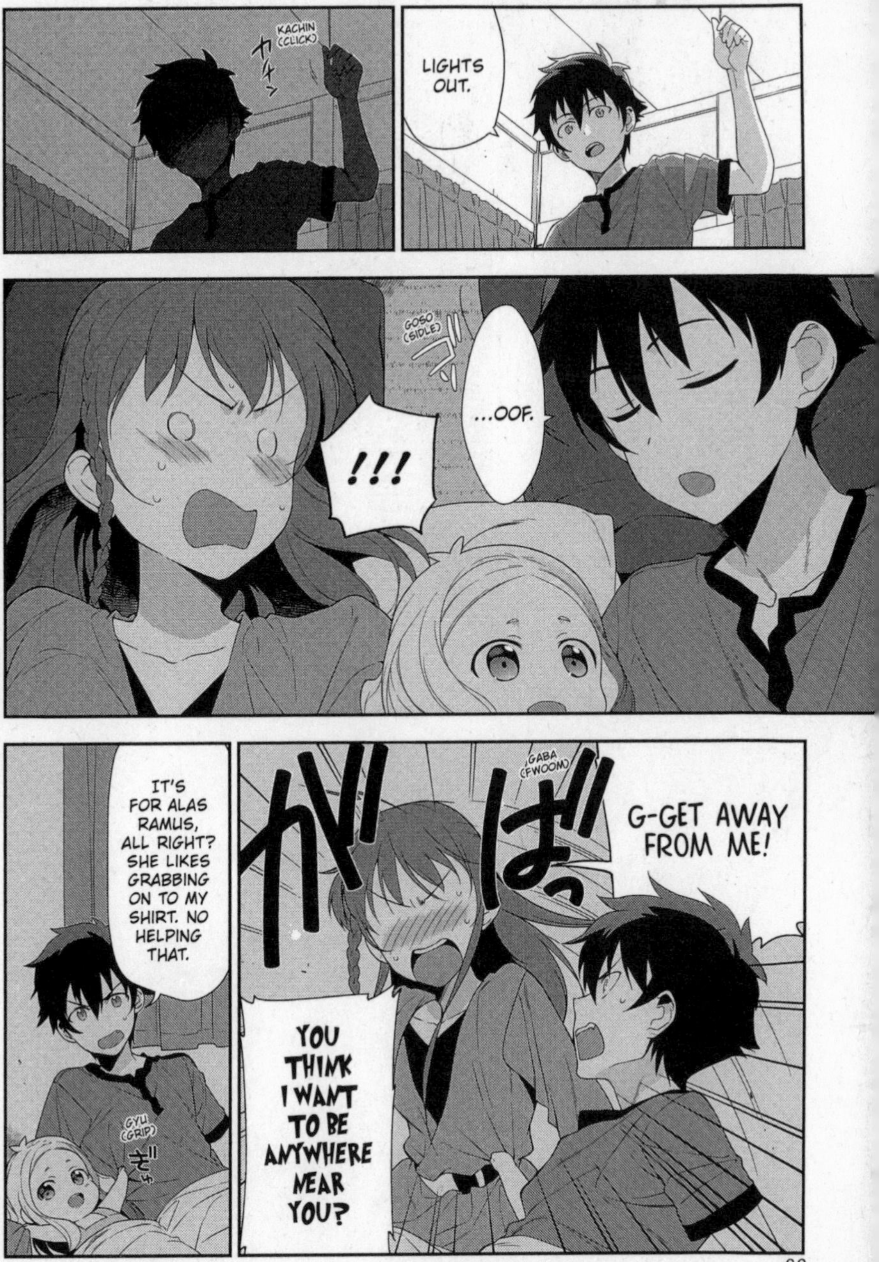
LIGHTS OUT.
KACHIN (CLICK)
GOSO (SIDLE)
...OOF.
!!!
GABA (FWOOM)
G-GET AWAY FROM ME!
YOU THINK I WANT TO BE ANYWHERE NEAR YOU?
IT'S FOR ALAS RAMUS, ALL RIGHT? SHE LIKES GRABBING ON TO MY SHIRT. NO HELPING THAT.
GYU (GRIP)

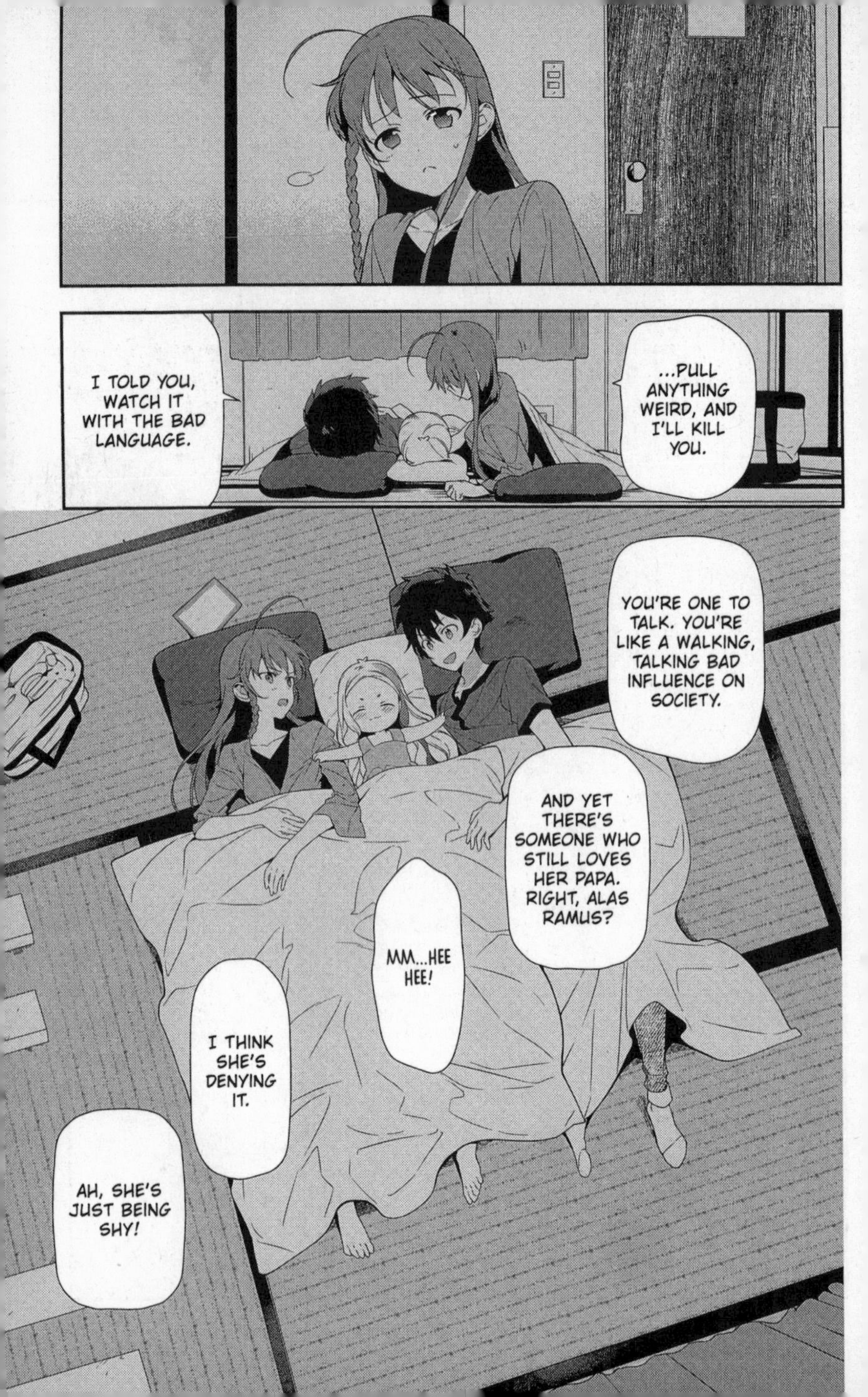
...PULL ANYTHING WEIRD, AND I'LL KILL YOU.
I TOLD YOU, WATCH IT WITH THE BAD LANGUAGE.
YOU'RE ONE TO TALK. YOU'RE LIKE A WALKING, TALKING BAD INFLUENCE ON SOCIETY.
AND YET THERE'S SOMEONE WHO STILL LOVES HER PAPA. RIGHT, ALAS RAMUS?
MM...HEE HEE!
I THINK SHE'S DENYING IT.
AH, SHE'S JUST BEING SHY!

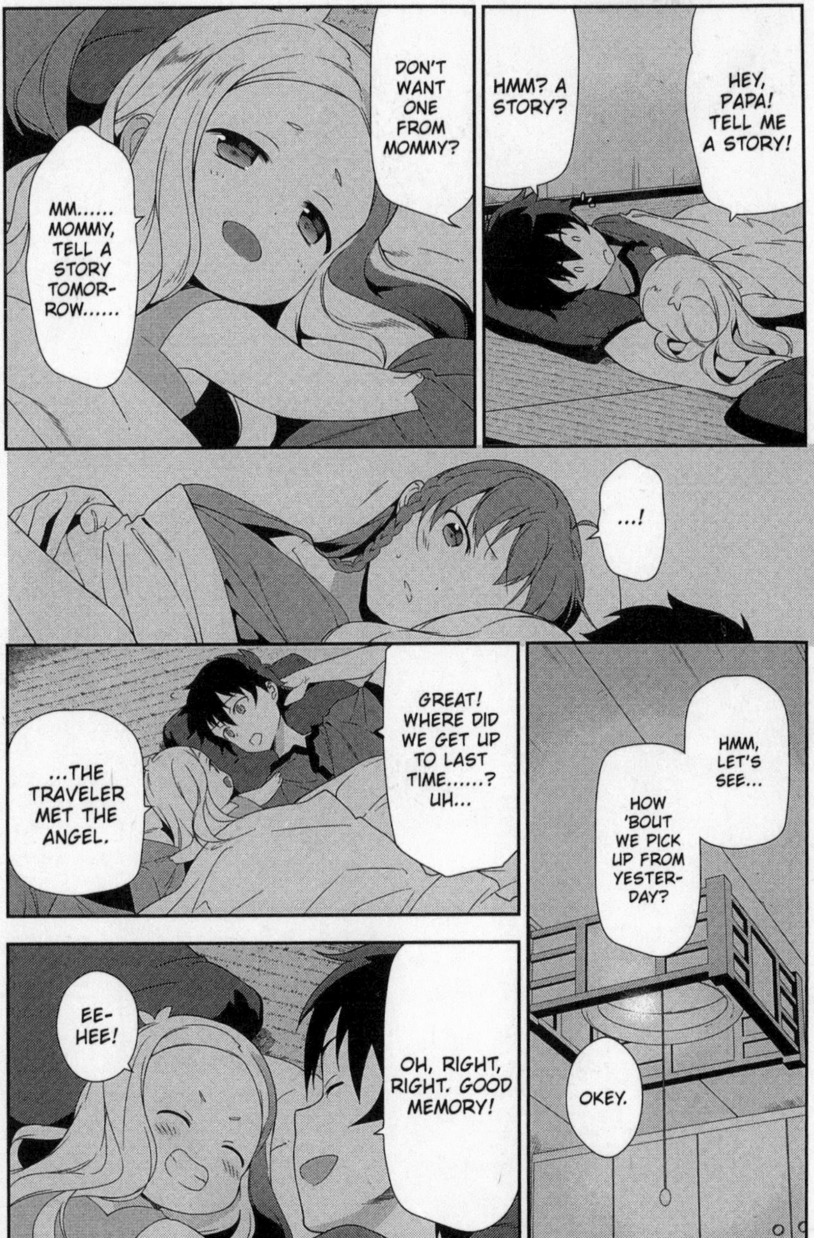
HEY, PAPA! TELL ME A STORY!
HMM? A STORY?
DON'T WANT ONE FROM MOMMY?
MM...... MOMMY, TELL A STORY TOMOR-ROW......
...!
HMM, LET'S SEE...
HOW 'BOUT WE PICK UP FROM YESTER-DAY?
OKEY.
GREAT! WHERE DID WE GET UP TO LAST TIME......? UH...
...THE TRAVELER MET THE ANGEL.
OH, RIGHT, RIGHT. GOOD MEMORY!
EE-HEE!

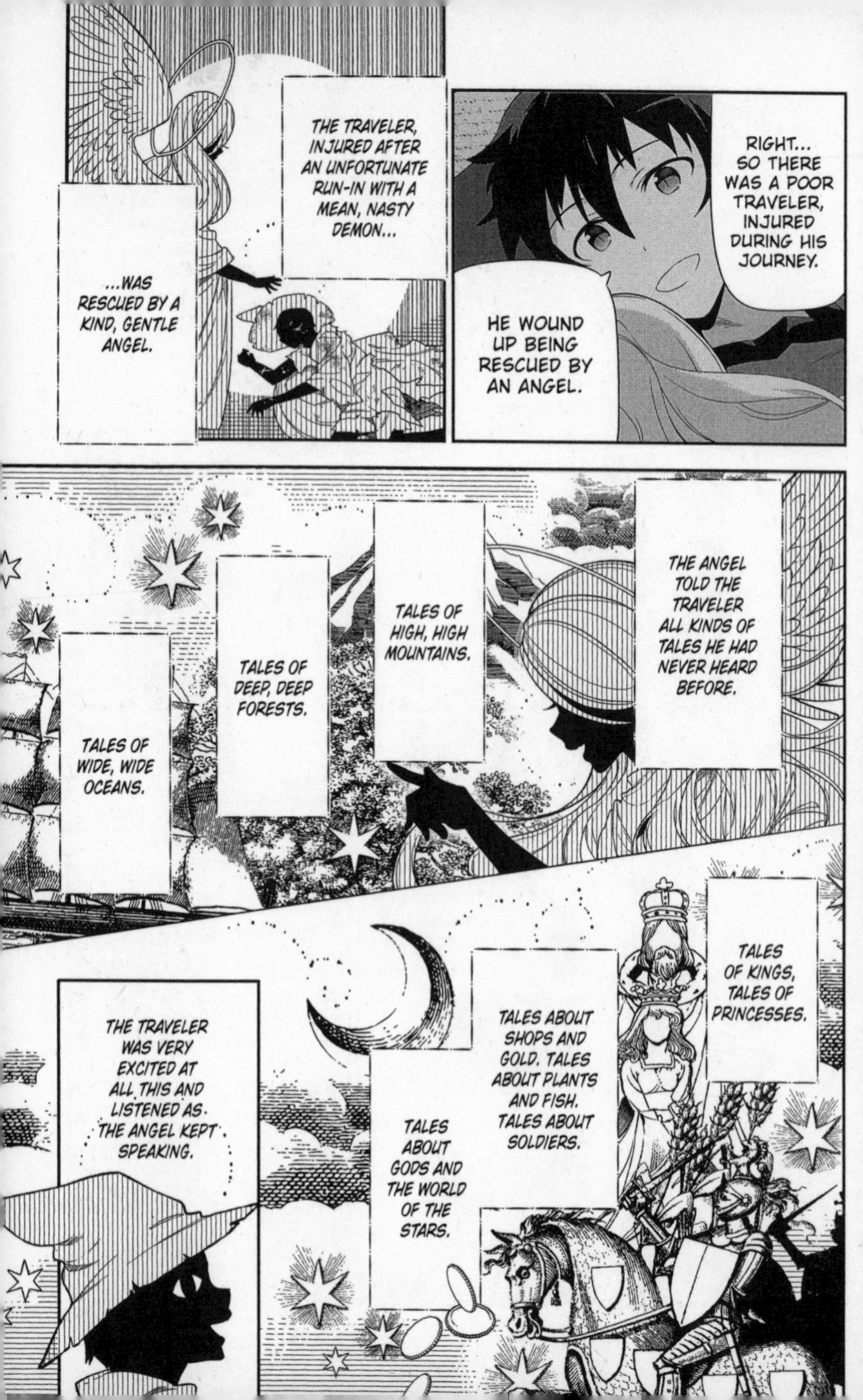
RIGHT... SO THERE WAS A POOR TRAVELER, INJURED DURING HIS JOURNEY.
HE WOUND UP BEING RESCUED BY AN ANGEL.
THE TRAVELER, INJURED AFTER AN UNFORTUNATE RUN-IN WITH A MEAN, NASTY DEMON...
...WAS RESCUED BY A KIND, GENTLE ANGEL.
THE ANGEL TOLD THE TRAVELER ALL KINDS OF TALES HE HAD NEVER HEARD BEFORE.
TALES OF HIGH, HIGH MOUNTAINS.
TALES OF DEEP, DEEP FORESTS.
TALES OF WIDE, WIDE OCEANS.
TALES OF KINGS, TALES OF PRINCESSES.
TALES ABOUT SHOPS AND GOLD. TALES ABOUT PLANTS AND FISH. TALES ABOUT SOLDIERS.
TALES ABOUT GODS AND THE WORLD OF THE STARS.
THE TRAVELER WAS VERY EXCITED AT ALL THIS AND LISTENED AS THE ANGEL KEPT SPEAKING.

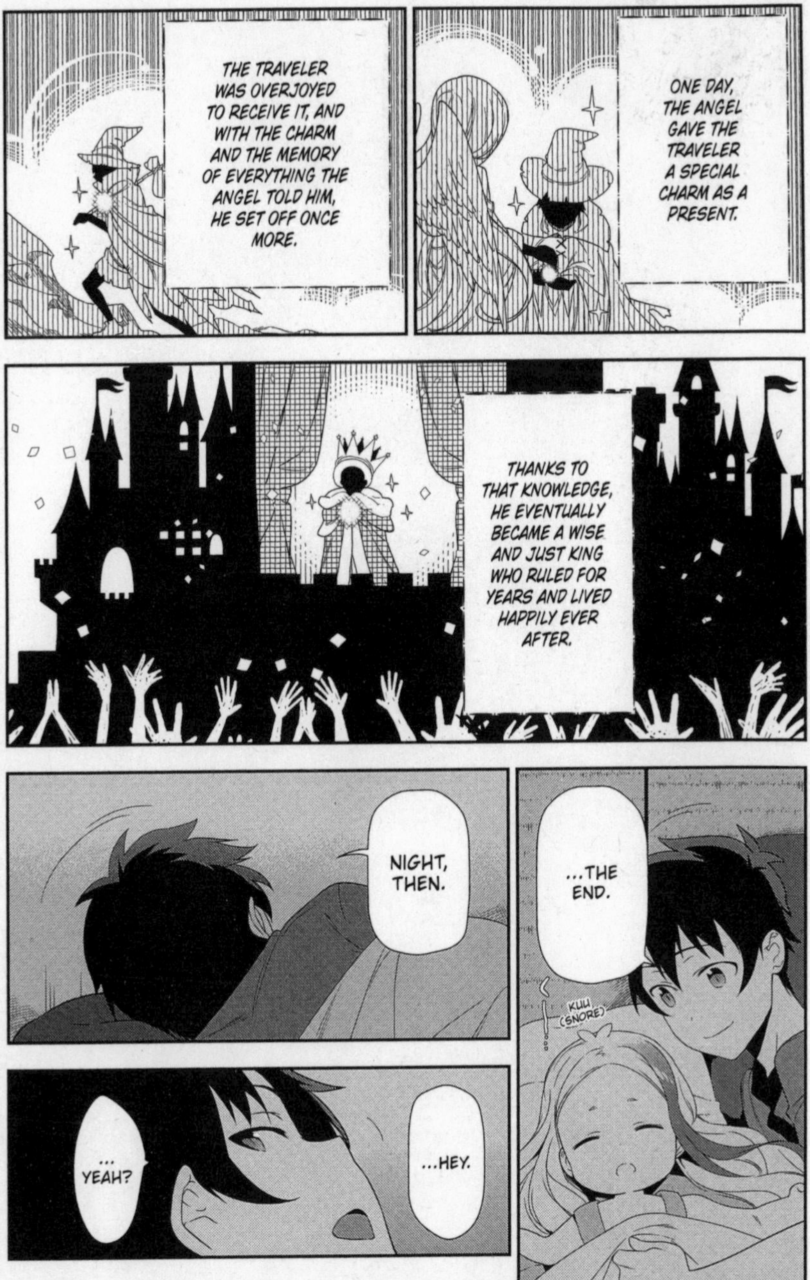
ONE DAY, THE ANGEL GAVE THE TRAVELER A SPECIAL CHARM AS A PRESENT.
THE TRAVELER WAS OVERJOYED TO RECEIVE IT, AND WITH THE CHARM AND THE MEMORY OF EVERYTHING THE ANGEL TOLD HIM, HE SET OFF ONCE MORE.
THANKS TO THAT KNOWLEDGE, HE EVENTUALLY BECAME A WISE AND JUST KING WHO RULED FOR YEARS AND LIVED HAPPILY EVER AFTER.
...THE END.
KUU (SNORE)
NIGHT, THEN.
...HEY.
... YEAH?

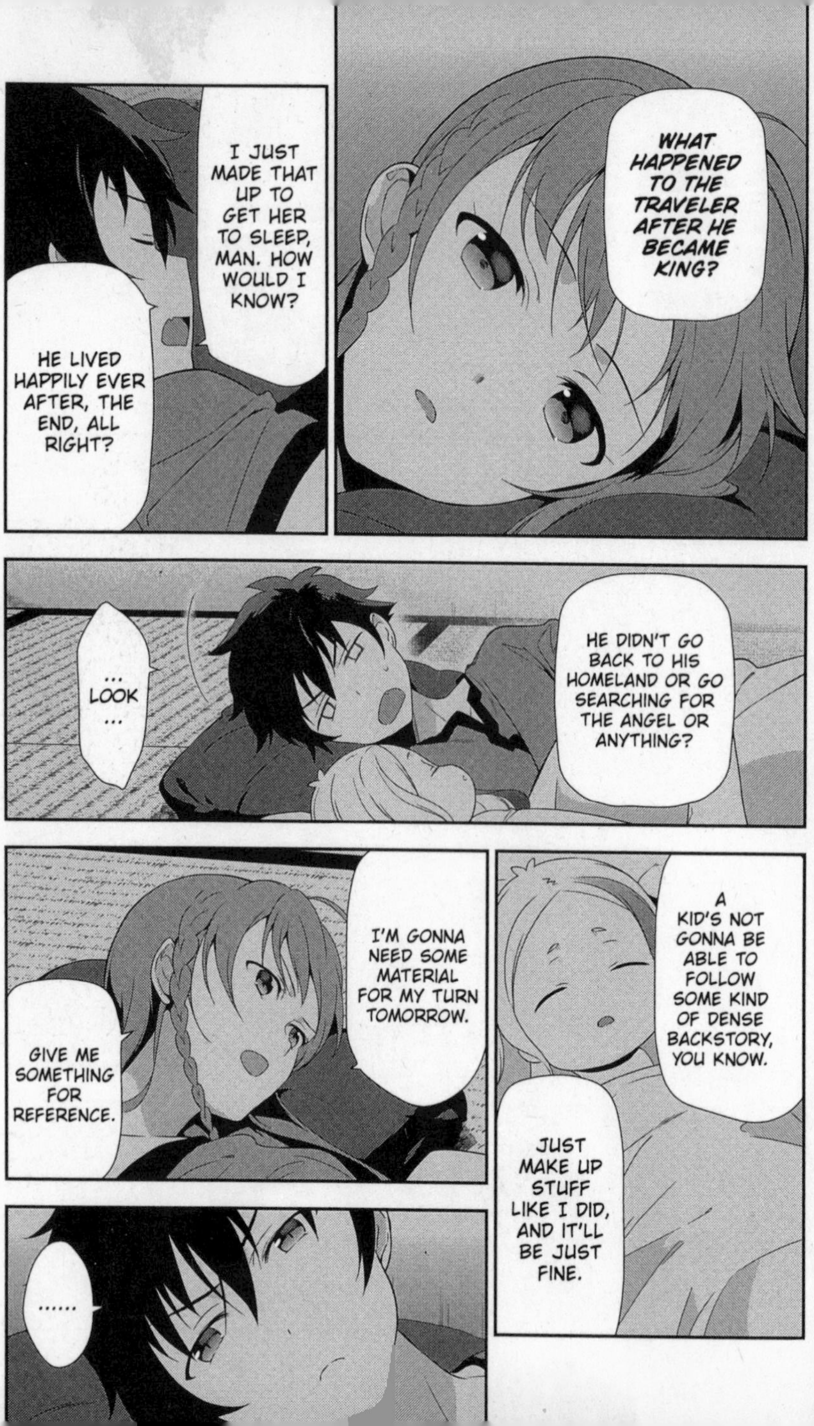
WHAT HAPPENED TO THE TRAVELER AFTER HE BECAME KING?
I JUST MADE THAT UP TO GET HER TO SLEEP, MAN. HOW WOULD I KNOW?
HE LIVED HAPPILY EVER AFTER, THE END, ALL RIGHT?
HE DIDN'T GO BACK TO HIS HOMELAND OR GO SEARCHING FOR THE ANGEL OR ANYTHING?
... LOOK ...
A KID'S NOT GONNA BE ABLE TO FOLLOW SOME KIND OF DENSE BACKSTORY, YOU KNOW.
JUST MAKE UP STUFF LIKE I DID, AND IT'LL BE JUST FINE.
I'M GONNA NEED SOME MATERIAL FOR MY TURN TOMORROW.
GIVE ME SOMETHING FOR REFERENCE.
......

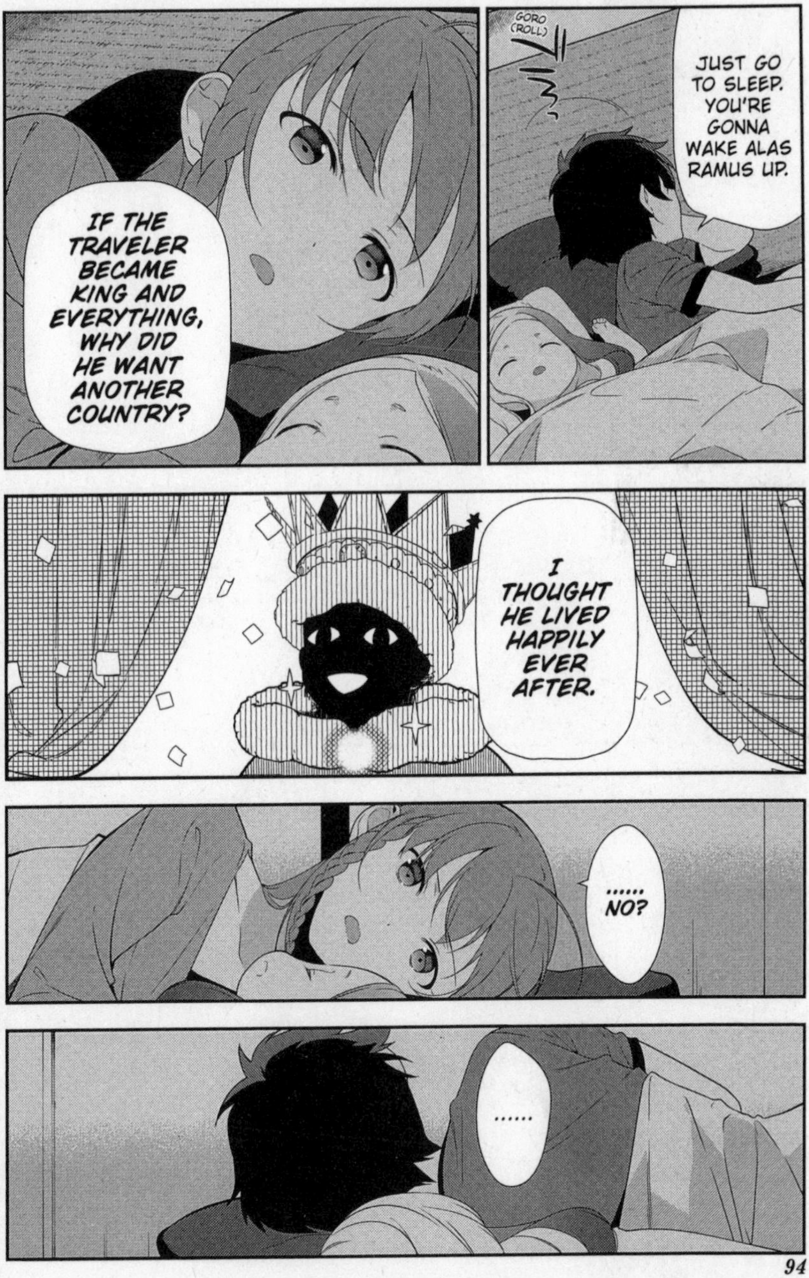
GORO (ROLL)
JUST GO TO SLEEP. YOU'RE GONNA WAKE ALAS RAMUS UP.
IF THE TRAVELER BECAME KING AND EVERYTHING, WHY DID HE WANT ANOTHER COUNTRY?
I THOUGHT HE LIVED HAPPILY EVER AFTER.
...... NO?
......

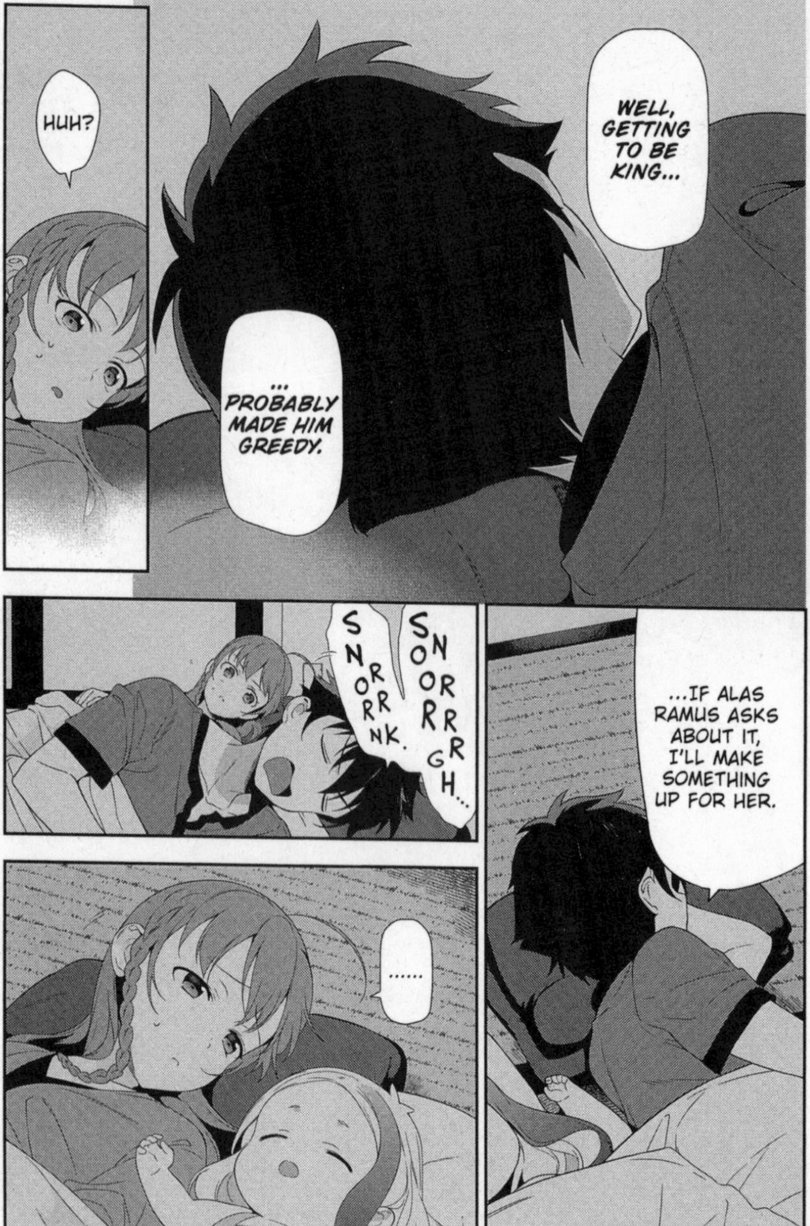
WELL, GETTING TO BE KING...
...PROBABLY MADE HIM GREEDY.
HUH?
...IF ALAS RAMUS ASKS ABOUT IT, I'LL MAKE SOMETHING UP FOR HER.
SNORRRRGH...
SNORRRNK.
......

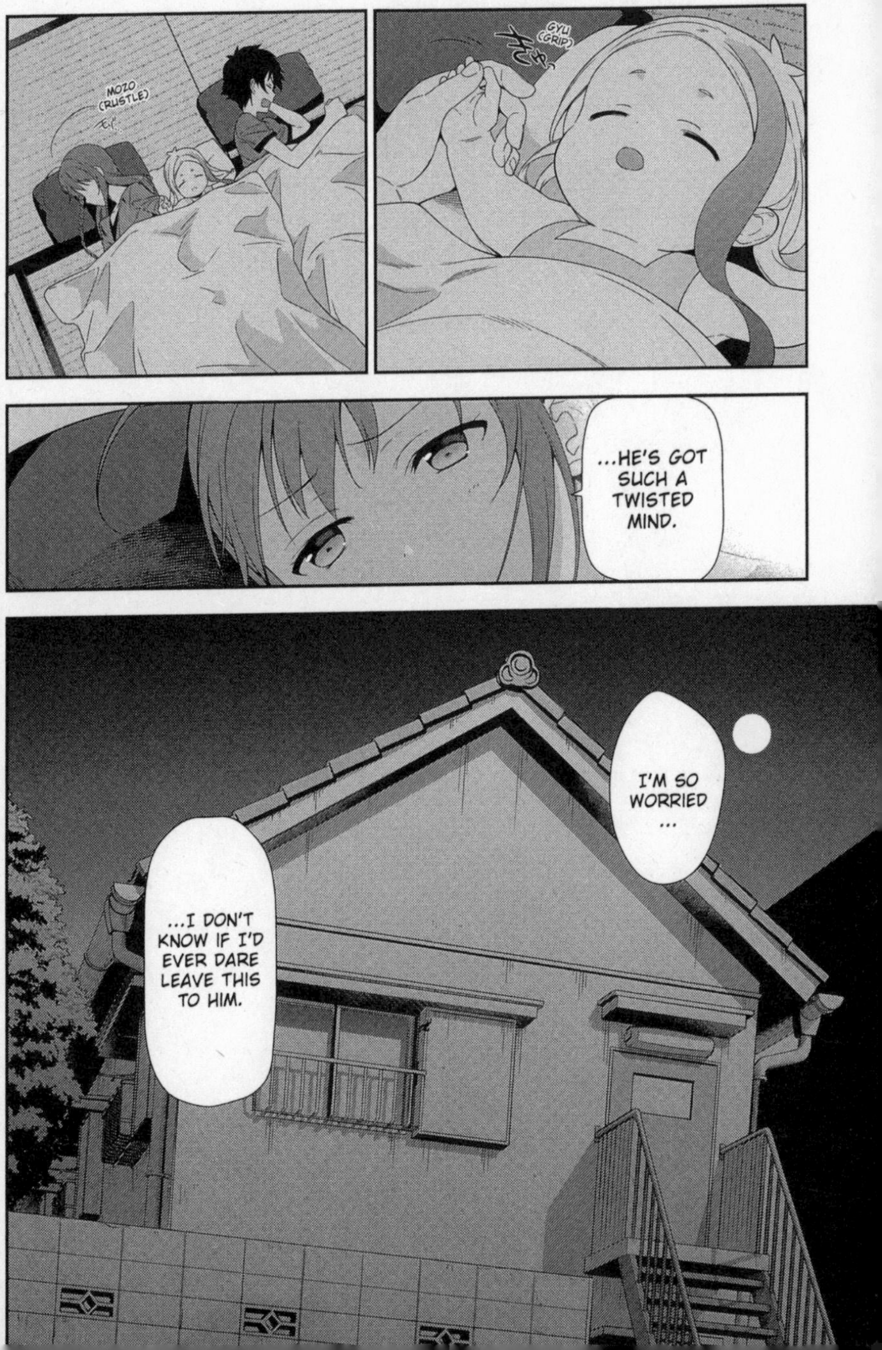
GYU (GRIP)
MOZO (RUSTLE)
...HE'S GOT SUCH A TWISTED MIND.
I'M SO WORRIED ...
...I DON'T KNOW IF I'D EVER DARE LEAVE THIS TO HIM.

Gabriel

THE DEVIL IS A PART-TIMER!

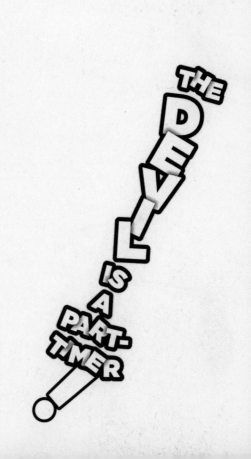

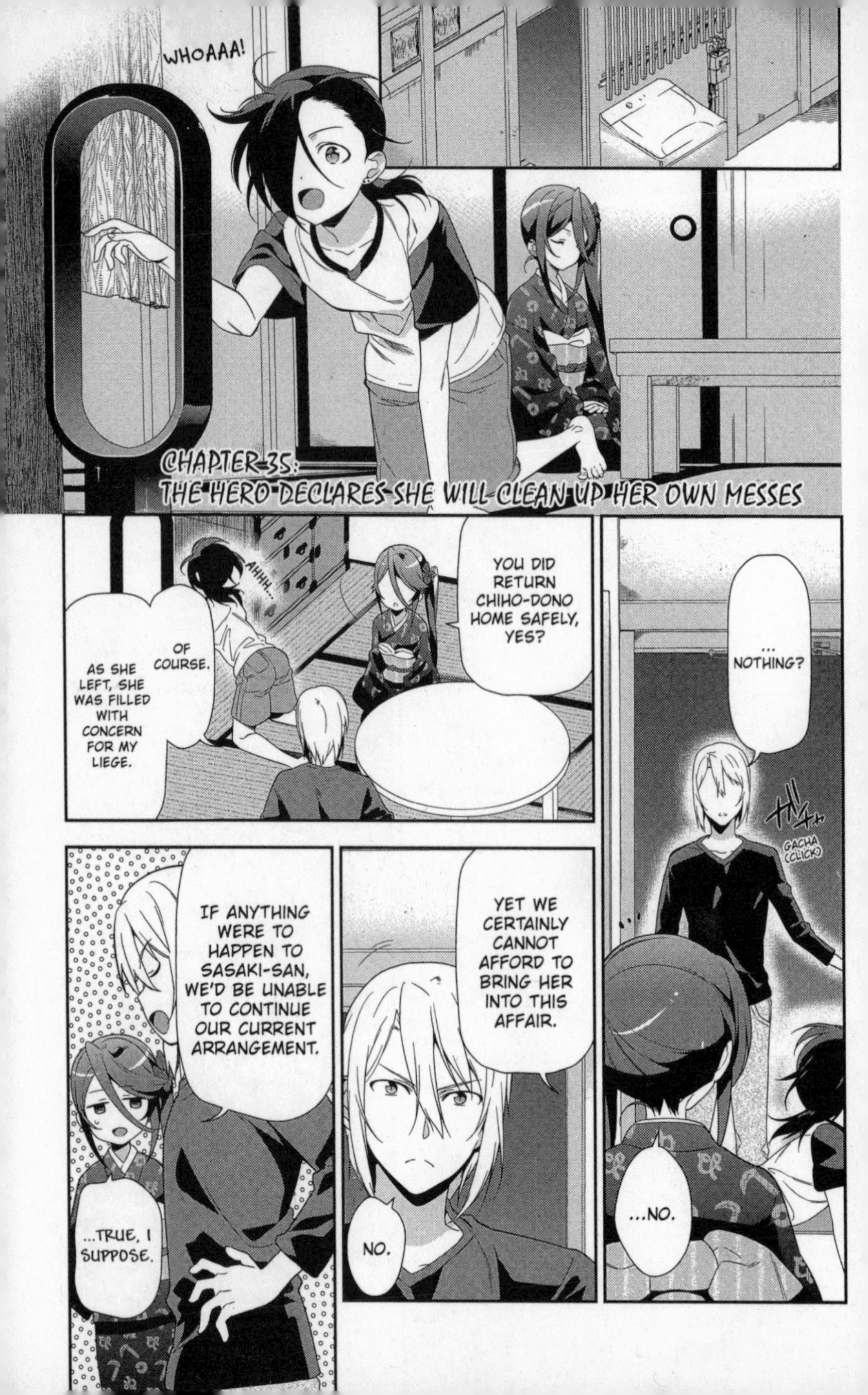
WHOAAA!
CHAPTER 35:
THE HERO DECLARES SHE WILL CLEAN UP HER OWN MESSES
... NOTHING?
GACHA (CLICK)
YOU DID RETURN CHIHO-DONO HOME SAFELY, YES?
AHHH...
OF COURSE.
AS SHE LEFT, SHE WAS FILLED WITH CONCERN FOR MY LIEGE.
...NO.
YET WE CERTAINLY CANNOT AFFORD TO BRING HER INTO THIS AFFAIR.
NO.
IF ANYTHING WERE TO HAPPEN TO SASAKI-SAN, WE'D BE UNABLE TO CONTINUE OUR CURRENT ARRANGEMENT.
...TRUE, I SUPPOSE.

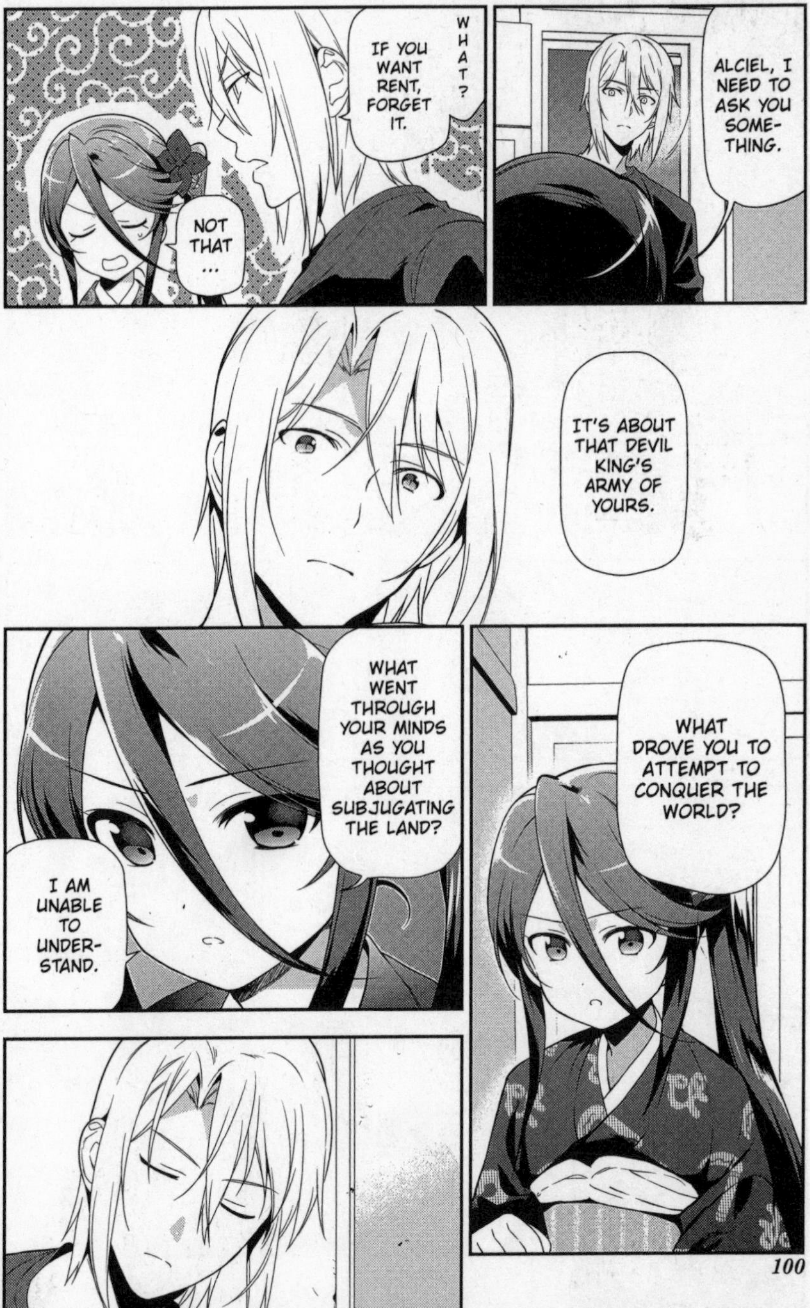
ALCIEL, I NEED TO ASK YOU SOME-THING.
WHAT?
IF YOU WANT RENT, FORGET IT.
NOT THAT ...
IT'S ABOUT THAT DEVIL KING'S ARMY OF YOURS.
WHAT DROVE YOU TO ATTEMPT TO CONQUER THE WORLD?
WHAT WENT THROUGH YOUR MINDS AS YOU THOUGHT ABOUT SUBJUGATING THE LAND?
I AM UNABLE TO UNDER-STAND.

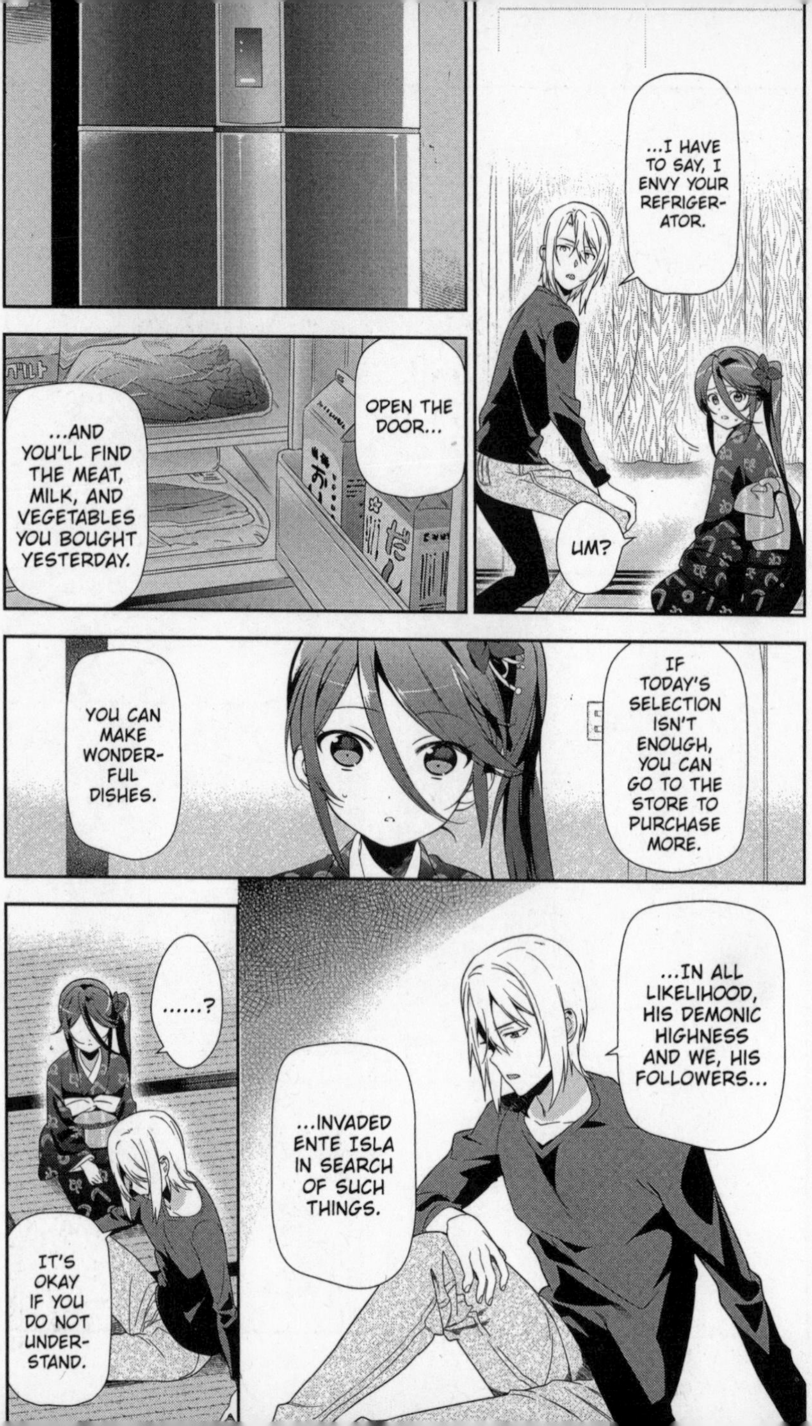
...I HAVE TO SAY, I ENVY YOUR REFRIGERATOR.
UM?
OPEN THE DOOR...
...AND YOU'LL FIND THE MEAT, MILK, AND VEGETABLES YOU BOUGHT YESTERDAY.
IF TODAY'S SELECTION ISN'T ENOUGH, YOU CAN GO TO THE STORE TO PURCHASE MORE.
YOU CAN MAKE WONDERFUL DISHES.
...IN ALL LIKELIHOOD, HIS DEMONIC HIGHNESS AND WE, HIS FOLLOWERS...
...INVADED ENTE ISLA IN SEARCH OF SUCH THINGS.
......?
IT'S OKAY IF YOU DO NOT UNDERSTAND.

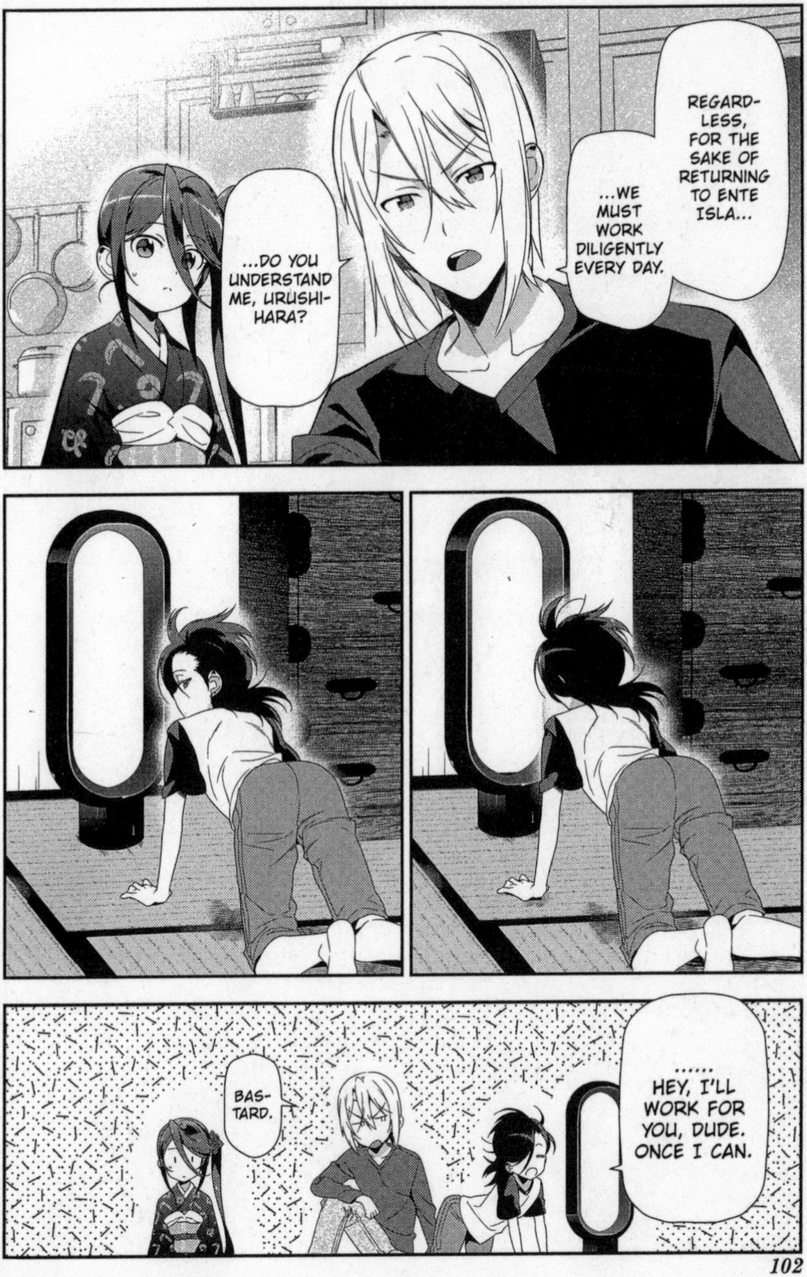
REGARD-LESS, FOR THE SAKE OF RETURNING TO ENTE ISLA...
...WE MUST WORK DILIGENTLY EVERY DAY.
...DO YOU UNDERSTAND ME, URUSHI-HARA?
......
HEY, I'LL WORK FOR YOU, DUDE. ONCE I CAN.
BAS-TARD.

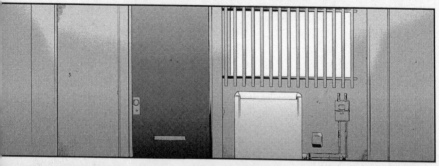

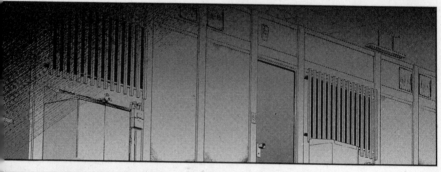

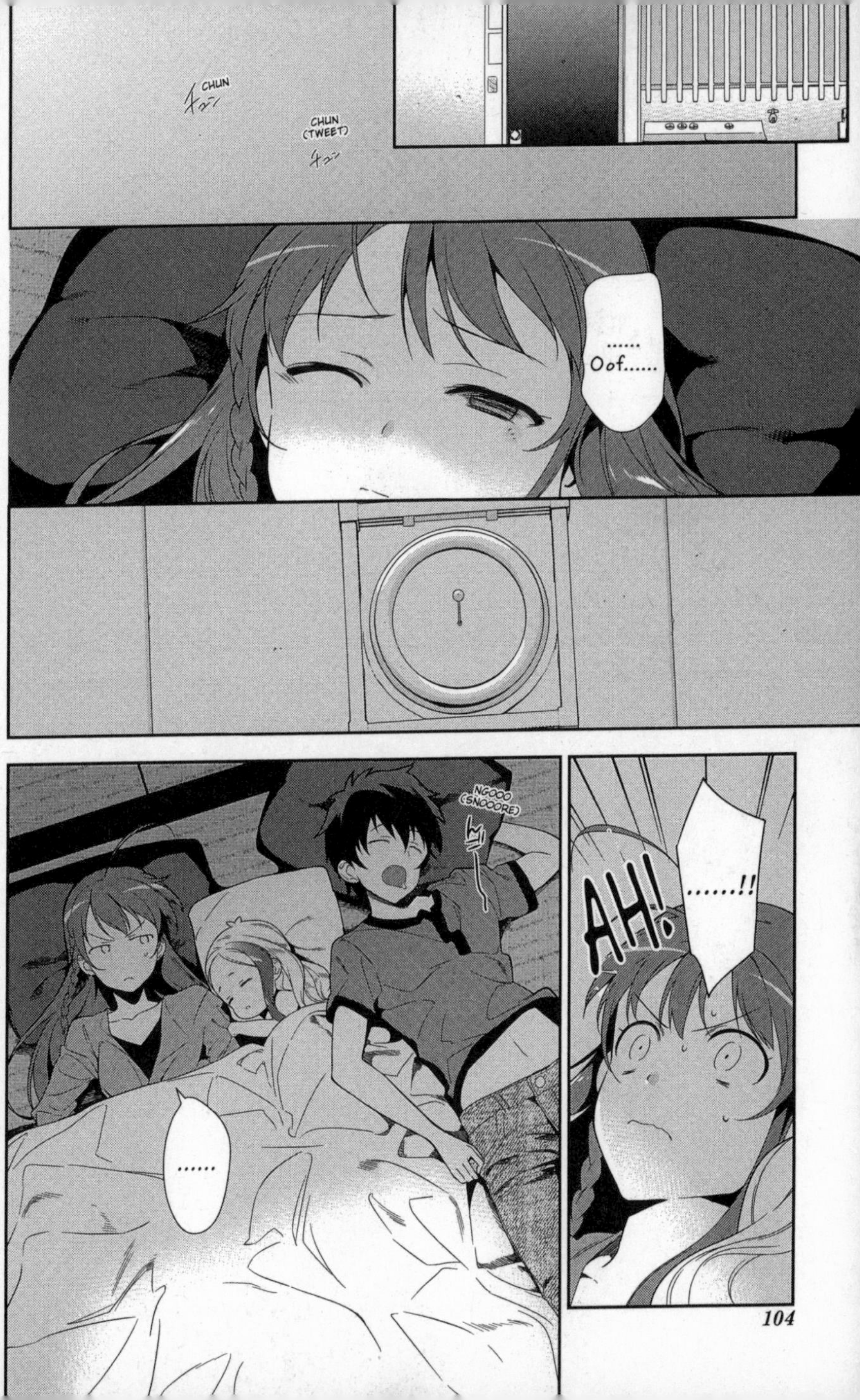
CHUN
チュン
CHUN (TWEET)
チュン
...... Oof......
......!!
AH!
NGOOO (SNOOORE)
......

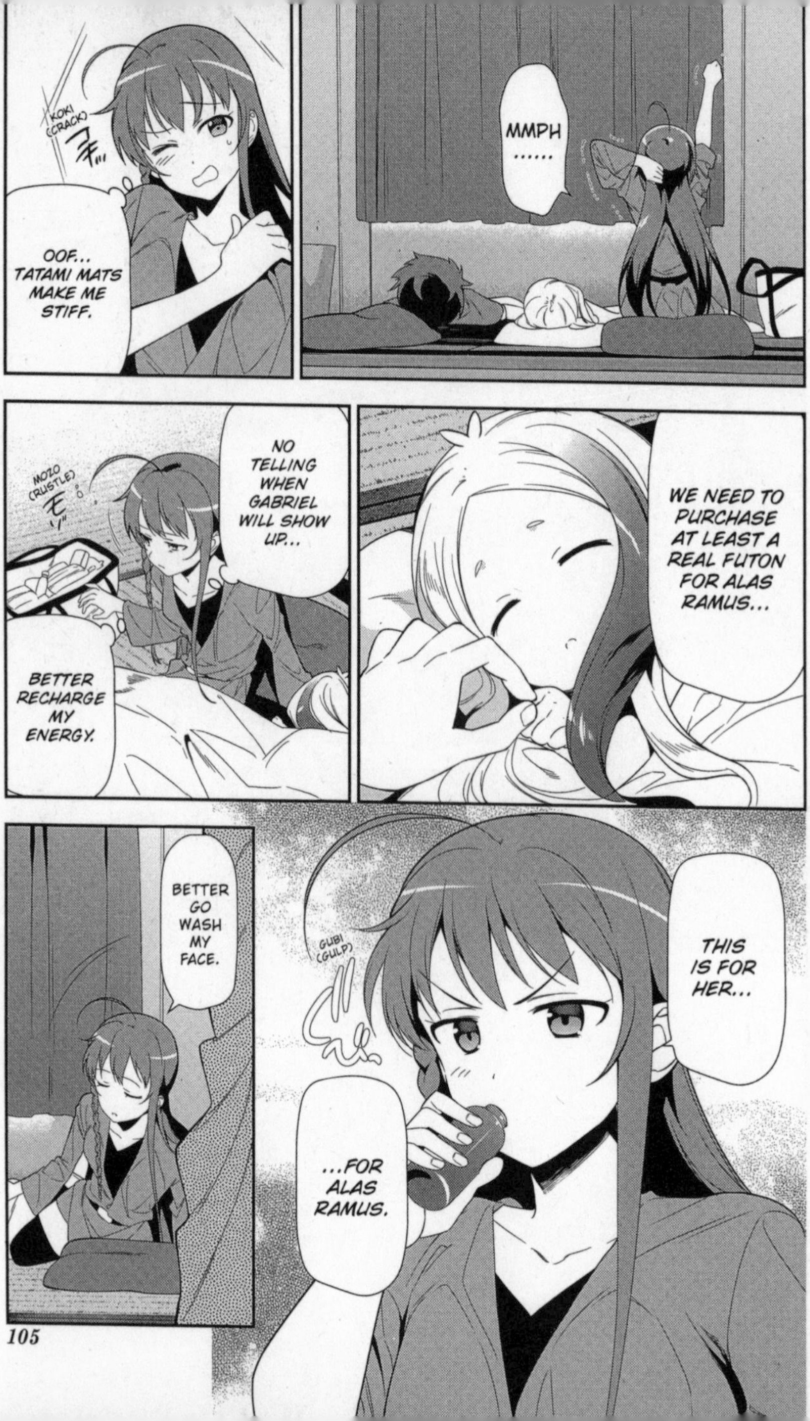
MMPH ......
KOKI (CRACK)
コキ
OOF... TATAMI MATS MAKE ME STIFF.
WE NEED TO PURCHASE AT LEAST A REAL FUTON FOR ALAS RAMUS...
NO TELLING WHEN GABRIEL WILL SHOW UP...
MOZO (RUSTLE)
モゾ
BETTER RECHARGE MY ENERGY.
THIS IS FOR HER...
GUBI (GULP)
...FOR ALAS RAMUS.
BETTER GO WASH MY FACE.

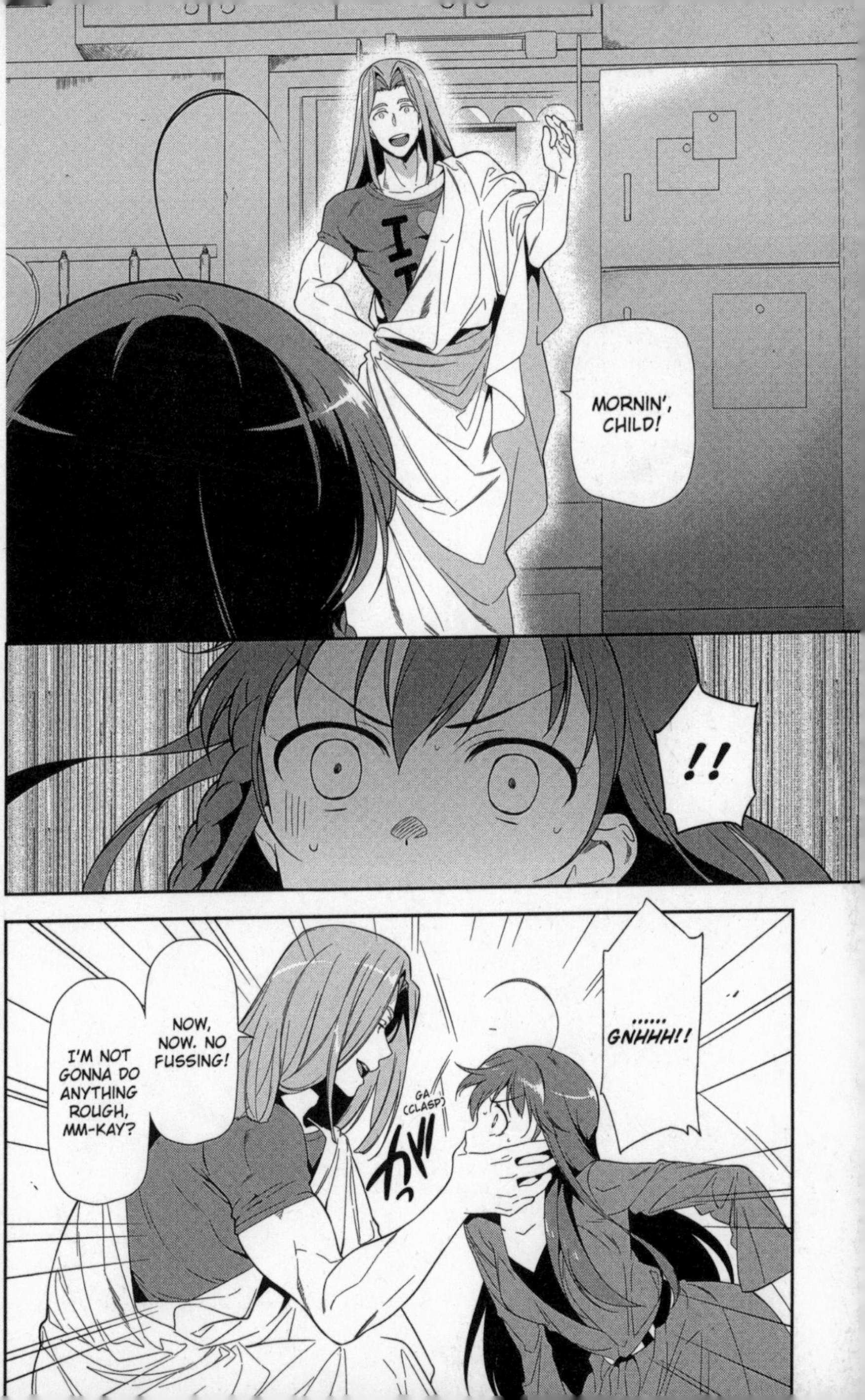
MORNIN', CHILD!
!!
......GNHHH!!
GA (CLASP)
NOW, NOW. NO FUSSING!
I'M NOT GONNA DO ANYTHING ROUGH, MM-KAY?

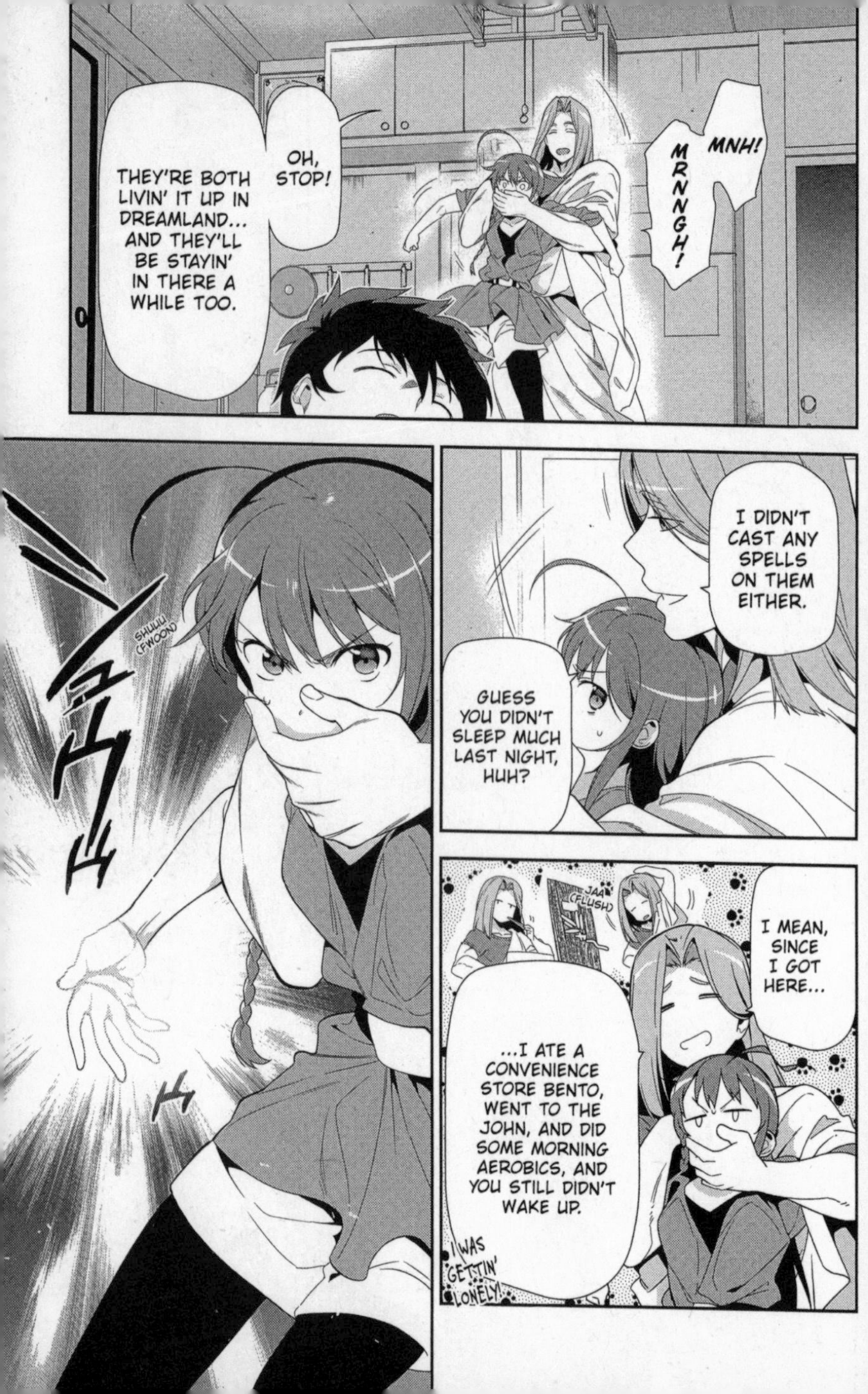
MNH!
MRNNGH!
OH, STOP!
THEY'RE BOTH LIVIN' IT UP IN DREAMLAND... AND THEY'LL BE STAYIN' IN THERE A WHILE TOO.
I DIDN'T CAST ANY SPELLS ON THEM EITHER.
GUESS YOU DIDN'T SLEEP MUCH LAST NIGHT, HUH?
I MEAN, SINCE I GOT HERE...
JAA (FLUSH)
...I ATE A CONVENIENCE STORE BENTO, WENT TO THE JOHN, AND DID SOME MORNING AEROBICS, AND YOU STILL DIDN'T WAKE UP.
I WAS GETTIN' LONELY!
SHUUU (FWOON)

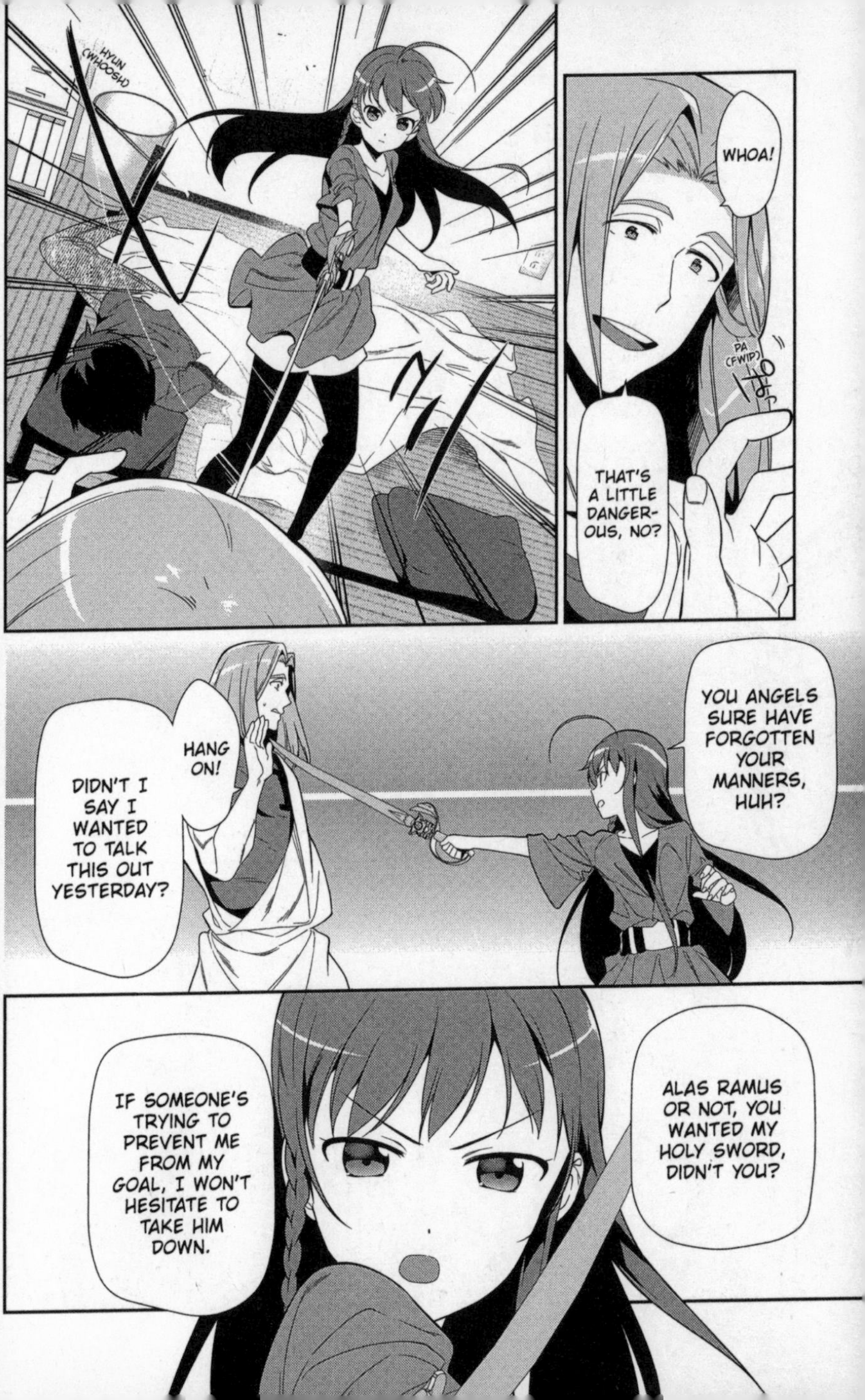
WHOA!
PA (FWIP)
THAT'S A LITTLE DANGER-OUS, NO?
HYUN (WHOOSH)
YOU ANGELS SURE HAVE FORGOTTEN YOUR MANNERS, HUH?
HANG ON!
DIDN'T I SAY I WANTED TO TALK THIS OUT YESTERDAY?
ALAS RAMUS OR NOT, YOU WANTED MY HOLY SWORD, DIDN'T YOU?
IF SOMEONE'S TRYING TO PREVENT ME FROM MY GOAL, I WON'T HESITATE TO TAKE HIM DOWN.

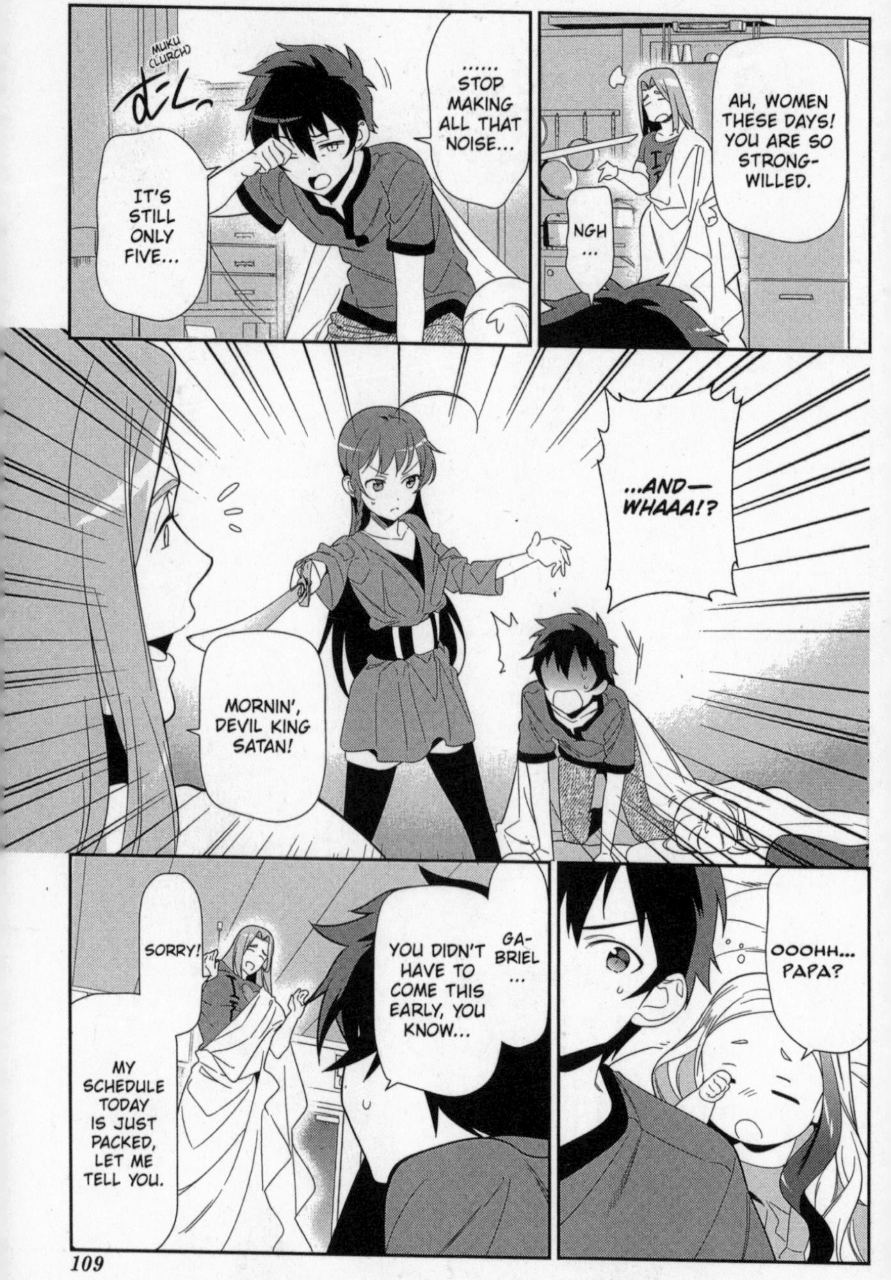
AH, WOMEN THESE DAYS! YOU ARE SO STRONG-WILLED.
NGH...
...... STOP MAKING ALL THAT NOISE...
MUKU (CLURCH)
IT'S STILL ONLY FIVE...
...AND— WHAAA!?
MORNIN', DEVIL KING SATAN!
OOOHH... PAPA?
GA-BRIEL...
YOU DIDN'T HAVE TO COME THIS EARLY, YOU KNOW...
SORRY!
MY SCHEDULE TODAY IS JUST PACKED, LET ME TELL YOU.

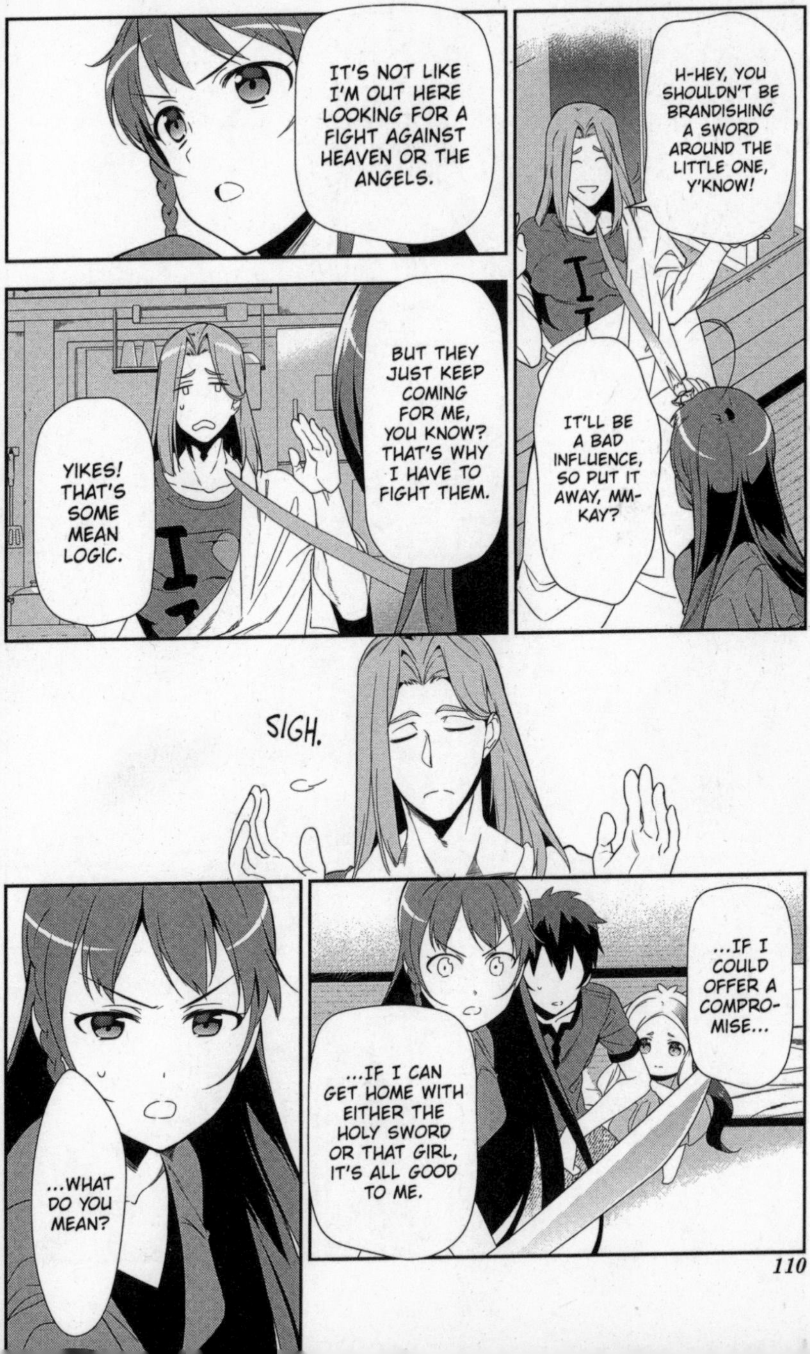
H-HEY, YOU SHOULDN'T BE BRANDISHING A SWORD AROUND THE LITTLE ONE, Y'KNOW!
IT'LL BE A BAD INFLUENCE, SO PUT IT AWAY, MM-KAY?
IT'S NOT LIKE I'M OUT HERE LOOKING FOR A FIGHT AGAINST HEAVEN OR THE ANGELS.
BUT THEY JUST KEEP COMING FOR ME, YOU KNOW? THAT'S WHY I HAVE TO FIGHT THEM.
YIKES! THAT'S SOME MEAN LOGIC.
SIGH.
...IF I COULD OFFER A COMPRO-MISE...
...IF I CAN GET HOME WITH EITHER THE HOLY SWORD OR THAT GIRL, IT'S ALL GOOD TO ME.
...WHAT DO YOU MEAN?

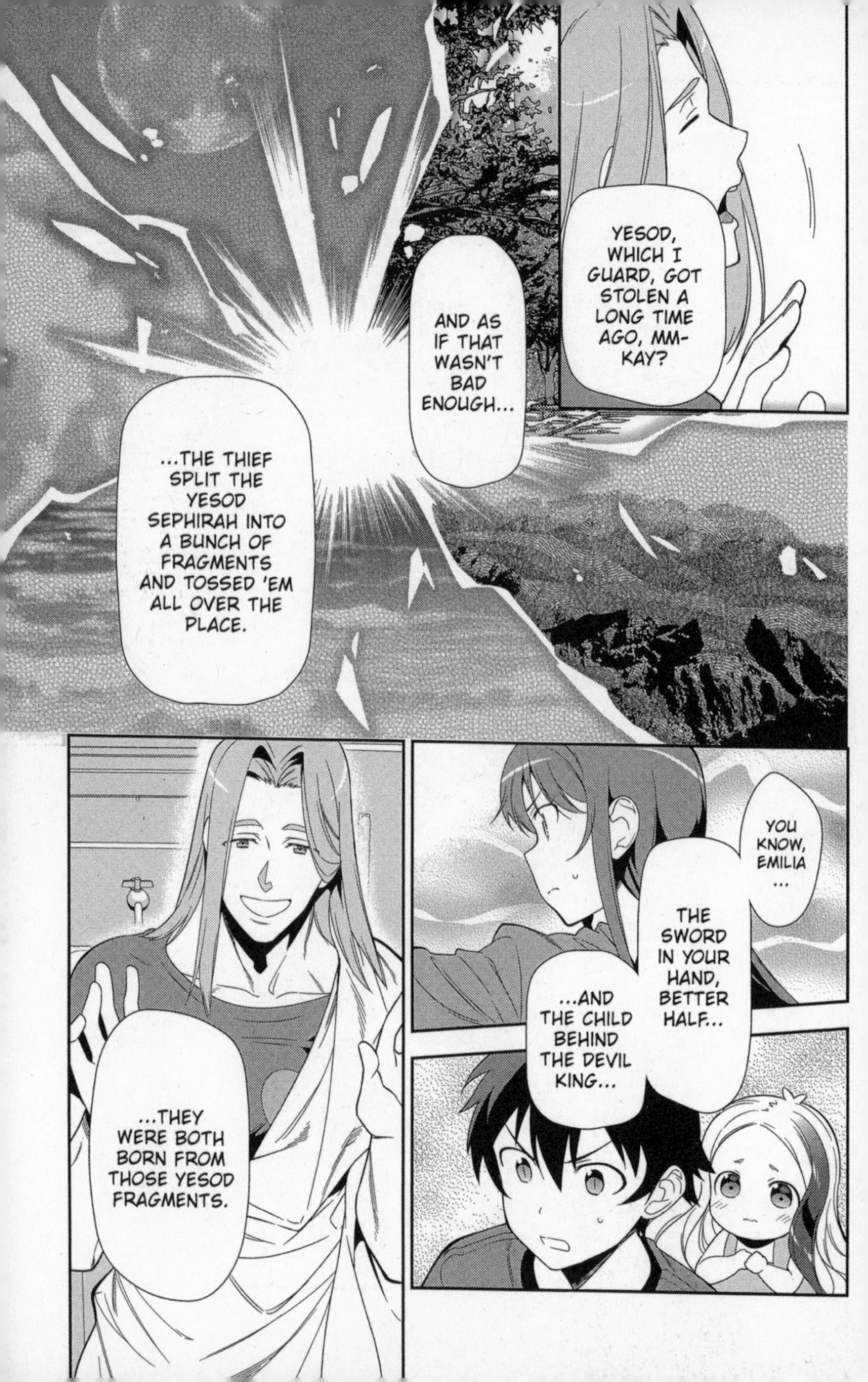
YESOD, WHICH I GUARD, GOT STOLEN A LONG TIME AGO, MM-KAY?
AND AS IF THAT WASN'T BAD ENOUGH...
...THE THIEF SPLIT THE YESOD SEPHIRAH INTO A BUNCH OF FRAGMENTS AND TOSSED 'EM ALL OVER THE PLACE.
YOU KNOW, EMILIA...
THE SWORD IN YOUR HAND, BETTER HALF...
...AND THE CHILD BEHIND THE DEVIL KING...
...THEY WERE BOTH BORN FROM THOSE YESOD FRAGMENTS.

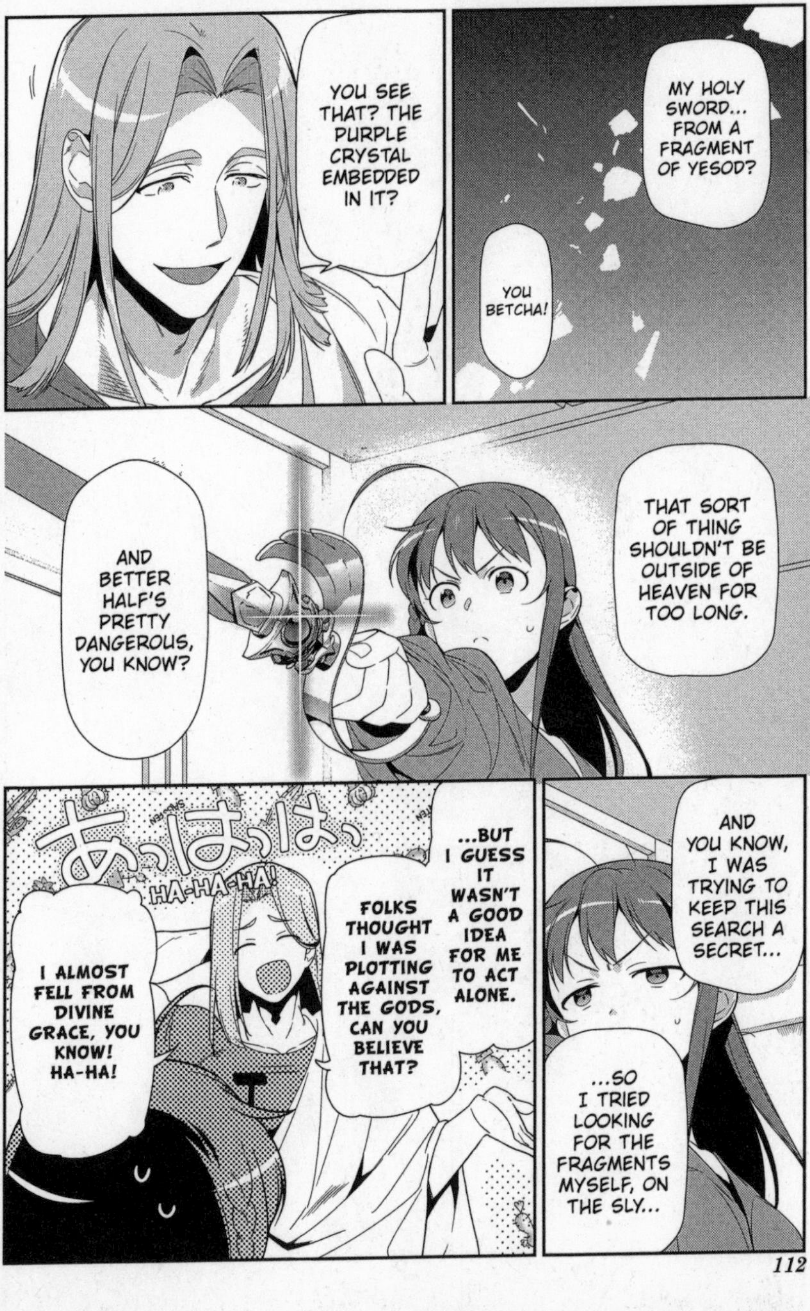
MY HOLY SWORD... FROM A FRAGMENT OF YESOD?
YOU BETCHA!
YOU SEE THAT? THE PURPLE CRYSTAL EMBEDDED IN IT?
THAT SORT OF THING SHOULDN'T BE OUTSIDE OF HEAVEN FOR TOO LONG.
AND BETTER HALF'S PRETTY DANGEROUS, YOU KNOW?
AND YOU KNOW, I WAS TRYING TO KEEP THIS SEARCH A SECRET...
...SO I TRIED LOOKING FOR THE FRAGMENTS MYSELF, ON THE SLY...
...BUT I GUESS IT WASN'T A GOOD IDEA FOR ME TO ACT ALONE.
FOLKS THOUGHT I WAS PLOTTING AGAINST THE GODS, CAN YOU BELIEVE THAT?
あっはっはっ
HA-HA-HA!
I ALMOST FELL FROM DIVINE GRACE, YOU KNOW! HA-HA!

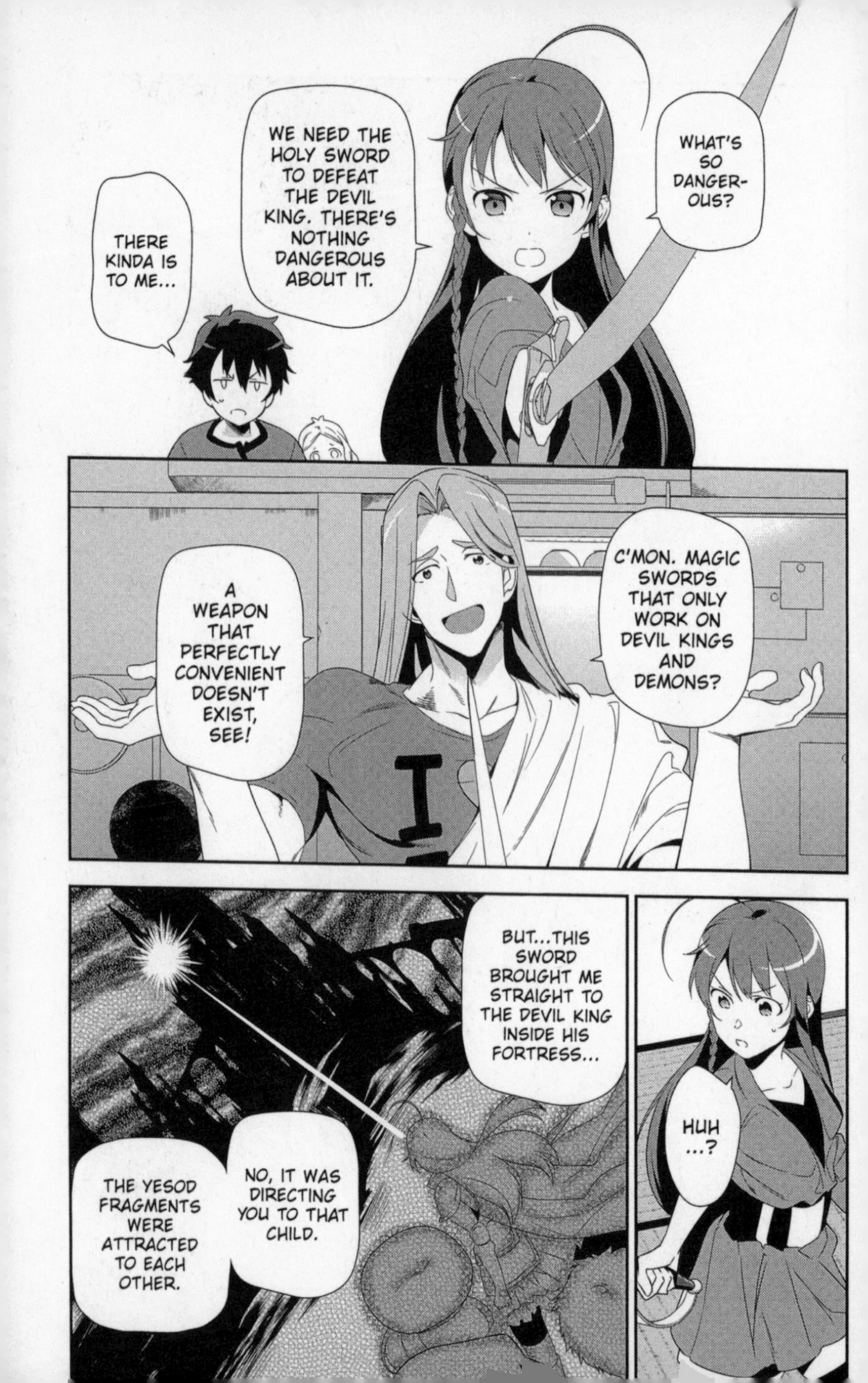
WHAT'S SO DANGER-OUS?
WE NEED THE HOLY SWORD TO DEFEAT THE DEVIL KING. THERE'S NOTHING DANGEROUS ABOUT IT.
THERE KINDA IS TO ME...
C'MON. MAGIC SWORDS THAT ONLY WORK ON DEVIL KINGS AND DEMONS?
A WEAPON THAT PERFECTLY CONVENIENT DOESN'T EXIST, SEE!
HUH ...?
BUT...THIS SWORD BROUGHT ME STRAIGHT TO THE DEVIL KING INSIDE HIS FORTRESS...
NO, IT WAS DIRECTING YOU TO THAT CHILD.
THE YESOD FRAGMENTS WERE ATTRACTED TO EACH OTHER.

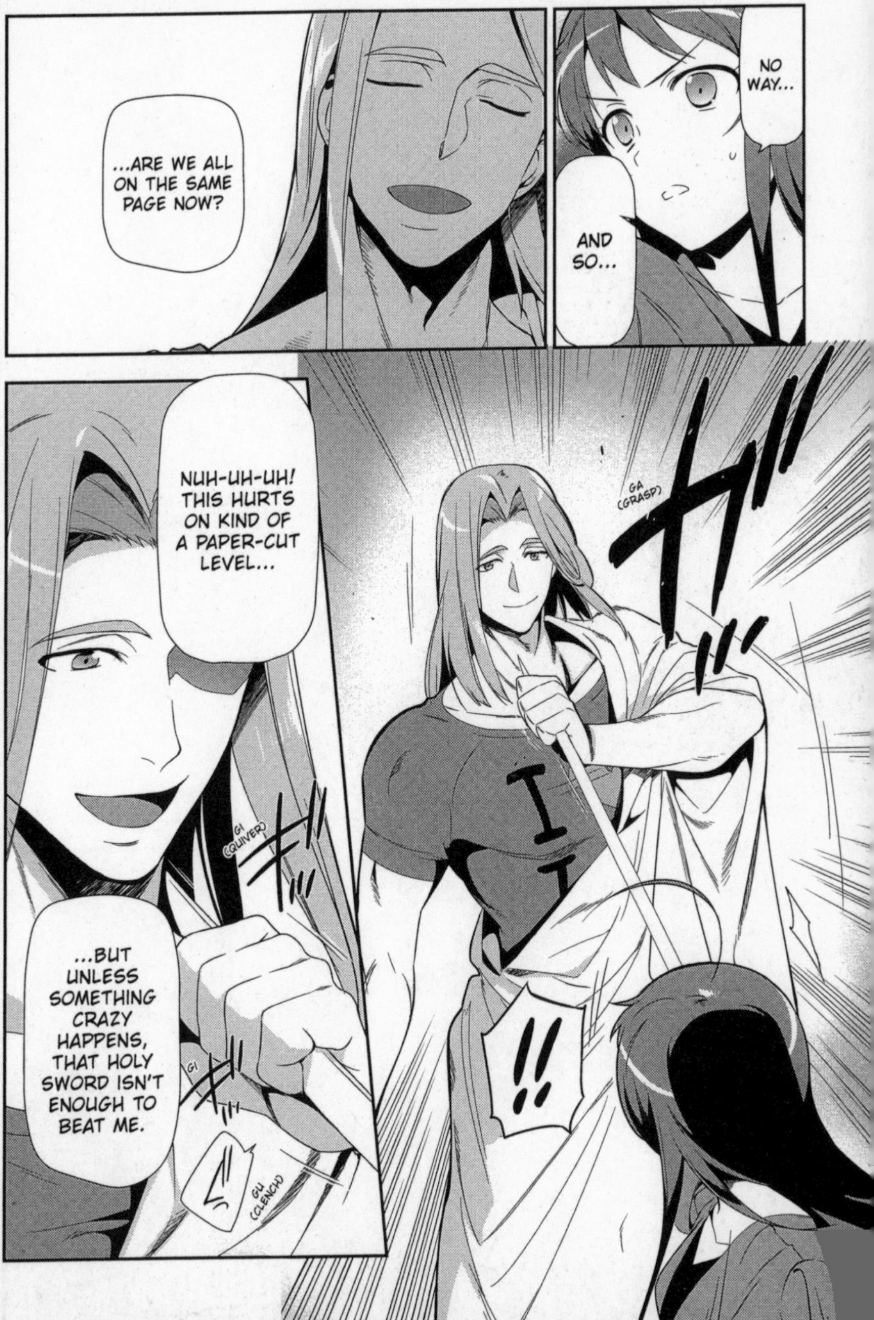
NO WAY...
AND SO...
...ARE WE ALL ON THE SAME PAGE NOW?
GA (GRASP)
!!
NUH-UH-UH! THIS HURTS ON KIND OF A PAPER-CUT LEVEL...
GI (QUIVER)
...BUT UNLESS SOMETHING CRAZY HAPPENS, THAT HOLY SWORD ISN'T ENOUGH TO BEAT ME.
GI
GU (CLENCH)

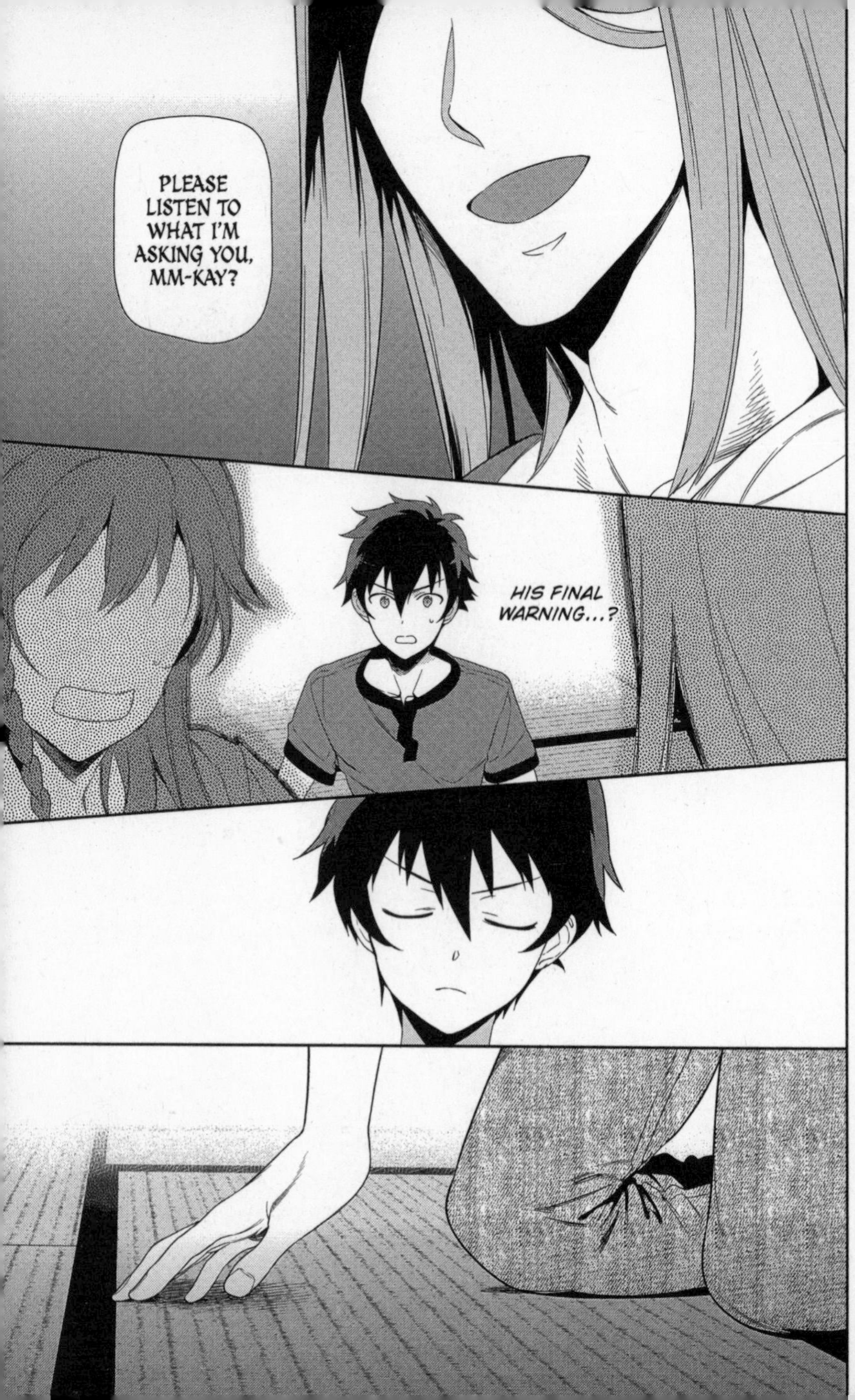
PLEASE LISTEN TO WHAT I'M ASKING YOU, MM-KAY?
HIS FINAL WARNING...?

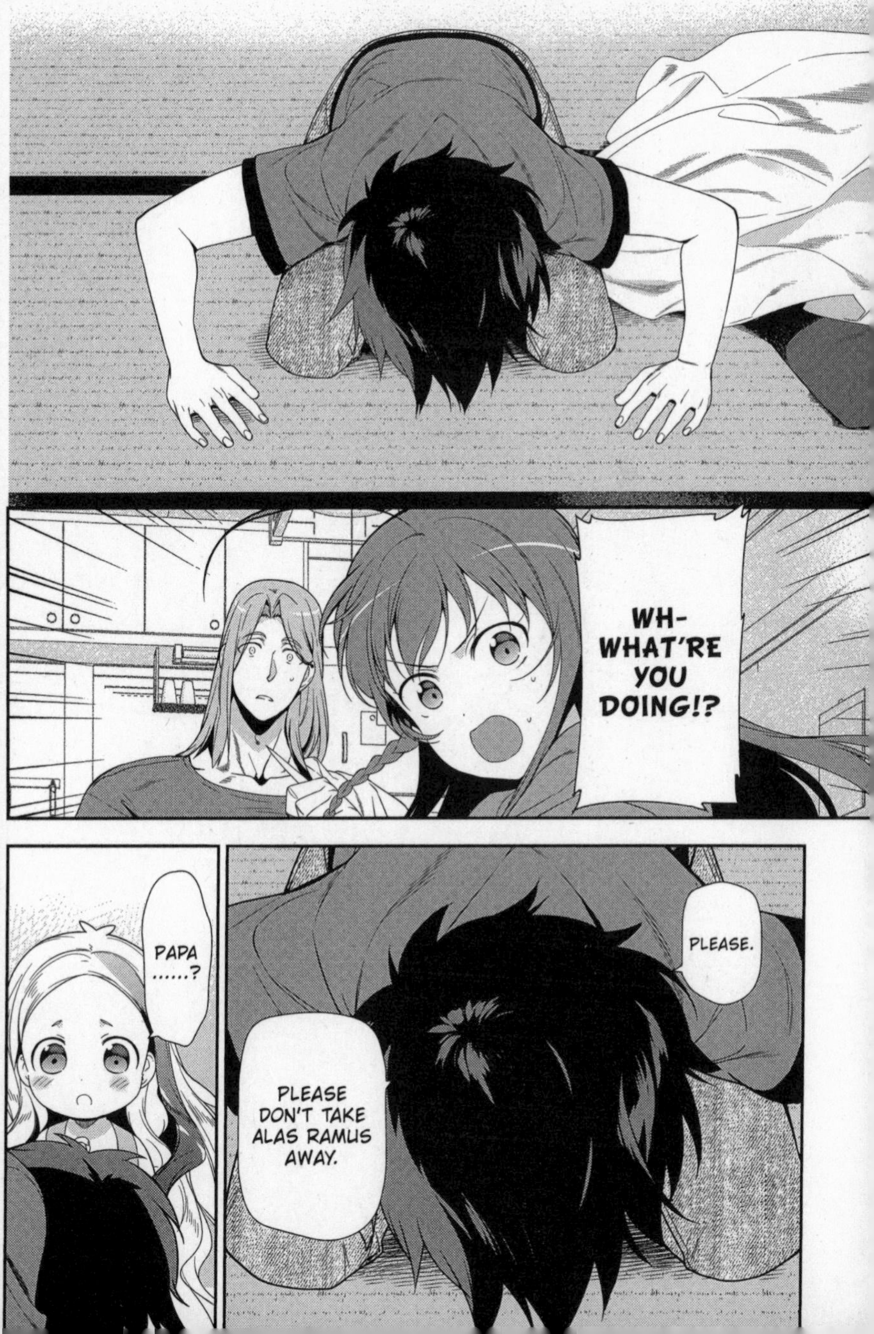
WH- WHAT'RE YOU DOING!?
PLEASE.
PLEASE DON'T TAKE ALAS RAMUS AWAY.
PAPA ......?

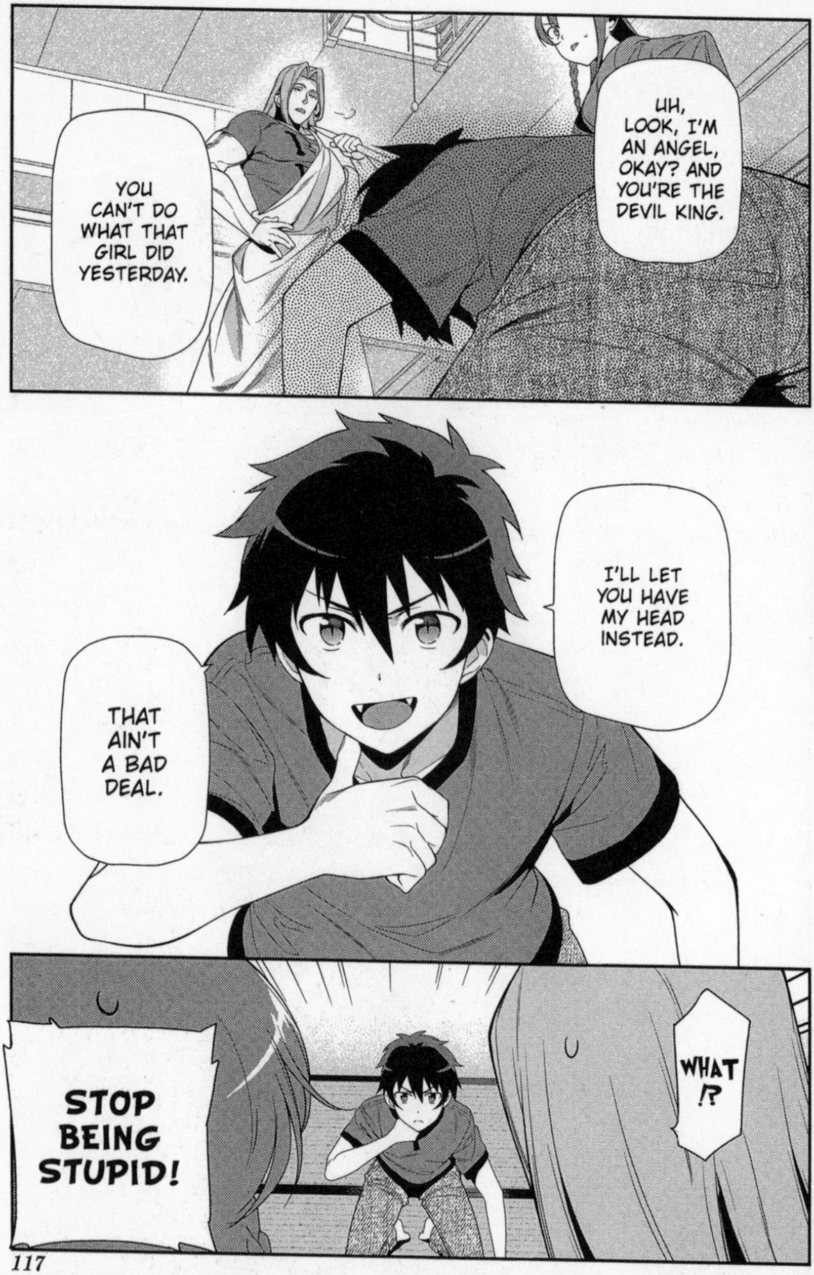
UH, LOOK, I'M AN ANGEL, OKAY? AND YOU'RE THE DEVIL KING.
YOU CAN'T DO WHAT THAT GIRL DID YESTERDAY.
I'LL LET YOU HAVE MY HEAD INSTEAD.
THAT AIN'T A BAD DEAL.
WHAT !?
STOP BEING STUPID!

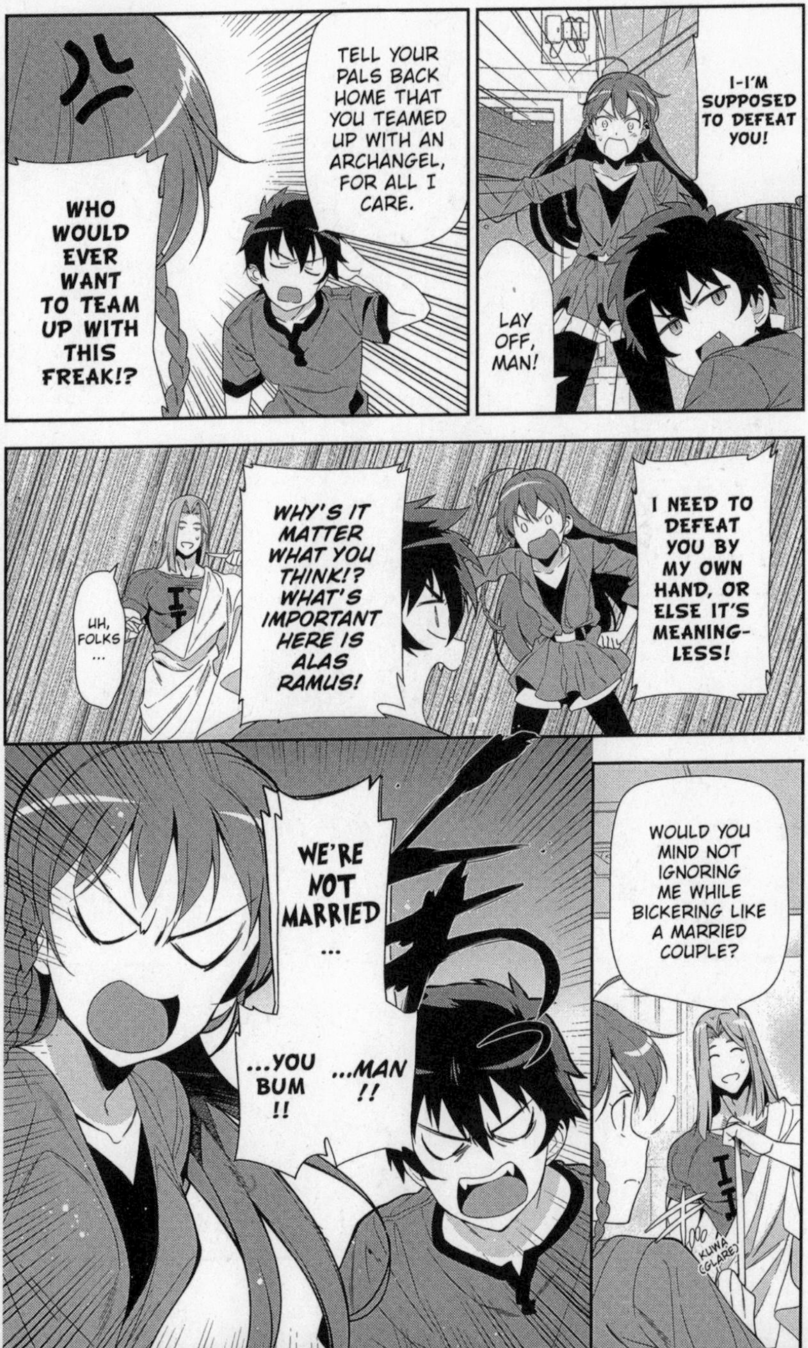
I-I'M SUPPOSED TO DEFEAT YOU!
LAY OFF, MAN!
TELL YOUR PALS BACK HOME THAT YOU TEAMED UP WITH AN ARCHANGEL, FOR ALL I CARE.
WHO WOULD EVER WANT TO TEAM UP WITH THIS FREAK!?
I NEED TO DEFEAT YOU BY MY OWN HAND, OR ELSE IT'S MEANING-LESS!
WHY'S IT MATTER WHAT YOU THINK!? WHAT'S IMPORTANT HERE IS ALAS RAMUS!
UH, FOLKS ...
WOULD YOU MIND NOT IGNORING ME WHILE BICKERING LIKE A MARRIED COUPLE?
KUWA (GLARE)
WE'RE NOT MARRIED ...
...MAN !!
...YOU BUM !!

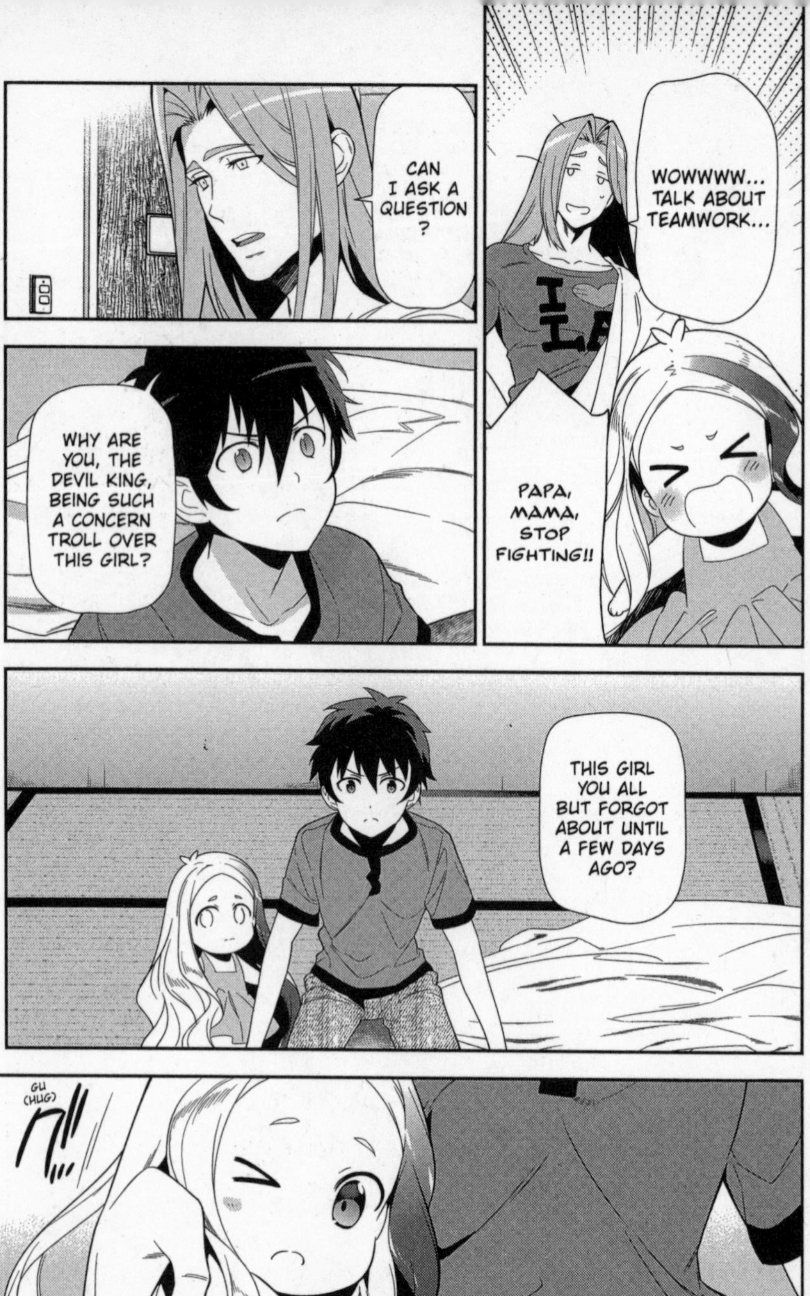
WOWWWW... TALK ABOUT TEAMWORK...
PAPA, MAMA, STOP FIGHTING!!
CAN I ASK A QUESTION?
WHY ARE YOU, THE DEVIL KING, BEING SUCH A CONCERN TROLL OVER THIS GIRL?
THIS GIRL YOU ALL BUT FORGOT ABOUT UNTIL A FEW DAYS AGO?
GU (HUG)

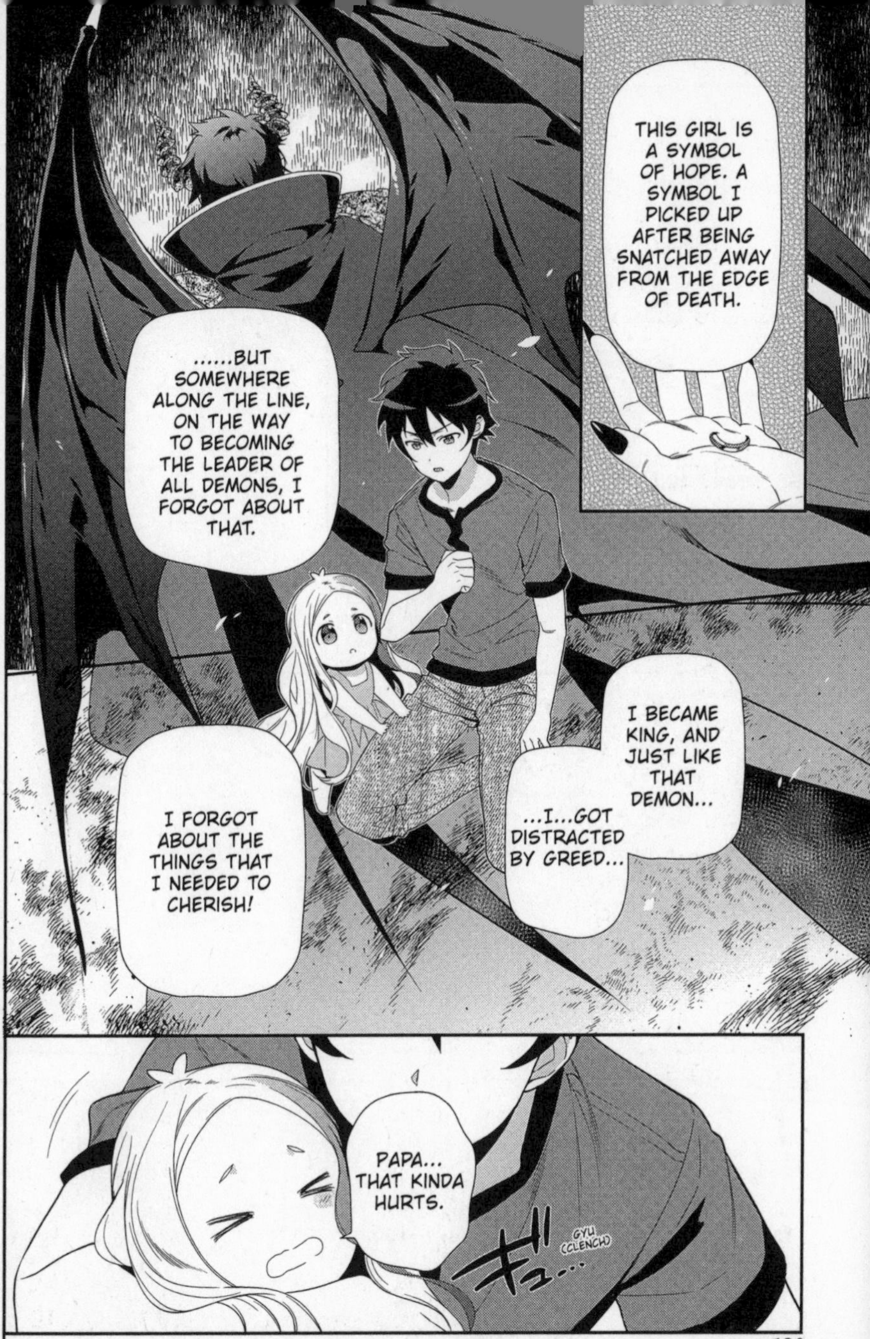
THIS GIRL IS A SYMBOL OF HOPE. A SYMBOL I PICKED UP AFTER BEING SNATCHED AWAY FROM THE EDGE OF DEATH.
......BUT SOMEWHERE ALONG THE LINE, ON THE WAY TO BECOMING THE LEADER OF ALL DEMONS, I FORGOT ABOUT THAT.
I BECAME KING, AND JUST LIKE THAT DEMON...
...I...GOT DISTRACTED BY GREED...
I FORGOT ABOUT THE THINGS THAT I NEEDED TO CHERISH!
PAPA... THAT KINDA HURTS.
GYU (CLENCH)

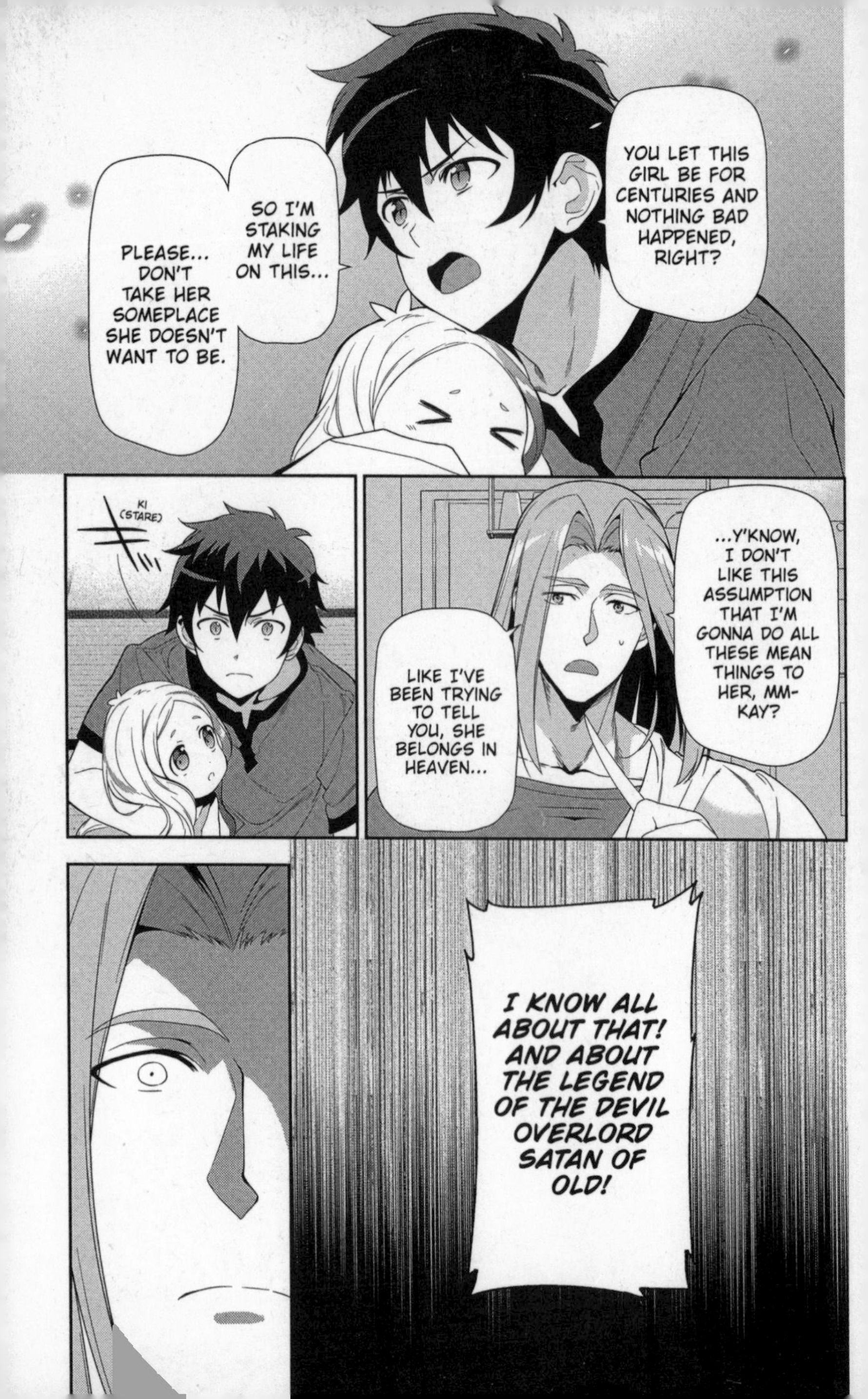
YOU LET THIS GIRL BE FOR CENTURIES AND NOTHING BAD HAPPENED, RIGHT?
SO I'M STAKING MY LIFE ON THIS...
PLEASE... DON'T TAKE HER SOMEPLACE SHE DOESN'T WANT TO BE.
...Y'KNOW, I DON'T LIKE THIS ASSUMPTION THAT I'M GONNA DO ALL THESE MEAN THINGS TO HER, MM-KAY?
LIKE I'VE BEEN TRYING TO TELL YOU, SHE BELONGS IN HEAVEN...
KI (STARE)
I KNOW ALL ABOUT THAT! AND ABOUT THE LEGEND OF THE DEVIL OVERLORD SATAN OF OLD!

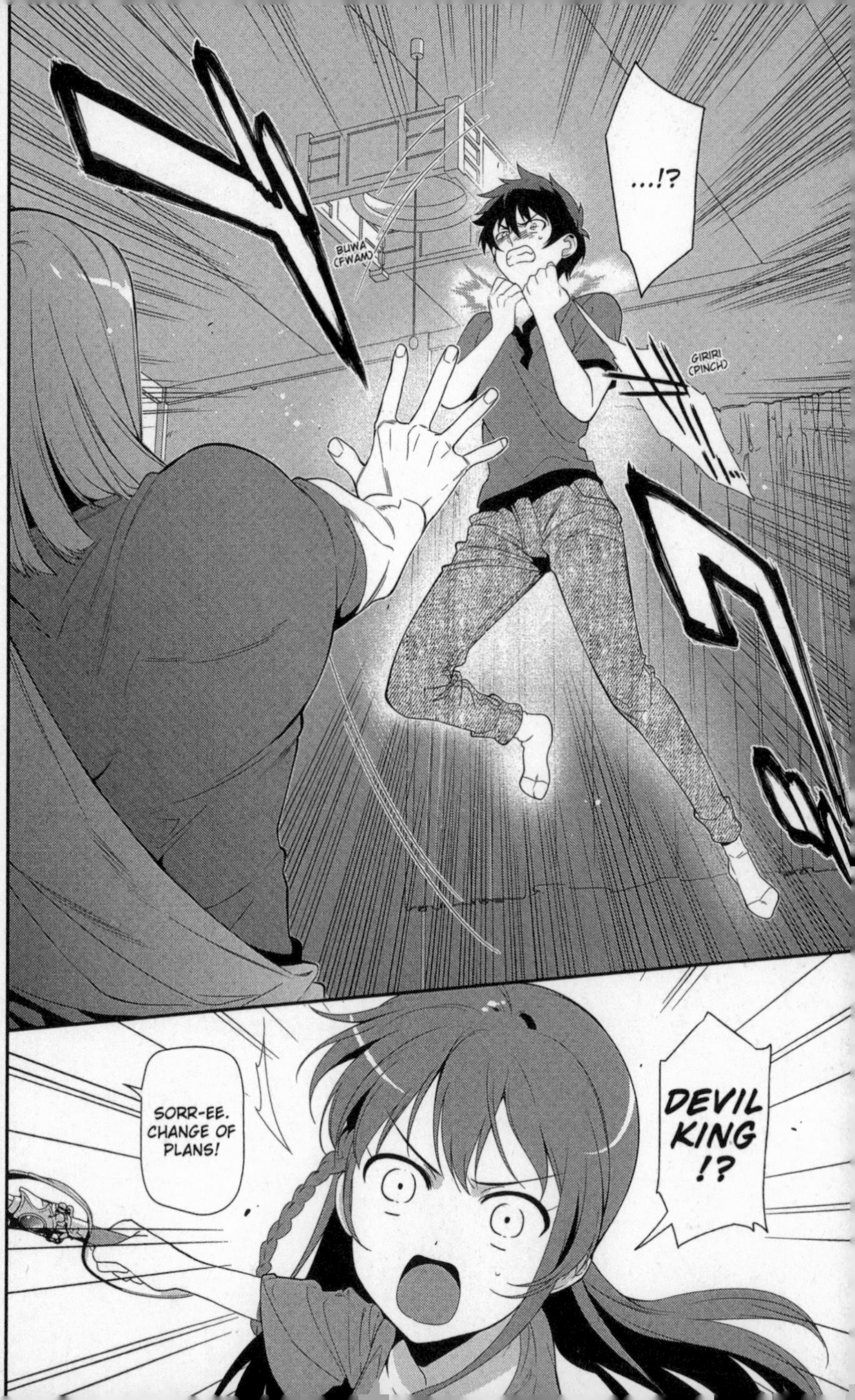
...!?
BUWA (FWAM)
GIRIRI (PINCH)
DEVIL KING !?
SORR-EE. CHANGE OF PLANS!

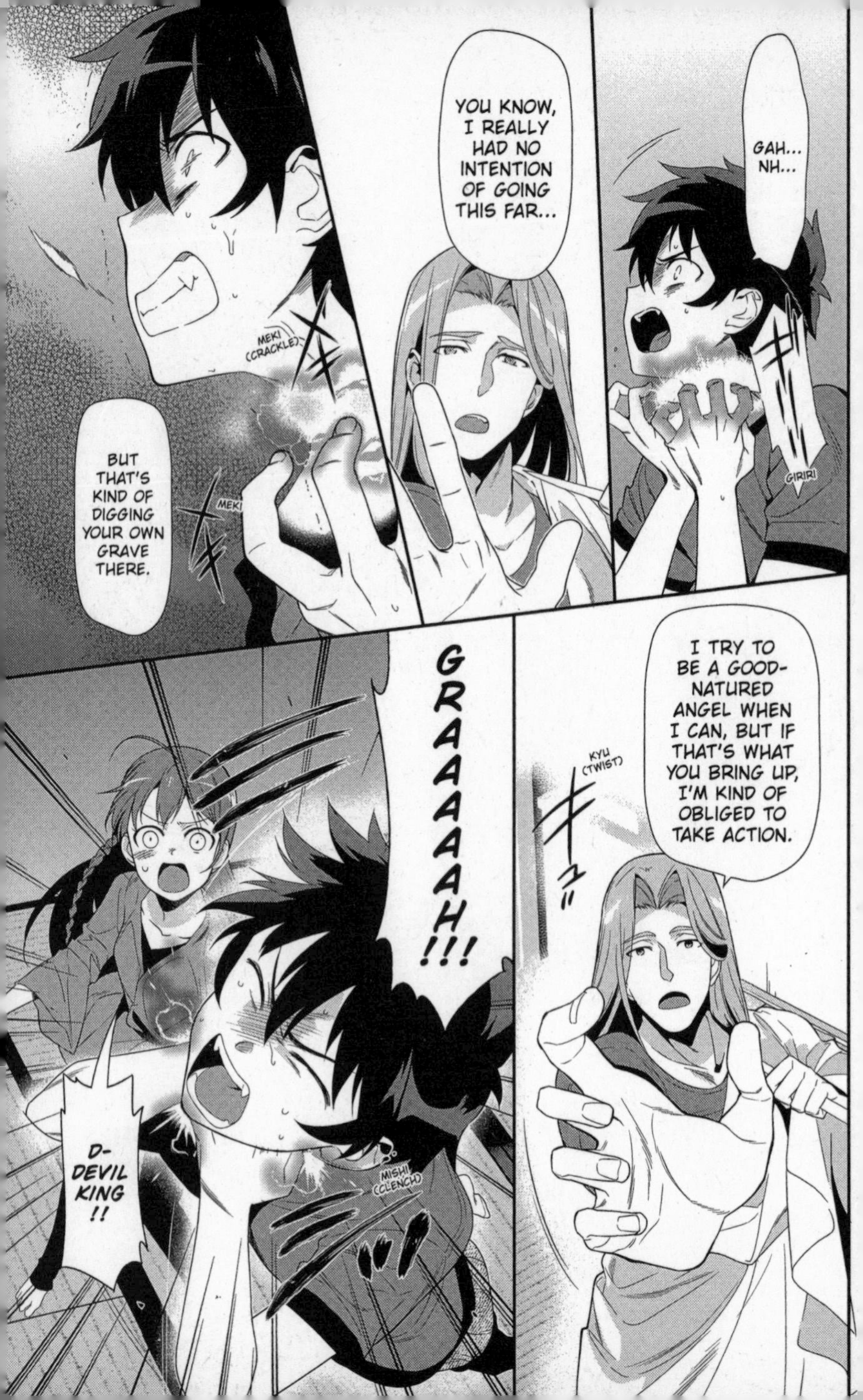
GAH... NH...
GIRIRI
YOU KNOW, I REALLY HAD NO INTENTION OF GOING THIS FAR...
MEKI (CRACKLE)
BUT THAT'S KIND OF DIGGING YOUR OWN GRAVE THERE.
MEKI
I TRY TO BE A GOOD-NATURED ANGEL WHEN I CAN, BUT IF THAT'S WHAT YOU BRING UP, I'M KIND OF OBLIGED TO TAKE ACTION.
KYU (TWIST)
GRAAAAAH!!!
D-DEVIL KING!!
MISHI (CLENCH)

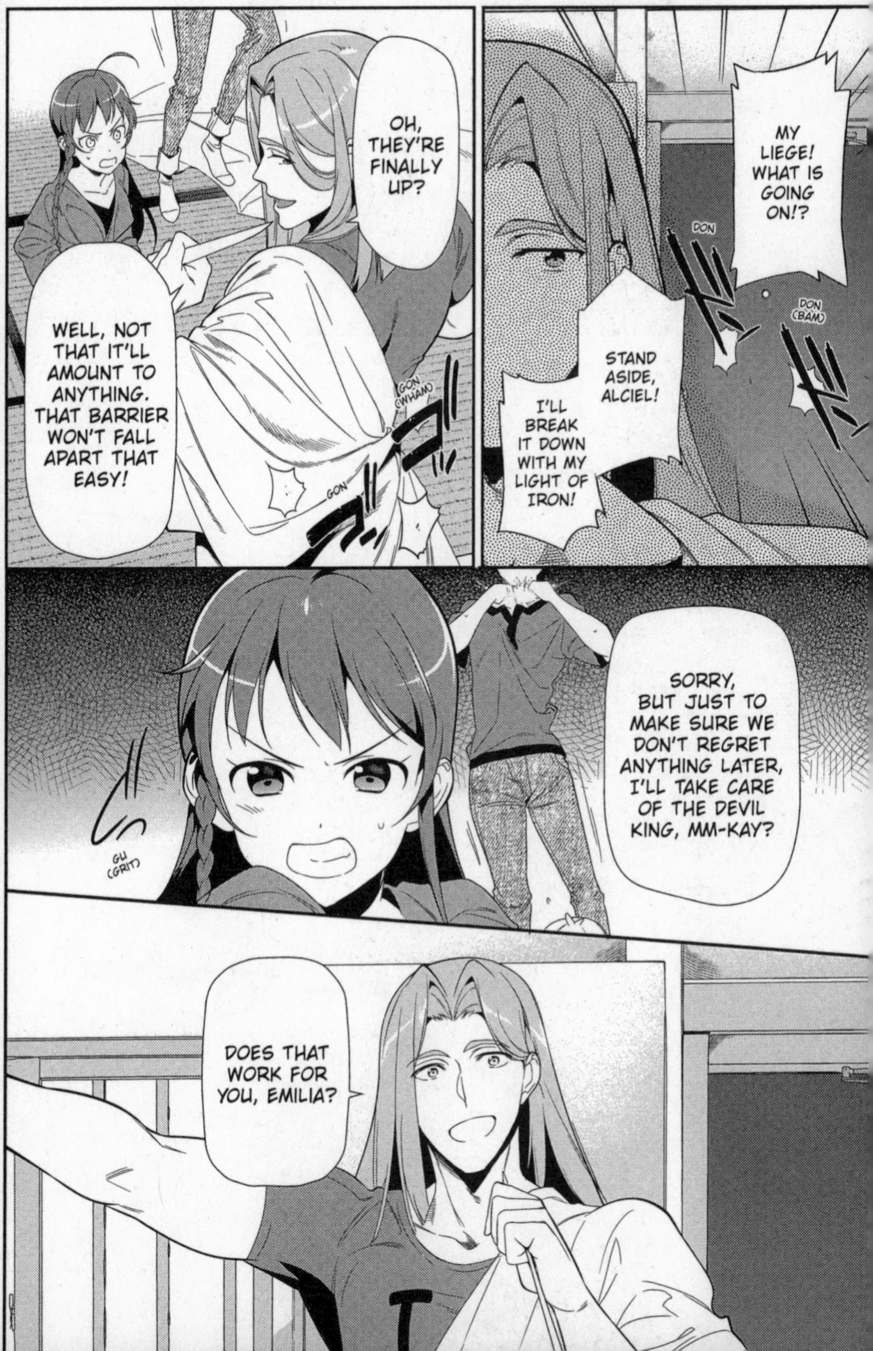
MY LIEGE! WHAT IS GOING ON!?
DON
DON (BAM)
STAND ASIDE, ALCIEL!
I'LL BREAK IT DOWN WITH MY LIGHT OF IRON!
OH, THEY'RE FINALLY UP?
GON (WHAM)
GON
WELL, NOT THAT IT'LL AMOUNT TO ANYTHING. THAT BARRIER WON'T FALL APART THAT EASY!
SORRY, BUT JUST TO MAKE SURE WE DON'T REGRET ANYTHING LATER, I'LL TAKE CARE OF THE DEVIL KING, MM-KAY?
GU (GRIT)
DOES THAT WORK FOR YOU, EMILIA?

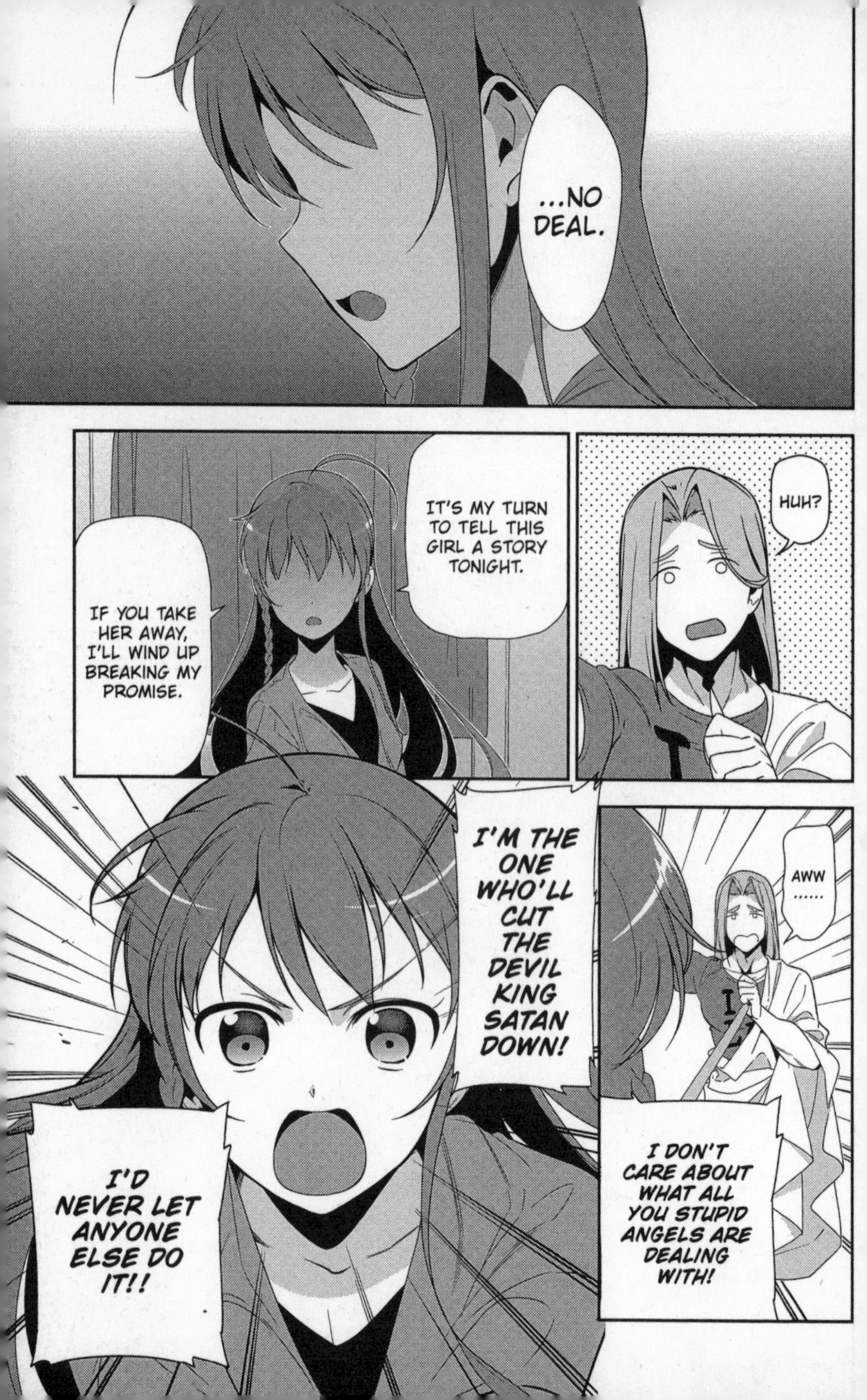
...NO DEAL.
HUH?
IT'S MY TURN TO TELL THIS GIRL A STORY TONIGHT.
IF YOU TAKE HER AWAY, I'LL WIND UP BREAKING MY PROMISE.
AWW ......
I DON'T CARE ABOUT WHAT ALL YOU STUPID ANGELS ARE DEALING WITH!
I'M THE ONE WHO'LL CUT THE DEVIL KING SATAN DOWN!
I'D NEVER LET ANYONE ELSE DO IT!!

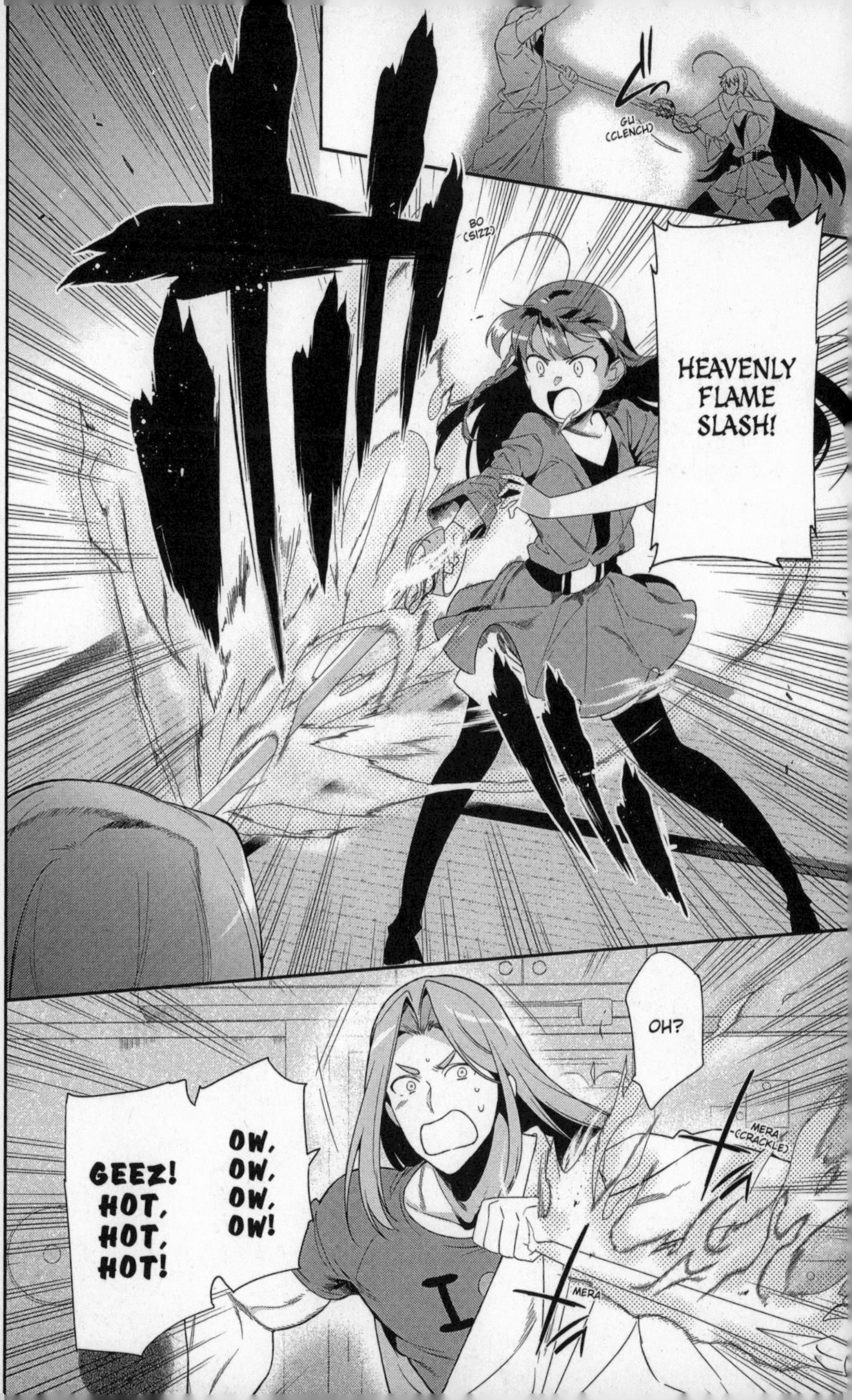
GU (CLENCH)
BO (SIZZ)
HEAVENLY FLAME SLASH!
OH?
MERA (CRACKLE)
OW, OW, OW, OW!
GEEZ! HOT, HOT, HOT!
MERA

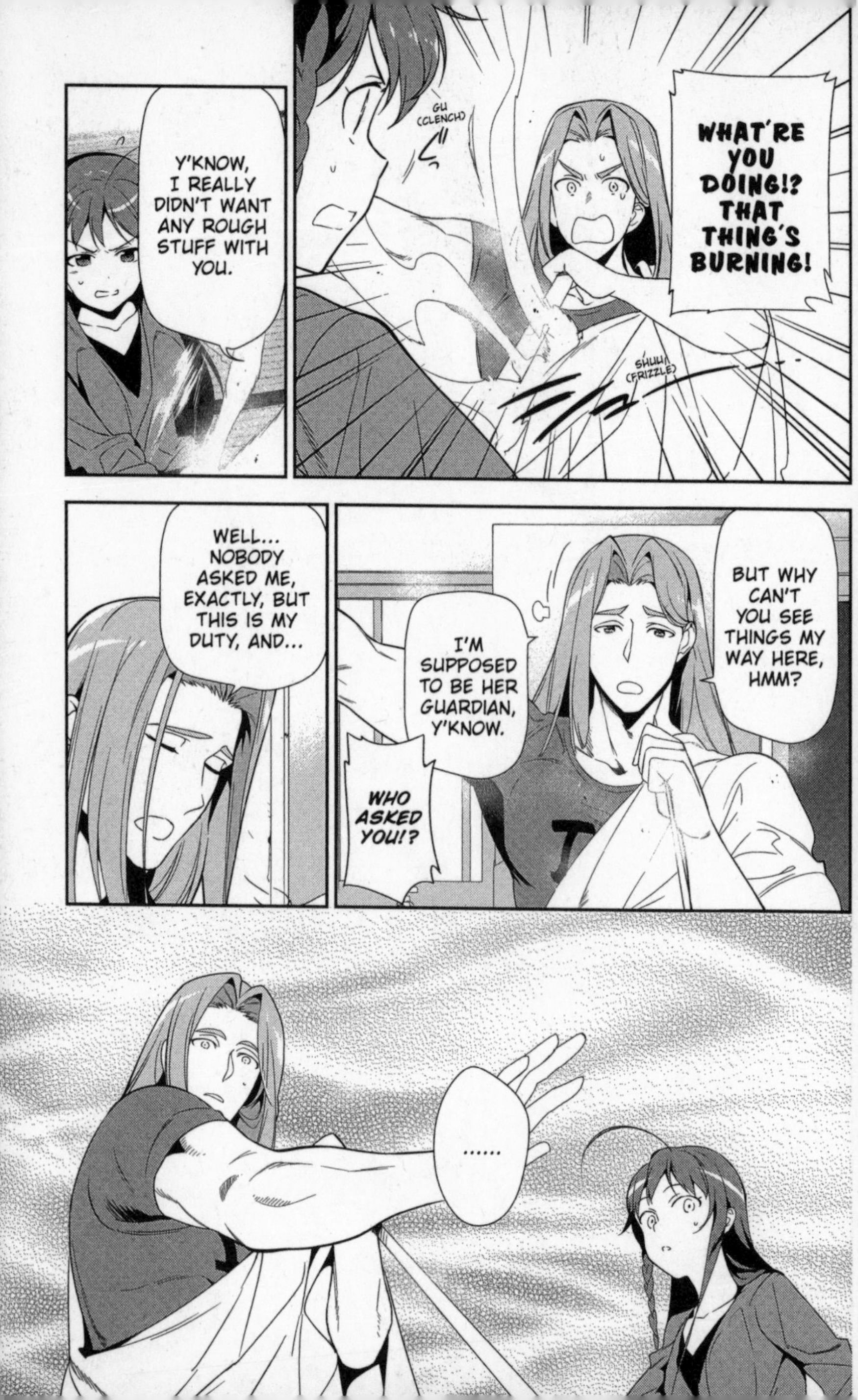
WHAT'RE YOU DOING!? THAT THING'S BURNING!
GU (CLENCH)
SHUU (FRIZZLE)
Y'KNOW, I REALLY DIDN'T WANT ANY ROUGH STUFF WITH YOU.
BUT WHY CAN'T YOU SEE THINGS MY WAY HERE, HMM?
I'M SUPPOSED TO BE HER GUARDIAN, Y'KNOW.
WHO ASKED YOU!?
WELL... NOBODY ASKED ME, EXACTLY, BUT THIS IS MY DUTY, AND...
......

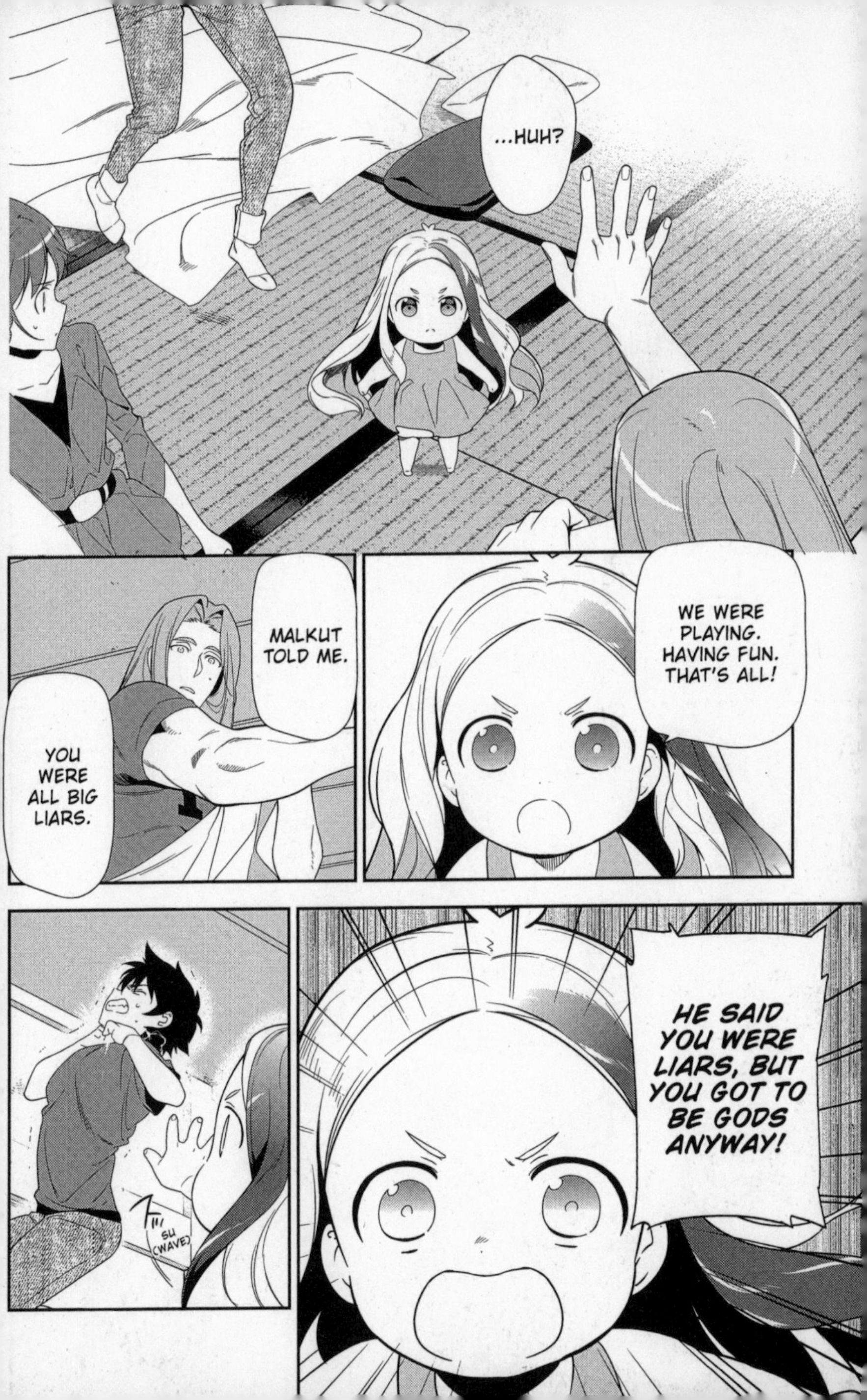
...HUH?
WE WERE PLAYING. HAVING FUN. THAT'S ALL!
MALKUT TOLD ME.
YOU WERE ALL BIG LIARS.
HE SAID YOU WERE LIARS, BUT YOU GOT TO BE GODS ANYWAY!
SU (WAVE)

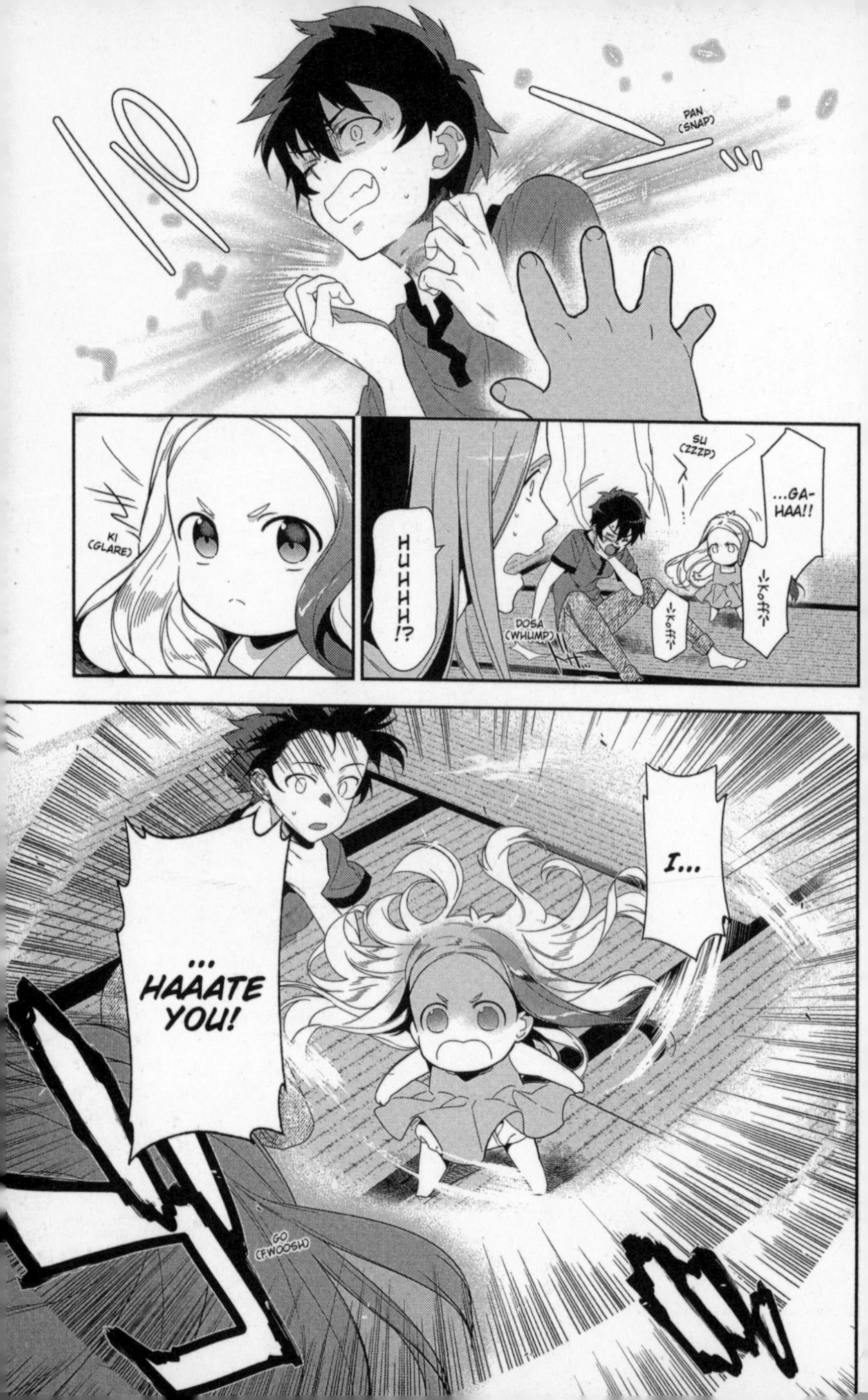
PAN (SNAP)
SU (ZZZP)
...GA-HAA!!
Koff
HUHHHH!?
Koff
DOSA (WHUMP)
KI (GLARE)
I...
...HAÄATE YOU!
GO (FWOOSH)

THE DEVIL IS A PART-TIMER!

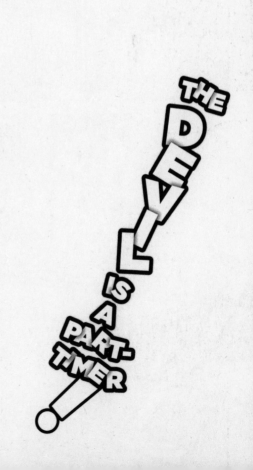

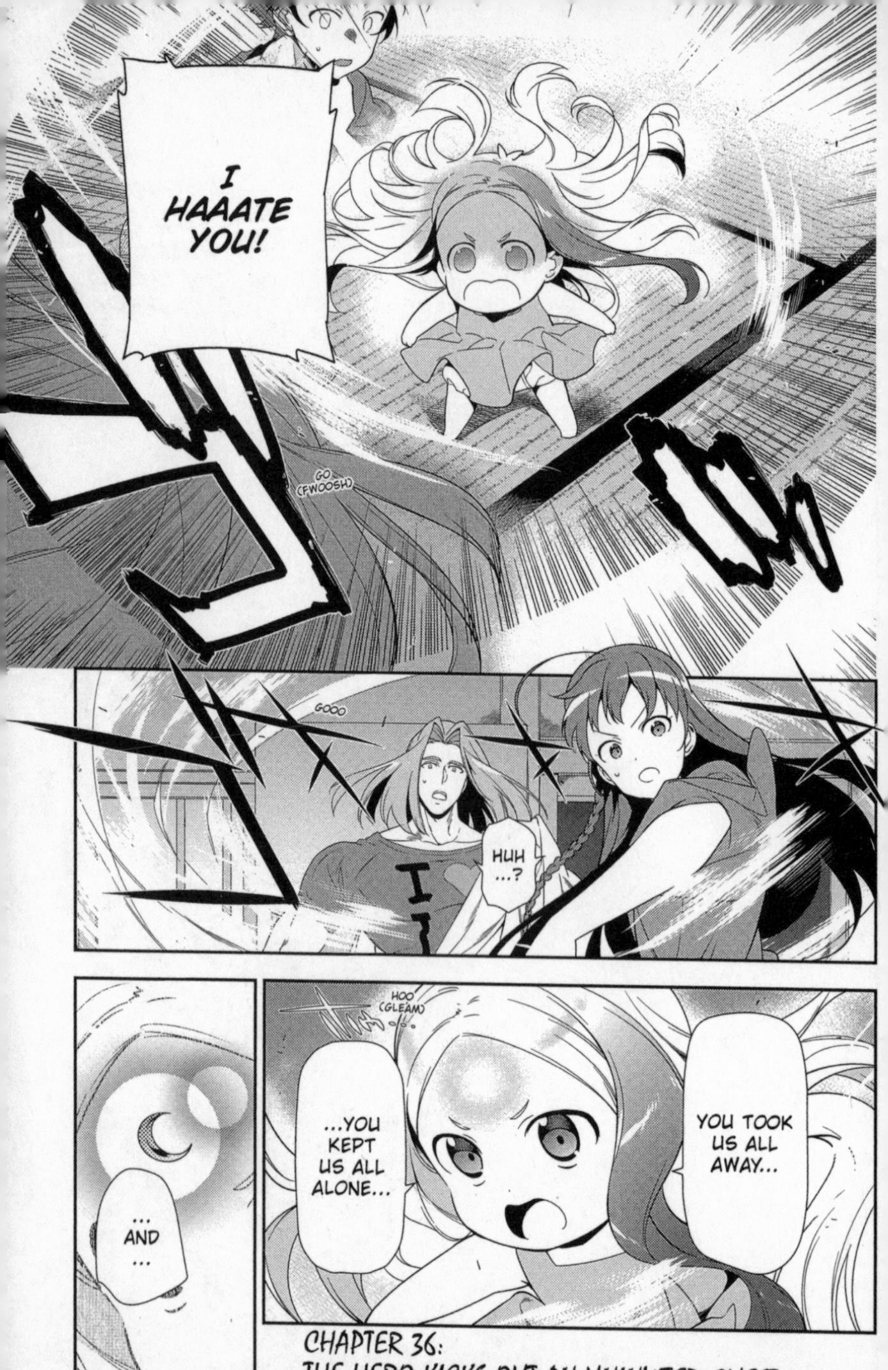
I HAAATE YOU!
GO (FWOOSH)
GOOO
HUH ...?
HOO (GLEAM)
YOU TOOK US ALL AWAY...
...YOU KEPT US ALL ALONE...
... AND ...

CHAPTER 36:
THE HERO KICKS OUT AN UNINVITED GUEST

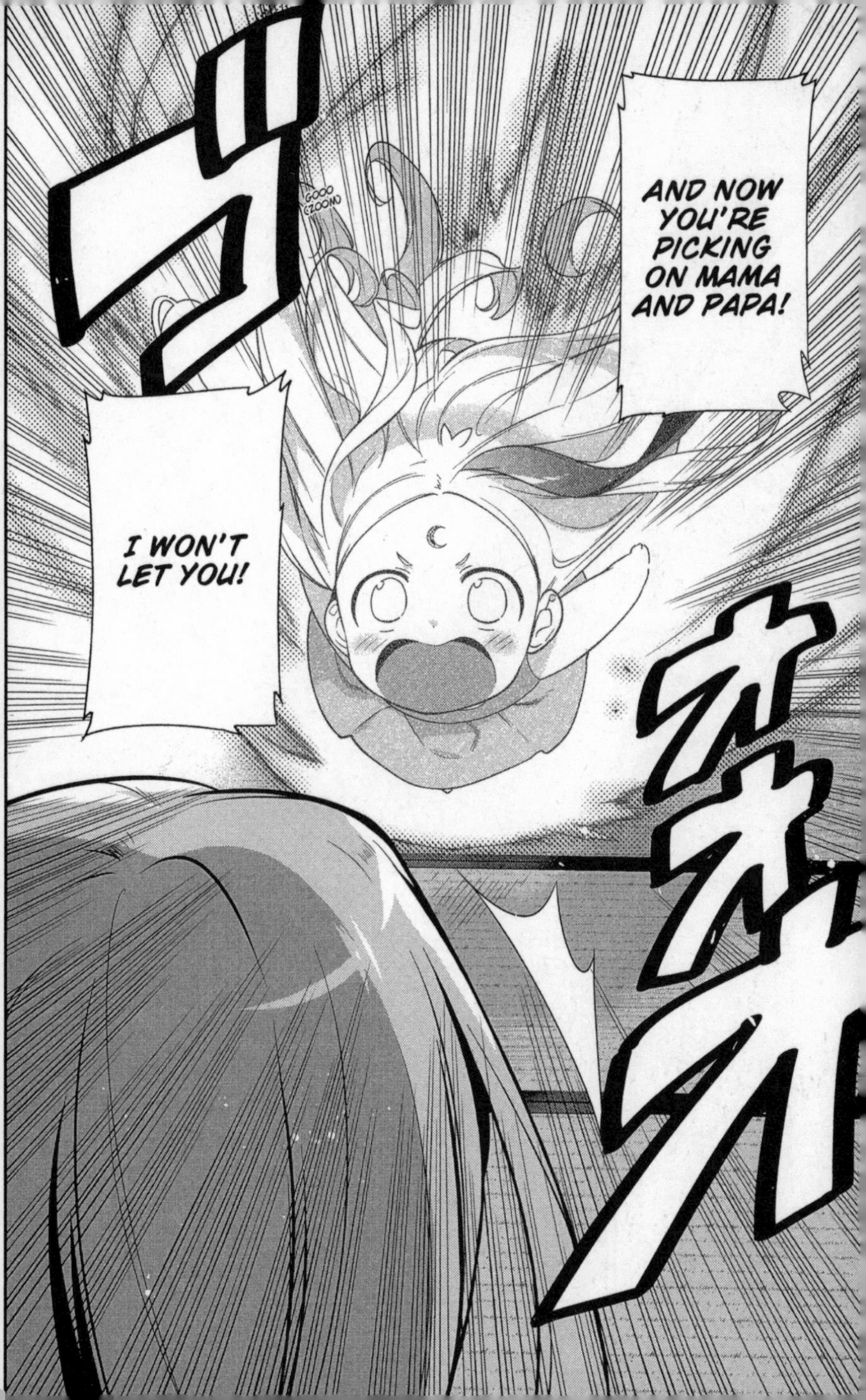
AND NOW YOU'RE PICKING ON MAMA AND PAPA!
GOOO (ZOOM)
I WON'T LET YOU!

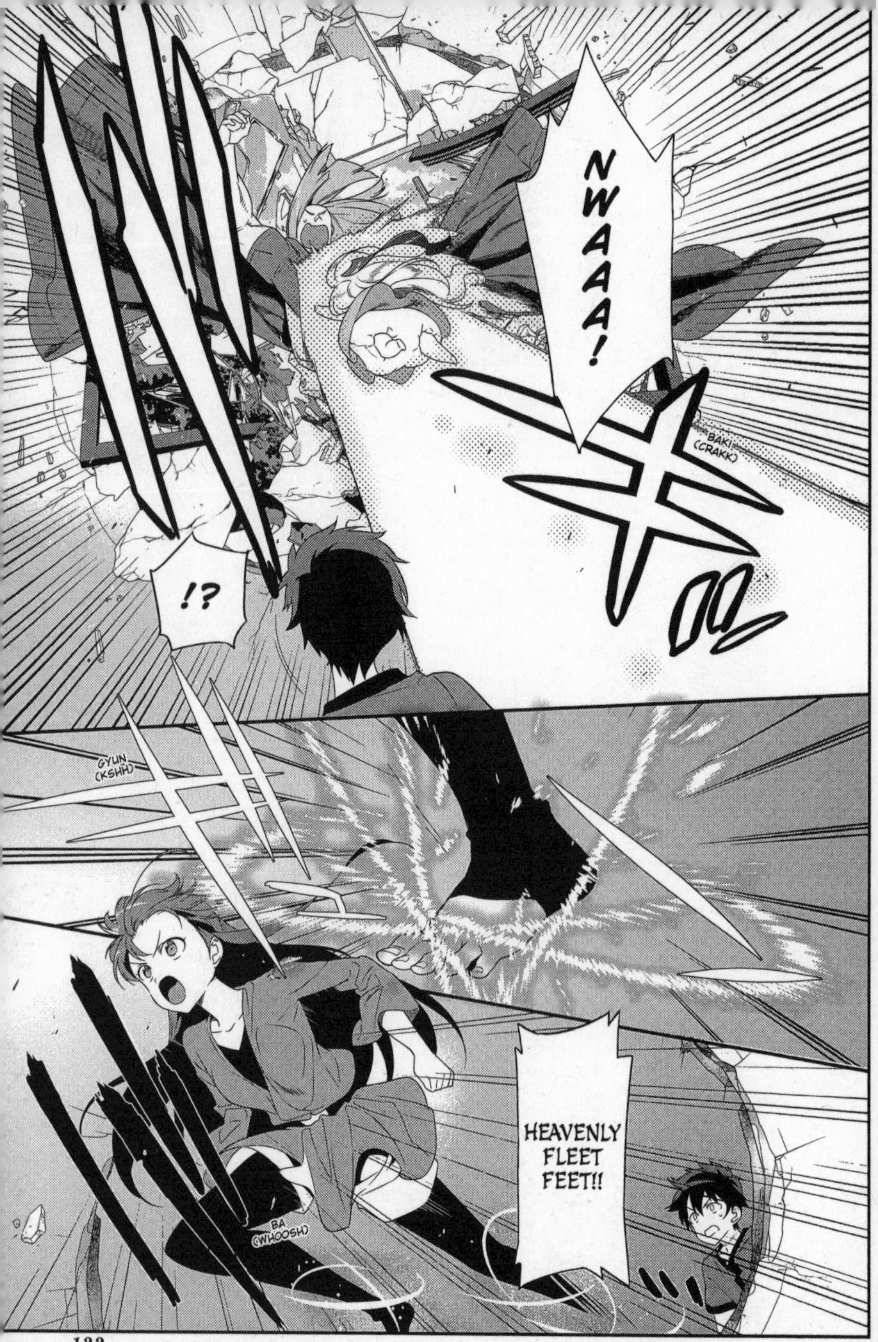
NWAAAA!
BAKI (CRAKK)
!?
GYUN (KSHH)
HEAVENLY FLEET FEET!!
BA (WHOOSH)

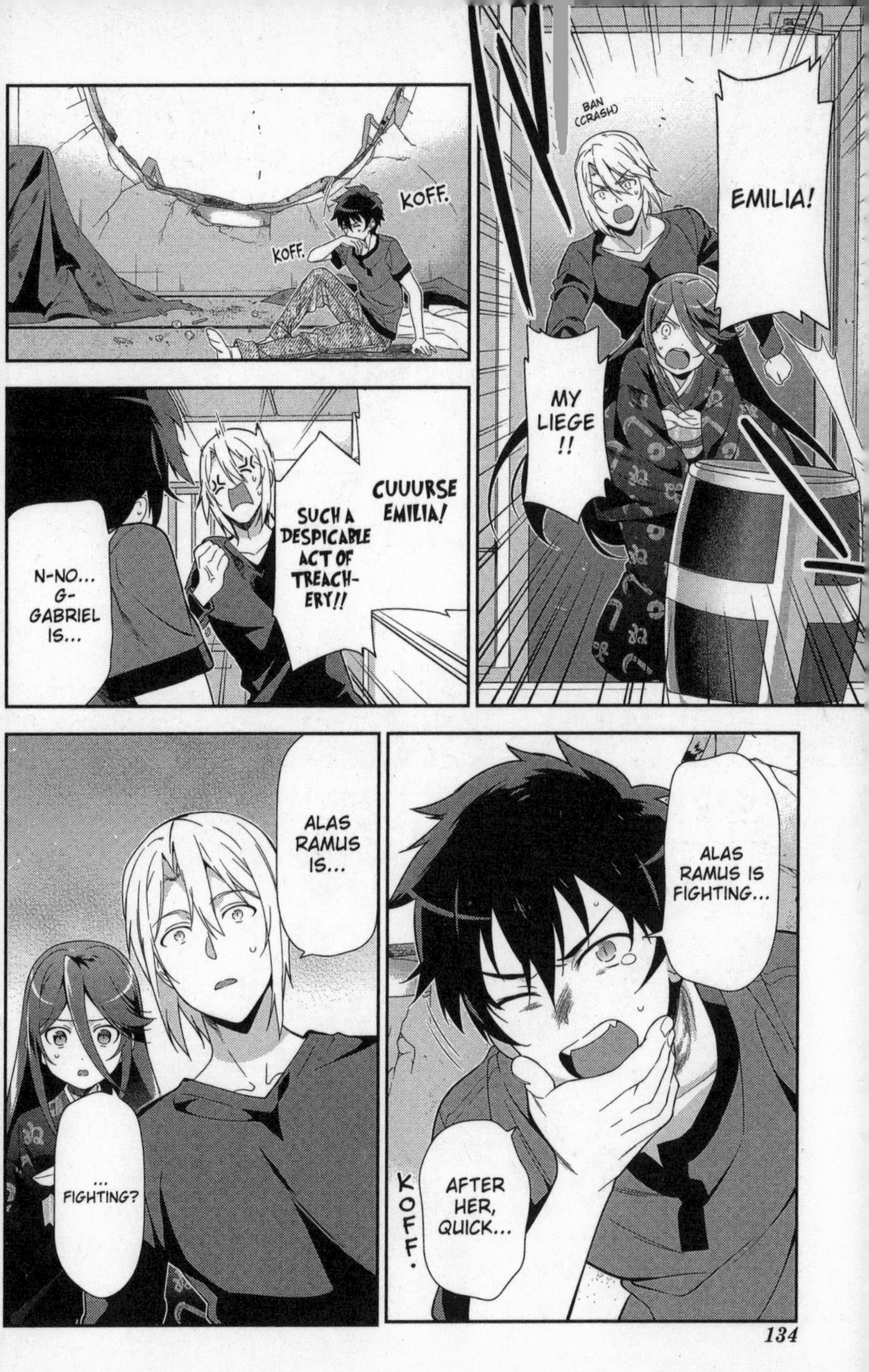
BAN (CRASH)
EMILIA!
MY LIEGE !!
KOFF.
KOFF.
CUUURSE EMILIA!
SUCH A DESPICABLE ACT OF TREACH-ERY!!
N-NO... G-GABRIEL IS...
ALAS RAMUS IS FIGHTING...
KOFF.
AFTER HER, QUICK...
ALAS RAMUS IS...
...FIGHTING?

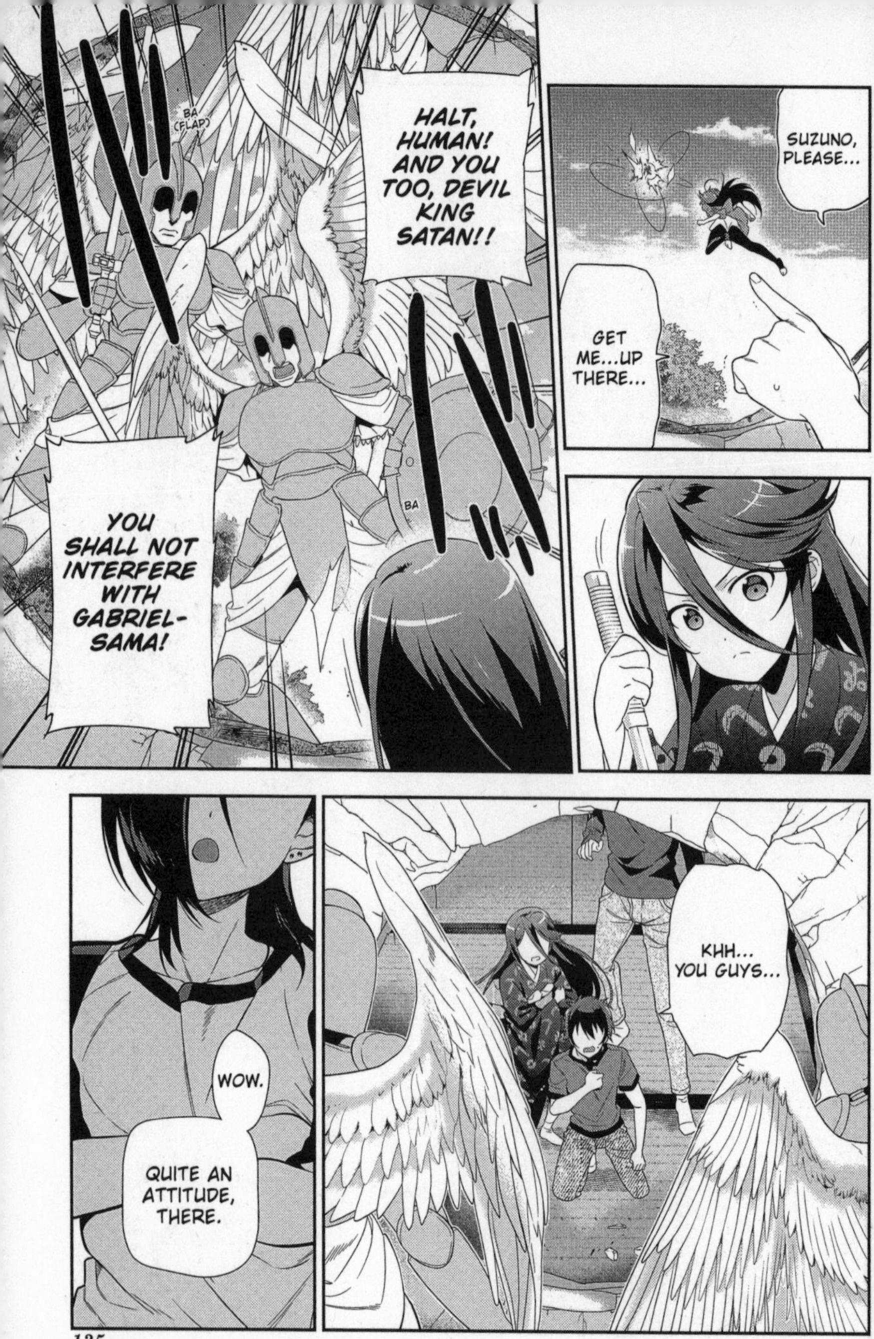
SUZUNO, PLEASE...
GET ME...UP THERE...
HALT, HUMAN! AND YOU TOO, DEVIL KING SATAN!!
BA (FLAP)
BA
YOU SHALL NOT INTERFERE WITH GABRIEL-SAMA!
KHH... YOU GUYS...
WOW.
QUITE AN ATTITUDE, THERE.

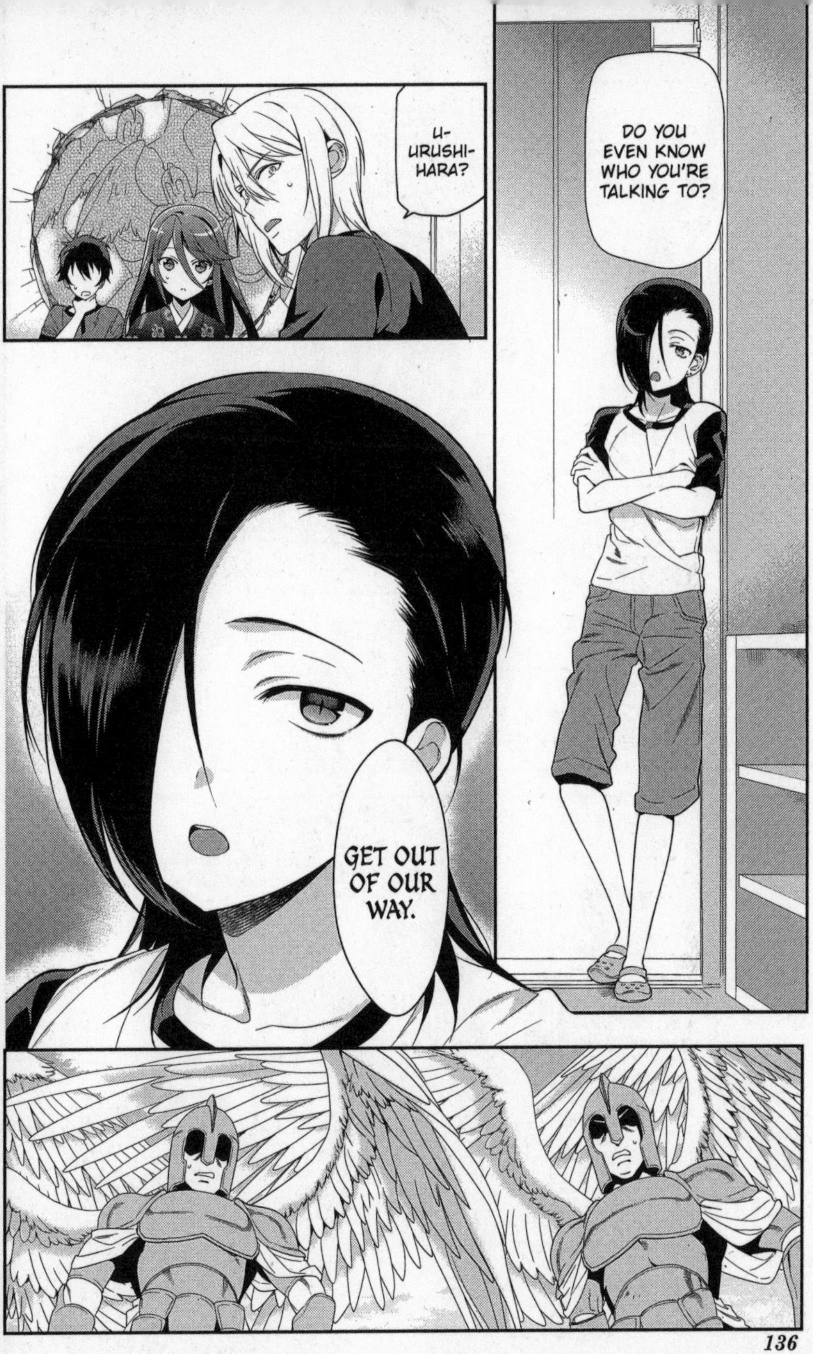
DO YOU EVEN KNOW WHO YOU'RE TALKING TO?
U-URUSHI-HARA?
GET OUT OF OUR WAY.

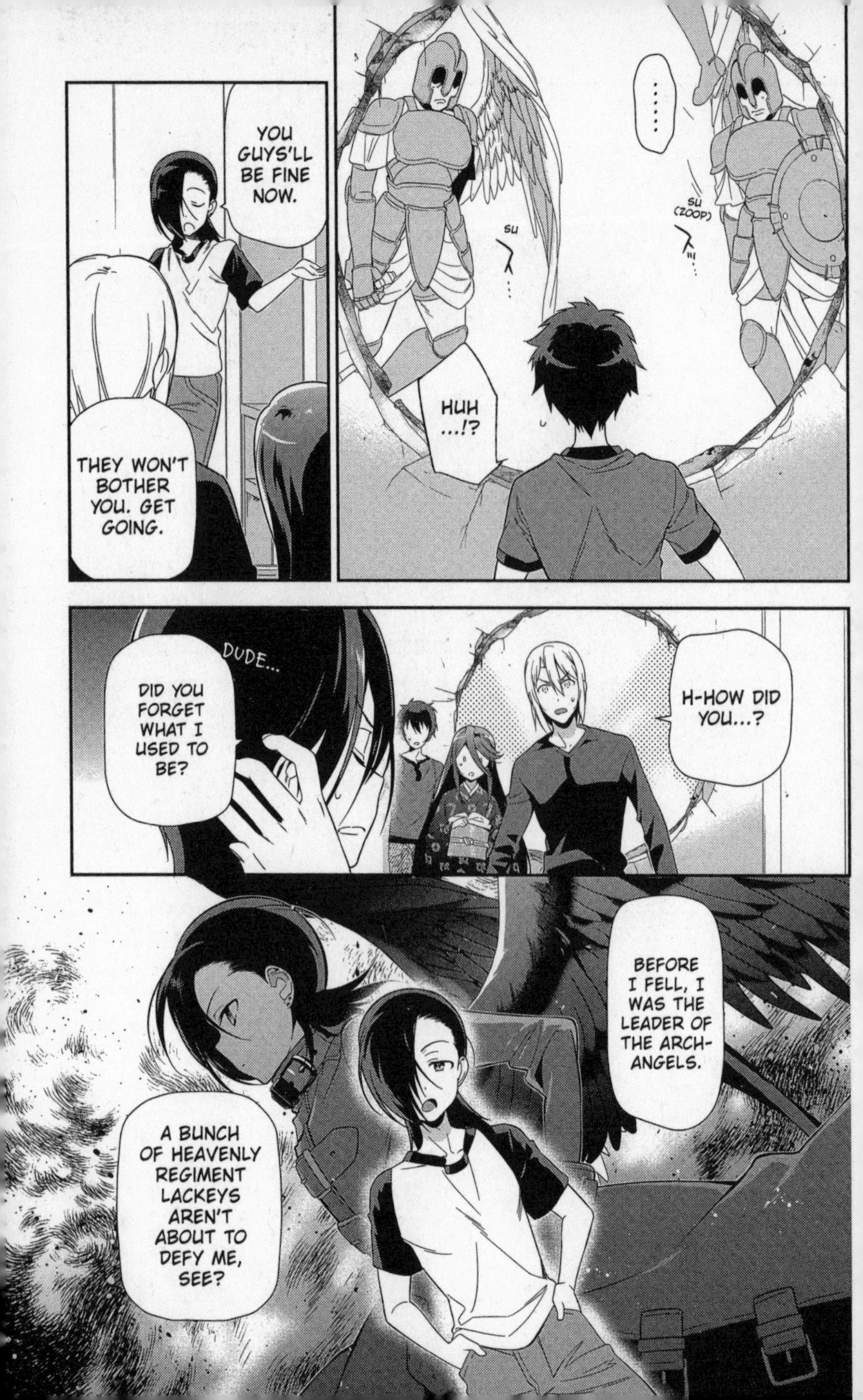
......
SU (ZOOP)
SU
HUH...!?
YOU GUYS'LL BE FINE NOW.
THEY WON'T BOTHER YOU. GET GOING.
H-HOW DID YOU...?
DUDE...
DID YOU FORGET WHAT I USED TO BE?
BEFORE I FELL, I WAS THE LEADER OF THE ARCH-ANGELS.
A BUNCH OF HEAVENLY REGIMENT LACKEYS AREN'T ABOUT TO DEFY ME, SEE?

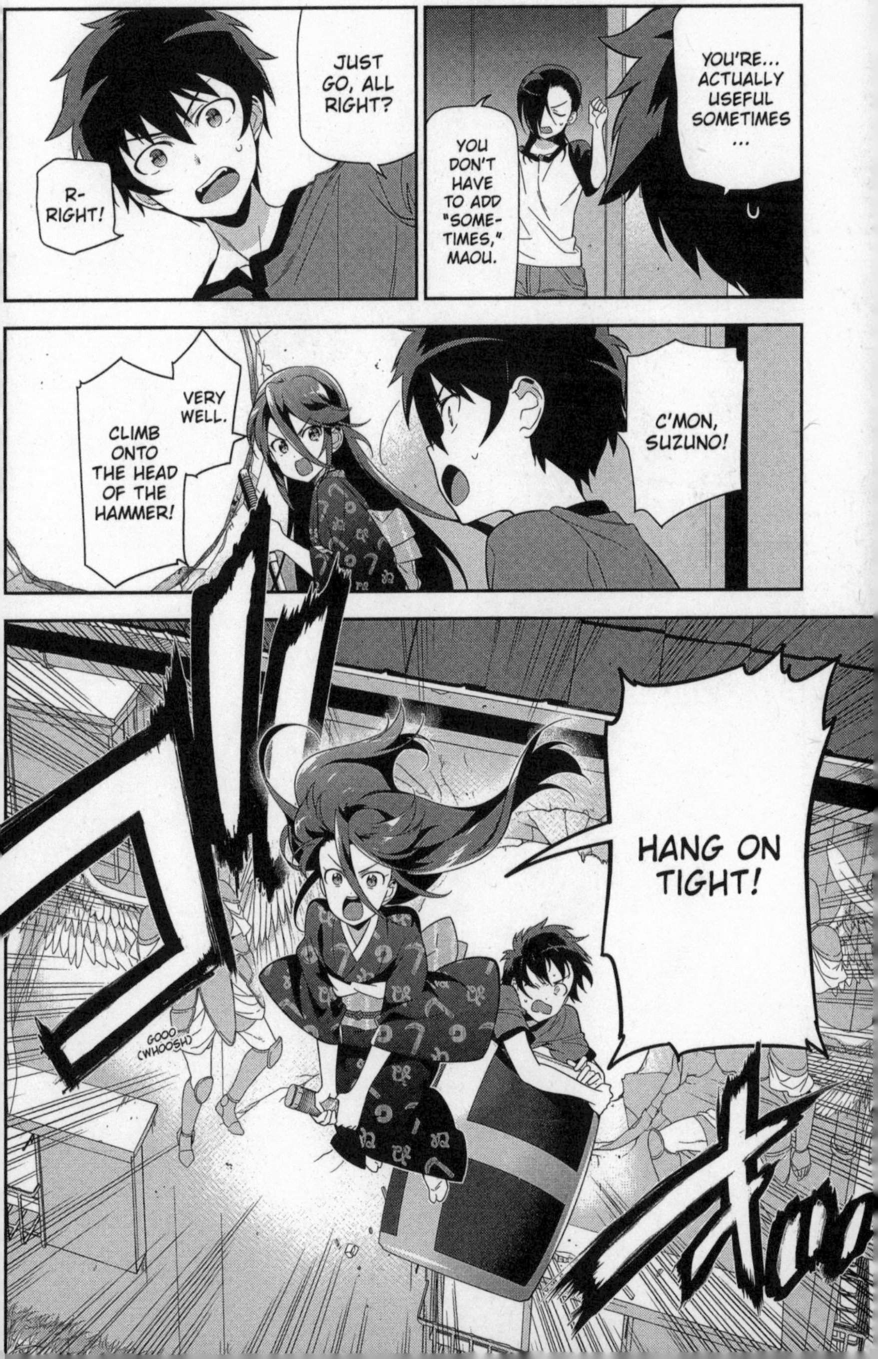
YOU'RE... ACTUALLY USEFUL SOMETIMES ...
YOU DON'T HAVE TO ADD "SOME-TIMES," MAOU.
JUST GO, ALL RIGHT?
R-RIGHT!
C'MON, SUZUNO!
VERY WELL.
CLIMB ONTO THE HEAD OF THE HAMMER!
HANG ON TIGHT!
GOOO (WHOOSH)

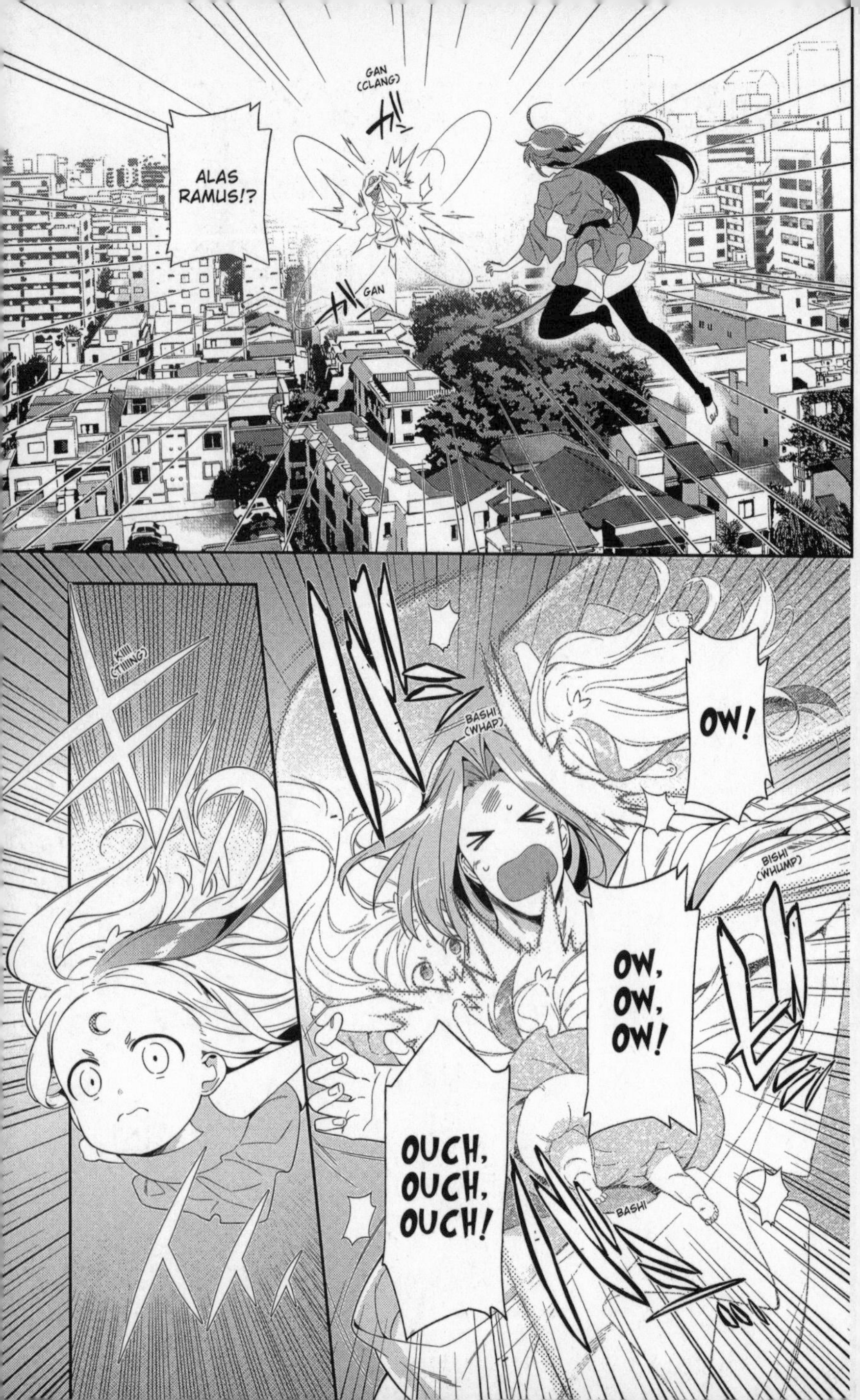
GAN (CLANG)
ALAS RAMUS!?
GAN
OW!
BASHI (WHAP)
BISHI (WHUMP)
OW, OW, OW!
KIIII (TIIIING)
OUCH, OUCH, OUCH!
BASHI

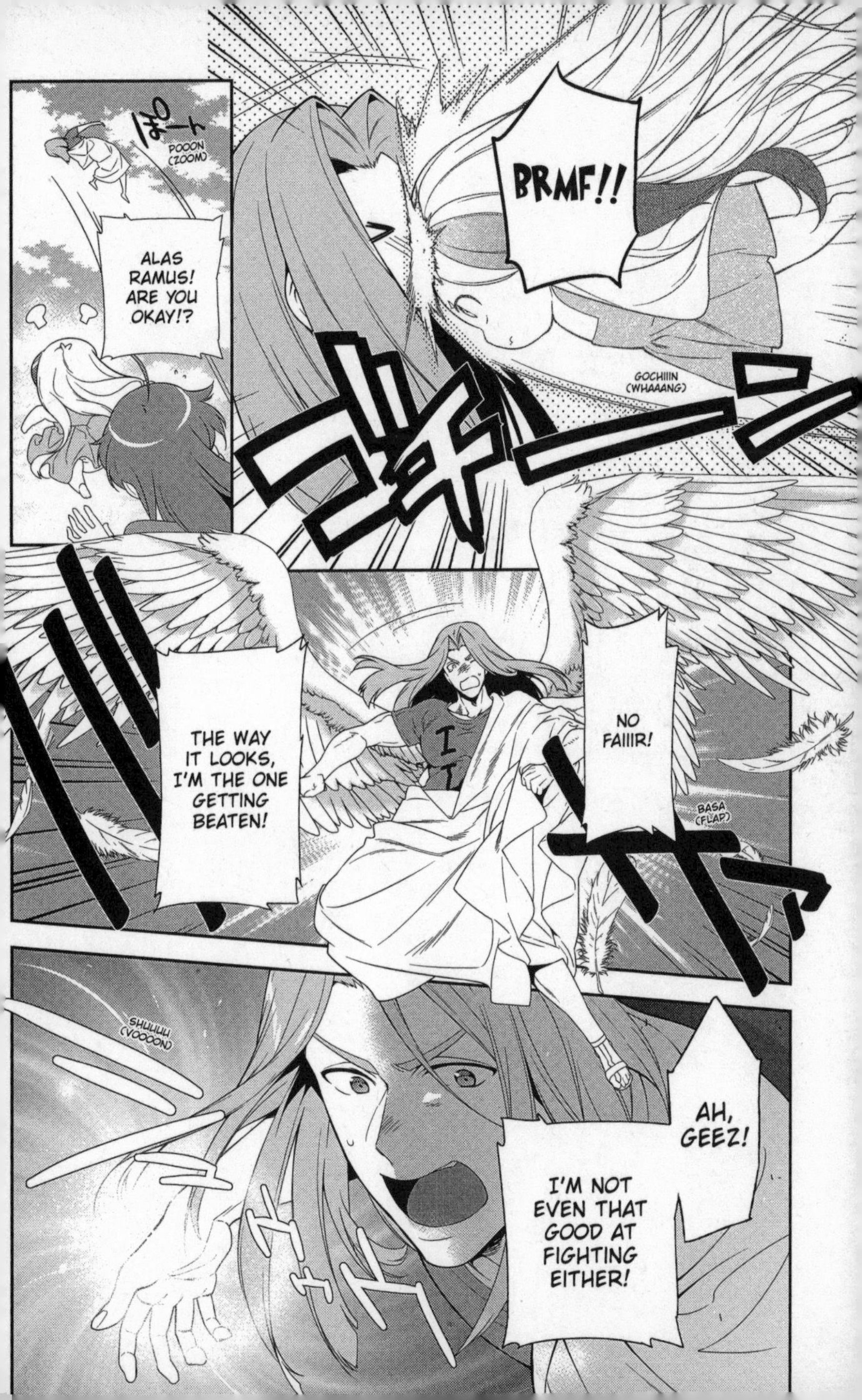
BRMF!!
GOCHIIIN (WHAAANG)
POOON (ZOOM)
ALAS RAMUS! ARE YOU OKAY!?
NO FAIIIR!
BASA (FLAP)
THE WAY IT LOOKS, I'M THE ONE GETTING BEATEN!
AH, GEEZ!
I'M NOT EVEN THAT GOOD AT FIGHTING EITHER!
SHUUUU (VOOOON)

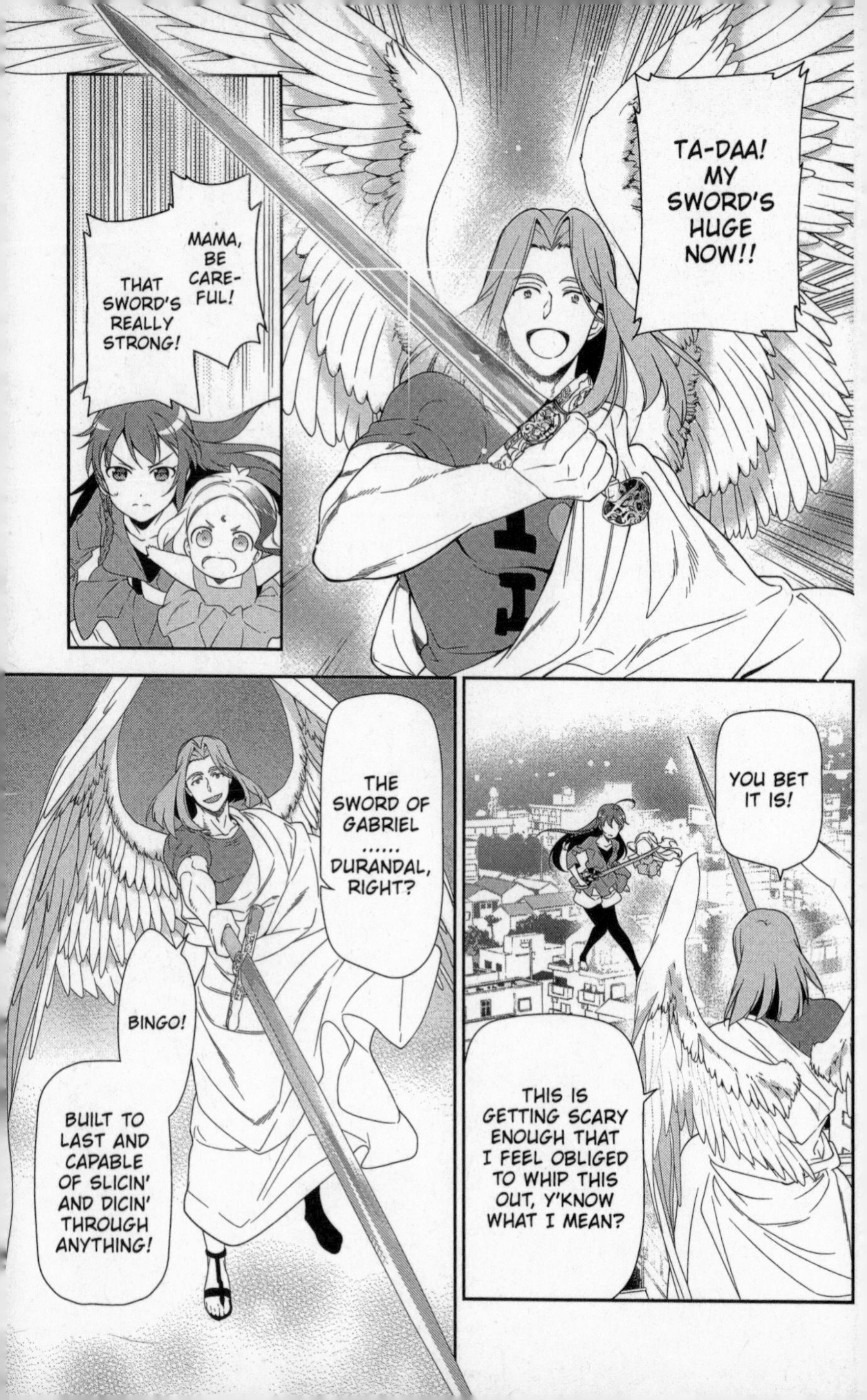

TA-DAA! MY SWORD'S HUGE NOW!!
MAMA, BE CAREFUL!
THAT SWORD'S REALLY STRONG!
YOU BET IT IS!
THIS IS GETTING SCARY ENOUGH THAT I FEEL OBLIGED TO WHIP THIS OUT, Y'KNOW WHAT I MEAN?
THE SWORD OF GABRIEL ...... DURANDAL, RIGHT?
BINGO!
BUILT TO LAST AND CAPABLE OF SLICIN' AND DICIN' THROUGH ANYTHING!

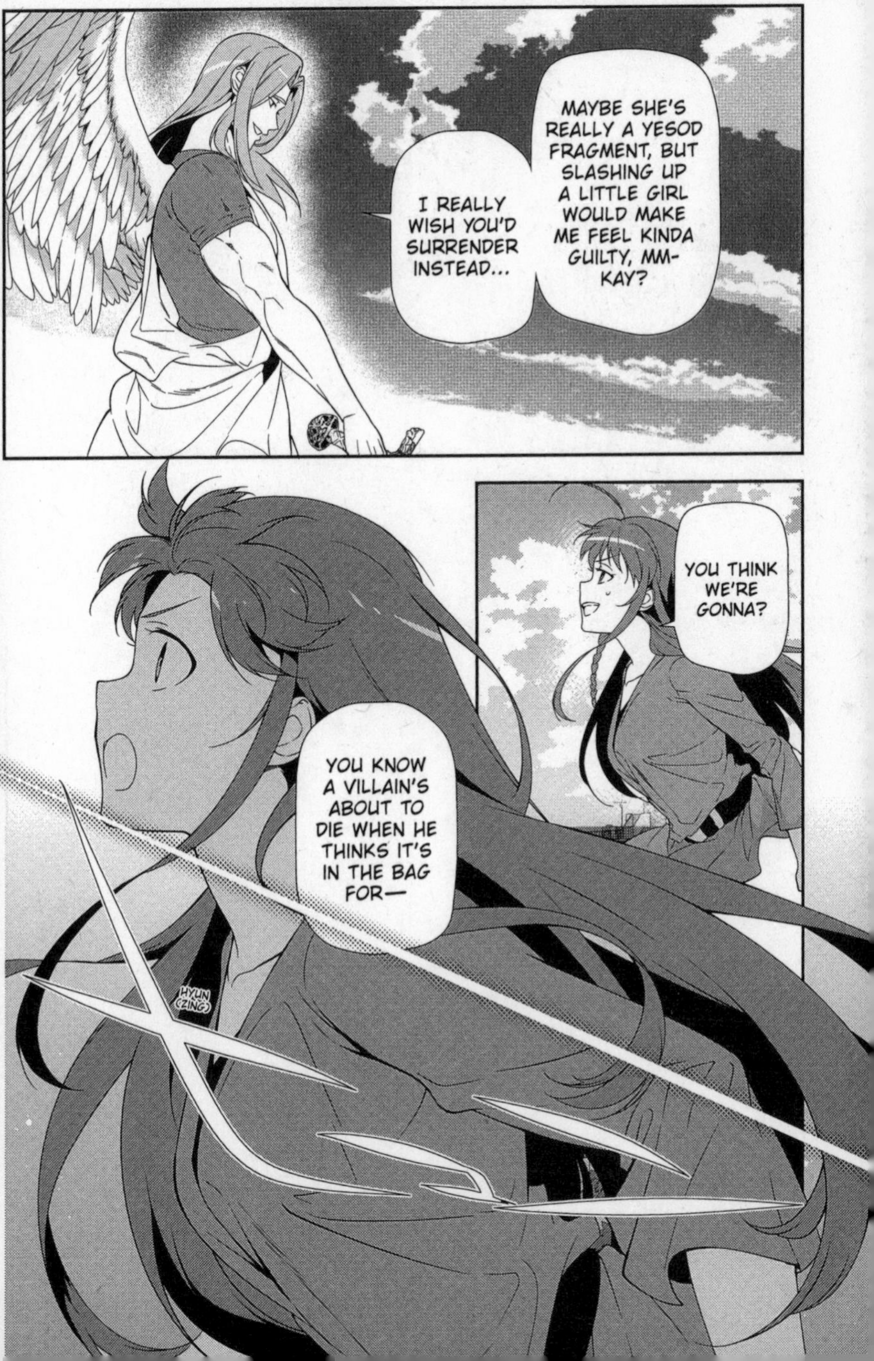
MAYBE SHE'S REALLY A YESOD FRAGMENT, BUT SLASHING UP A LITTLE GIRL WOULD MAKE ME FEEL KINDA GUILTY, MM-KAY?
I REALLY WISH YOU'D SURRENDER INSTEAD...
YOU THINK WE'RE GONNA?
YOU KNOW A VILLAIN'S ABOUT TO DIE WHEN HE THINKS IT'S IN THE BAG FOR—
HYUN (ZING)

!!
PIKI (CRACK)
FU (VANISH)
MAMA!!
FUWA (SWOOP)
AS LONG AS I GET THE YESOD FRAGMENT HOUSED INSIDE, EVERY-THING'S HUNKY-DORY!
PON (TAP)
SO I REALLY DON'T CARE WHAT HAPPENS TO THAT SWORD, Y'KNOW.
OW! I CUT MY SHOUL-DER!

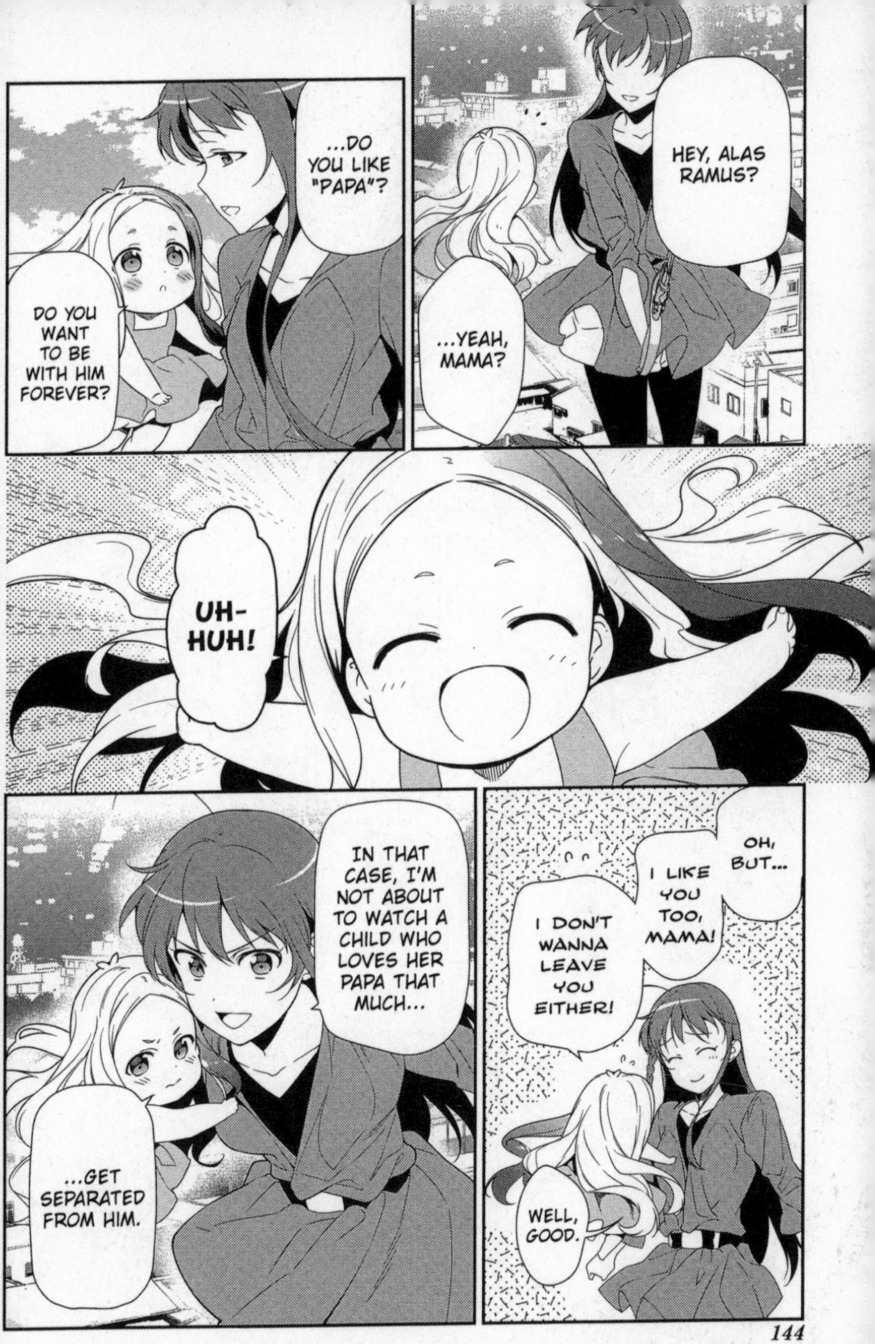
HEY, ALAS RAMUS?
...YEAH, MAMA?
...DO YOU LIKE "PAPA"?
DO YOU WANT TO BE WITH HIM FOREVER?
UH-HUH!
OH, BUT...
I LIKE YOU TOO, MAMA!
I DON'T WANNA LEAVE YOU EITHER!
WELL, GOOD.
IN THAT CASE, I'M NOT ABOUT TO WATCH A CHILD WHO LOVES HER PAPA THAT MUCH...
...GET SEPARATED FROM HIM.

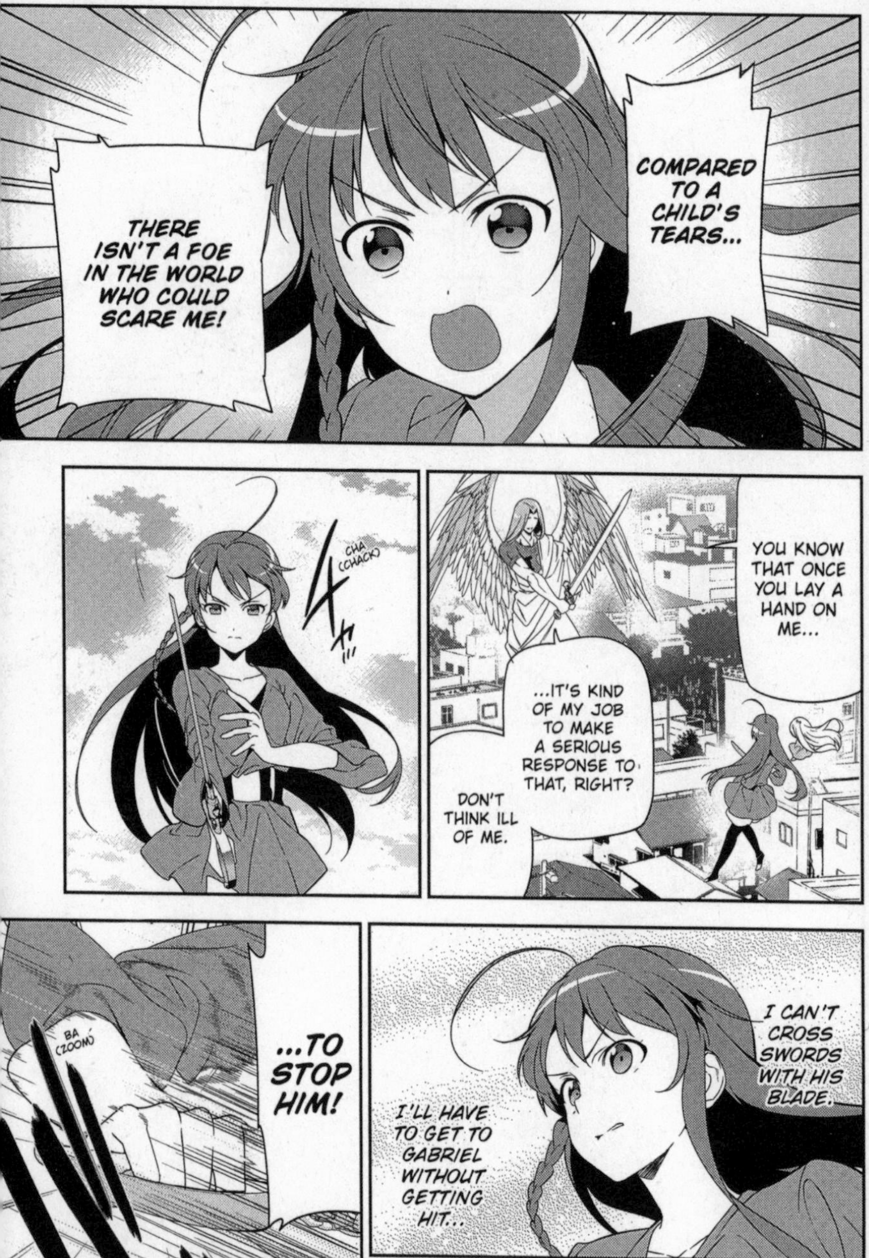
COMPARED TO A CHILD'S TEARS...
THERE ISN'T A FOE IN THE WORLD WHO COULD SCARE ME!
YOU KNOW THAT ONCE YOU LAY A HAND ON ME...
...IT'S KIND OF MY JOB TO MAKE A SERIOUS RESPONSE TO THAT, RIGHT?
DON'T THINK ILL OF ME.
CHA (CHACK)
I CAN'T CROSS SWORDS WITH HIS BLADE.
I'LL HAVE TO GET TO GABRIEL WITHOUT GETTING HIT...
...TO STOP HIM!
BA (ZOOM)

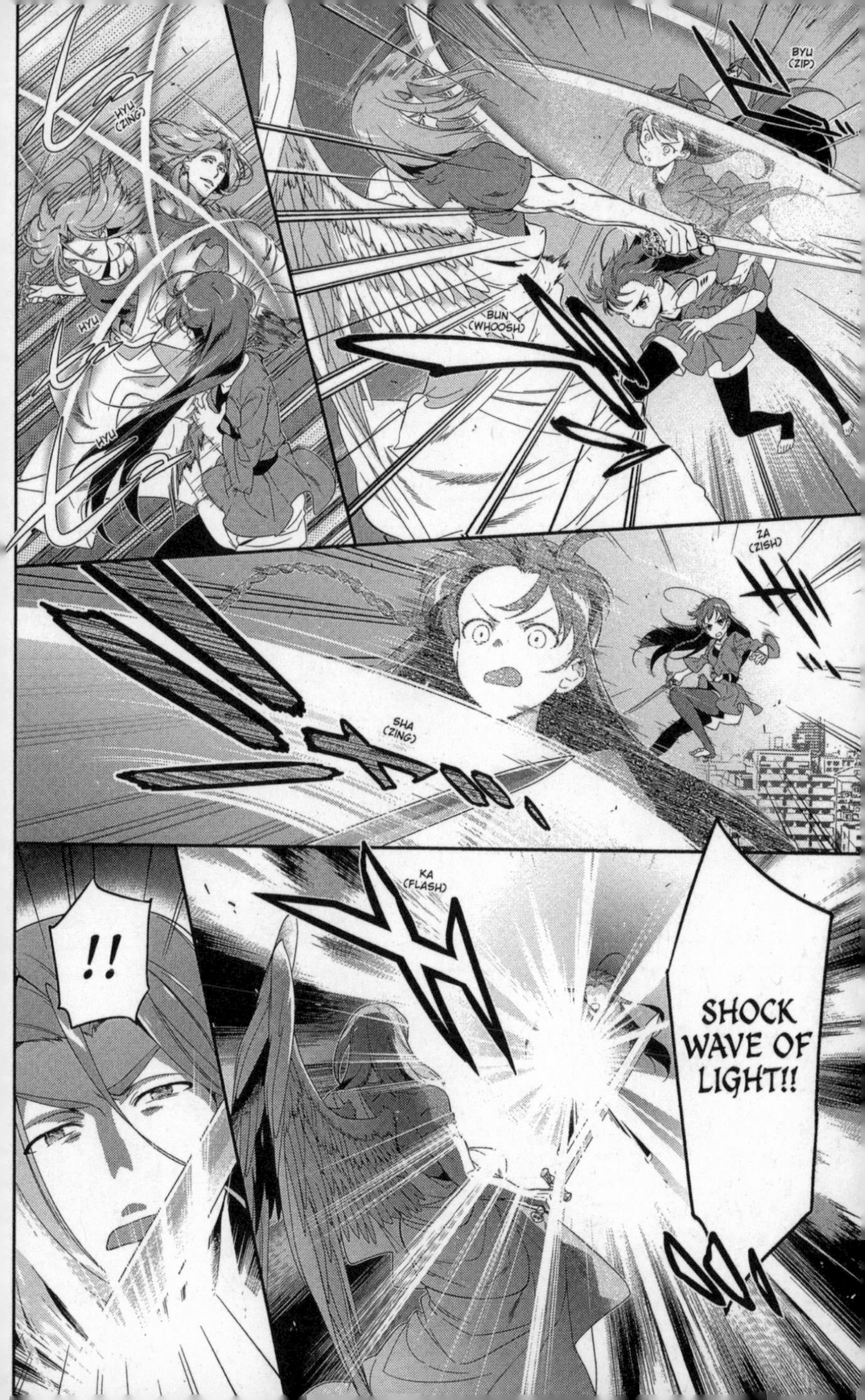
BYU (ZIP)
BUN (WHOOSH)
HYU (ZING)
HYU
HYU
ZA (ZISH)
SHA (ZING)
SHOCK WAVE OF LIGHT!!
KA (FLASH)
!!

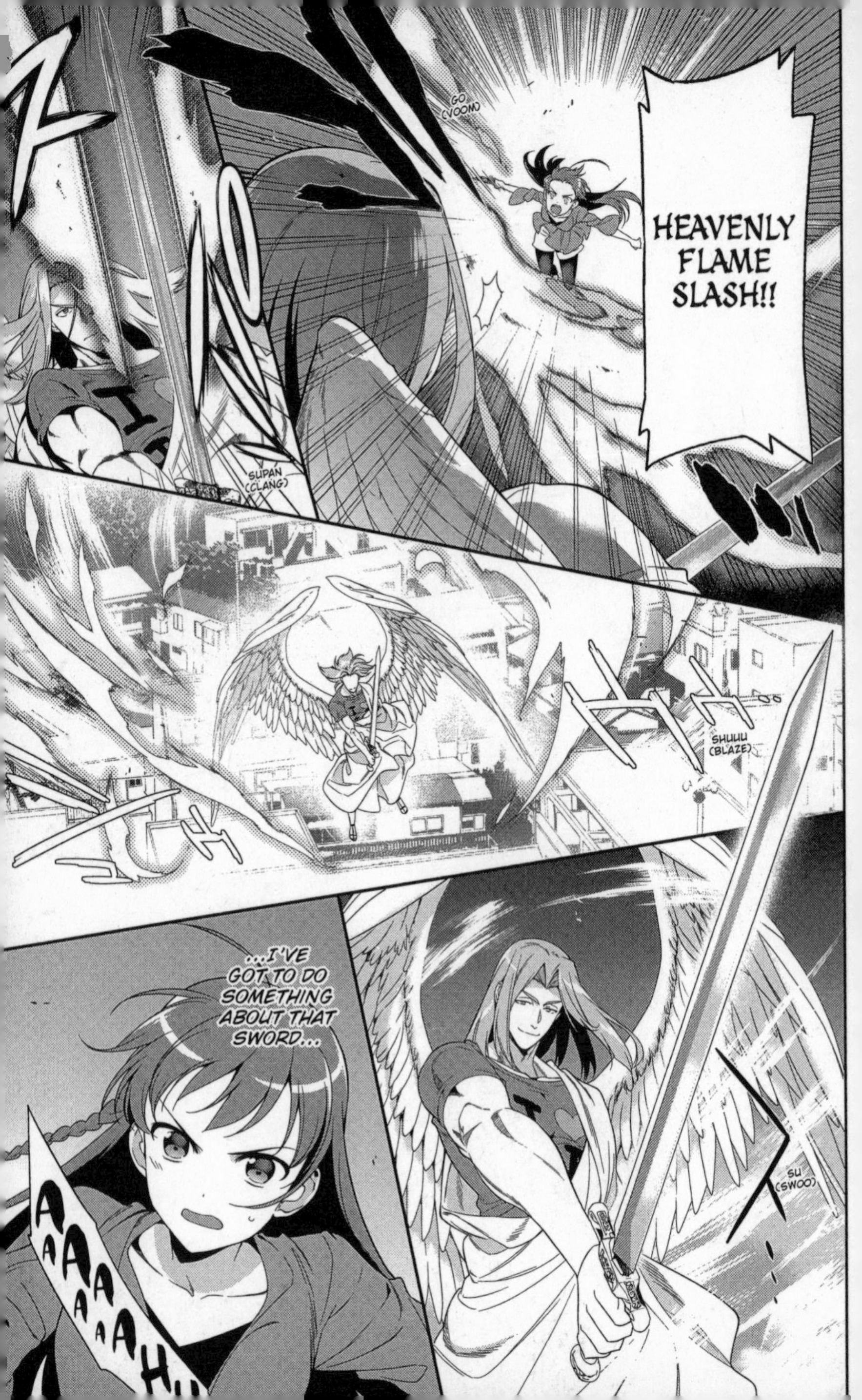
HEAVENLY FLAME SLASH!!
GO (VOOM)
SUPAN (CLANG)
SHUUU (BLAZE)
SU (SWOO)
...I'VE GOT TO DO SOMETHING ABOUT THAT SWORD...
AAAAAAAAAH!!

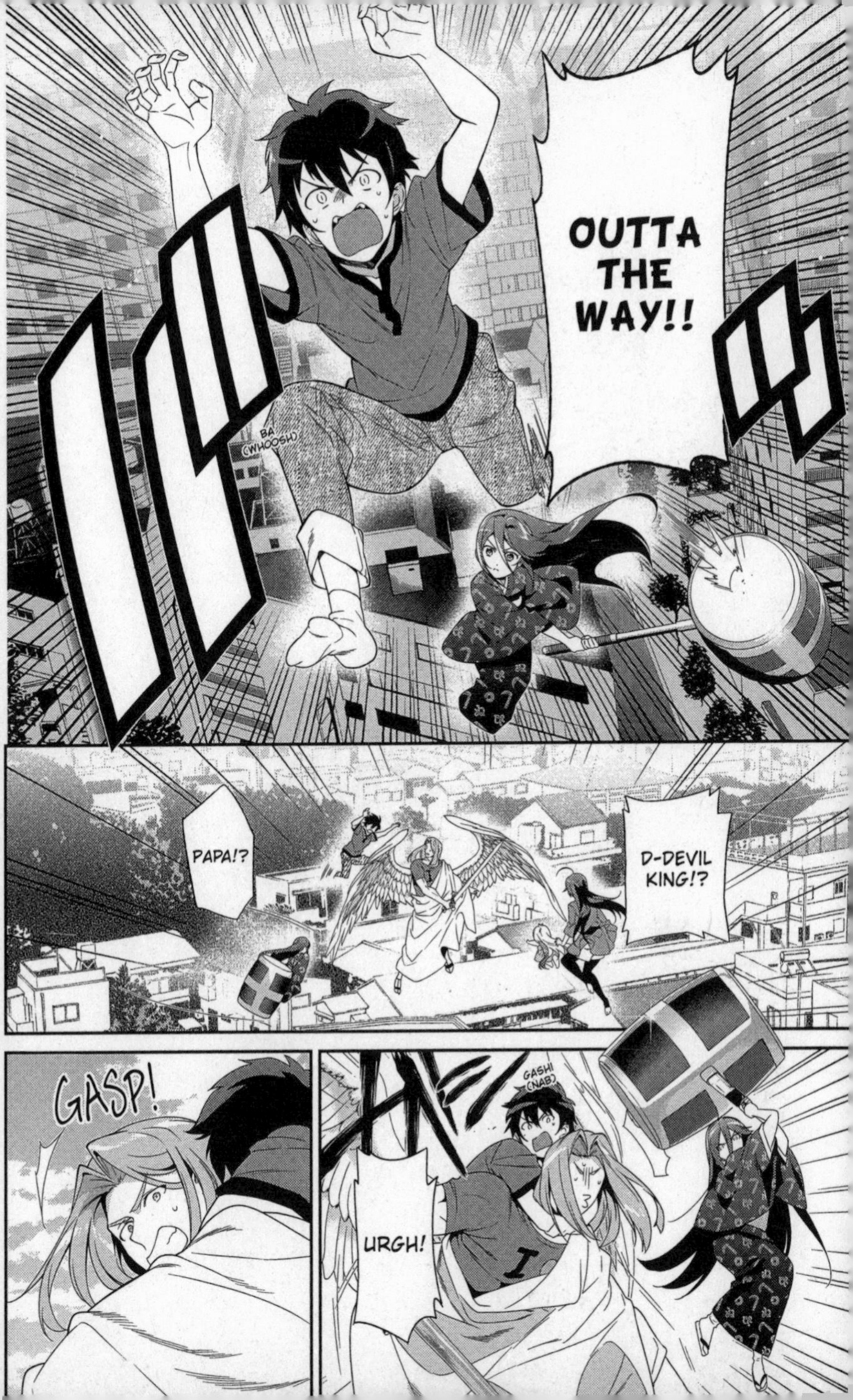
OUTTA THE WAY!!
BA (WHOOSH)
D-DEVIL KING!?
PAPA!?
GASHI (NAB)
URGH!
GASP!

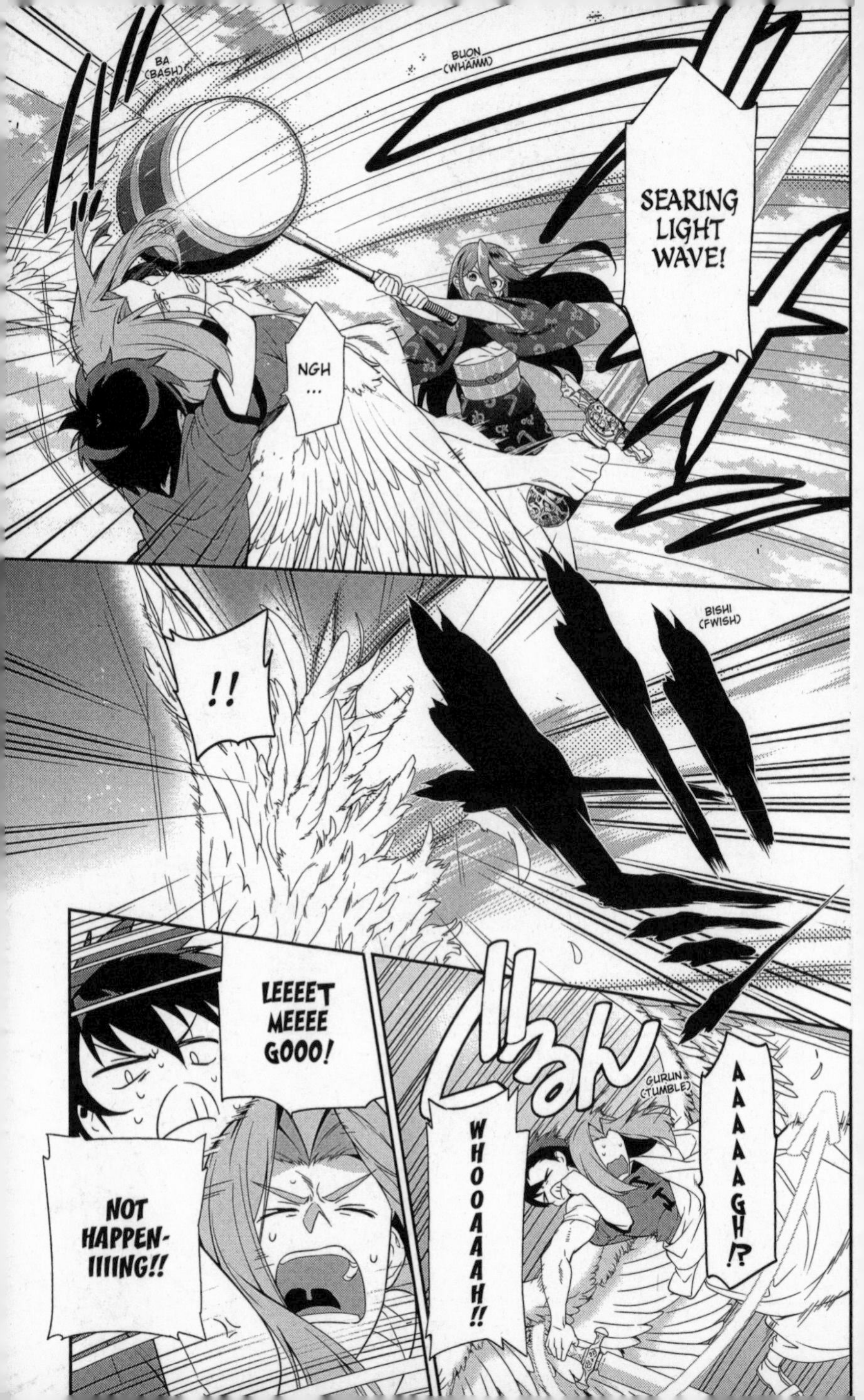
SEARING LIGHT WAVE!
BUON (WHAMM)
BA (BASH)
NGH ...
BISHI (FWISH)
!!
AAAAAGH!?
GURUN (TUMBLE)
WHOOOAAAAH!!
LEEEET MEEEE GOOO!
NOT HAPPEN-IIIING!!

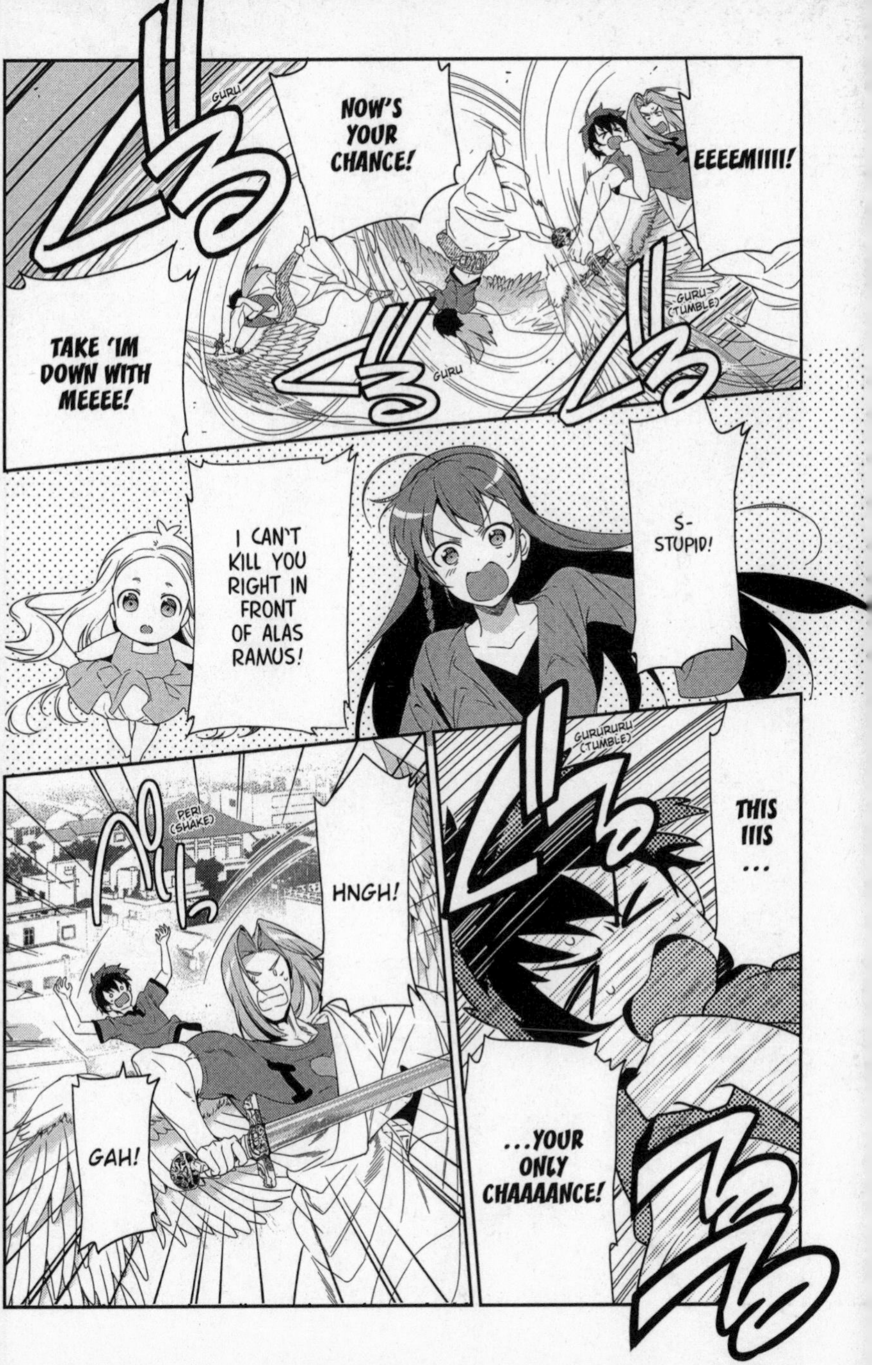
EEEEMIIII!
GURU (TUMBLE)
NOW'S YOUR CHANCE!
GURU
GURU
TAKE 'IM DOWN WITH MEEEE!
S-STUPID!
I CAN'T KILL YOU RIGHT IN FRONT OF ALAS RAMUS!
GURURURU (TUMBLE)
THIS IIIS...
...YOUR ONLY CHAAAANCE!
PERI (SHAKE)
HNGH!
GAH!

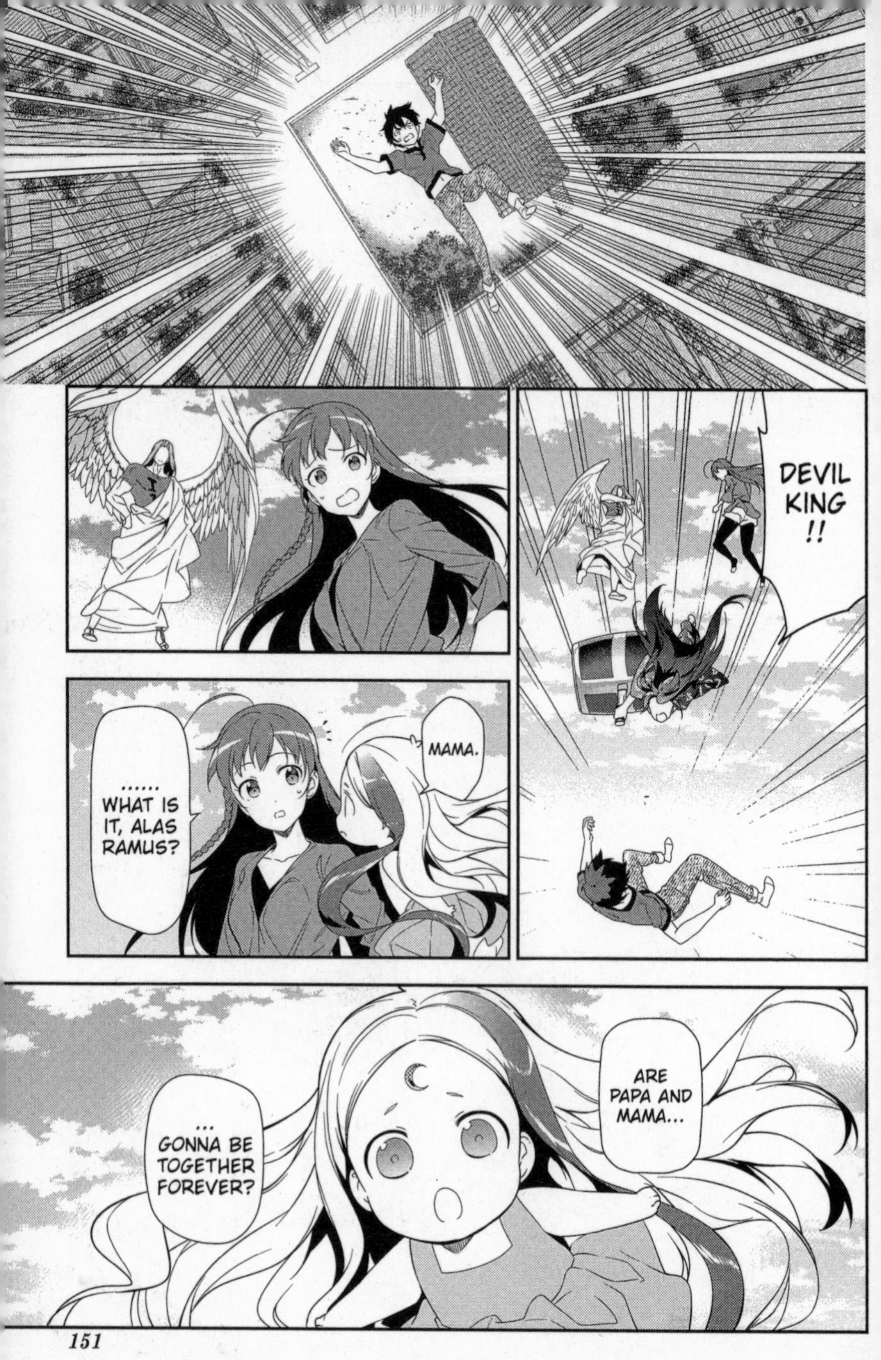
DEVIL KING !!
MAMA.
...... WHAT IS IT, ALAS RAMUS?
ARE PAPA AND MAMA...
... GONNA BE TOGETHER FOREVER?

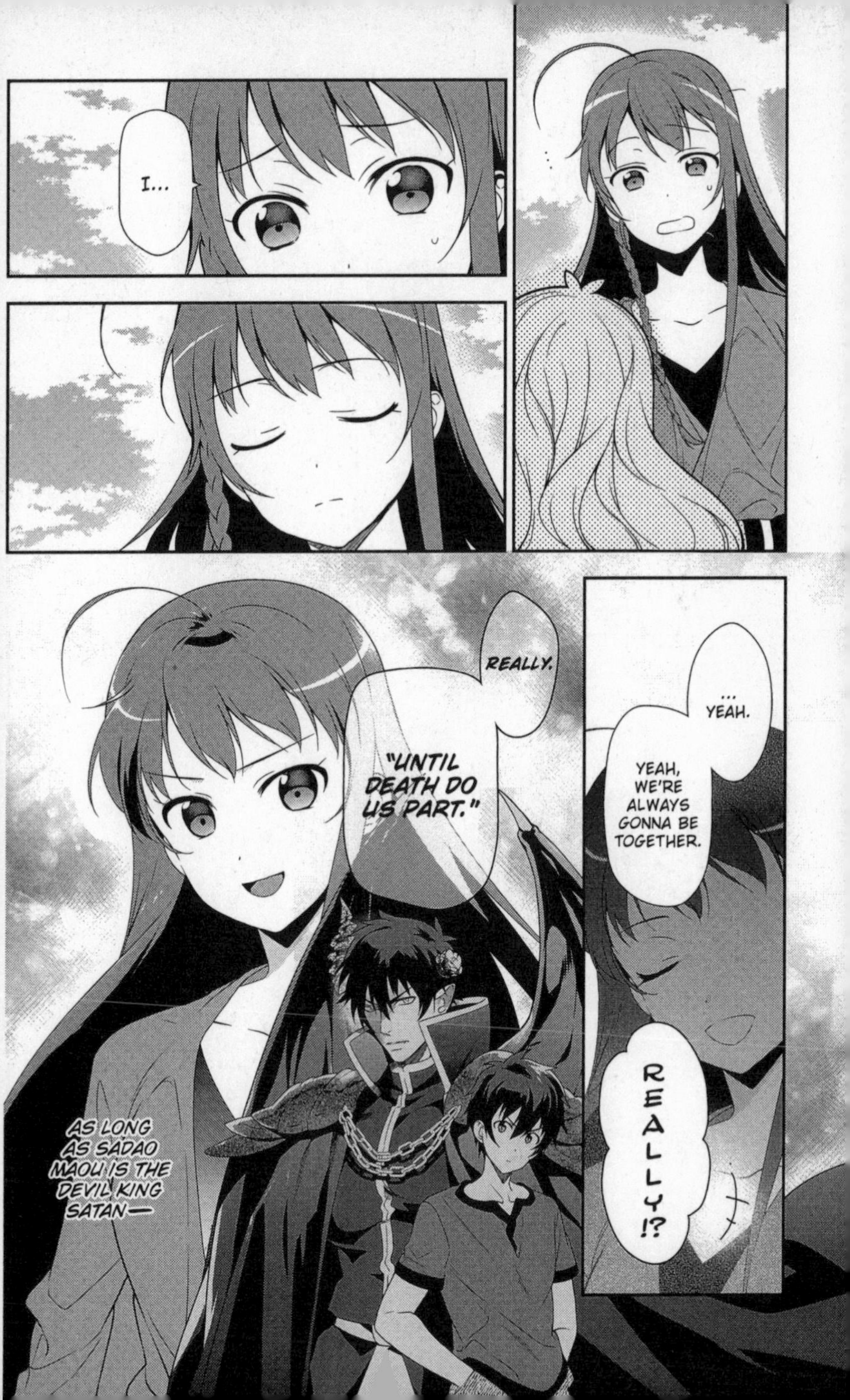
I...
...
YEAH.
YEAH, WE'RE ALWAYS GONNA BE TOGETHER.
REALLY!?
REALLY.
"UNTIL DEATH DO US PART."
AS LONG AS SADAO MAOU IS THE DEVIL KING SATAN—

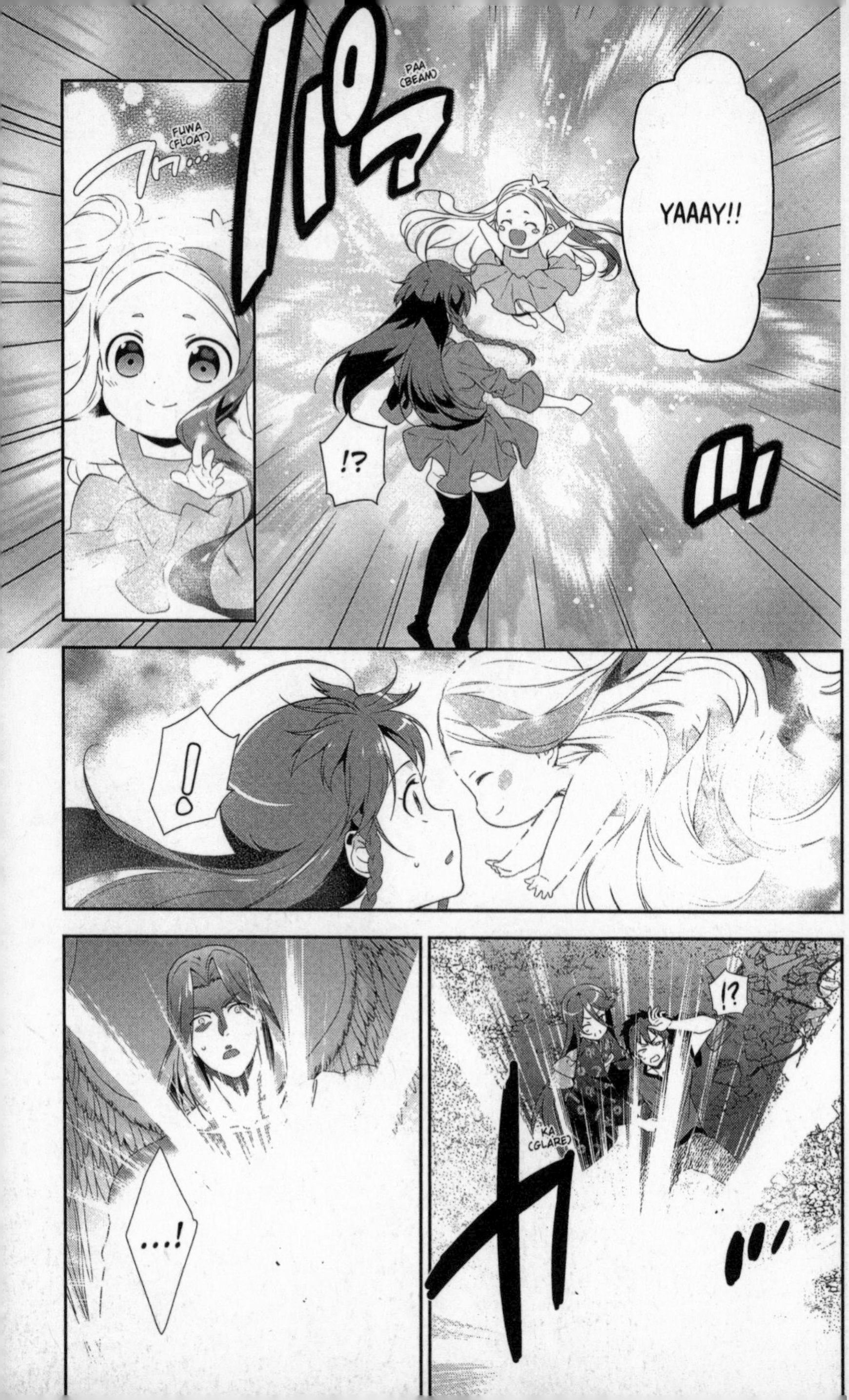
YAAAY!!
PAA (BEAM)
!?
FUWA (FLOAT)
!
!?
KA (GLARE)
...!

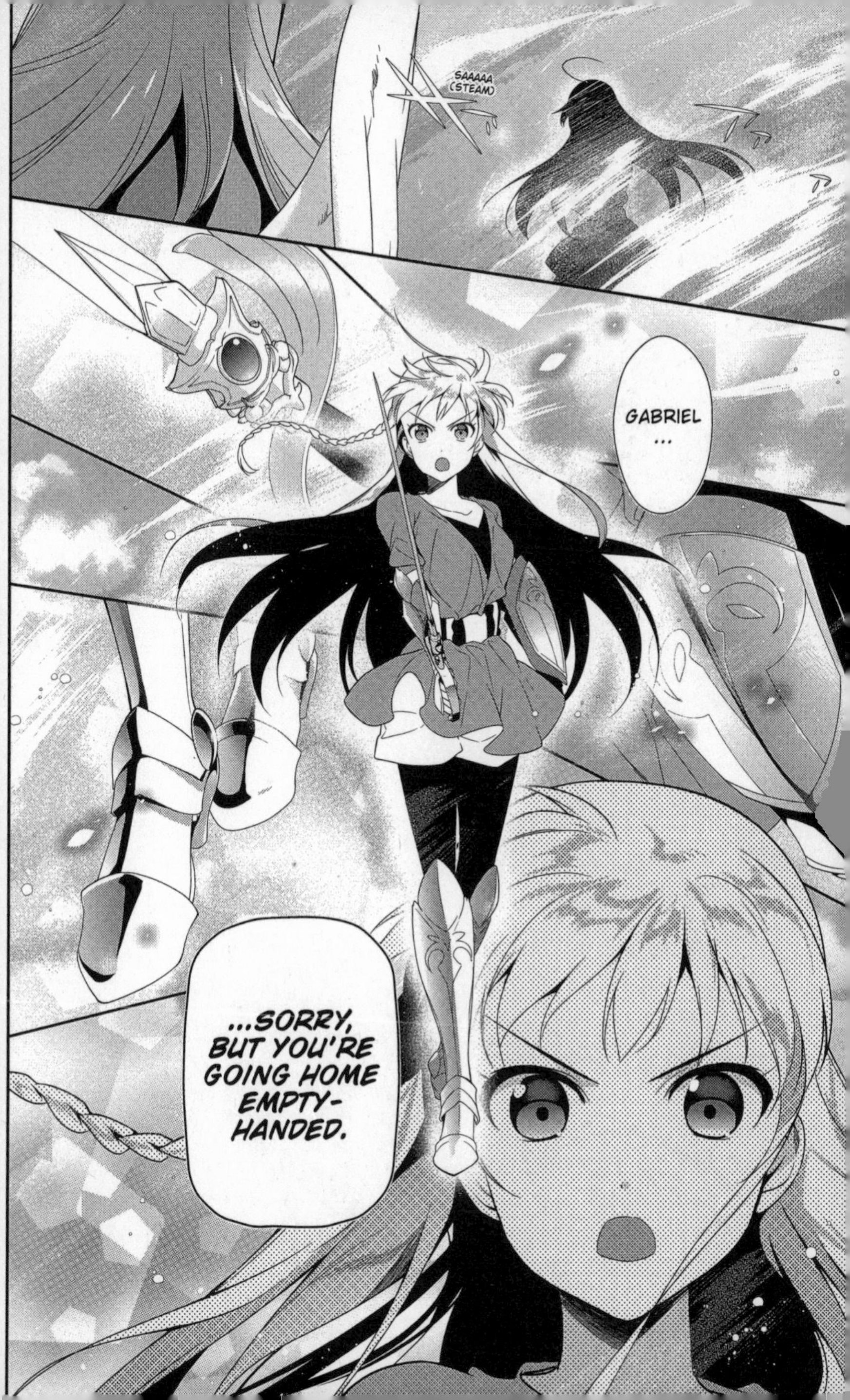
SAAAAA (STEAM)
GABRIEL ...
...SORRY, BUT YOU'RE GOING HOME EMPTY-HANDED.

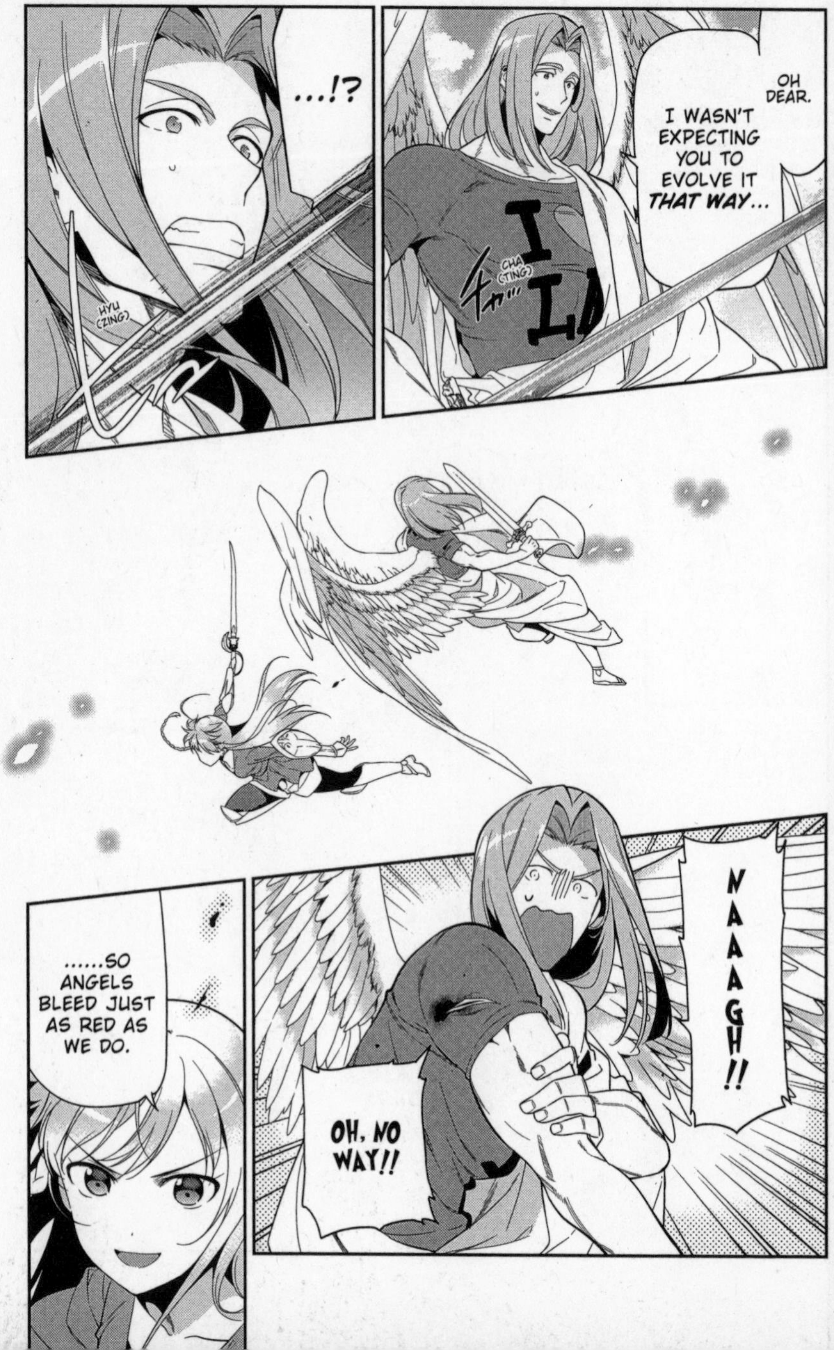
OH DEAR.
I WASN'T EXPECTING YOU TO EVOLVE IT THAT WAY...
CHA (TING)
...!?
HYU (ZING)
NAAAAGH!!
OH, NO WAY!!
......SO ANGELS BLEED JUST AS RED AS WE DO.

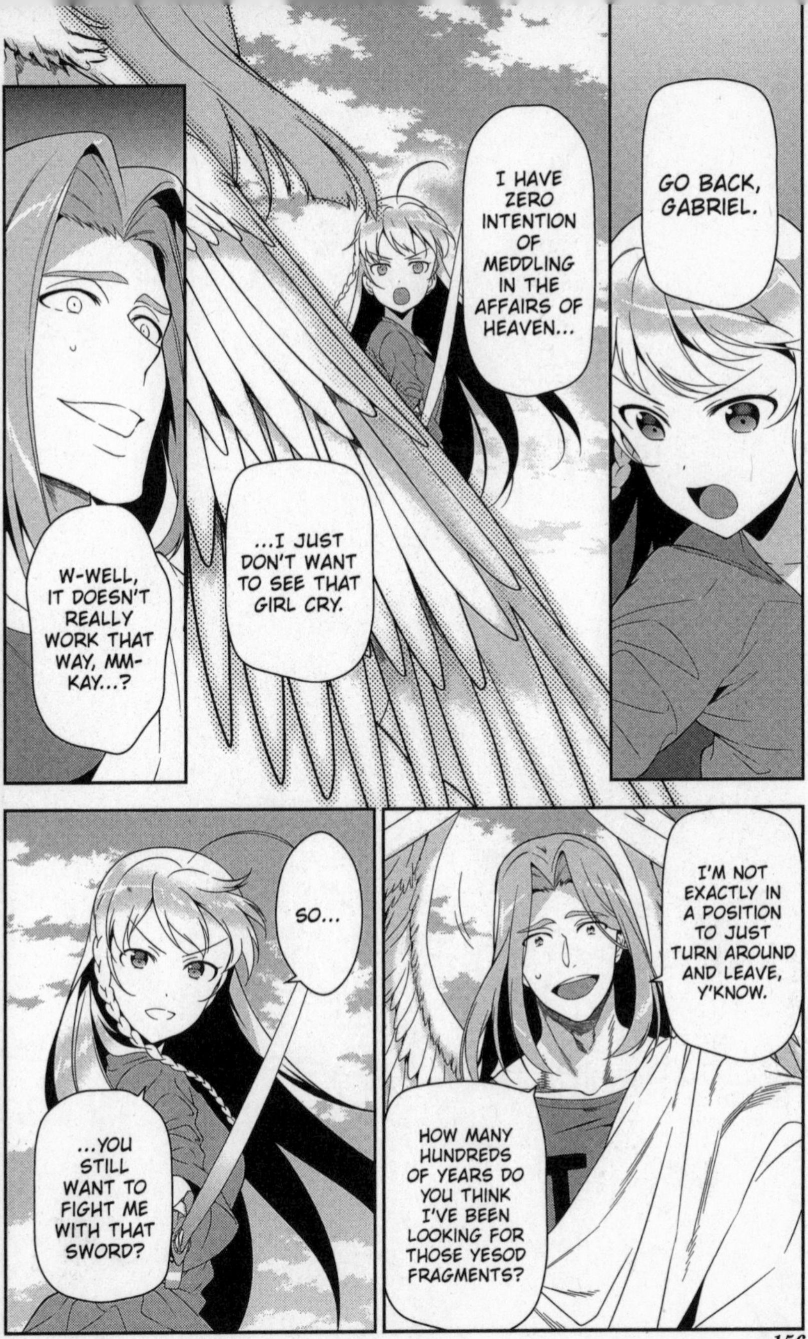
GO BACK, GABRIEL.
I HAVE ZERO INTENTION OF MEDDLING IN THE AFFAIRS OF HEAVEN...
...I JUST DON'T WANT TO SEE THAT GIRL CRY.
W-WELL, IT DOESN'T REALLY WORK THAT WAY, MM-KAY...?
I'M NOT EXACTLY IN A POSITION TO JUST TURN AROUND AND LEAVE, Y'KNOW.
HOW MANY HUNDREDS OF YEARS DO YOU THINK I'VE BEEN LOOKING FOR THOSE YESOD FRAGMENTS?
SO...
...YOU STILL WANT TO FIGHT ME WITH THAT SWORD?

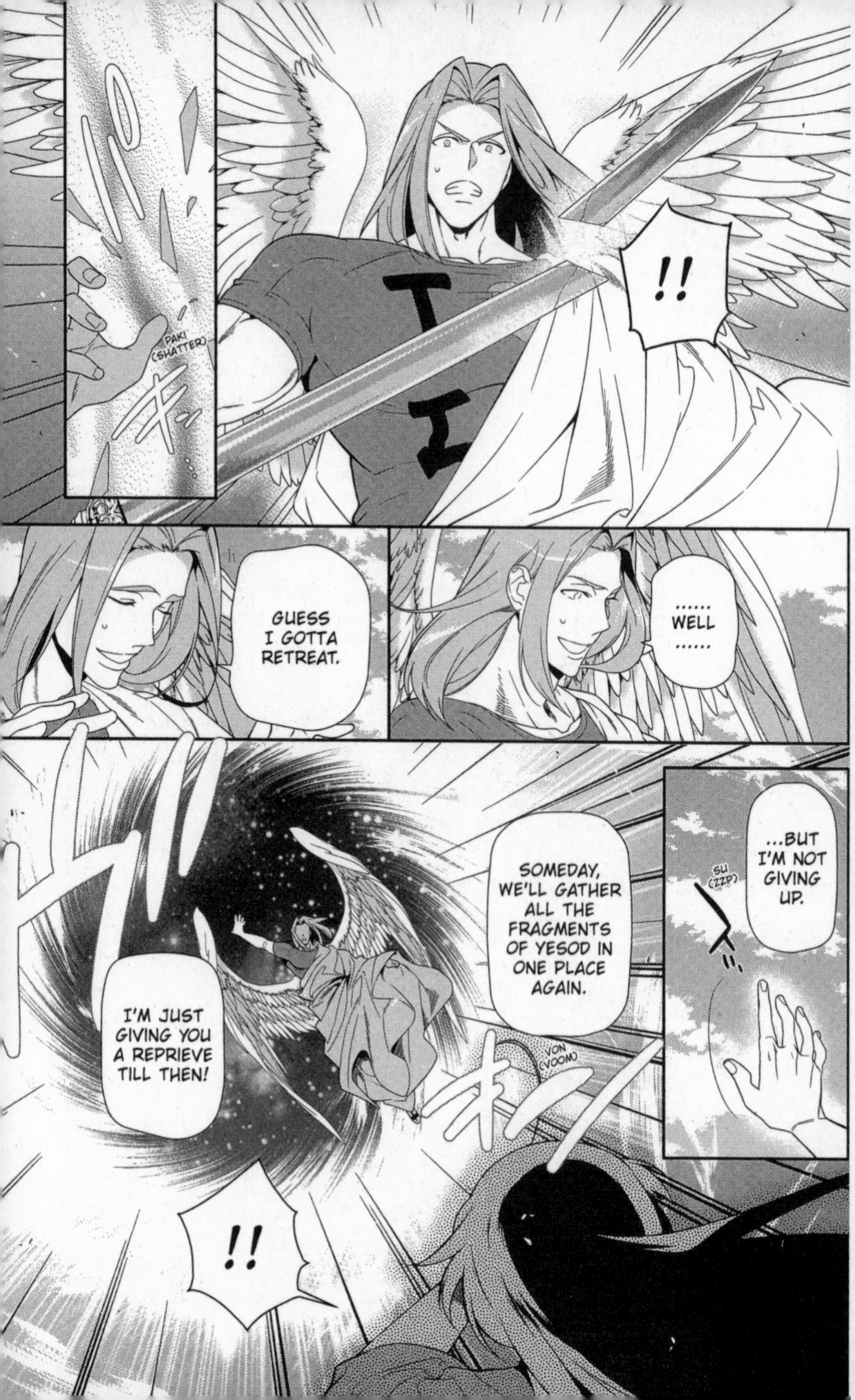
!!
PAKI (SHATTER)
...... WELL ......
GUESS I GOTTA RETREAT.
...BUT I'M NOT GIVING UP.
SU (ZZP)
SOMEDAY, WE'LL GATHER ALL THE FRAGMENTS OF YESOD IN ONE PLACE AGAIN.
VON (VOOM)
I'M JUST GIVING YOU A REPRIEVE TILL THEN!
!!

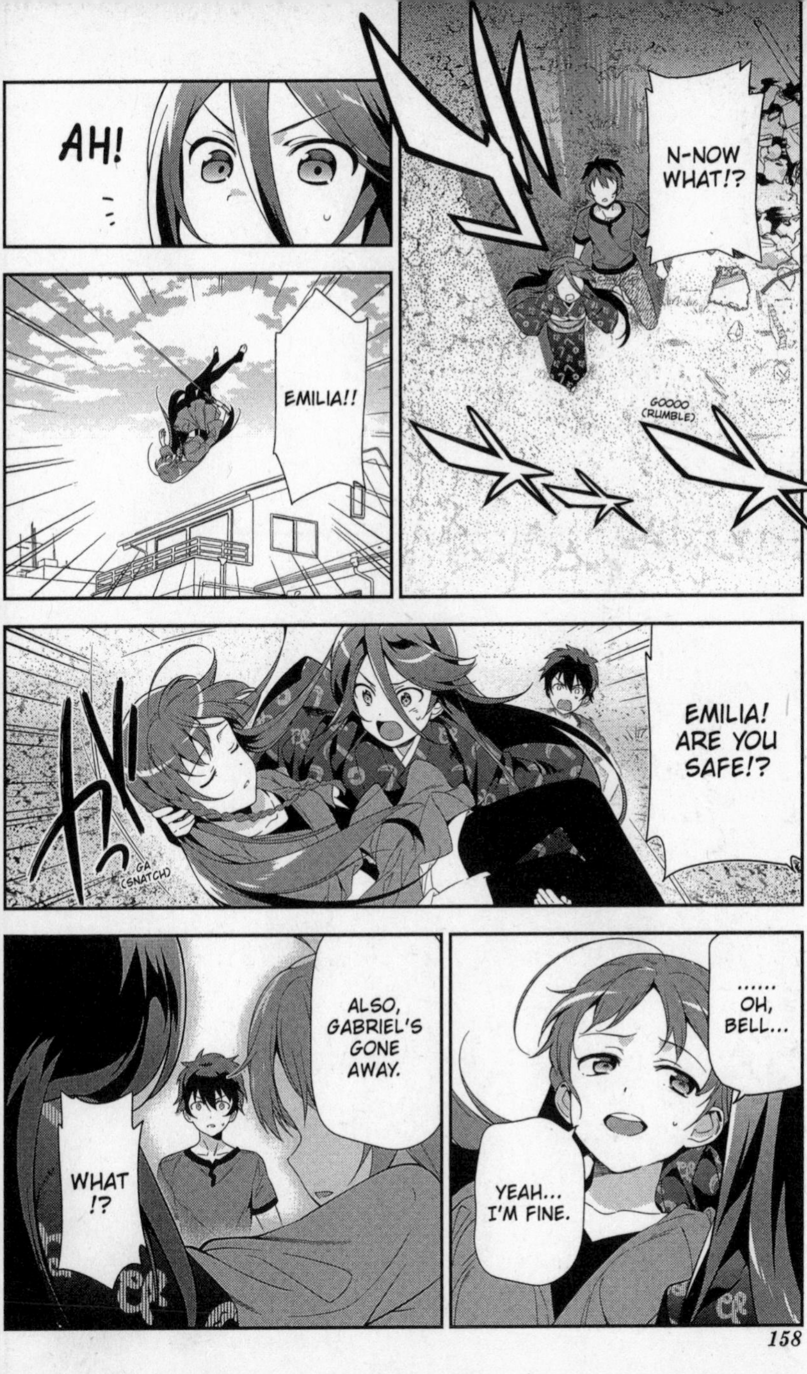
N-NOW WHAT!?
GOOOO (RUMBLE)
AH!
EMILIA!!
EMILIA! ARE YOU SAFE!?
GA (SNATCH)
...... OH, BELL...
YEAH... I'M FINE.
ALSO, GABRIEL'S GONE AWAY.
WHAT !?

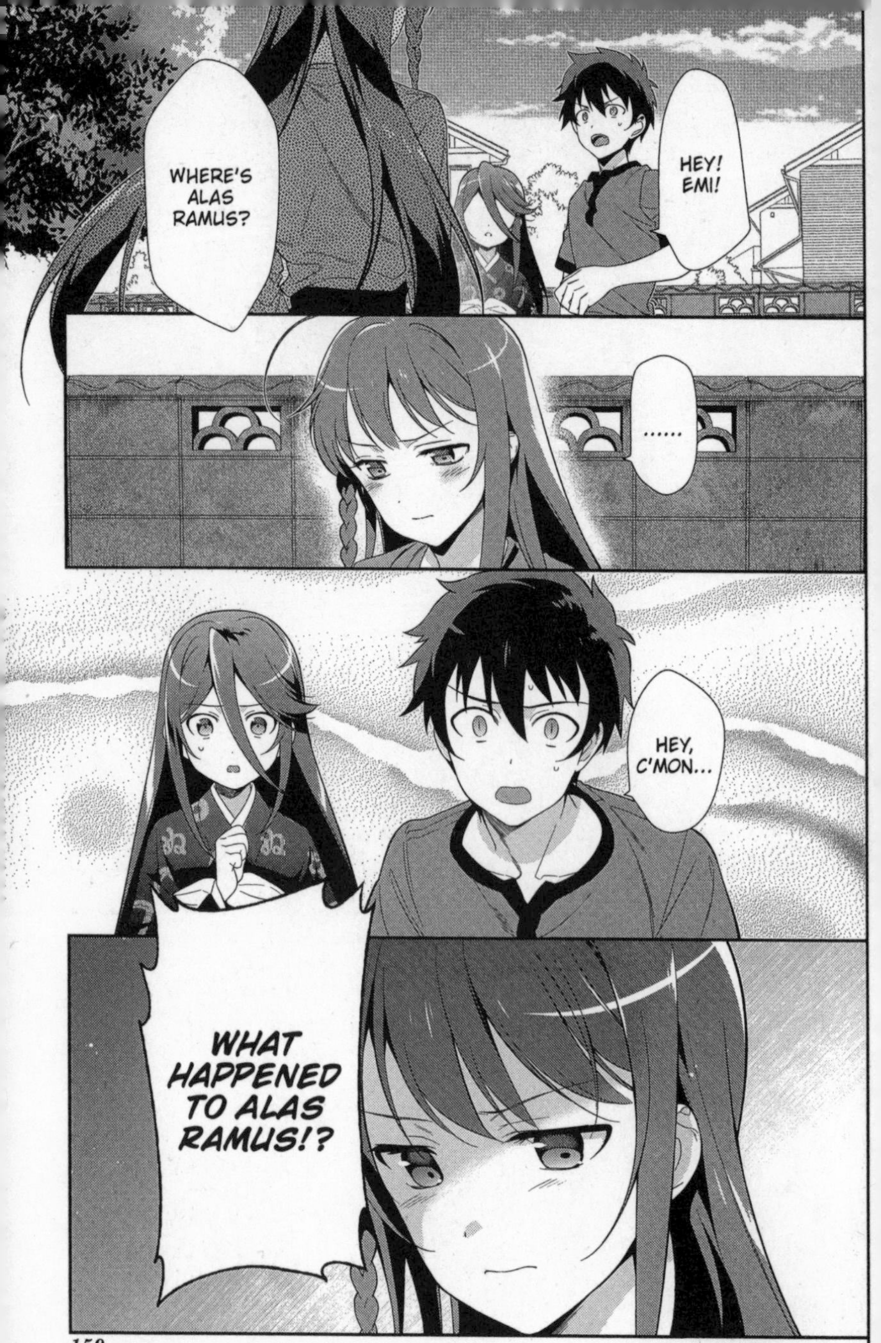
HEY! EMI!
WHERE'S ALAS RAMUS?
......
HEY, C'MON...
WHAT HAPPENED TO ALAS RAMUS!?

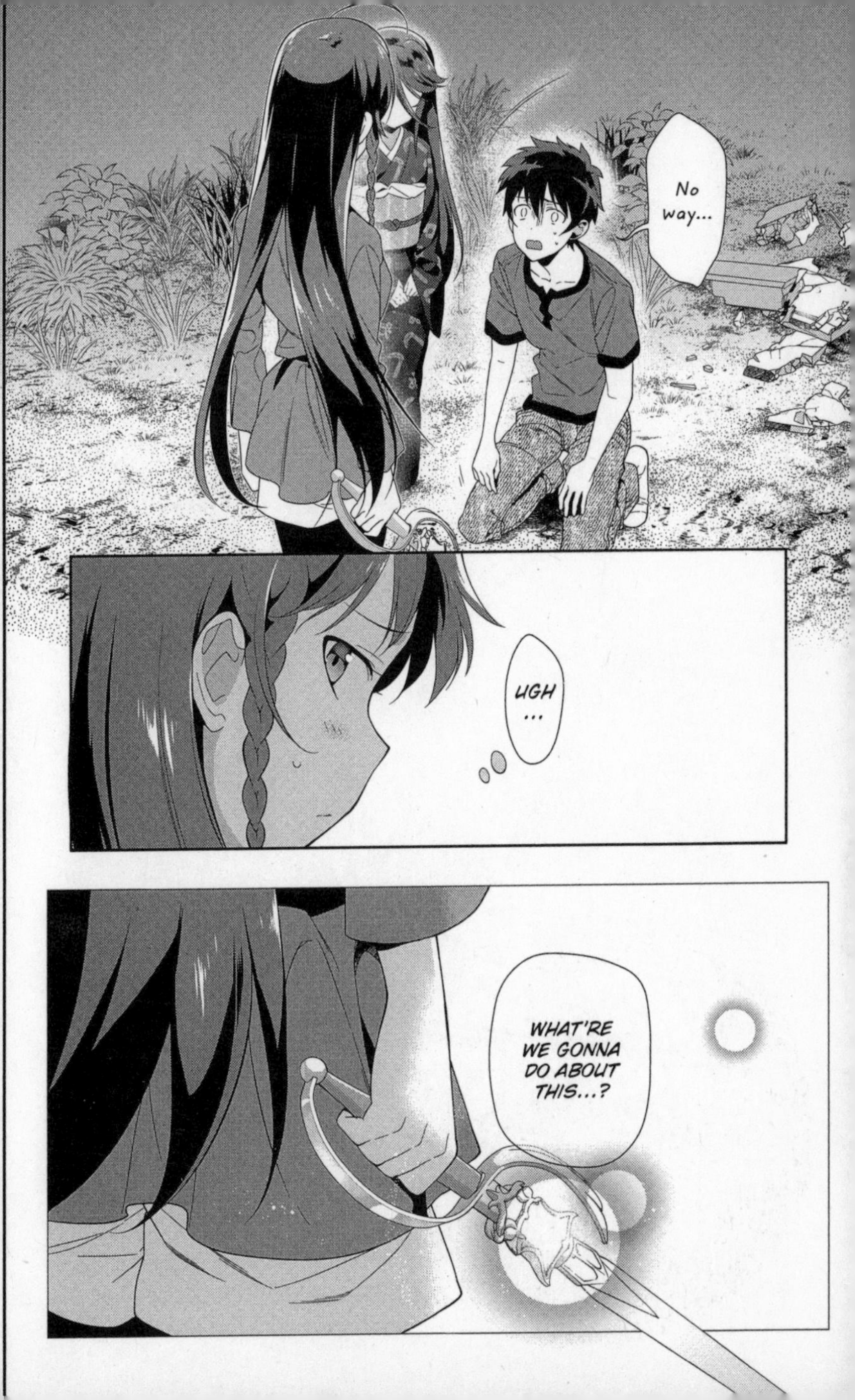
No way...
UGH ...
WHAT'RE WE GONNA DO ABOUT THIS...?

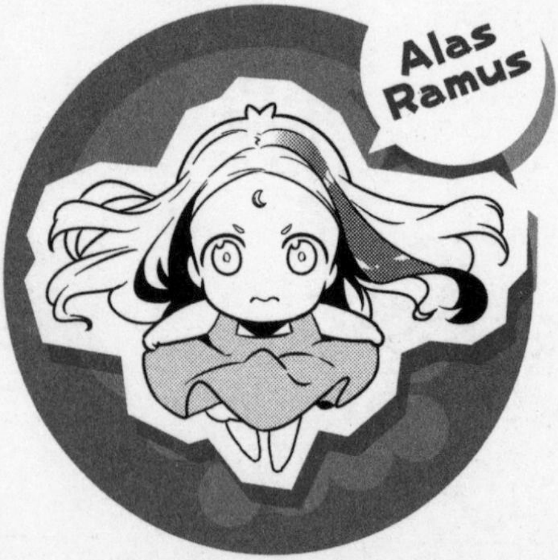
Alas
Ramus

THE DEVIL IS A PART-TIMER!

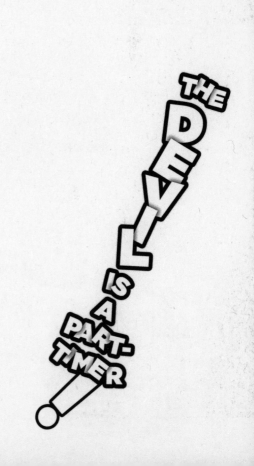

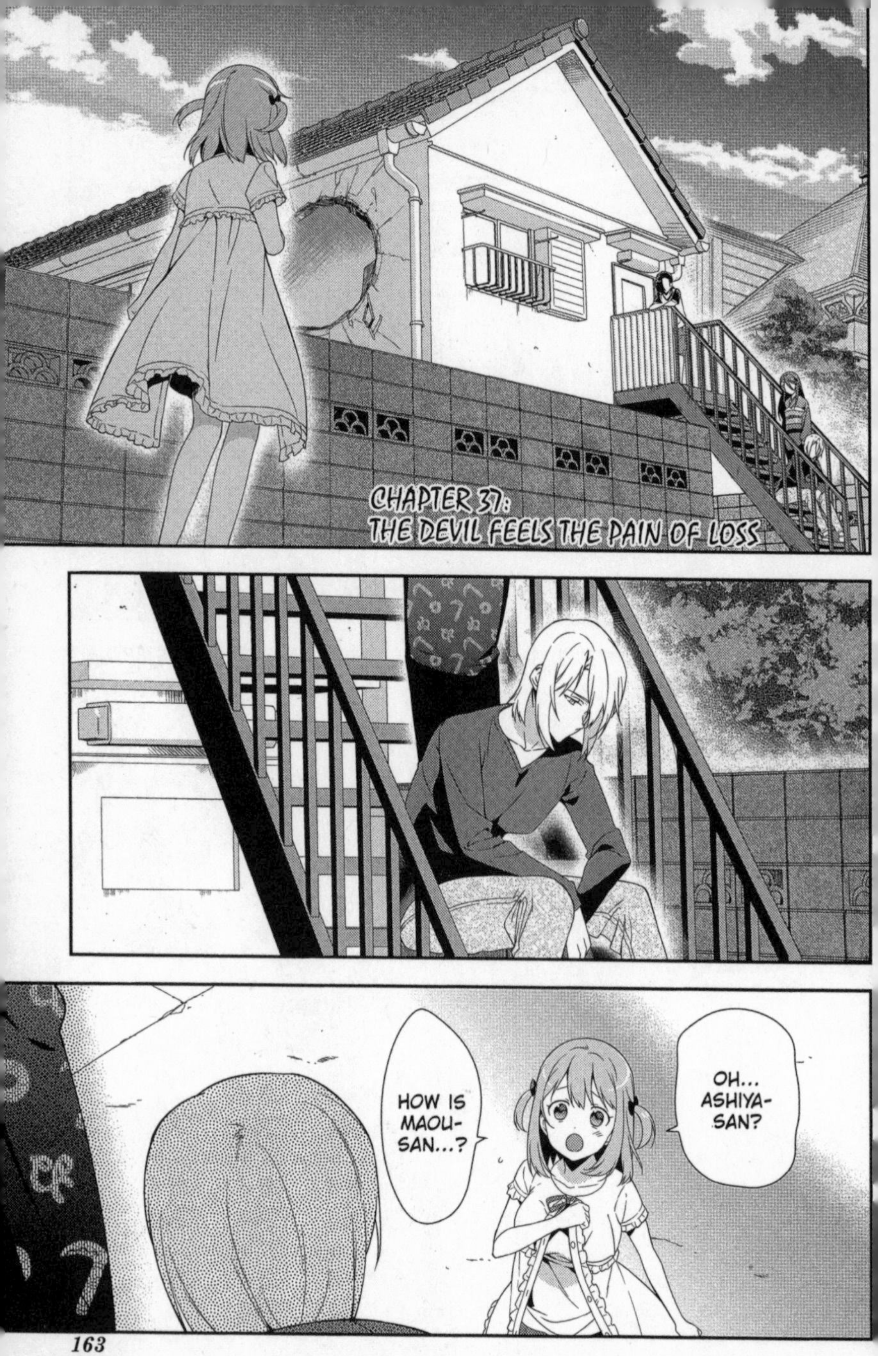
CHAPTER 37:
THE DEVIL FEELS THE PAIN OF LOSS
OH... ASHIYA-SAN?
HOW IS MAOU-SAN...?

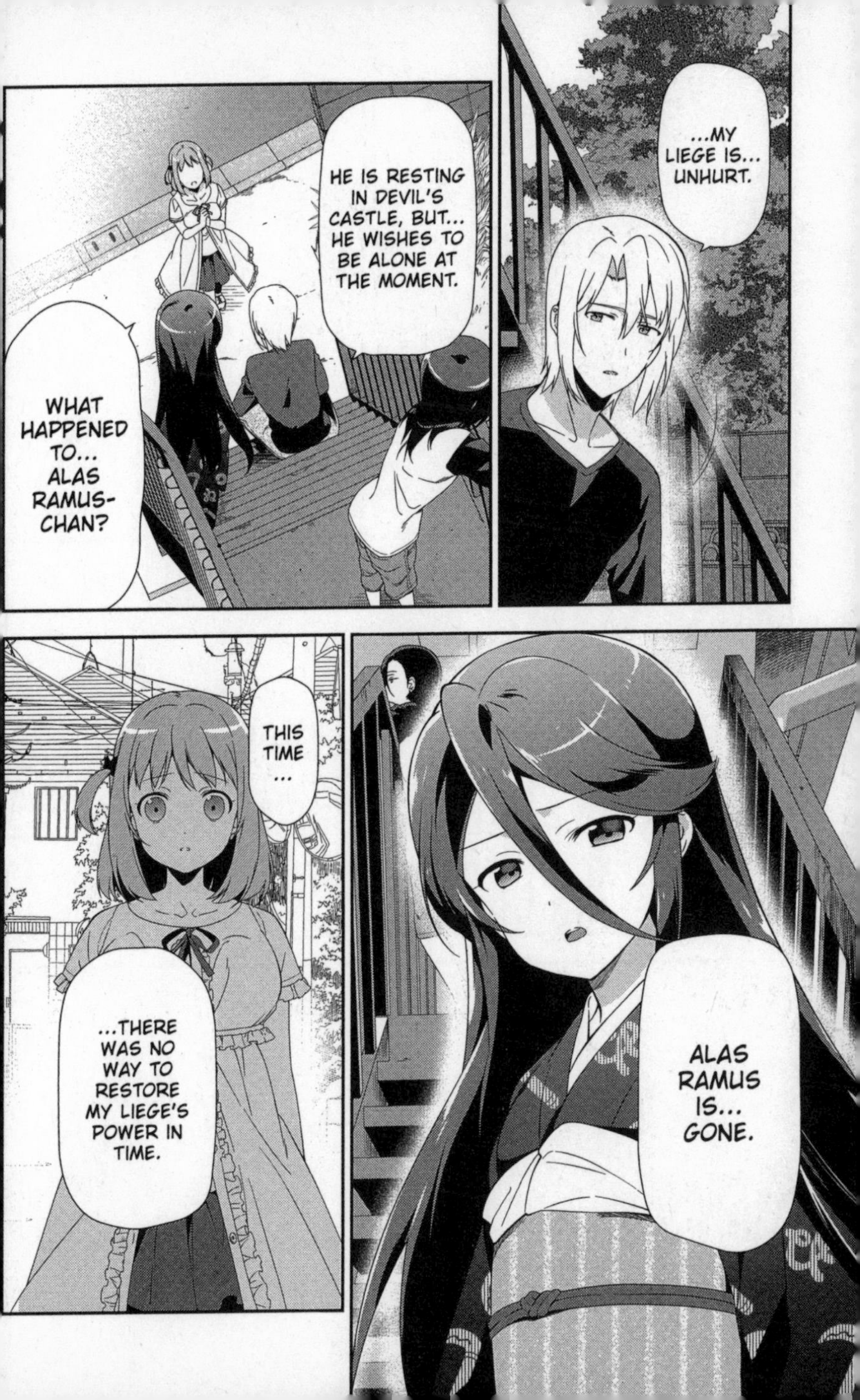

...MY LIEGE IS... UNHURT.
HE IS RESTING IN DEVIL'S CASTLE, BUT... HE WISHES TO BE ALONE AT THE MOMENT.
WHAT HAPPENED TO... ALAS RAMUS-CHAN?
ALAS RAMUS IS... GONE.
THIS TIME...
...THERE WAS NO WAY TO RESTORE MY LIEGE'S POWER IN TIME.

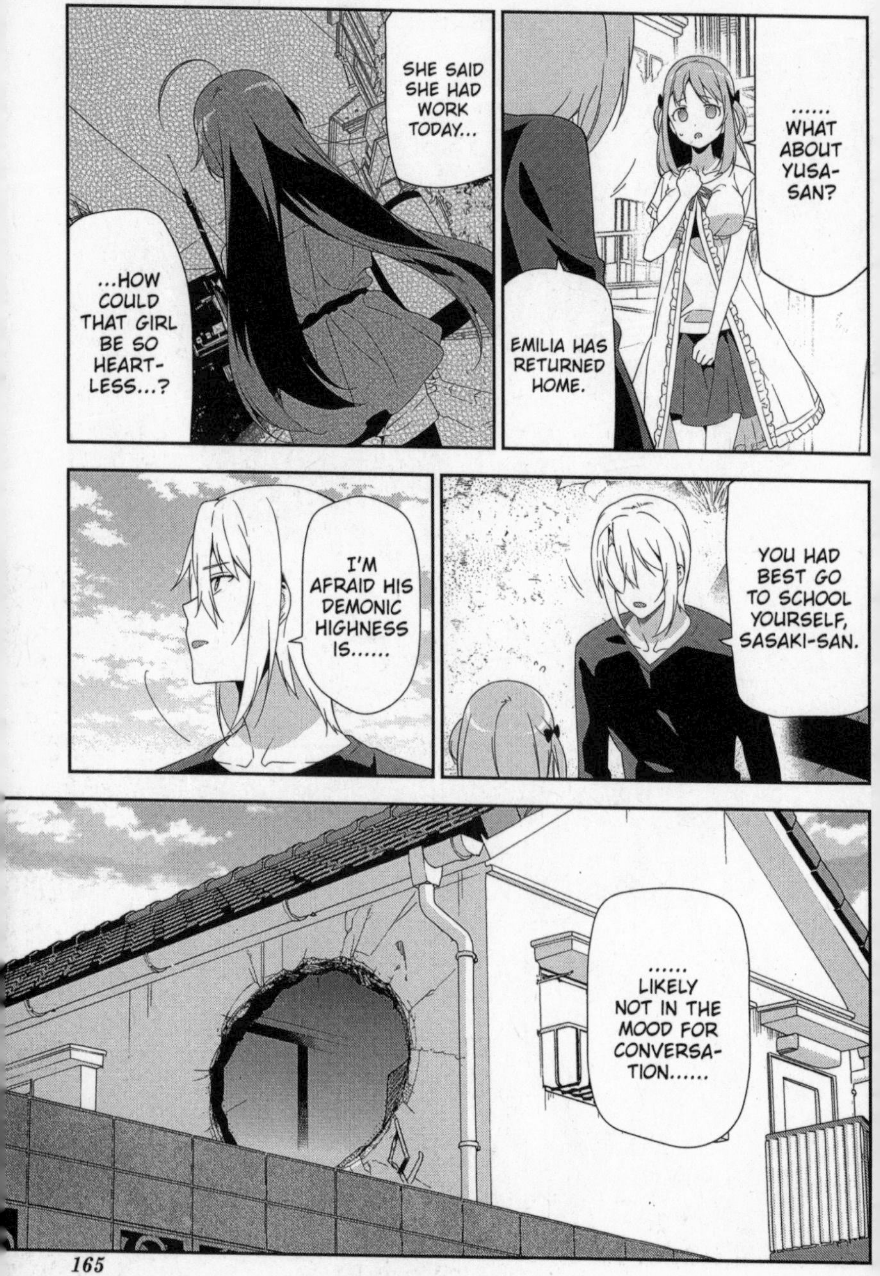
...... WHAT ABOUT YUSA-SAN?
EMILIA HAS RETURNED HOME.
SHE SAID SHE HAD WORK TODAY...
...HOW COULD THAT GIRL BE SO HEARTLESS...?
YOU HAD BEST GO TO SCHOOL YOURSELF, SASAKI-SAN.
I'M AFRAID HIS DEMONIC HIGHNESS IS......
...... LIKELY NOT IN THE MOOD FOR CONVERSATION......

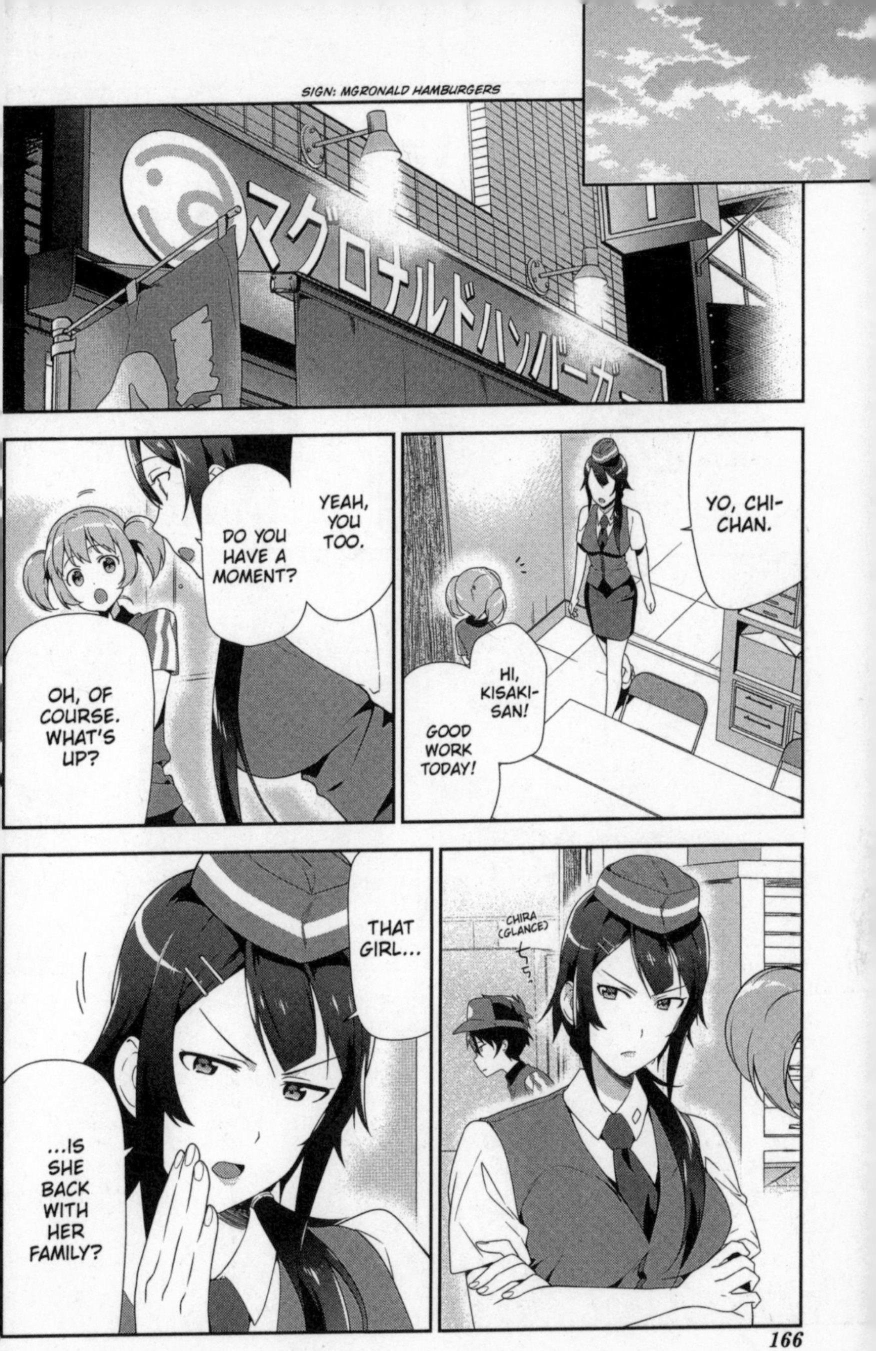
SIGN: MGRONALD HAMBURGERS
マグロナルドハンバーガー
YO, CHI-CHAN.
HI, KISAKI-SAN!
GOOD WORK TODAY!
YEAH, YOU TOO.
DO YOU HAVE A MOMENT?
OH, OF COURSE. WHAT'S UP?
CHIRA (GLANCE)
THAT GIRL...
...IS SHE BACK WITH HER FAMILY?

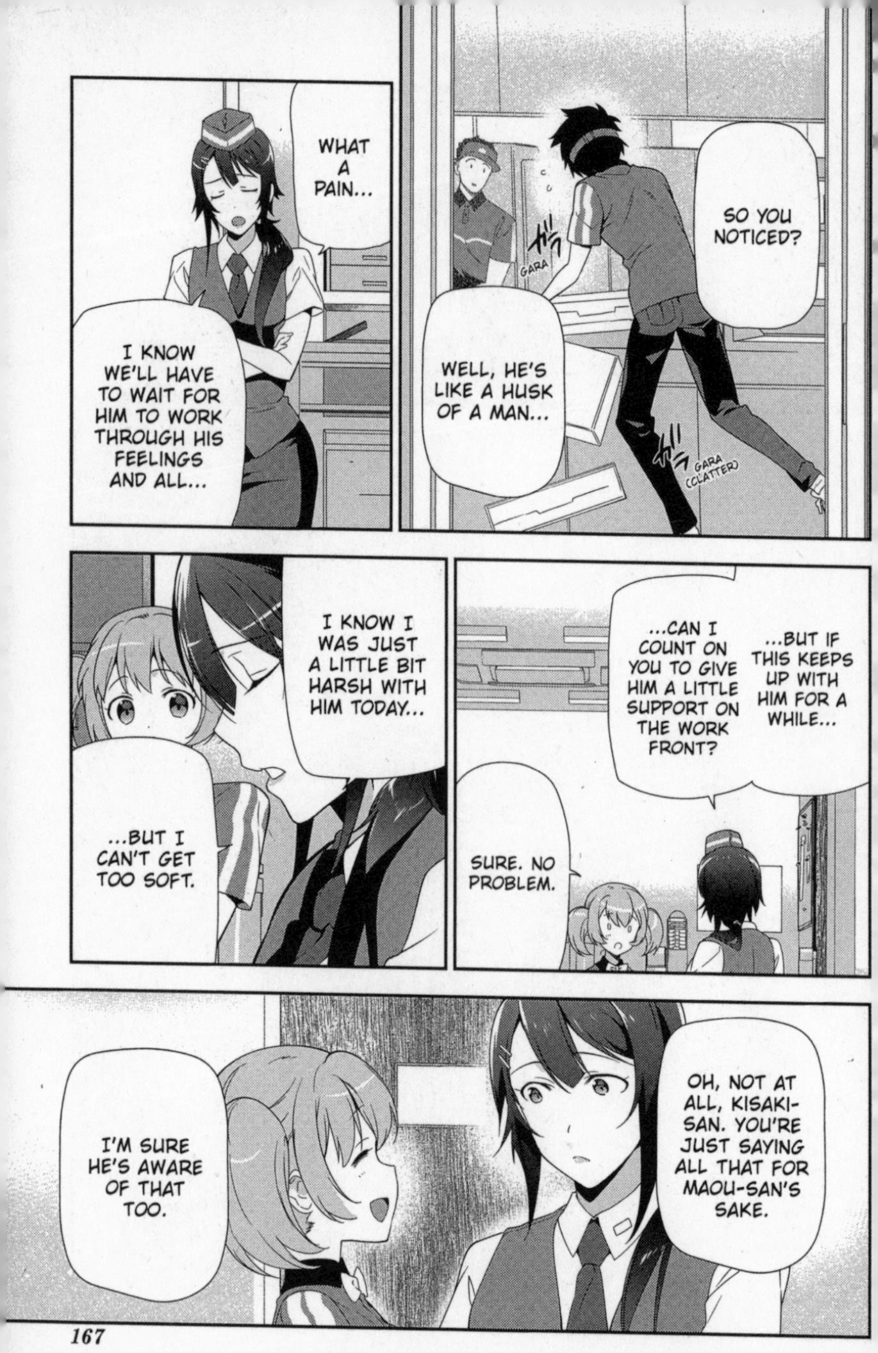
SO YOU NOTICED?
GARA
WELL, HE'S LIKE A HUSK OF A MAN...
GARA (CLATTER)
WHAT A PAIN...
I KNOW WE'LL HAVE TO WAIT FOR HIM TO WORK THROUGH HIS FEELINGS AND ALL...
...BUT IF THIS KEEPS UP WITH HIM FOR A WHILE...
...CAN I COUNT ON YOU TO GIVE HIM A LITTLE SUPPORT ON THE WORK FRONT?
SURE. NO PROBLEM.
I KNOW I WAS JUST A LITTLE BIT HARSH WITH HIM TODAY...
...BUT I CAN'T GET TOO SOFT.
OH, NOT AT ALL, KISAKI-SAN. YOU'RE JUST SAYING ALL THAT FOR MAOU-SAN'S SAKE.
I'M SURE HE'S AWARE OF THAT TOO.

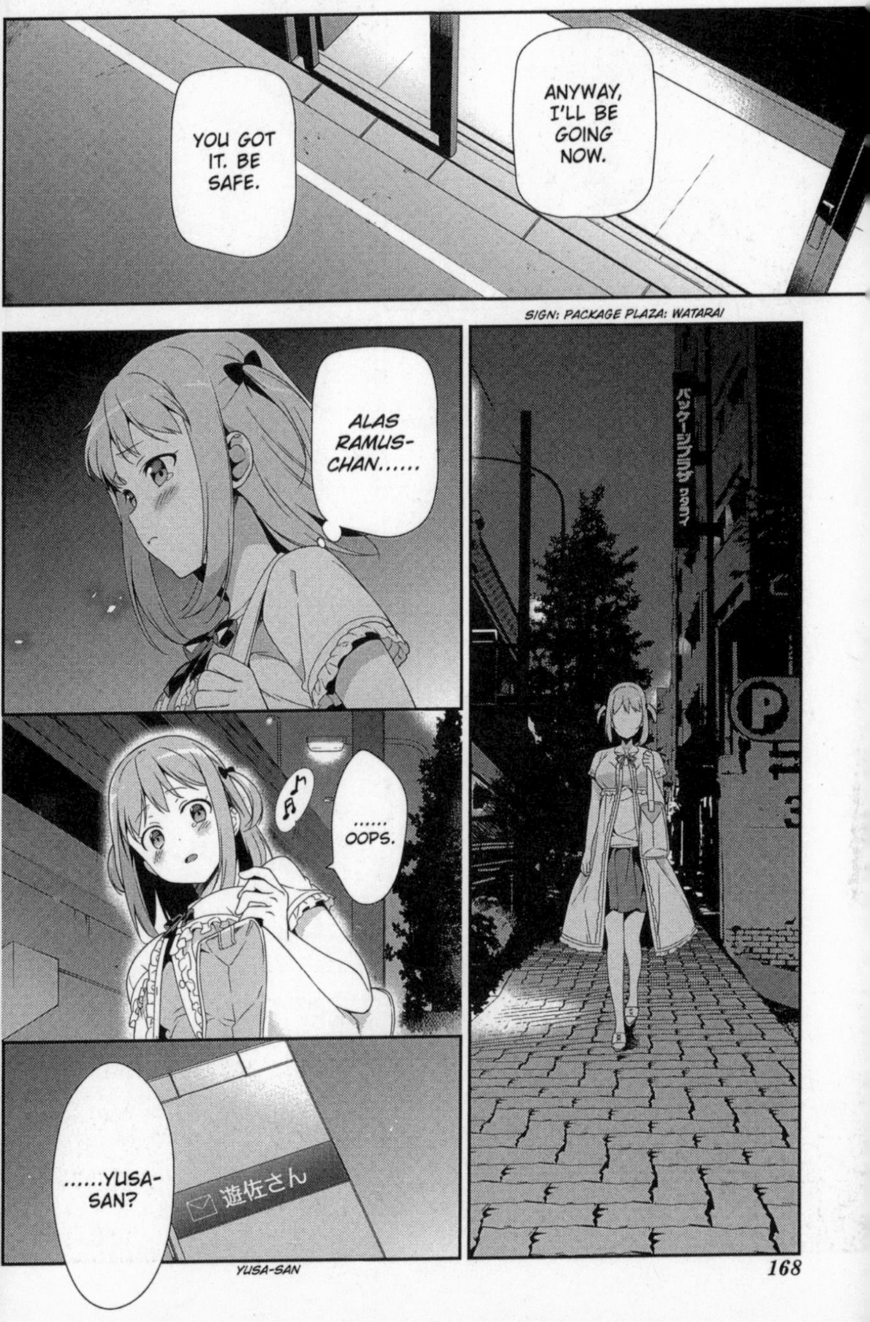
ANYWAY, I'LL BE GOING NOW.
YOU GOT IT. BE SAFE.
SIGN: PACKAGE PLAZA: WATARAI
パッケージプラザ
ALAS RAMUS-CHAN......
......OOPS.
......YUSA-SAN?
遊佐さん
YUSA-SAN

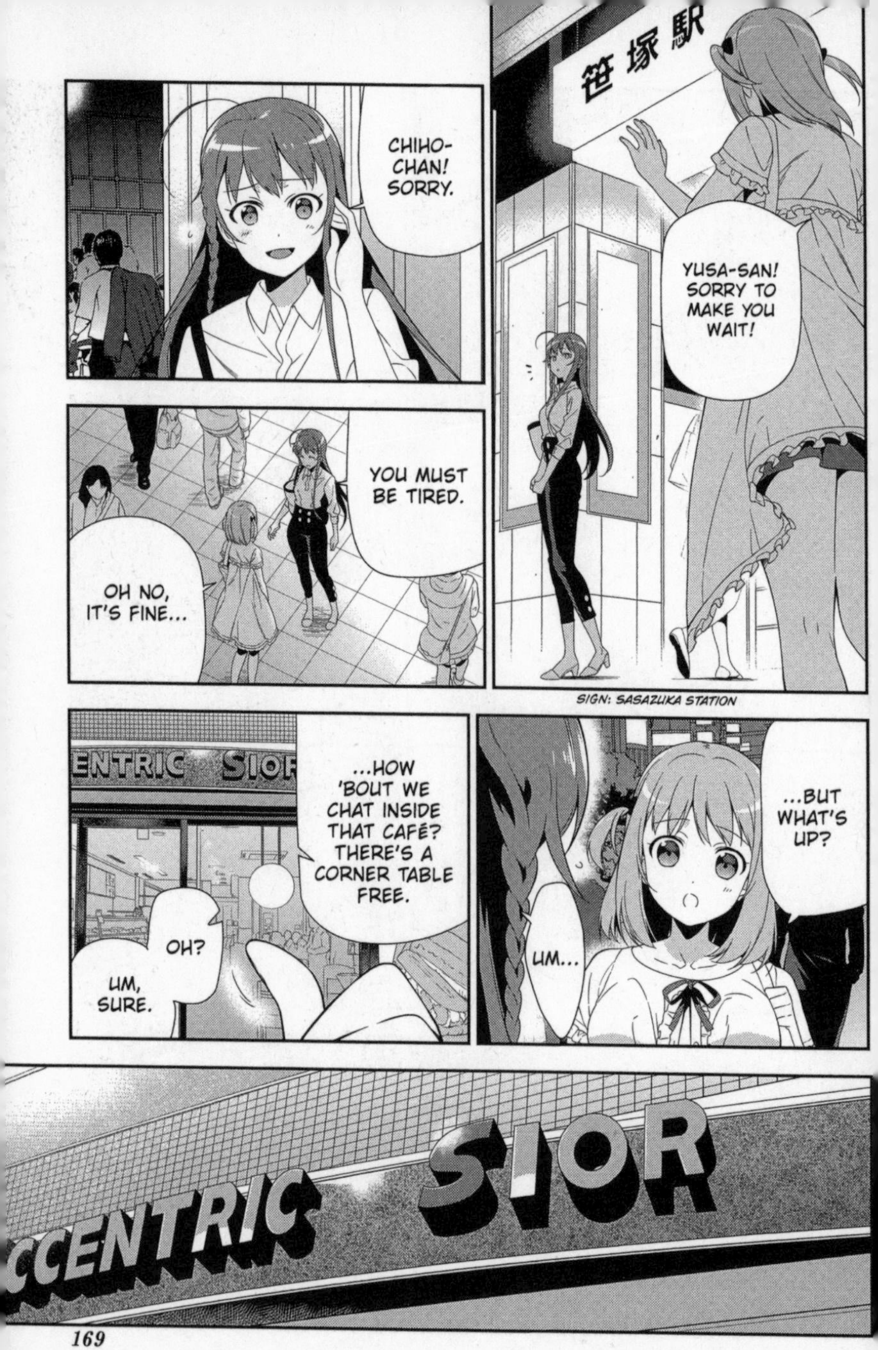
笹塚駅
YUSA-SAN! SORRY TO MAKE YOU WAIT!
SIGN: SASAZUKA STATION
CHIHO-CHAN! SORRY.
YOU MUST BE TIRED.
OH NO, IT'S FINE...
...BUT WHAT'S UP?
UM...
ENTRIC SIOR
...HOW 'BOUT WE CHAT INSIDE THAT CAFÉ? THERE'S A CORNER TABLE FREE.
OH?
UM, SURE.
CCENTRIC SIOR

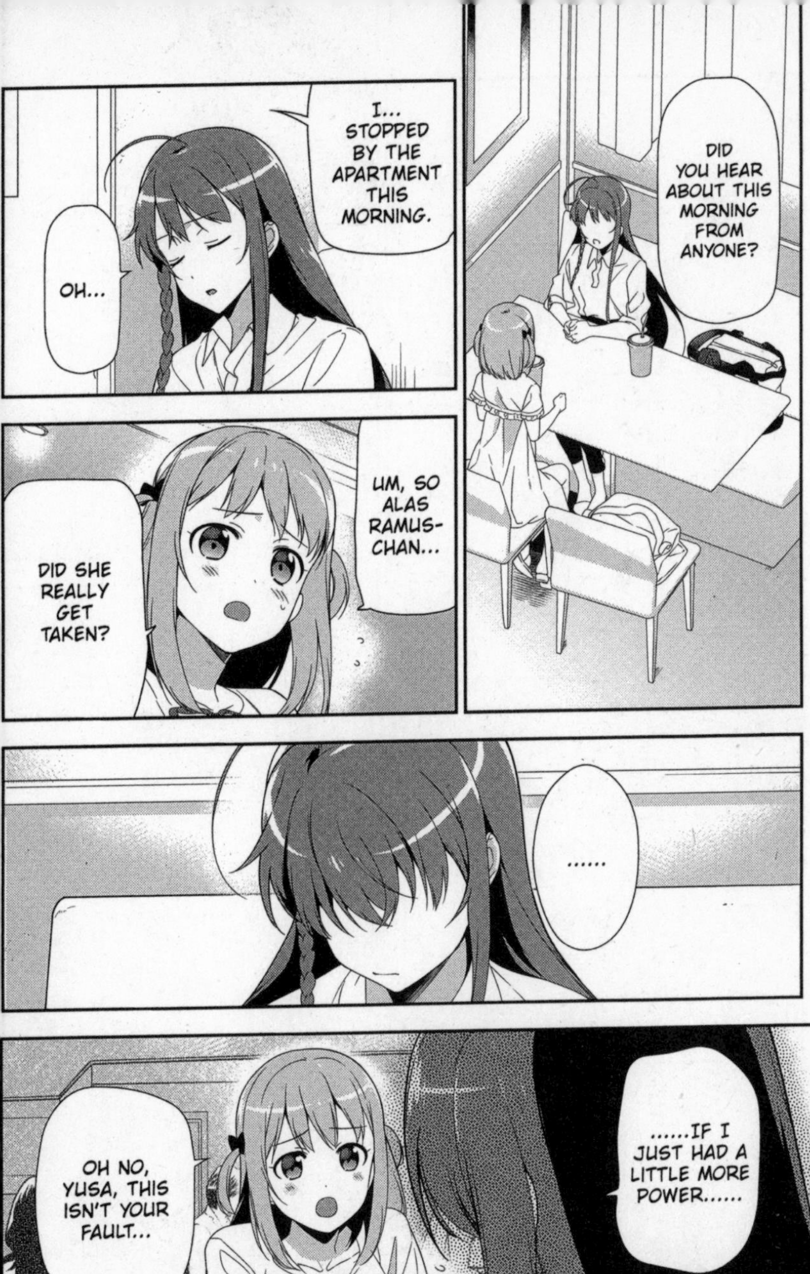
DID YOU HEAR ABOUT THIS MORNING FROM ANYONE?
I... STOPPED BY THE APARTMENT THIS MORNING.
OH...
UM, SO ALAS RAMUS-CHAN...
DID SHE REALLY GET TAKEN?
......
......IF I JUST HAD A LITTLE MORE POWER......
OH NO, YUSA, THIS ISN'T YOUR FAULT...

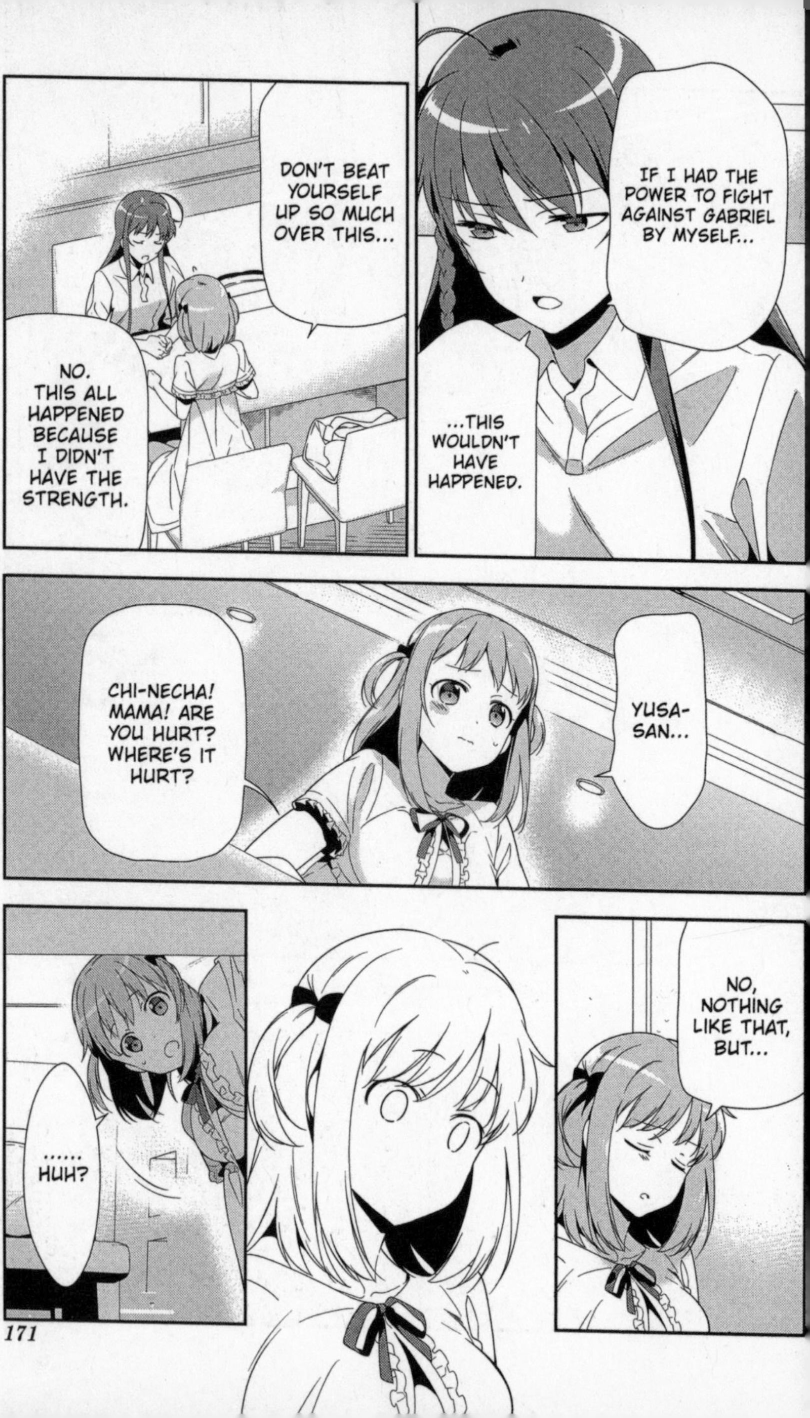
IF I HAD THE POWER TO FIGHT AGAINST GABRIEL BY MYSELF...
...THIS WOULDN'T HAVE HAPPENED.
DON'T BEAT YOURSELF UP SO MUCH OVER THIS...
NO. THIS ALL HAPPENED BECAUSE I DIDN'T HAVE THE STRENGTH.
YUSA-SAN...
CHI-NECHA! MAMA! ARE YOU HURT? WHERE'S IT HURT?
NO, NOTHING LIKE THAT, BUT...
......
HUH?

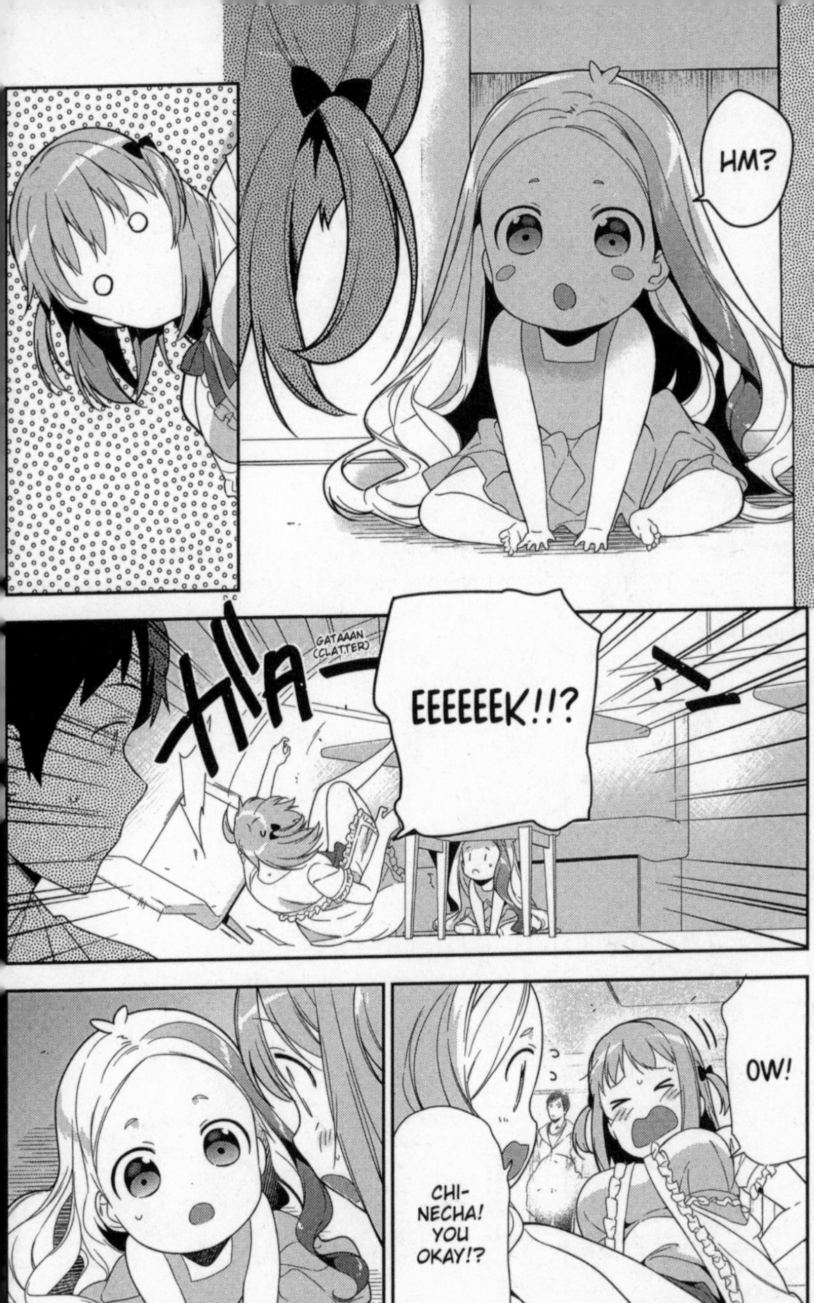
HM?
GATAAAN (CLATTER)
HYA—
EEEEEEK!!?
OW!
CHI-NECHA! YOU OKAY!?

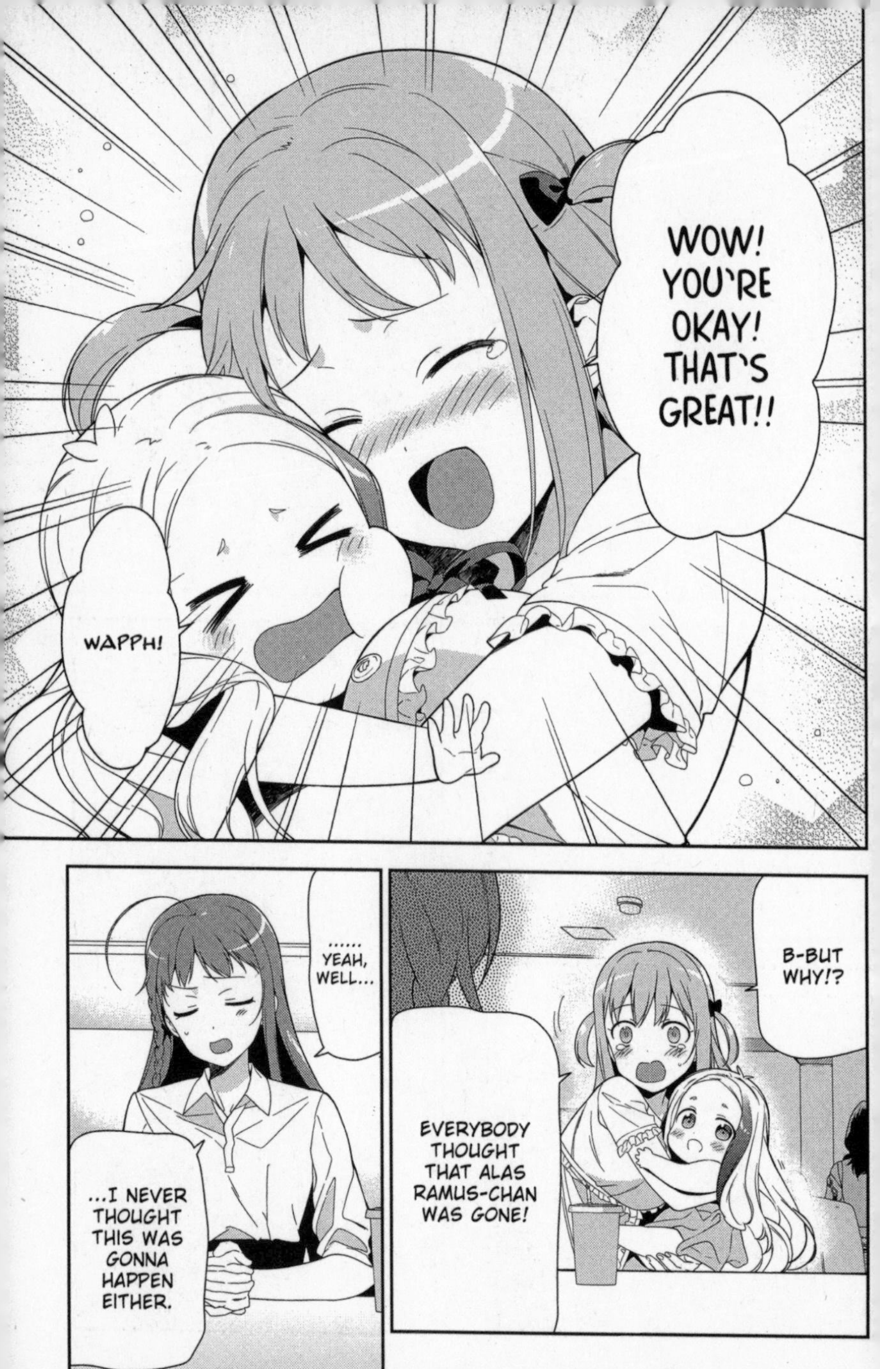
WOW! YOU'RE OKAY! THAT'S GREAT!!
WAPPH!
B-BUT WHY!?
EVERYBODY THOUGHT THAT ALAS RAMUS-CHAN WAS GONE!
...... YEAH, WELL...
...I NEVER THOUGHT THIS WAS GONNA HAPPEN EITHER.

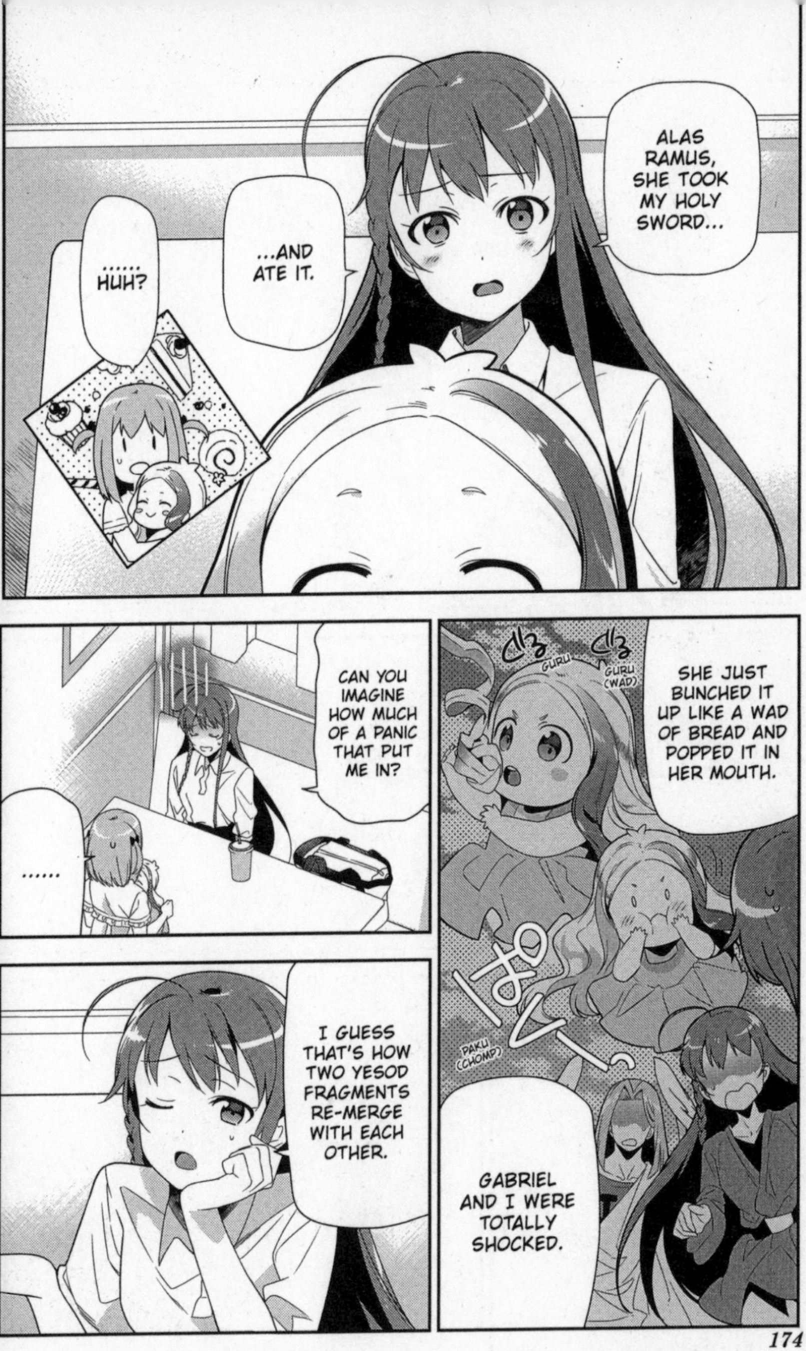

ALAS RAMUS, SHE TOOK MY HOLY SWORD...
...AND ATE IT.
......HUH?
ぐる GURU
ぐる GURU (WAD)
SHE JUST BUNCHED IT UP LIKE A WAD OF BREAD AND POPPED IT IN HER MOUTH.
ぱくっ PAKU (CHOMP)
GABRIEL AND I WERE TOTALLY SHOCKED.
CAN YOU IMAGINE HOW MUCH OF A PANIC THAT PUT ME IN?
......
I GUESS THAT'S HOW TWO YESOD FRAGMENTS RE-MERGE WITH EACH OTHER.

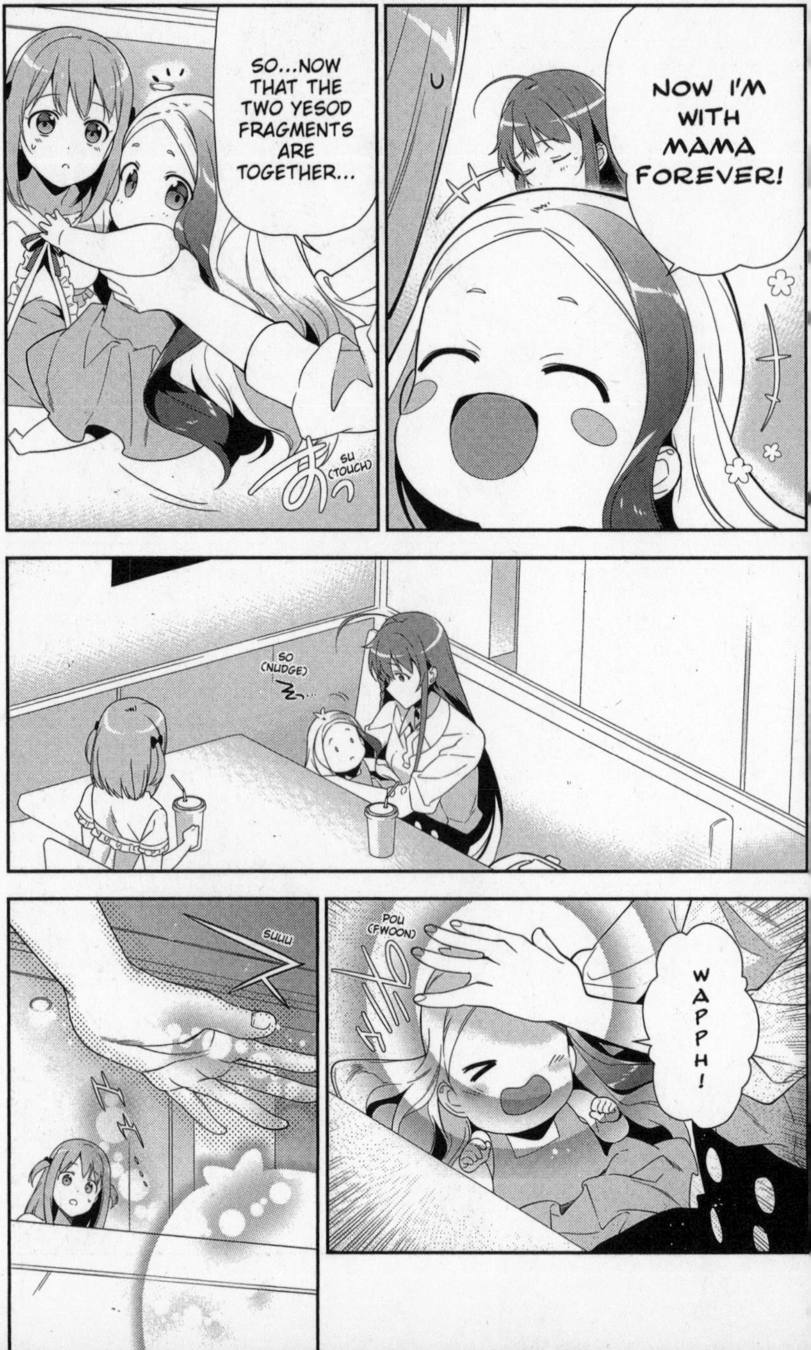
NOW I'M WITH MAMA FOREVER!
SO...NOW THAT THE TWO YESOD FRAGMENTS ARE TOGETHER...
SU (TOUCH)
SO (NUDGE)
POU (FWOON)
WAPPH!
SUUU

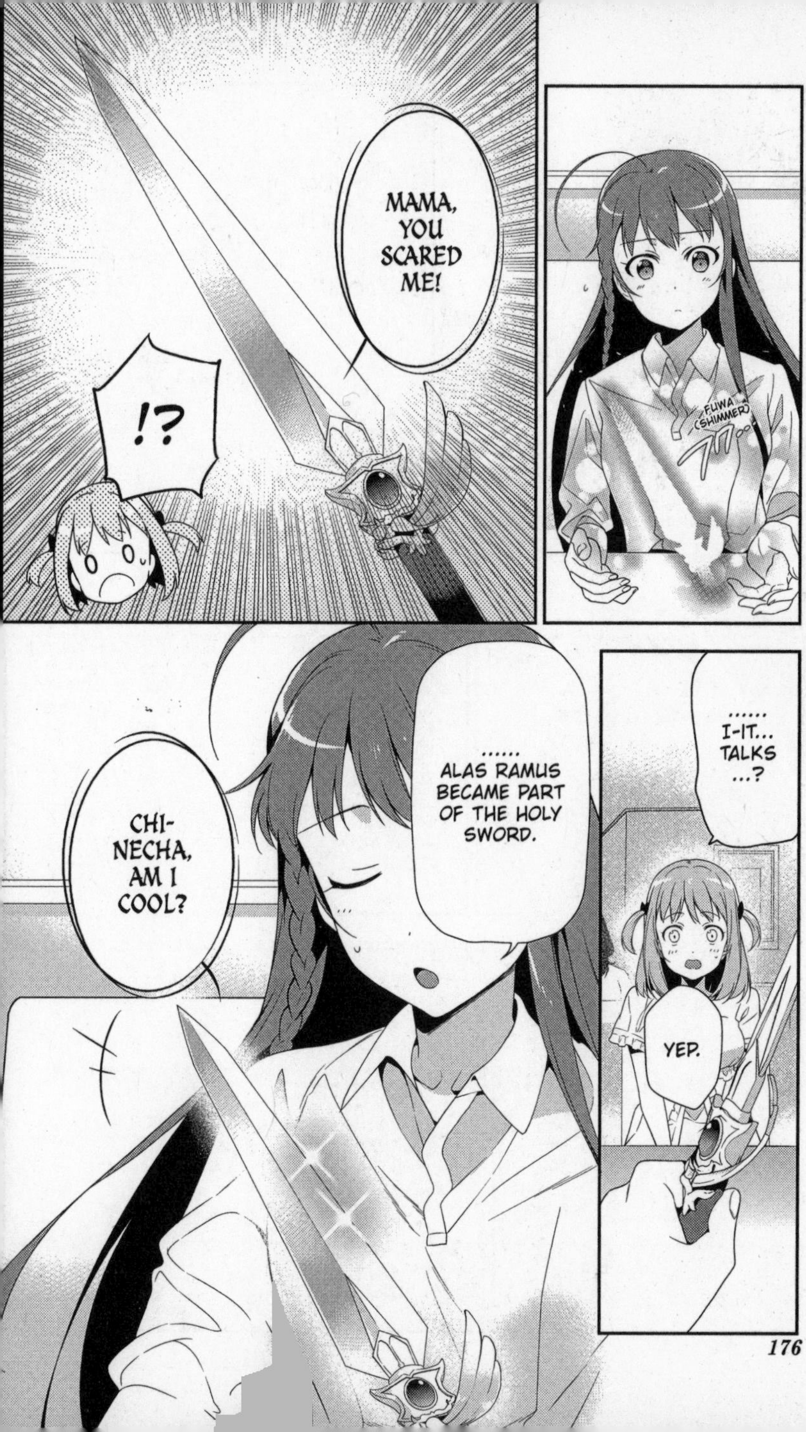
FUWA (SHIMMER)
MAMA, YOU SCARED ME!
!?
...... I-IT... TALKS ...?
YEP.
...... ALAS RAMUS BECAME PART OF THE HOLY SWORD.
CHI-NECHA, AM I COOL?

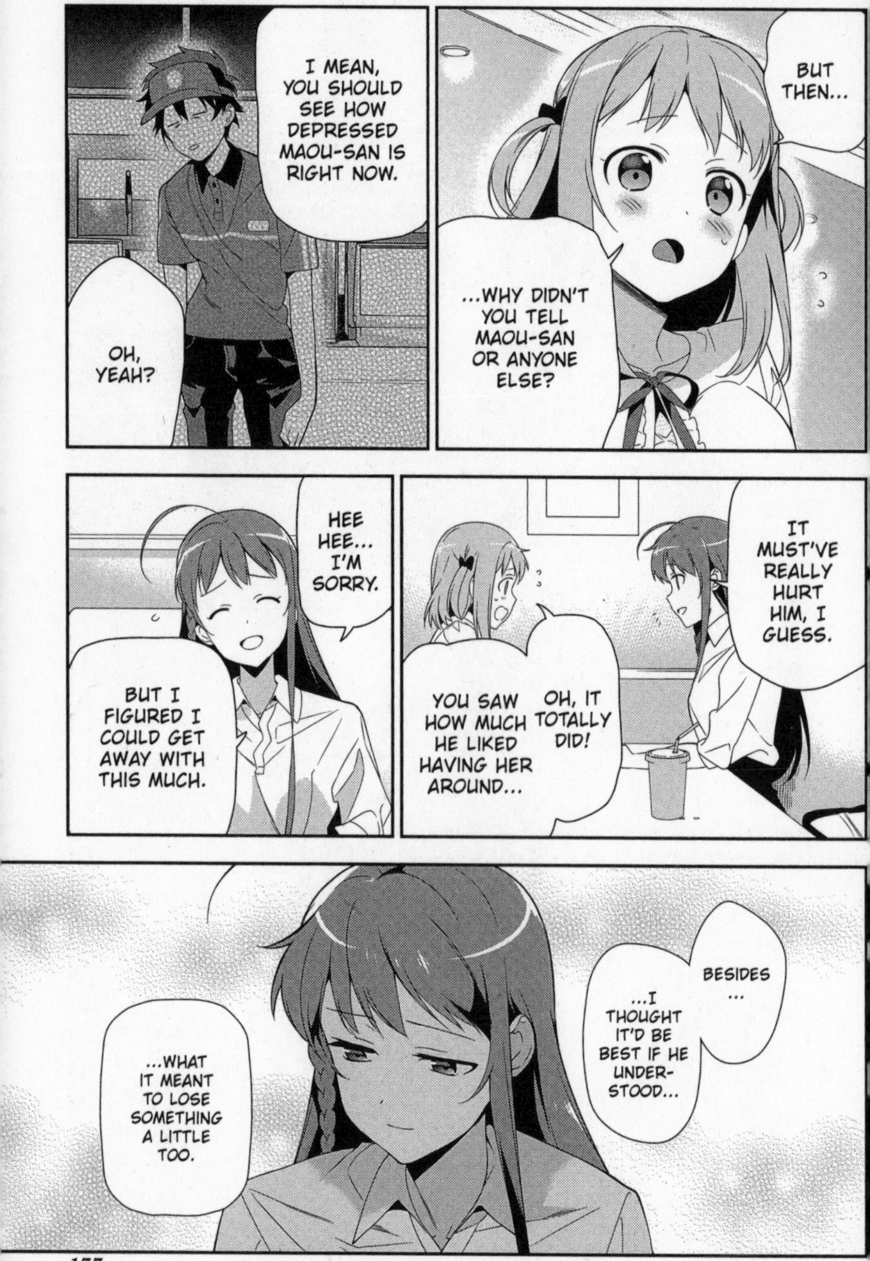
BUT THEN...
...WHY DIDN'T YOU TELL MAOU-SAN OR ANYONE ELSE?
I MEAN, YOU SHOULD SEE HOW DEPRESSED MAOU-SAN IS RIGHT NOW.
OH, YEAH?
IT MUST'VE REALLY HURT HIM, I GUESS.
OH, IT TOTALLY DID!
YOU SAW HOW MUCH HE LIKED HAVING HER AROUND...
HEE HEE... I'M SORRY.
BUT I FIGURED I COULD GET AWAY WITH THIS MUCH.
BESIDES...
...I THOUGHT IT'D BE BEST IF HE UNDER-STOOD...
...WHAT IT MEANT TO LOSE SOMETHING A LITTLE TOO.

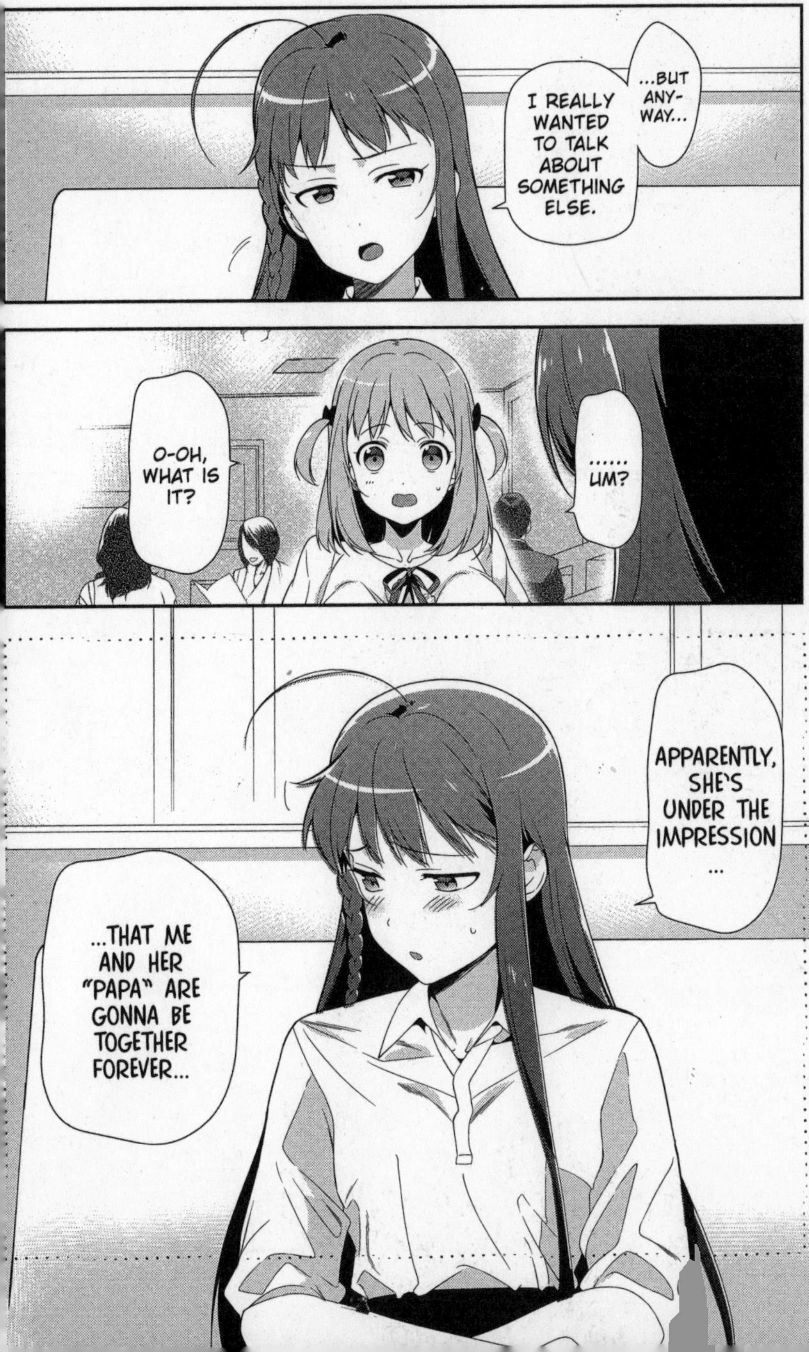
...BUT ANY-WAY...
I REALLY WANTED TO TALK ABOUT SOMETHING ELSE.
...... UM?
O-OH, WHAT IS IT?
APPARENTLY, SHE'S UNDER THE IMPRESSION ...
...THAT ME AND HER "PAPA" ARE GONNA BE TOGETHER FOREVER...

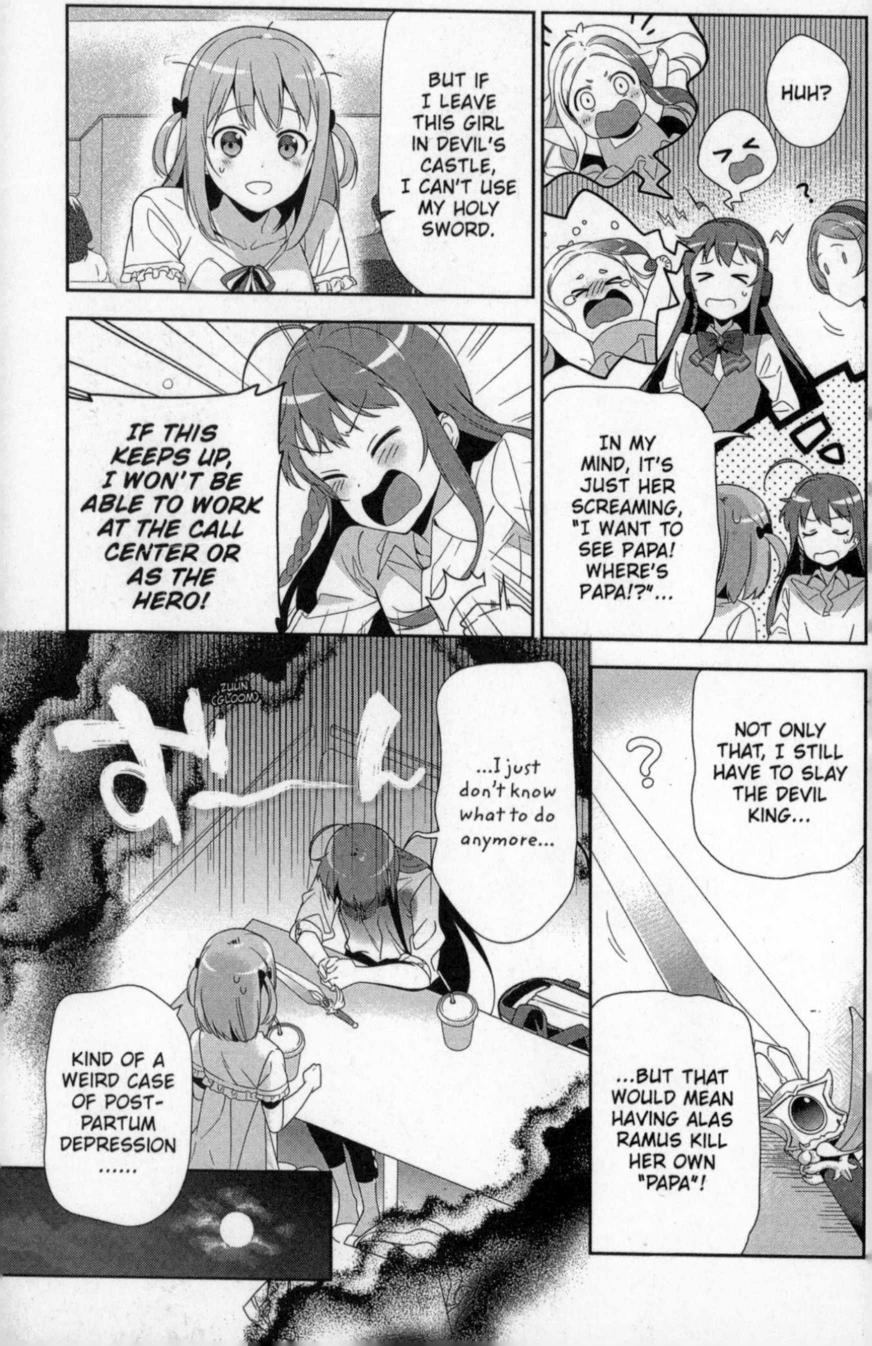
HUH?
IN MY MIND, IT'S JUST HER SCREAMING, "I WANT TO SEE PAPA! WHERE'S PAPA!?"...
BUT IF I LEAVE THIS GIRL IN DEVIL'S CASTLE, I CAN'T USE MY HOLY SWORD.
IF THIS KEEPS UP, I WON'T BE ABLE TO WORK AT THE CALL CENTER OR AS THE HERO!
NOT ONLY THAT, I STILL HAVE TO SLAY THE DEVIL KING...
...BUT THAT WOULD MEAN HAVING ALAS RAMUS KILL HER OWN "PAPA"!
ZUUN (GLOOM)
...I just don't know what to do anymore...
KIND OF A WEIRD CASE OF POST-PARTUM DEPRESSION ......

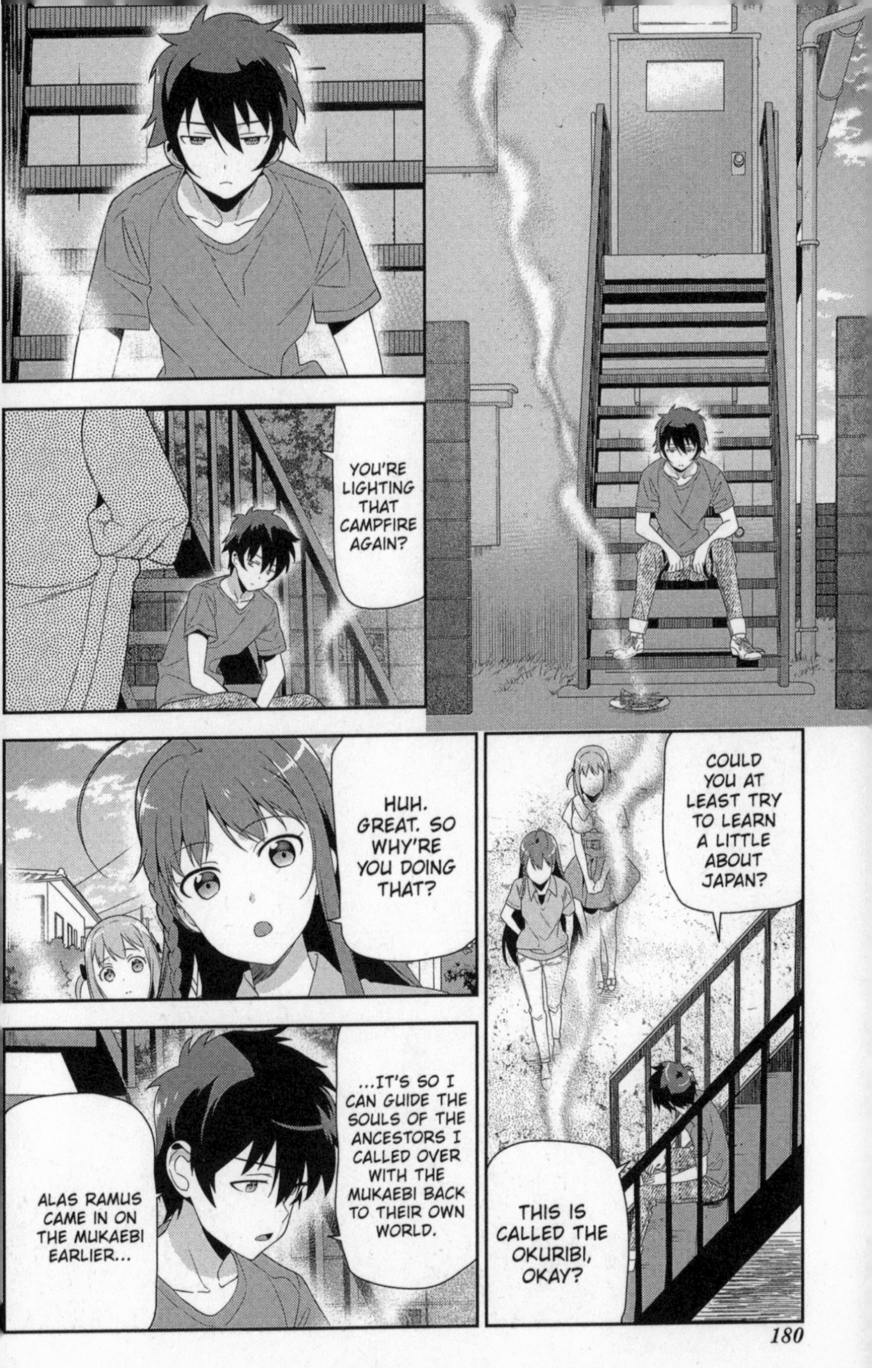
YOU'RE LIGHTING THAT CAMPFIRE AGAIN?
COULD YOU AT LEAST TRY TO LEARN A LITTLE ABOUT JAPAN?
THIS IS CALLED THE OKURIBI, OKAY?
HUH. GREAT. SO WHY'RE YOU DOING THAT?
...IT'S SO I CAN GUIDE THE SOULS OF THE ANCESTORS I CALLED OVER WITH THE MUKAEBI BACK TO THEIR OWN WORLD.
ALAS RAMUS CAME IN ON THE MUKAEBI EARLIER...

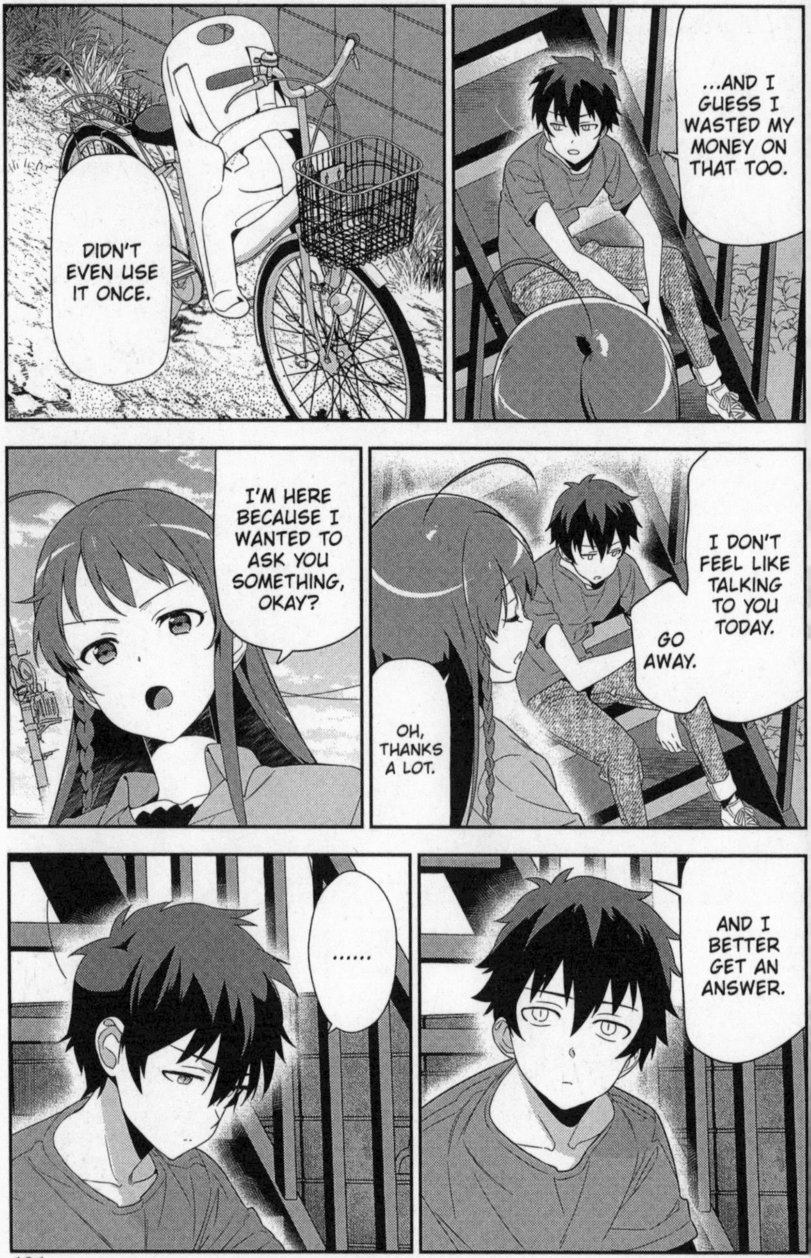
...AND I GUESS I WASTED MY MONEY ON THAT TOO.
DIDN'T EVEN USE IT ONCE.
I DON'T FEEL LIKE TALKING TO YOU TODAY.
GO AWAY.
OH, THANKS A LOT.
I'M HERE BECAUSE I WANTED TO ASK YOU SOMETHING, OKAY?
AND I BETTER GET AN ANSWER.
......

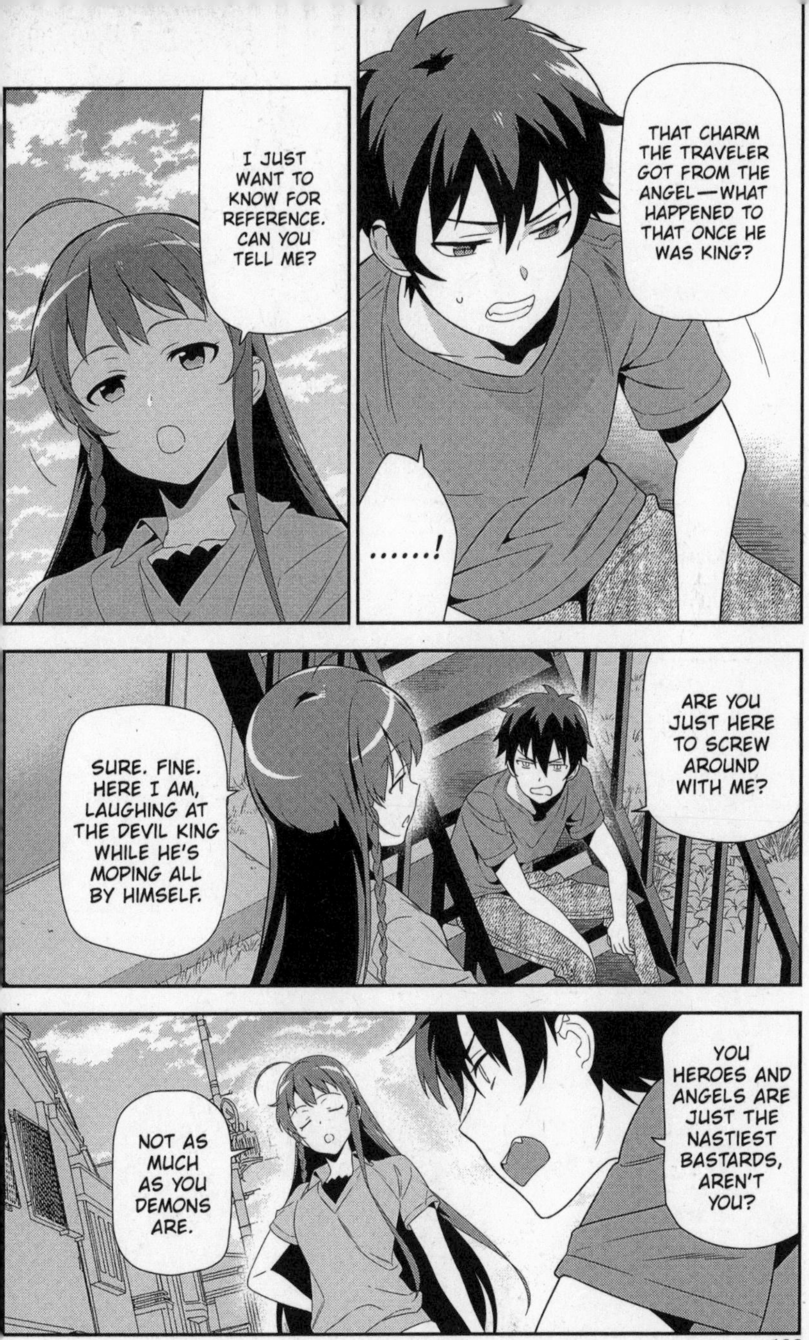
THAT CHARM THE TRAVELER GOT FROM THE ANGEL—WHAT HAPPENED TO THAT ONCE HE WAS KING?
......!
I JUST WANT TO KNOW FOR REFERENCE. CAN YOU TELL ME?
ARE YOU JUST HERE TO SCREW AROUND WITH ME?
SURE. FINE. HERE I AM, LAUGHING AT THE DEVIL KING WHILE HE'S MOPING ALL BY HIMSELF.
YOU HEROES AND ANGELS ARE JUST THE NASTIEST BASTARDS, AREN'T YOU?
NOT AS MUCH AS YOU DEMONS ARE.

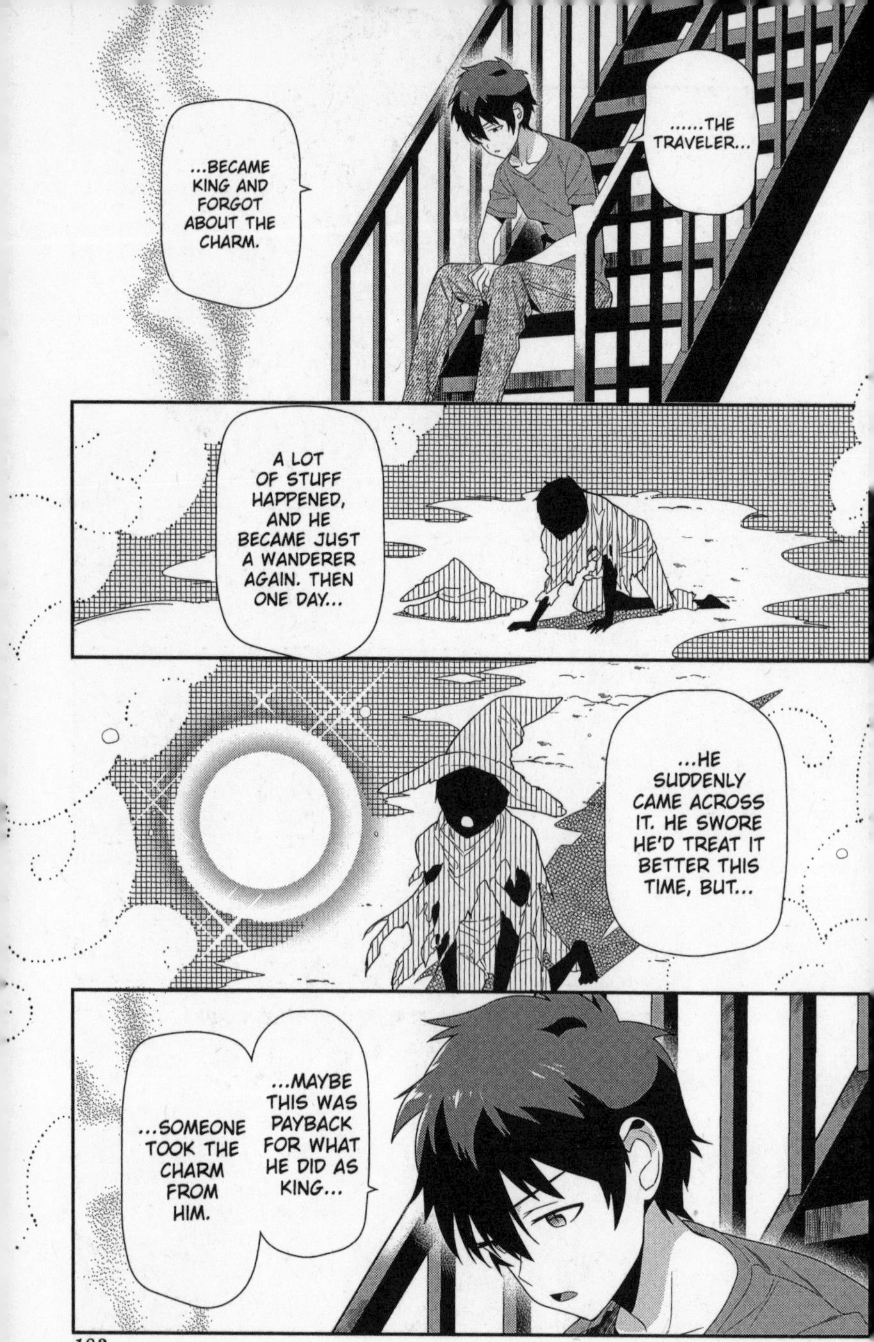
......THE TRAVELER...
...BECAME KING AND FORGOT ABOUT THE CHARM.
A LOT OF STUFF HAPPENED, AND HE BECAME JUST A WANDERER AGAIN. THEN ONE DAY...
...HE SUDDENLY CAME ACROSS IT. HE SWORE HE'D TREAT IT BETTER THIS TIME, BUT...
...MAYBE THIS WAS PAYBACK FOR WHAT HE DID AS KING...
...SOMEONE TOOK THE CHARM FROM HIM.

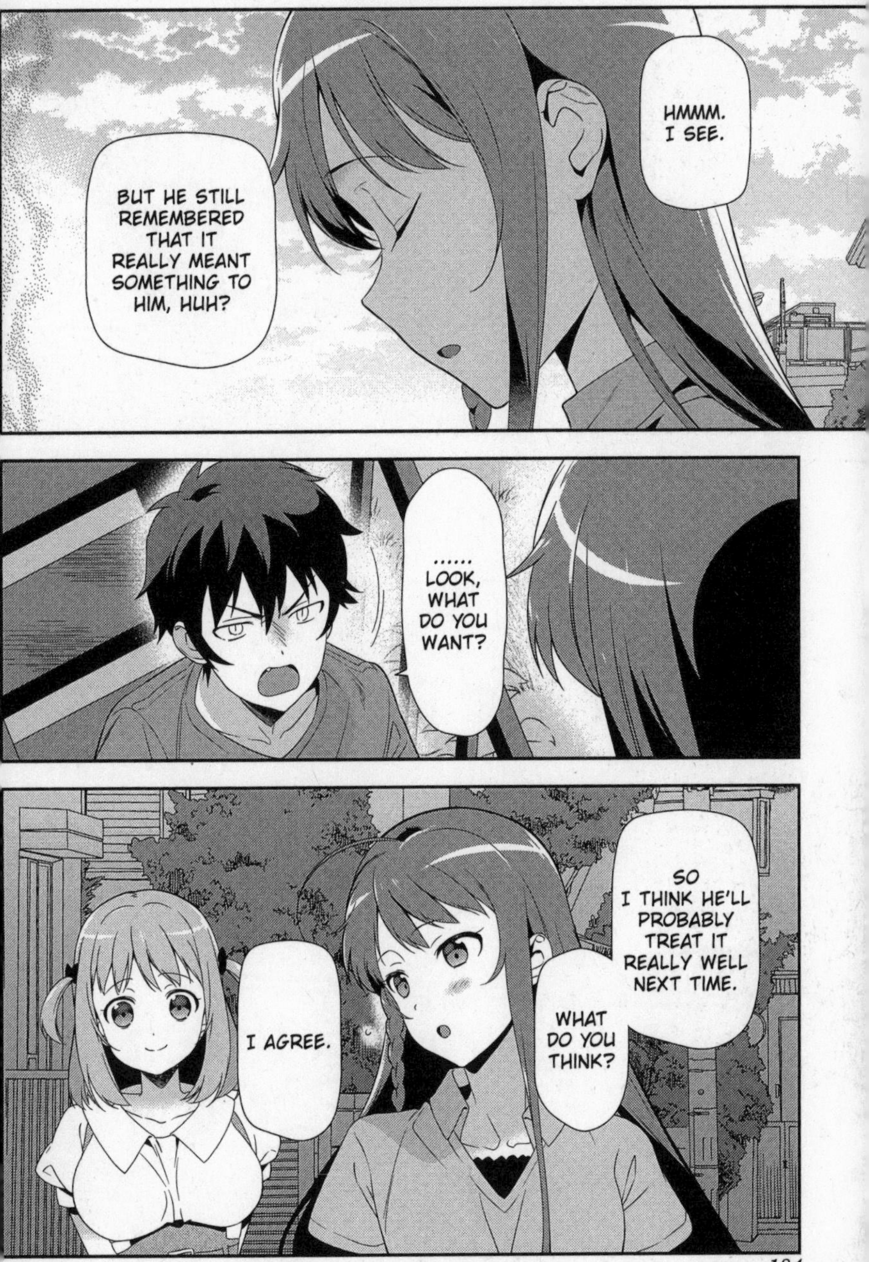
HMMM. I SEE.
BUT HE STILL REMEMBERED THAT IT REALLY MEANT SOMETHING TO HIM, HUH?
...... LOOK, WHAT DO YOU WANT?
SO I THINK HE'LL PROBABLY TREAT IT REALLY WELL NEXT TIME.
WHAT DO YOU THINK?
I AGREE.

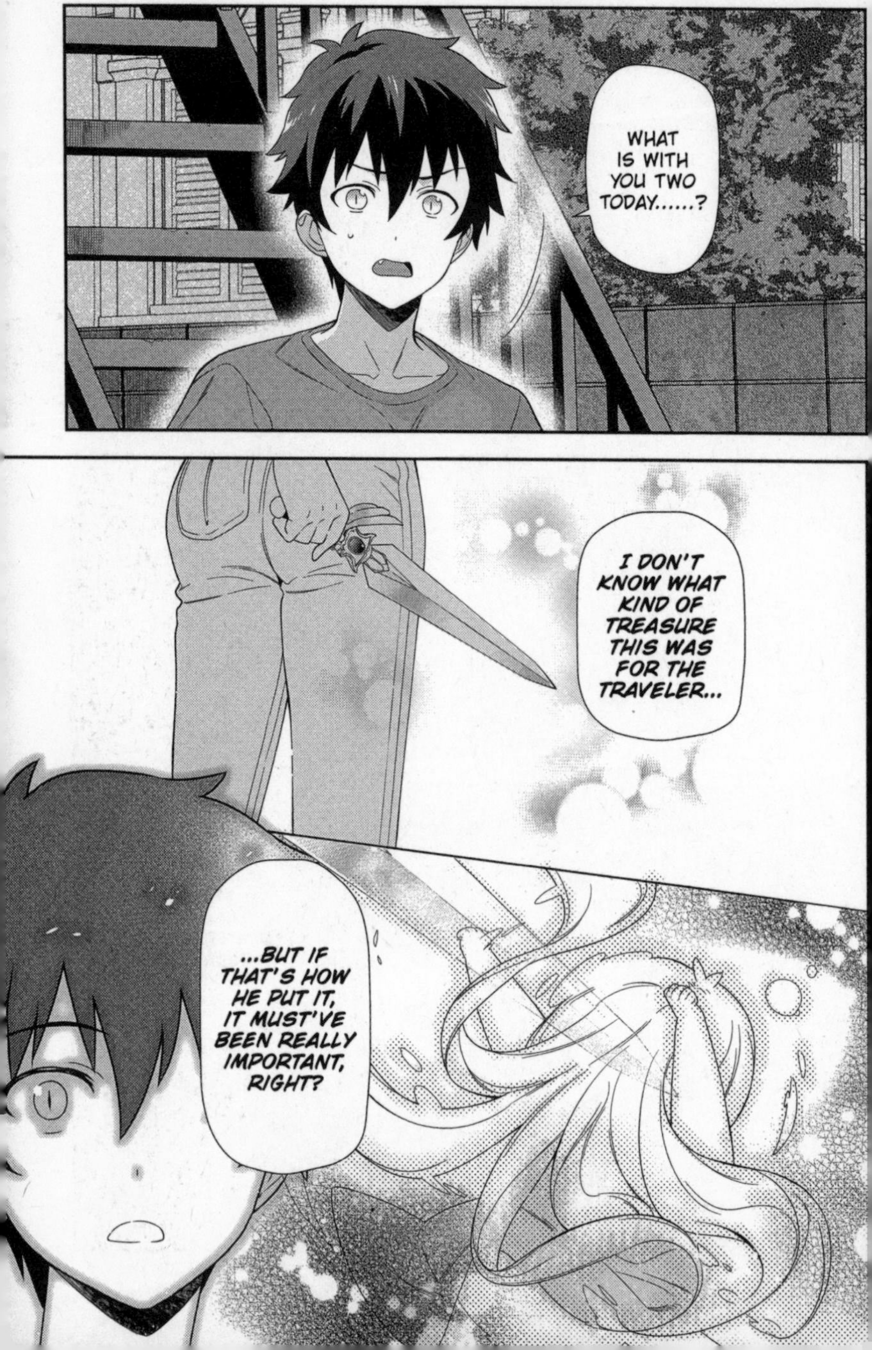
WHAT IS WITH YOU TWO TODAY......?
I DON'T KNOW WHAT KIND OF TREASURE THIS WAS FOR THE TRAVELER...
...BUT IF THAT'S HOW HE PUT IT, IT MUST'VE BEEN REALLY IMPORTANT, RIGHT?

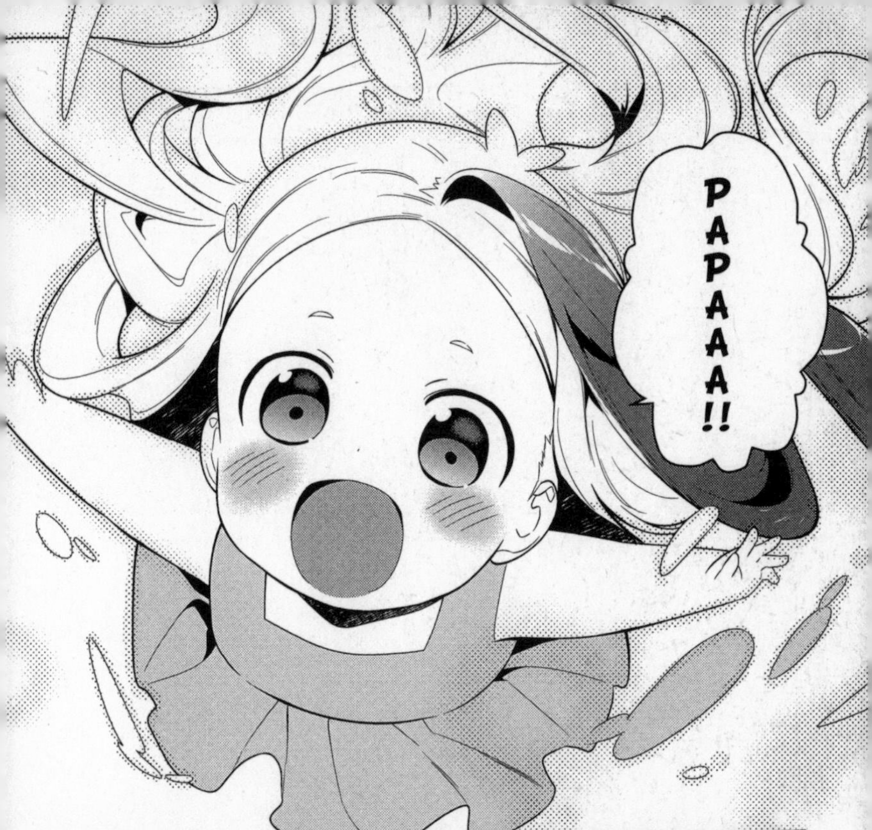
PAPAAA!!
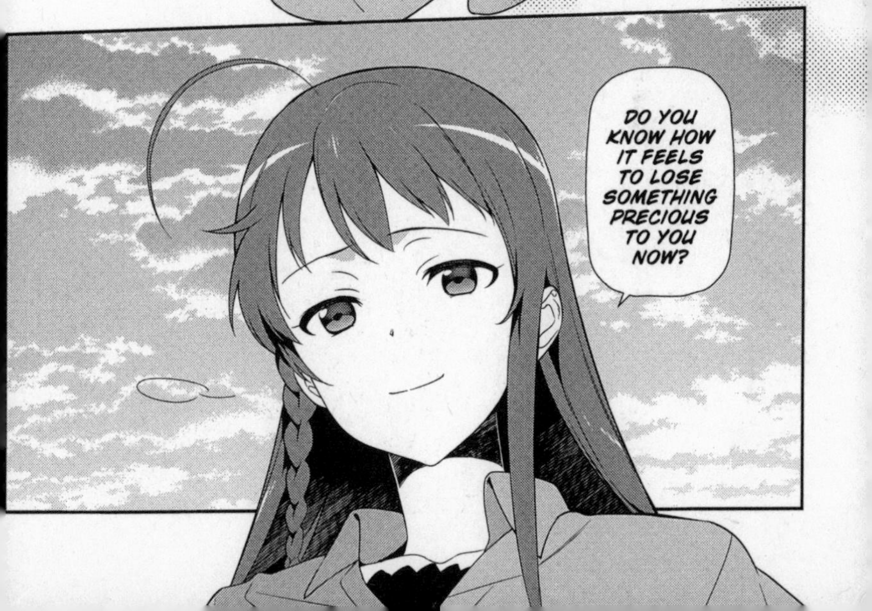
DO YOU KNOW HOW IT FEELS TO LOSE SOMETHING PRECIOUS TO YOU NOW?

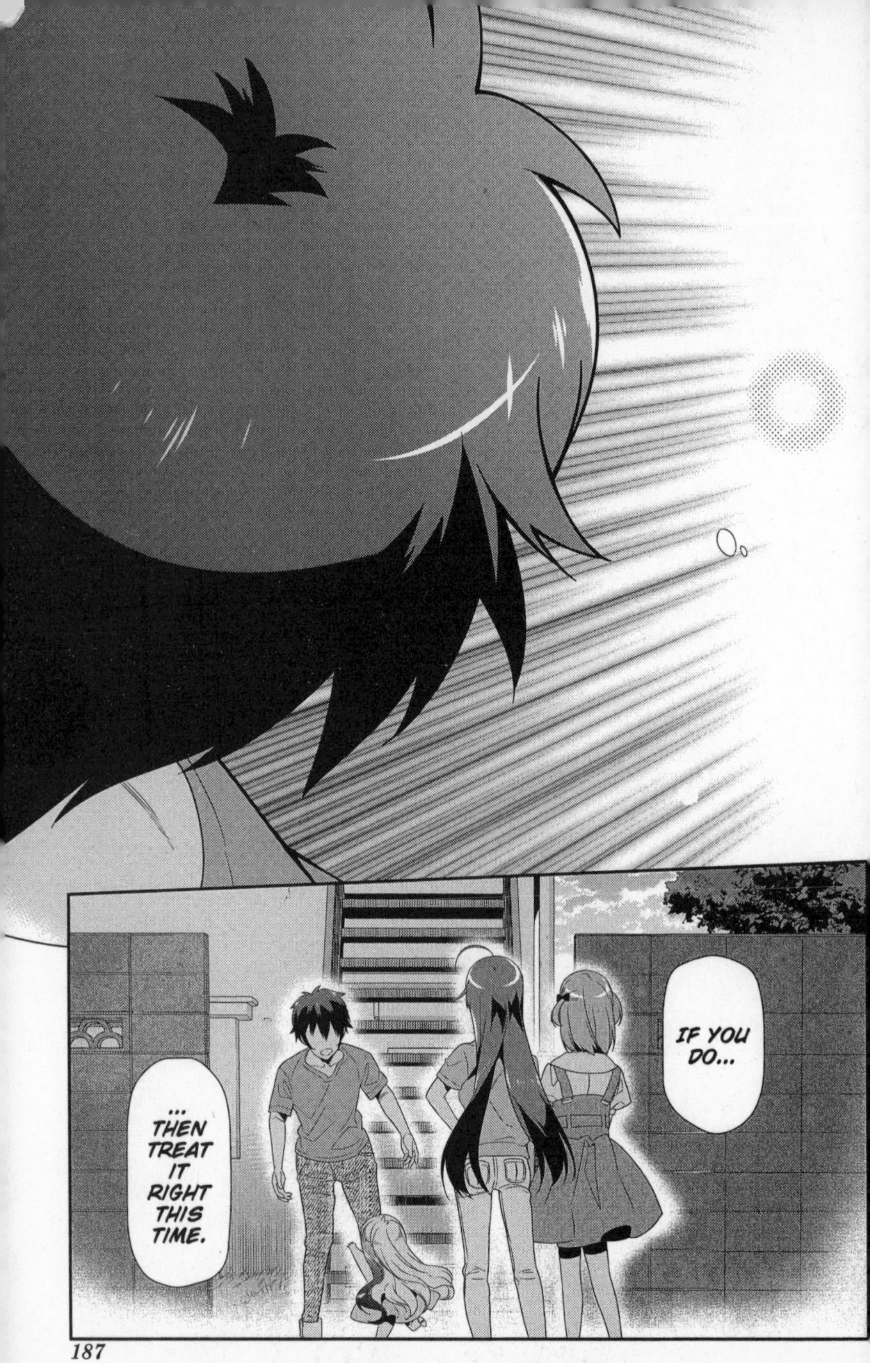
IF YOU DO...
...THEN TREAT IT RIGHT THIS TIME.

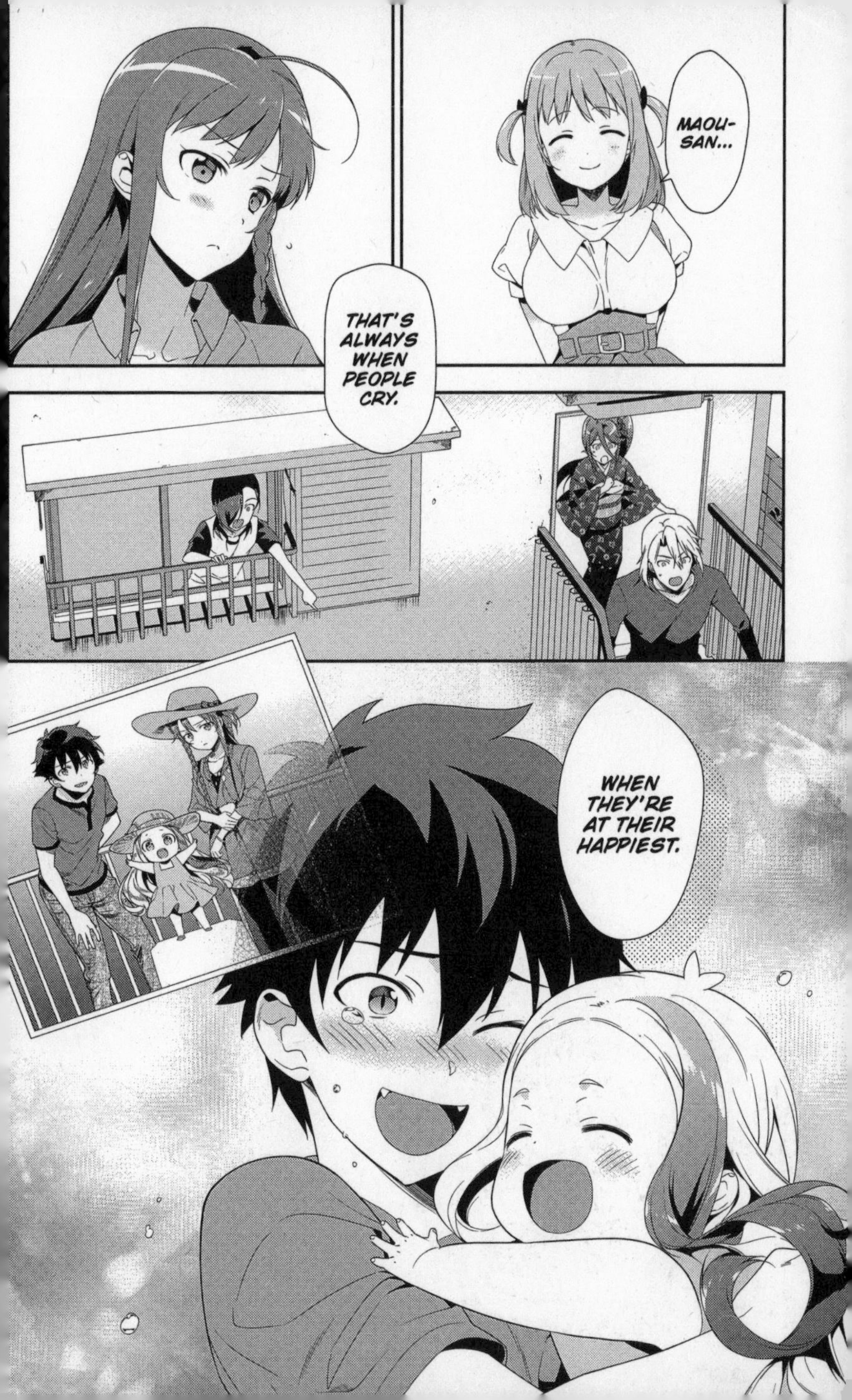
MAOU-SAN...
THAT'S ALWAYS WHEN PEOPLE CRY.
WHEN THEY'RE AT THEIR HAPPIEST.

Suzuno
Kamazuki

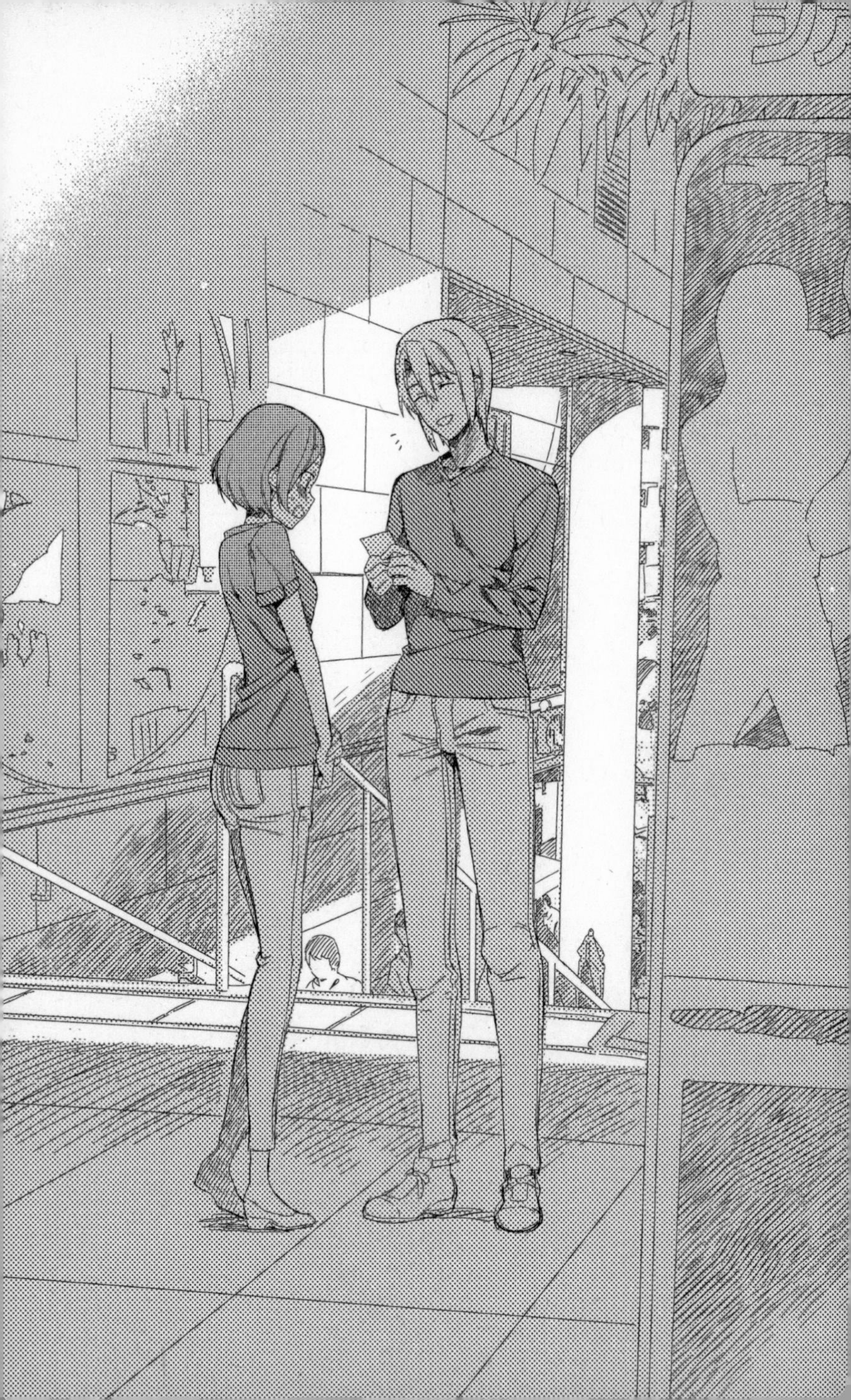

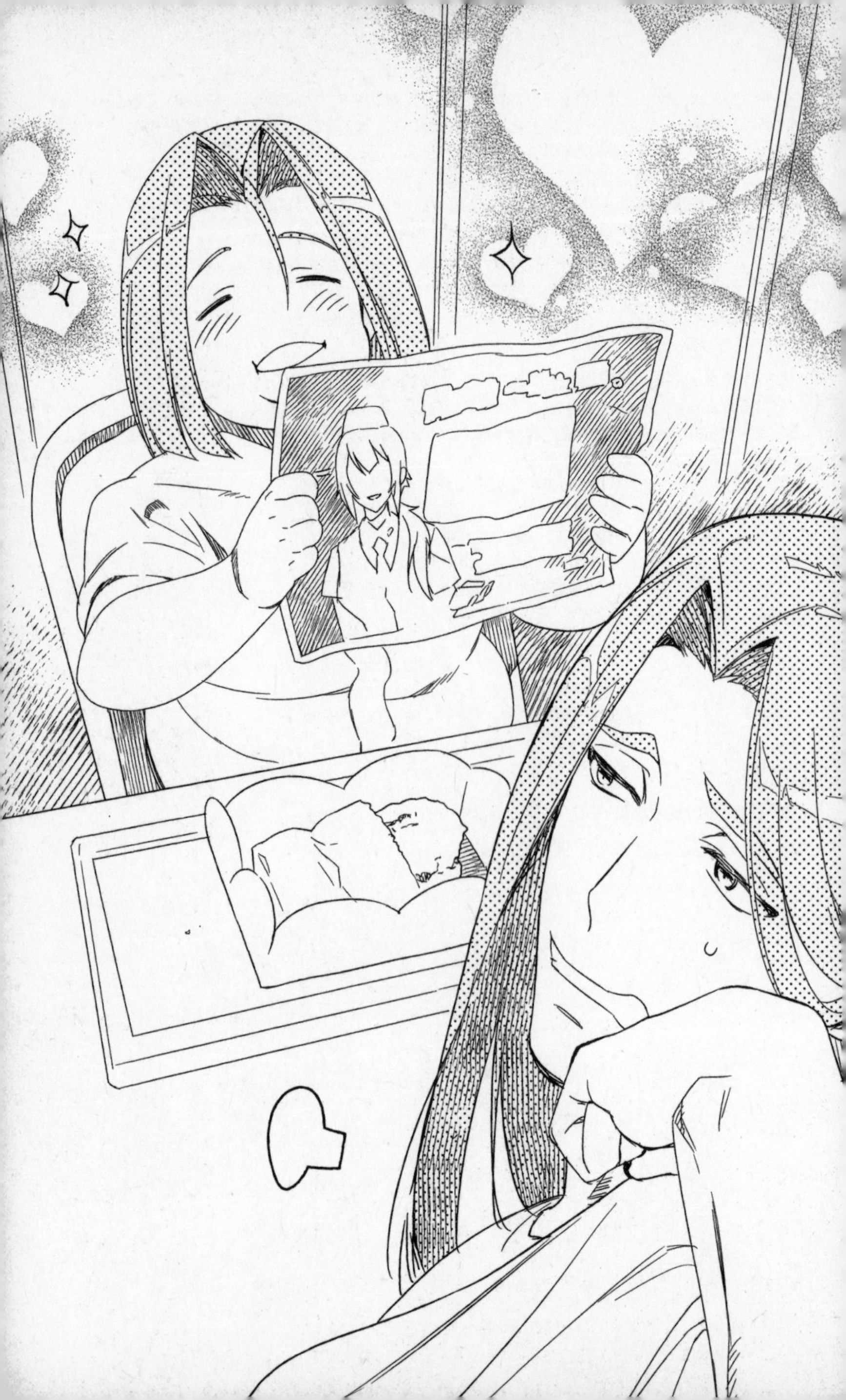

I WROTE IN THE LAST VOLUME ABOUT HOW IT WAS "ALREADY VOLUME 6," BUT THE NEXT THING I KNOW, WE'RE AT VOLUME 7. WITH THIS BOOK, I'VE MANAGED TO COVER EVERYTHING UP TO VOLUME 3 OF THE ORIGINAL NOVELS. MY DEEPEST THANKS GO OUT TO EVERYONE WHO ALWAYS GIVES ME SUPPORT, AS WELL AS WAGAHARA-SENSEI, 029-SENSEI, AND OF COURSE, THE READERS.

FOR THE END OF THIS VOLUME, I DID A COUPLE PAGES OF ILLUSTRATIONS THAT I REGRETTABLY HAD TO CUT OUT OF THE MAIN MANGA'S STORY. I REALLY WANTED TO ADD THESE SCENES TO THE MANGA TOO...!

STARTING WITH THE NEXT BOOK, WE'LL BE DIVING INTO VOLUME 4 OF THE NOVEL, MOSTLY SET IN THE OHGURO-YA SNACK BAR OFF THE CHOSHI COASTLINE. I'M REALLY LOOKING FORWARD TO IT—THERE ARE A LOT OF EPISODES FROM THAT BOOK THAT I PERSONALLY LIKE A LOT. I ALWAYS DAYDREAMED ABOUT DRAWING THIS VOLUME (AND HOW NICE IT WOULD BE IF THEY LET ME), BUT SEEING IT BECOME A REALITY MAKES ME SO OVERJOYED. I HOPE YOU'LL ALL KEEP SUPPORTING ME GOING FORWARD!

SPECIAL THANKS!

ART STAFF: SHIBA, TAKASHI YAMANO

3D: TAKASHI YAMANO, WINGLAYER

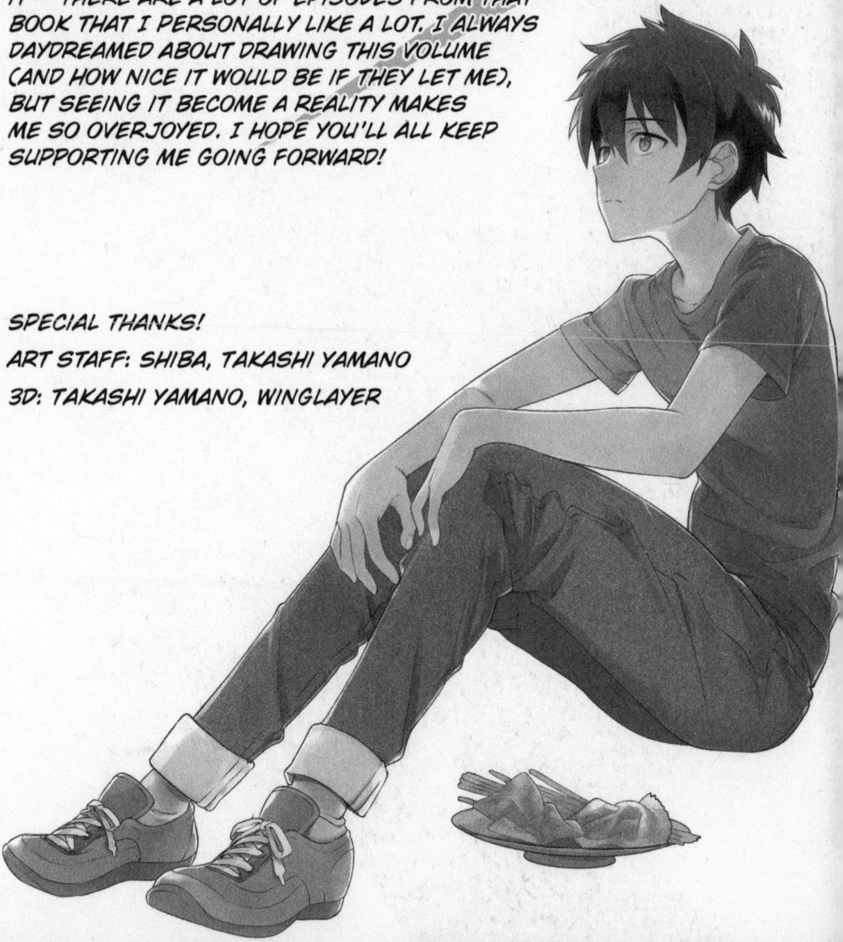

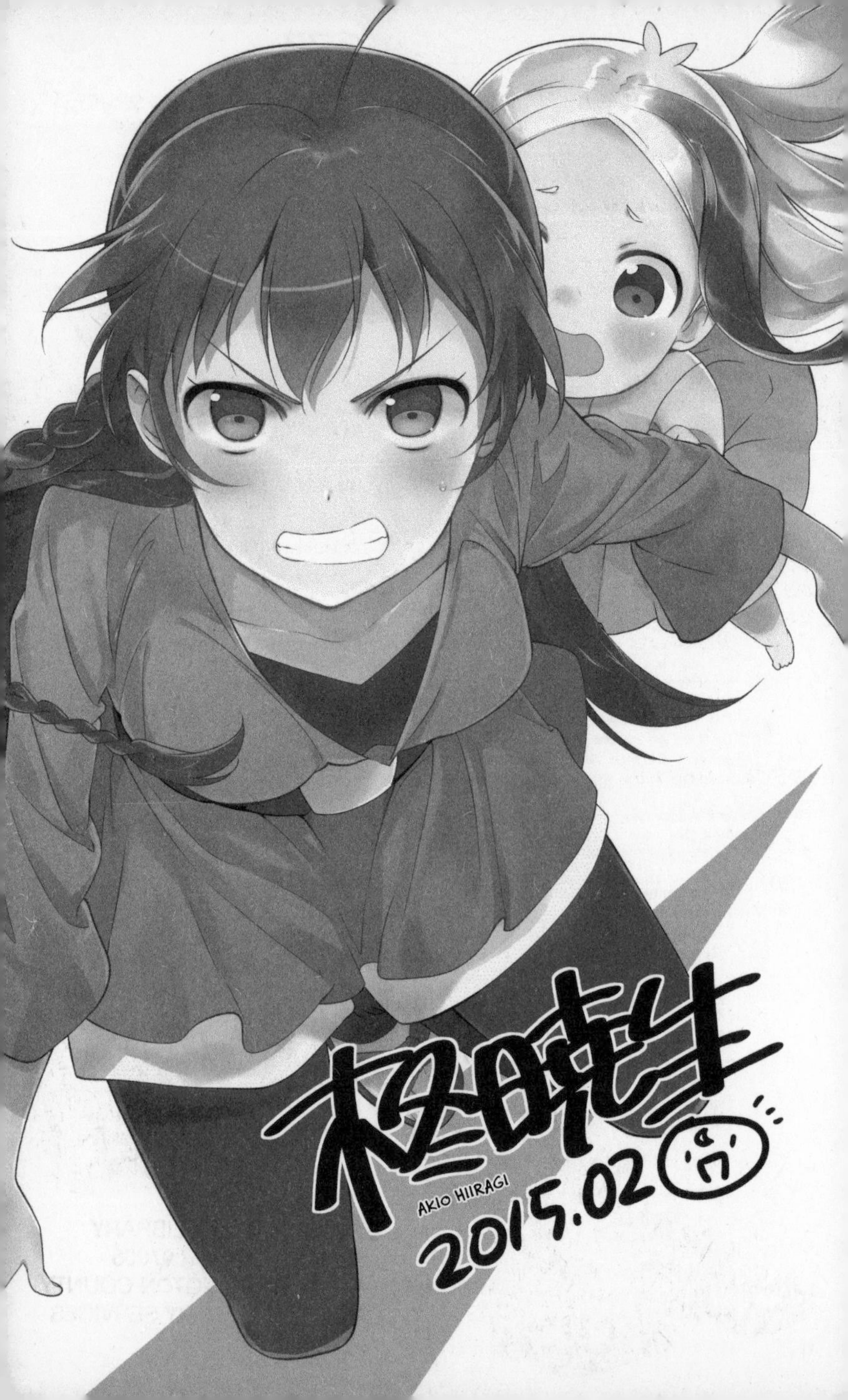
柊暁生
AKIO HIIRAGI
2015.02

600 7 4

P9-CBC-726

THE DEVIL IS A PART-TIMER! 7

ART: AKIO HIIRAGI
ORIGINAL STORY: SATOSHI WAGAHARA
CHARACTER DESIGN: 029 (ONIKU)

Translation: Kevin Gifford

Lettering: Brndn Blakeslee

This book is a work of fiction. Names, characters, places, and incidents are the product of the author's imagination or are used fictitiously. Any resemblance to actual events, locales, or persons, living or dead, is coincidental.

HATARAKU MAOUSAMA! Vol. 7
© SATOSHI WAGAHARA / AKIO HIIRAGI 2015
All rights reserved.
Edited by ASCII MEDIA WORKS
First published in Japan in 2015 by KADOKAWA CORPORATION, Tokyo.
English translation rights arranged with KADOKAWA CORPORATION, Tokyo,
through Tuttle-Mori Agency, Inc., Tokyo.

English translation © 2016 by Yen Press, LLC

Yen Press
1290 Avenue of the Americas
New York, NY 10104

Visit us at yenpress.com
facebook.com/yenpress
twitter.com/yenpress
yenpress.tumblr.com
instagram.com/yenpress

First Yen Press Edition: October 2016

Yen Press is an imprint of Yen Press, LLC.
The Yen Press name and logo are trademarks of Yen Press, LLC.

The publisher is not responsible for websites (or their content) that are not owned by the publisher.

Library of Congress Control Number: 2014504637

ISBNs: 978-0-316-36015-9 (paperback)
       978-0-316-39822-0 (ebook)
       978-0-316-39824-4 (app)

10 9 8 7 6 5 4 3 2 1

BVG

Printed in the United States of America